D1138911

For Reference Only

This volume must not
be removed from the Library
without the express permission
of the Librarian

University of Central Lancashire Library
Preston PR1 2HE
Telephone: 01772 892279

SOCIAL LAW AND POLICY
IN AN EVOLVING EUROPEAN UNION

Social Law and Policy in an Evolving European Union

Edited by
JO SHAW

·HART·
PUBLISHING

OXFORD – PORTLAND
2000

Hart Publishing
Oxford and Portland, Oregon

Published in North America (US and Canada) by
Hart Publishing c/o
International Specialized Book Services
5804 NE Hassalo Street
Portland, Oregon
97213-3644
USA

Distributed in the Netherlands, Belgium and Luxembourg by
Intersentia, Churchillaan 108
B2900 Schoten
Antwerpen
Belgium

Hart Publishing is a specialist legal publisher based in Oxford, England.
To order further copies of this book or to request a list of other
publications please write to:

Hart Publishing Ltd, Salter's Boatyard,
Folly Bridge, Abingdon Road, Oxford OX1 4LB
Telephone: +44 (0)1865 245533 or Fax: +44 (0)1865 794882
e-mail: mail@hartpub.co.uk
WEBSITE: http//www.hartpub.co.uk

British Library Cataloguing in Publication Data
Data Available
ISBN 1–84113–107–5 (hardback)

Typeset by Hope Services (Abingdon) Ltd.
Printed and bound in Great Britain on acid-free paper by
Biddles Ltd, www.biddles.co.uk

Contents

Acknowledgements

A number of the papers published in this volume were originally presented in earlier versions at a Conference on "The United Kingdom and the Social Dimension of the European Union: Perspectives and Prospects after the UK General Election and after the Treaty of Amsterdam", held at the University of Leeds in November 1997. I am grateful to the primary sponsors of that event: the University Association for Contemporary University Studies, the University of Leeds Academic Development Fund and the European Commission. Further papers were presented at a meeting of the Society of Public Teachers of Law, EC Law Section, held in Oxford in March 1999, and at the Socio-Legal Studies Association Annual Conference in Loughborough in April 1999. A number of additional and complementary papers have been commissioned to complete the publication. Many thanks to all the contributors to the volume for bearing with some delays and for responding positively to most, if not quite all, of my suggestions. Many thanks also to Anthea Connolly for diligent editorial work.

List of Contributors

Catherine Barnard is University Lecturer in Law and a Fellow of Trinity College, Cambridge.

Mark Bell is Lecturer in Law at the University of Leicester.

Nick Bernard is Reader in Law at the Queen's University of Belfast.

Fiona Beveridge is Lecturer in Law, Feminist Legal Research Unit, University of Liverpool.

Niklas Bruun is Professor of European Labour Law with special focus on Nordic labour relations at Hanken School of Economics in Helsinki and Arbetslivsinstitutet (National Institute for Working Life), Stockholm.

Simon Deakin is Reader in Economic Law and Assistant Director of the ESRC Centre for Business Research at the University of Cambridge.

Barry Fitzpatrick is Jean Monnet Professor of European Law, School of Public Policy, Economics and Law, University of Ulster.

Sandra Fredman is Professor of Law at the University of Oxford and a Fellow of Exeter College.

Tamara Hervey is Professor of Law at the University of Nottingham.

Clare McGlynn is Reader in Law at the University of Durham.

Sue Nott is Senior Lecturer in Law, Feminist Legal Research Unit, University of Liverpool.

Miguel Poiares Maduro is Professor, Faculdade de Direito, Universidade Nova de Lisboa.

Hannah Reed is Junior Research Fellow at the ESRC Centre for Business Research, University of Cambridge.

Jo Shaw is Professor of European Law and Jean Monnet Chair of European Law and Integration at the University of Leeds.

Helen Stalford is Lecturer in Law at the University of Liverpool.

Kylie Stephen works in the Women's Unit, Cabinet Office, UK Government.

Carl F Stychin is Professor of Law and Social Theory at the University of Reading.

Phil Syrpis is Lecturer in Law at the University of Bristol.

Erika Szyszczak is Jean Monnet Professor of European Law at the University of Nottingham.

Chloë J Wallace is Lecturer in Law at the University of Leeds.

PART I
Introduction

Introduction

JO SHAW

The overall aim of this collection is to explore the legal dimensions of European Union ("EU") social policy. The term "EU social policy" as used here covers a rather loosely bundled group of topics. A non-inclusive list of the areas covered would include labour market policy, regulation of the employment relationship, the role of the social partners and of governmental authorities in industrial relations, those aspects of the free movement of persons touching upon social issues, especially family policy and human capital formation and development, social inclusion and inter-regional redistributive policies, the impact of the internal market upon (national) welfare states, and policies and practices aimed at promoting principles of non-discrimination and societal and labour market equity. However, the book does not provide a comprehensive account of the legal aspects of the policies pursued by the EU separately or in partnership with the Member States, or indeed a systematic account of these policies themselves. It attempts the more limited task of reflecting upon the function, content, role and effects of law and legal institutions, instruments and practices in relation to this broad framework of EU social policy. This task necessitates steps beyond legal analysis alone, and requires the adoption of approaches—illustrated in many of the essays—which place law and legal institutions in their socio-economic and political context, which problematise the gap between law "in the books" and law "in action". This is especially so where EU law requires national implementation. Such approaches highlight the differentiating effects of national legal and other cultures, and reflect upon the ideological and normative premises which inform both the legal framework of the EU and its interpretation by key actors such as the Court of Justice, national courts and the EU political institutions.

More specifically, the objectives of the collection relate to the task of identifying and investigating tensions and contestations within EU social policy. Social law and policy are keenly contested domains. For example, should the EU really be concerned with "more than economics" at all, or is social policy properly the domain of the Member States? What is the scope of EU social policy, and in particular what are the links between the so-called "European social model", which is a rather diffuse amalgam of ideas and principles constructed principally by the Commission to justify social policy interventions on the part of the EU, and the labour market orientation for social policy which has tended to dominate in the Council since it began to fast-track the evolution of the Employment provisions introduced by the Treaty of Amsterdam in 1997? What or who are the relevant actors in EU social policy? What powers do they have and how do they apply those powers? What legitimacy can they claim? How are conflicts between them resolved? Who are the subjects of EU social policy? Can a concentration in terms of policy agendas upon a labour market orientation—and thus upon those who are actually or potentially employed—be successfully reconciled with the parallel increase in commitment claimed by the EU institutions to excluded groups such as those in poverty, children, third country nationals, racial and ethnic minorities and other groups such as the disabled or gays and lesbians? Above all exactly *what is* EU social policy, beyond the descriptive reference points about the policy areas and activities which it covers which have already been employed in this Introduction? Is there a core of concepts, ideas or principles which structures the field of EU social policy and, therefore, EU social law, which can be derived, for example, from the general goals of the EU as an integration project and emerging polity? What role do social rights play in the formulation of a conception of EU social policy, and what is their position within the evolving EU constitutional framework?

One recent trend is, however, clear: despite the persistence of these areas of contestation, social law and policy have been moving increasingly into the mainstream of the EU, both in terms of the policy-making agenda and the conditions under which law and policy is made, and in terms of academic reflection upon that law and policy. One reason for this process of mainstreaming stems from the important changes to the Treaty framework for enacting social policy, especially with the 1997 Treaty of Amsterdam which entered into force in May 1999. These changes have given the EU institutions greater powers to adopt social policy measures in many of the fields of policy outlined above. One element of the overall pattern of changes has comprised amendments to the goals of the EU, principally as expressed in the Treaties, but also as reflected in a shift towards mainstreaming social policy issues onto the agendas of key actors such as the Commission and the Council Presidency. A good example is provided by the so-called *e*Europe summit of the European Council held in March 2000 in Lisbon by the Portuguese Presidency. The European Council agreed a new strategic goal for the Union of strengthening employment, economic reform and social cohesion as part of a knowledge-based economy. The social aspects of this goal—investing in people and building an active welfare state—were given equal prominence in public statements about this new goal as the economic aspects such as the knowledge economy, financial markets, the promotion of small and medium sized businesses and the generation of innovation.

Changes in relation to the Treaty regime for enacting social policy measures can be tracked through the Single European Act and the Treaty of Maastricht (including the Social Policy Protocol and the Social Policy Agreement which provided the UK with its infamous opt-out operative between 1993 and 1997), and the Treaty of Amsterdam. For those unfamiliar with the current status quo, a brief restatement setting out the key elements of the Treaty regime for social policy-making will be useful.

Beginning with the Treaty on European Union, Article 2 TEU marks out a number of social goals for the EU within its framework of objectives, including economic and social progress, a high level of employment, economic and social cohesion, the introduction of a citizenship of the Union, and the promotion of the free movement of persons. Turning to the EC Treaty, these goals are broadly matched in Article 2 EC, which states the tasks of the European Community ("EC"), adding to that list the search for equality between men and women and the raising of the standard of living and quality of life. The normative significance of these goals are addressed in a number of essays, notably those by Poiares Maduro and Fitzpatrick.

Article 3 EC, listing the activities of the EC, cites—in addition to the market-making activities which have for so long tended to dominate the work of the EC and now the EU—a number of areas of social policy. These include measures concerning the entry and movement of persons, the approximation of the laws of the Member States to the extent required for the functioning of the common market, the promotion of coordination between employment policies of the Member States with a view to enhancing their effectiveness by developing a coordinated strategy for employment, a policy in the social sphere comprising a European Social Fund and the strengthening of economic and social cohesion, and contributions to health protection and education and training of quality. Article 3(2) "mainstreams" gender equality by requiring that in all its activities the "Community shall aim to eliminate inequalities, and to promote equality, between men and women".

As a broad political principle concerned with issues of the dispersal of power, subsidiarity clearly has an important constitutional impact upon social policy-making, evident since the 1989 Community Charter of Fundamental Social Rights of Workers referred to the principle of subsidiarity as supporting the assertion that many of the social rights contained in the Charter would require implementation at national rather than Community level. In addition, in its narrower "comparative efficiency" guise determining the exercise of competences shared between the EU and the Member States (Article 5 EC, *ex* Article 3b EC), subsidiarity in this sense of determining the optimum level for regulation is a factor which must be taken into account by the legislative organs of the EU before they may validly adopt legislative measures.

Powers to adopt measures aimed at the achievement of the social goals outlined above vary across the different policy areas as regards the procedures to be adopted, the nature of the measures which may be adopted, and the contents of the policies to be implemented. It remains an ongoing debate at the level of principle, as demonstrated by Syrpis' opening essay in this collection, whether EU social policy has, or should have, a social or an economic rationale. The dominant ideological premise of the early years, informed by the OECD Ohlin

Committee findings, was that social progress would be the natural correlative of the economic progress fostered by the benefits of a common market and closer economic integration between the Member States, suggesting that an interventionist social policy on the part of the European Communities themselves would in fact be counterproductive. This laissez-faire approach resonated neatly over the years with national concerns to preserve welfare state sovereignty because of the fundamental fiscal and budgetary concerns thereby implicated. In practice, the laissez-faire rationale has gradually waned, as the Member States have—as legislators—used existing provisions to adopt measures with a frank social aspiration where economic justifications have come a poor second (e.g. in the area of sex equality or in relation to employment protection) and have—through Treaty amendments—introduced a wider range of social aspirations into the opening Articles of the Treaties and greater possibilities for social policy-making using qualified majority voting.

Although Title XI of Part Three of the EC Treaty is headed "Social Policy, Education, Vocational Training and Youth", leading the eye to focus upon those provisions in the expectation of here finding the definitive statement regarding EU social policy, in practice powers for the adoption of social policies are more dispersed rather widely across the Treaty. Some are of a general nature; others are more specific. In the first place, Article 13 EC—a new law-making power introduced by the Treaty of Amsterdam—allows for the adoption of measures to combat discrimination on a number of grounds including sex, race, ethnic origin, disability, age and sex orientation. This measure is analysed by Bell in his essay, and its significance is touched upon in a number of other essays including Stychin's. Moreover, as the essays by Stalford and McGlynn make clear, there are important powers to adopt social policy measures in the provisions on the free movement of persons, especially in relation to human capital development through the transferability of qualifications and the patchwork regulation of the family in the context of migration. Additionally, the analysis in Hervey's essay addresses the effects of internal market liberalisation (i.e. the impact of negative integration through Treaty-based freedoms) coupled with EU competition policies which have significant marketisation impacts upon some areas of public service provision, upon *national* welfare states. The principles of non-discrimination on grounds of nationality and the free movement of goods, persons and services are necessitating a rethinking of national policies for allocating public goods and EU responses such as the principle of social solidarity.

The general provisions allowing for the approximation of laws in relation to the creation of the common market have been of particular historical significance for the evolution of social policy, especially before the more specific law-making powers of the newly reworded Title XI were introduced, but more often than not such measures have required adoption by unanimous vote. These provisions are of less significance now that there exist more specialised social policy provisions, a point that can also be made about Article 308 EC (*ex* Article

235 EC) which is a residual law-making provision allowing for the adoption of measures necessary to achieve the objectives of the European Community where no other specific power has been provided in the Treaty. Article 308 is little used in the social policy field today, and Article 95 EC, which allows the adoption of harmonisation measures in relation to the development of the single market, is largely excluded from use in the arena of social policy by the exceptions in paragraph 2 relating to the free movement of persons and the "rights and interests of employed persons", exceptions which now matter much less in the changed institutional economy of qualified majority voting under Title XI. The issues of principle about the purposes and effects of the approximation of laws are addressed in the essays by Syrpis and Barnard, and touched upon in relation to specific national conditions in the essay by Bruun. The essays by Syrpis and Barnard also highlight the important tension between social policy-making and the normative content of the building of a single market in which commodities and factors of production can flow without obstacles being erected by the Member States, but where in practice notwithstanding the free movement provisions market failures resulting from differences between national regulatory structures may still arise.

The Treaty of Amsterdam provided a significant innovation in relation to labour market policy, by introducing a specific Title on Employment (Title VIII of Part Three), suggested by many to be a correlate of the Treaty of Maastricht provisions on economic and monetary union, and what was—at the time the new Title was agreed in 1997—the still planned introduction of the single currency (achieved as of January 1 1999 in eleven Member States). The Employment policy provisions (analysed in the essays by Szyszczak and Deakin and Read) do not concern harmonisation of national measures, but a "softer" form of approximation of national policies intended to improve the flexibility and responsiveness to changing conditions within the national labour markets in a global economy, as well as to combat market failures such as the gendered division of labour or skills shortages. Deakin and Read examine the interaction between flexiblisation and market failure.

As alluded to already, there is now a significant grouping of social policy-making provisions and principles in Title XI, headed by a restatement of the EU's overall social goals in Article 136 EC. This provision mentions for the first time in the main body of the EC Treaty the Community Charter of Fundamental Social Rights of Workers of 1989, as an inspiration for EU policy, notwithstanding that it was never formally "agreed" by the United Kingdom. A notable feature of this revised framework of provisions is a generalised competence on the part of the EU to support and complement the activities of the Member States in many of the classic social policy fields and—especially—in relation to the regulation of the employment relationship, working conditions and key aspects of industrial relations such as the information and consultation of workers. An overlap with the Employment policy provisions is apparent so far as the EU may adopt measures to combat the exclusion of persons from the labour market and to promote the labour market opportunities of men and women. Some areas are excluded from qualified majority decision-making in the Council and co-decision between Council and Parliament, notably those clustering closer to the traditional social policy sovereignty of the Member States such as social security and the social protection of workers, and issues relating to the employment conditions of legally resident third country nationals. However, compared to the general position since the Single European Act which introduced qualified majority voting only for health and safety at work measures (although without prejudice to the special provisions of the Social Policy Agreement in force after the Treaty of Maastricht, with an opt-out for the UK, which instituted more widespread qualified majority voting after 1993), this represents a significant change in terms of the mainstream Treaty provisions. Following on from the introduction of the social dialogue into the EC Treaty by the Single European Act, and the use of the social partner mechanism in the Social Policy Agreement, Articles 138 and 139 mainstream the social dialogue as a basis for agreement between the social partners over the contents of EU measures, and institute a procedure for a contractual agreement between the partners involved in the social dialogue to be adopted as a formal EU measure. The significance of this procedure for democratisation of the EU is discussed in the essay by Bernard, as it represents a significant departure from the EC Treaty norm for decision-making.

A principle which has long been at the forefront of EU social policy is that of equality between men and women, now buttressed by the mainstreaming provision in Article 3(2) EC. The process of mainstreaming at EU and—especially— at national level is discussed in the essay by Beveridge, Nott and Stephen. The longstanding guarantee of equal treatment at least in relation to matters of pay (Article 141 EC, *ex* Article 119 EC) has been strengthened by the Treaty of Amsterdam with the addition of a specific law-making power in the field of equal treatment in the employment sphere (by means of Council-Parliament co-decision) and a rider intended to "save" certain types of national positive action measures introduced to promote women's employment in particular which had been endangered by Court of Justice case law on the principle of equal treatment. These developments are discussed in the essay by Fredman. The precise scope of the equality principle remains highly contested terrain, as Stychin's discussion of its usage by those campaigning against sexual orientation discrimination highlights. Likewise, McGlynn contests the gender stereotypes which have often infused EU sex equality law especially as a result of interventions on the part of the Court of Justice. Fitzpatrick's essay shows how the value systems which come through the Court of Justice's case law can stand as a cypher for a wider conception of the whole EU social constitution as contrasted to national social constitutions. The conditioning of the effects of EU sex equality law by reference to the national settings in which it must be implemented is apparent in the essay by Wallace. The proliferation of essays addressing the subject of sex equality law and policy highlights the overall contribution which it has made to the construction of a body of EU social law, and its intertwining with general principles of EU law such as the principle of direct effect and the role of national courts in the EU legal order.

Also contained in Title XI are provisions on the European Social Fund—which needs to be viewed in the context of the wider regional policy or economic and social cohesion policy governed by Title XVII of Part Three—and provisions on training and education. The latter are discussed in the essay by Stalford. One can also ascribe to the broad category of social policy the Treaty provisions on Public Health (Title XIII) and consumer protection (Title XIV) although these are not directly discussed in this volume. Finally, it should not be assumed that all the EU social policy provisions are exclusively contained in the EC Treaty. As McGlynn's discussion of an emerging family law and policy highlights, it is important to view the EU treaties in this context as a unity, so far as the provisions in the area of Justice and Home Affairs in particular are leading to the regulation of national procedural questions such as the enforceability of national judgments in non-national courts and the creation of a single "judicial area" not only in the civil law field (now in the EC Treaty), but also in the criminal field with implications for questions such as combatting domestic violence or trafficking in persons.

This subject-oriented overview of the framework of Treaty provisions setting goals and establishing policy competences in the area of EU social policy provides only a starting point for introducing the key themes of this collection. Such an overview has a strictly limited capacity to answer the types of questions posed at the beginning of this Introduction or to engage with the principal tensions inherent in EU social policy and law. Taken together, the essays do indeed range across many of the fields in which policy and legal development at the EU level has substantially affected the achievement of what are the widely acknowledged goals of social policy in liberal democratic states with mixed economy systems in the areas of fairness, justice, solidarity and social protection. They illustrate the practical evidence of spillover from the EU's market-making policies into a social dimension historically primarily shaped by economic imperatives. They revisit also crucial legal questions, such as the nature and scope of the Treaty-based competences granted to the institutions, the interpretation of those powers by the Court of Justice, and the extent of legally enforceable social rights, duties and tasks enshrined in EU law, whether originating in the Treaties, secondary EU legislation or national law. These legal questions have generally been at the heart of most discussion of EU social law; they remain so here, but they are conditioned by an awareness that over the years the centre of gravity in terms of the legal analysis of EU social policy has shifted. For example, the advent of constitutional principles such as subsidiarity and of a wider range of "original" social powers means de-emphasising the role of the Court of Justice as a driving force of social policy (in particular through its activist case law on the equal opportunities provisions and on the Acquired Rights Directive of 1977), and emphasising instead the crucial role of the legislature in the broadest sense, encompassing the interinstitutional balance between the Commission, the Parliament and the Council, and the various formal and informal roles taken by the social partners and other interest groups which are permitted an input into the substance, if not always the process, of policy-making. Indeed, tensions between courts and legislatures in policy-making are evident in many of the essays. Moreover, the nature of the governance project as a whole in the EU has changed radically, with a move towards softer forms of "coordination" in preference to the harsher disciplines of "approximation". This is well illustrated by the Employment Policy domain.

Yet at the same time, there are other crucial factors conditioning the evolution of EU social policy. The forms of policy spillover are no longer confined to the links between the "economic" and the "social" (with the historical juxtaposition of the "European market" with the "national welfare state"). They extend also to increasing linkages between the political and constitutional dimensions of the EU and its evolving social policy dimension. Thus, it is vital to examine the full range of constraints upon action by the EU institutions, the ongoing national dimensions of EU social policy, and the challenges faced in terms of reformulating social policy goals in the light of economic globalisation and the political reality of the EU as internal market and (partial) economic and monetary union, with claims to recognition as a constitutionalised polity. The book is accordingly organised into sections which address the principal constraints upon social law and policy-making, place the evolution of EU social policy in its national context, highlight the centrality of policies promoting anti-discrimination and employment equity, touch upon an emerging agenda relating to the family and family formations, and explore the normative challenges facing EU social policy-making.

By way of amplification of the approach taken, it is useful to place developments in relation to social law and policy in the wider context of the evolving European Union, and to bear in mind the profound impact of the historical "learning curve" of EU social policy. A brief contextual and historical analysis of the framework of social policy in EU provides the best means to demonstrate how deeply EU social policy is embedded within the broader frame of the EU as an emerging non-state and postnational polity as well as more a longstanding framework of economic integration, and to reinforce the intense interdependencies of the social, economic and political dimensions of the EU.

The content and conditions of EU social law and policy have changed radically across a historical frame measuring some fifty years, although change has been especially rapid in the last twenty years. The social policy debates of the 1970s were undertaken in the context of a stagnant European Community but accompanied by a gradual disruption at national level of the postwar socio-economic and political consensus; those of the 1980s were overshadowed by the euphoria of the *relance communautaire* and the 1992 single market programme and accompanied by a distinct shift towards the right in many of the domestic political arenas along with policies of monetary discipline and privatisation of publicly owned sectors of the economy as well as public utilities. In turn, the social policy debates of the third millenium are just as sharply shaped by economic and political circumstances.

Examining the exogenous factors which currently shape EU social policy, what stands out are the substantial achievements of a European Union of fifteen Member States in which the broad regulatory conditions for a single market for goods, services, persons and capital have largely been in place since the mid-1990s; where eleven out of those fifteen states have shared a single currency since 1999 and are bound together in an evolving economic and monetary union; and where frontier-free travel has substantially been achieved in thirteen states and where the project to solidify and extend the achievements in relation to the free movement of persons and associated systems of transnational social control such as criminal law now stands at the head of the Union's agenda. These factors certainly might be expected to create more propitious circumstances for social policy-making in the sense of having created a stronger bond of commonality between the Member States. Indeed there is some limited evidence of this in relation to measures related to the labour market which are closely linked to the enhancement of economic prosperity and the modernisation of economies, and certain flagship areas such as anti-discrimination policy seen as part of the construction of the area of freedom, security and justice announced by the Treaty of Amsterdam as much as they are constructed as elements of social policy itself. But alongside the "achievements" in relation to EU goals cited here (and indeed these are not always applauded as achievements in every corner of the EU), there stand the contested terrains of enlargement (especially to the east) and of flexibility. For Member States continue to show divergent levels of commitment towards the core and peripheral goals of the (pan-)European integration project and to insist upon divergent interpretations of its pasts, its presents and its futures. Although flexibility as regards participants is—since the Treaty of Amsterdam—no longer a feature of EU social policy-making, it continues to cast a shadow especially when viewed in the light of anticipated future enlargement(s) to create a much more heterogenous EU. Substantively, for example, employment policy anticipates highly flexible governance structures.

A further crucial pillar of the background to evolving EU social law and policy comprises the constitutional pretensions of the European Union. Central to the contention of a form of EU constitutionalism has, historically, been the claim that the EU constitutes a "new type" of Treaty-based legal order, based on principles of legal supremacy and the direct applicability of EU law upheld by the Court of Justice and a conception of shared or pooled sovereignty between the Member States and the EU. Grafted more recently onto this contention has been the argument that the EU, although not a state in any conventional sense, in fact imitates some other essential elements of a constitutionalised polity such as judicial review, protection of fundamental rights, a concept of citizenship, and autonomous powers and decision-making structures and institutions subject to the rule of law. Yet the sum total of these pretensions remains still an inchoate, uncertain and contested polity. The key anchors of the constitutional framework conventionally visible within the national model, such as the *demos* or people, the political community and spaces in which competing political ideas are exchanged and debated, and the structures to promote legitimacy and democracy as core principles of constitutional government, are all to a very substantial extent still lacking.

One by-product of the mainstreaming of EU social policy is that it has become clear that this as yet incomplete constitutional framework is central to the further development of the EU as "social polity". Historically, the development of policies of social protection and social justice has been irrevocably tied to the development of (nation) states as protective shells, taking care of the health and welfare of their "own" citizens in particular, but also, to a lesser extent, the welfare of all those who are resident within the geographical borders of that polity. This is no longer the case. The governance of the social sphere across the EU and its Member States must now be approached taking into account the competing claims of the various levels where governmental authority is exercised (including the subnational level in many Member States) to be legitimate sites of governance. There has thus been a significant element of mutual spillover between the evolving constitutional pretensions of the EU and its evolving social dimension.

Thus far the "social policy" of the EU in its core sense has necessarily been very limited, as the "welfare state" as protective framework for securing basic social justice remains largely a national (taxation-based) project. But already it is being increasingly disrupted by the disciplines of the internal market freedoms. In some ways the strongly divergent characteristics and principles of the national welfare states which have been one of the distinctive strengths of "European model" are threatening to become weaknesses as the risks of regulatory competition and uncontrollable welfare or health care burdens resulting from the free movement of persons and services and the principle of non-discrimination on grounds of nationality become ever more intense. EU integration places the claims of resident non-nationals—and even those who visit on a temporary basis in order to enjoy services or benefits of a social or welfare nature— on an entirely different basis, provided only that such persons are nationals of another Member State (i.e. they are EU citizens) or are members of a set of limited categories of protected third country nationals who enjoy derived rights. Pressures and forces generated by the market-making aspects of the EU integration project are compounded by the growing pressures on all welfare states (especially in the areas of pensions and umemployment) resulting from demographic changes and the processes of economic restructuring on a global scale. Furthermore, the dilemmas of social policy-making are intensively interconnected with other social choices, e.g. in relation to fiscal policy, the scope of public management of the economy and of economic activities as well as public service provision, redistributive policies such as regional policy, and other conservatory policies such as environmental policy. Many of these are fields in which the EU now claims important regulatory or redistributive competences. The welfare state is not, therefore, an isolated beacon which can be treated separately from other areas of policy-making. Welfare state security itself can increasingly no longer be taken for granted, as notions of state responsibility for individual citizens are now frequently rejected within political discourse as both financially unviable and psychologically ineffective. In sum, it is no longer realistic either to view social policy as an "essentially" national matter in which EU interference can only grudgingly be admitted or to take a longterm minimalist view of the need for EU-level responses to all of these challenges to the level of security which welfare states can or indeed should give to individuals. The EU will increasingly evolve as a form of "social polity", although the nature of the changes which will occur and the forms of constitutional and democratic control needed to ensure the legitimacy and effectiveness of policy actions remain highly contested territory. The enquiries undertaken by the essays in this collection make a modest contribution to sketching out the bare outlines of the contests and debates of the future of social law and policy in an evolving European Union.

PART II

Social Policy in
a Climate of Economic Constraints

1

The Integrationist Rationale for European Social Policy

PHIL SYRPIS[1]

"Both at the level of terminology and at a deeper ideological level, there is no single clear or accepted policy agenda for employment law in the European Union."[2]

INTRODUCTION

The lack of a "clear or accepted policy agenda" has had the effect of stunting the evolution of European social policy. This chapter sets itself a modest task. It seeks to develop a coherent rationale for European social policy, in an attempt to enable it to flourish within clearly demarcated boundaries.

Throughout the history of the European Community and now the European Union, many alternative rationales for European level social policy have been discussed. Labour lawyers have tended to advocate a social rationale, and have harnessed the seductive language of human rights (particularly the apparently more seductive language of "fundamental" human rights), democracy and citizenship to that rationale.[3] More recently, it has been economic rationales which have been to the fore. European social policy, of a very different nature to that based on a social rationale, can now be aimed at the achievement of employment-creating and competitiveness-enhancing objectives.[4]

---

[1] A version of this chapter was presented at the WG Hart Workshop on Legal Regulation of the Employment Relation at the Institute of Advanced Legal Studies in July 1999. Thanks go to Paul Davies, Tonia Novitz and Paul Skidmore for their valuable comments at various stages in the gestation of this chapter. All the usual disclaimers apply.

[2] M Freedland, "Employment Policy", in P Davies *et al* (eds), *European Community Labour Law: Principles and Perspectives; Liber Amicorum Lord Wedderburn* (Oxford, Clarendon Press, 1996) 278. See also J Shaw, "Twin-Track Social Europe—the Inside Track" in D O'Keeffe and P Twomey (eds), *Legal Issues of the Maastricht Treaty* (Chichester, Wiley, 1994) 298: "It is exceedingly difficult, therefore, for the outsider to point to common themes in Community Social Policy".

[3] See, e.g., B Bercusson *et al*, "Manifesto for a Social Europe", reproduced in summary form in (1997) 3 *ELJ* 189.

[4] See S Deakin and F Wilkinson, "Rights vs. Efficiency? The Economic Case for Transnational Labour Standards", (1994) 23 *ILJ* 289; Commission White Paper, *Growth, Competitiveness, Employment* (COM(93) 700).

In this chapter I consider a different order of justification for European social policy; one which draws its ideological strength from a functionalist interpretation of the purpose of the European Union. Action based on the integrationist rationale aims to establish, or to improve the functioning of, the market in Europe. Paul Davies has argued that a Community social policy "subservient to the process of integration of markets" is inherently unambitious.[5] Others assume that the integrationist agenda demands the harmonization or approximation of the laws of the Member States so that a "level playing field" may be created across Europe. This overly simplistic assumption leads them to the justified conclusion that this objective is undesirable,[6] and to a rejection of the integrationist rationale in the social policy context. In this chapter, I challenge these views. I endeavour to identify the variety of ways in which it is argued that European social policy can make a contribution to the establishment and functioning of the market in Europe. I argue that the integrationist rationale, when properly formulated, is able to provide the conceptual clarity which European social policy has been missing.

Grounding Community action on the integrationist rationale has one significant, arguably decisive, advantage. Action based on the integrationist rationale has a more secure basis in the Treaties than action based on the economic or social rationales. It is now common to speak in terms of a multi-level system of governance in Europe, or at least of a two-tier polity in which competence is divided between the supranational and the national spheres.[7] The challenge in the European Union, as in other federal systems, is to determine the manner in which the regulatory space ought to be shared. The principle of subsidiarity provides, at the least, a useful starting point.[8] Article 5 (ex 3b) EC states that:

> "In areas which do not fall within its exclusive competence, the Community shall take action, in accordance with the principle of subsidiarity, only if and insofar as the objectives of the proposed action cannot be sufficiently achieved by the Member States and can therefore, by reason of the scale or effects of the proposed action, be better achieved by the Community".

Thus, both legally,[9] and more significantly, politically,[10] the Community institutions are vulnerable whenever the objectives of the action which they seek

---

[5] P Davies, "The Emergence of European Labour Law" in Lord McCarthy (ed.), *Legal Intervention in Industrial Relations: Gains and Losses* (Oxford, Basil Blackwell, 1992) 344.

[6] European Commission, *Medium Term Social Action Programme 1995–97* (COM(95) 134) at 2; "Total harmonization of social policies . . . is not an objective of the Commission or of the Union".

[7] W Streeck, "Neo-Voluntarism: A New European Social Policy Regime?", (1995) 1 *ELJ* 31 at 34.

[8] See G Bermann, "Taking Subsidiarity Seriously: Federalism in the European Community and the United States", (1994) 94 *Columbia Law Review* 331; and G De Burca, "Reappraising Subsidiarity's Significance after Amsterdam", (1999) *Jean Monnet Paper* 7/99, Harvard Law School.

[9] The discussion of subsidiarity in Case C–84/94 *UK* v. *Council* [1996] ECR I–5755 at para. 47 and Opinion of AG Leger at para. 129, is wholly unconvincing.

[10] UNICE's refusal to negotiate with the ETUC and CEEP in the context of the Commission's proposals on national information and consultation was premised on "the non-conformity of such a move with the principle of subsidiarity"; COM(98) 612 at 1. See also *EIRR* 291 (March 1998) at 3; and *EIRR* 298 (November 1998) at 2.

to take can be sufficiently achieved by the Member States. The subsidiarity principle operates more strongly against Community action based on the social and economic rationales than against Community action informed by the integrationist rationale.[11] It is easier for the Community institutions to demonstrate that Member State action alone is insufficient in the context of the establishment and functioning of the market in Europe, than it is to show that Member State action alone is incapable of achieving any given social and economic objectives.

The integrationist rationale is concerned with measures which seek to make the European economy function like a single, integrated unit. The EC Treaty does not identify the role which social policy might play in this process. Accordingly, views differ. I consider the extent to which both harmonisation and flexible framework measures, with which students of Community social policy are becoming increasingly familiar, can contribute to the realisation of integrationist objectives.

The most significant obstacles to the establishment and functioning of the market are "barriers to free movement" and "distortions of competition". Action which eliminates either barriers to free movement or distortions of competition can be adopted on the basis of the integrationist rationale. However, the definition of both terms is contested. The scope which these terms are given affects the need for Community level legislation and the form which such legislation may take. It also defines the scope for freedom of action at the Member State level and below.

This chapter argues that the term "barrier to free movement" should not be defined in an overly broad way. Member State laws which do not discriminate against imported products and which do not *prevent* the market access of such products do not constitute barriers to free movement. The Community should encourage competition between national regulatory regimes. However, where such competition produces "destructive" outcomes, the EU has the competence to intervene to eliminate what may be termed a "distortion of competition". In particular, the EU can act to prevent Member States from lowering their standards to sub-optimal levels in an attempt to gain competitive advantage. The challenge for the Community institutions lies in articulating the appropriate policy response.

THE ELIMINATION OF BARRIERS TO FREE MOVEMENT

It is common knowledge that the existence of barriers to free movement between the Member States affects the establishment and functioning of the market in Europe. The European Court of Justice has held that the free movement provisions of the EC Treaty catch not only Member State rules which discriminate (directly or indirectly) against imported factors of production, but

---

[11] S Simitis and G Lyon-Caen, "Community Labour Law: A Critical Introduction to its History", in Davies *et al*, above n. 2, at 10.

also all non-discriminatory rules which actually or potentially hinder inter-State trade.[12] There are three possible outcomes to consider in the context of cases brought under the free movement provisions of the EC Treaty. First, it may be held that national rules are not barriers to free movement. In this case, national regulation escapes scrutiny, except as regards the primary definitional question, and Community level action to remove barriers to free movement is, of course, not required. Secondly, the rules may be held to hinder free movement, and not to be justifiable.[13] In such cases it will, again, not be necessary to adopt Community level legislation. "No harmonization measures [are] required with respect to those national measures which would be condemned under the *Cassis* reasoning."[14] Thirdly, it may be held that national rules hinder free movement, but are also justified. National rules are justified where they are applied in a non-discriminatory manner; are justified by imperative requirements in the general interest; are suitable for securing the attainment of the objective which they pursue; and do not, in terms of the restriction on intra-Community trade, go beyond what is necessary in order to attain that objective.[15] It is in this third case that Community legislation may be required. Community legislative competence "is triggered each time there is a *prima facie* transgression by a state of the *Dassonville* formula, even when, necessarily, the state measure in question is justified".[16]

The primary task is to determine whether or not a national rule is capable of hindering inter-State trade. This fundamental question has, somewhat perplexingly, never received a clear answer. Certainly, in many cases, the European Court has drawn the net widely. In *Alpine Investments* and *Bosman* the Court held that national rules which *directly affect* access to markets of any of the factors of production in other Member States are capable of impeding free movement.[17] However, this approach has not been followed in all cases. *Peralta* and *Commune di Bassano* suggest that there may be a *de minimis* test. In *Peralta*, the Court held that where the purpose of a national rule is not to regulate trade and

---

[12] Case 8/74 *Procureur du Roi* v. *Dassonville* [1974] ECR 837. Thus far, the Court has stopped short of holding that rules which restrict free movement *within* a Member State are capable of hindering trade. The inexorable logic of the internal market suggests that this may be subject to change.

[13] The equalisation of laws in the Community simply by removing restrictive national rules is known as "negative harmonisation". See A McGee and S Weatherill, "The Evolution of the Single Market—Harmonisation or Liberalisation", (1990) 53 *MLR* 578 at 580. Negative harmonisation is "politically attractive to the legislature since the burden of further enactment is removed . . . It similarly proves advantageous to the process of market integration since barriers are thus set aside without the need for a prior harmonization of divergent regulatory concepts": C Joerges, "Product Safety in the European Community: Market Integration, Social Regulation and Legal Structures", (1992) 39 *Journal of Behavioural Sciences* 132 at 142.

[14] P Craig and G De Burca, *EU Law: Text, Cases and Materials* (2nd edn., Oxford, Clarendon Press, 1998) 1126.

[15] See Case C–55/94 *Gebhard* [1995] ECR I–4165 at para. 37.

[16] J Weiler, "The Constitution of the Common Market Place: Text and Context in the Evolution of the Free Movement of Goods", in P Craig and G De Burca (eds), *The Evolution of EU Law* (Oxford, OUP, 1999) 362.

[17] See Case C–384/93 *Alpine Investments BV* v. *Minister van Financiën* [1995] ECR I–1141 at para. 38; Case C–415/93 *Bosman* [1995] ECR I–4921 at para. 103.

the restrictive effects which it might have on free movement are too uncertain and indirect, the rule is not to be regarded as being of a nature to hinder trade between Member States.[18] *Keck* represents a different approach. It is well known that in *Keck* the European Court decided that "national provisions restricting or prohibiting certain selling arrangements", fall outside the scope of the free movement provisions (so long as they do not discriminate against imports).[19] It is rather less well known that in order to come to this conclusion, the Court adopted new reasoning. The Court did not argue that rules relating to selling arrangements fall outside the scope of the free movement provisions because they do not affect market access. Indeed, it conceded that the national legislation at issue may restrict the volume of sales of products from other Member States.[20] The Court held that rules relating to selling arrangements fall outside the scope of the free movement provisions because their application to the sale of products from other Member States "is not by nature such as to *prevent* their access to the market or to impede access any more than it impedes the access of domestic products".[21]

There is a difference between a test which is based on whether or not access to markets is *affected*, even significantly affected, and one based on whether it is *prevented*. Rules which restrict the volume of trade may affect market access, but they do not prevent it. Joseph Weiler has argued in favour of a test based on the prevention of market access. He has stated that rules which do not discriminate against imports should only be caught if they *prevent* access to markets in other Member States: "Market regulation rules—whether selling arrangements or otherwise—that do not bar market access should not be caught unless discriminatory in law or in fact".[22]

There have been few cases which have analysed whether national labour law rules amount to barriers to free movement. In the most important of them, *Rush Portuguesa*, the Court baldly stated that:

> "Community law does not preclude Member States from extending their legislation, or collective labour agreements entered into by both sides of industry, to any person who is employed, even temporarily, within their territory, no matter in which country the employer is established".[23]

This holding appears to make it clear that, notwithstanding the free movement provisions of the EC Treaty, a host Member State is entitled to impose its own legislation on enterprises from other Member States who are operating in

---

[18] In Case C–379/92 *Peralta* [1994] ECR I–3453 at para. 24, and Cases C–140–142/94 *Commune di Bassano* [1995] ECR I–3257 at para. 29.

[19] Cases C–267 and C–268/91 *Keck & Mithouard* [1993] ECR I–6097 at para. 16.

[20] *Ibid.* at para. 13.

[21] *Ibid.* at para. 17 (emphasis added).

[22] Weiler, above n. 16, at 372.

[23] Case C–113/89 *Rush Portuguesa* v. *Office Nationale d'Immigration* [1990] ECR I–1417 at para. 18. See also Case C–43/93 *Vander Elst* v. *Office des Migrations Internationales* [1994] ECR I–3803 and Case C–272/94 *Guiot & Climatec* [1996] ECR I–1905.

its territory.[24] There are only two possible interpretations of the judgment, the first consistent with the *preventing* market access test, the second with the *affecting* market access test. According to the first, national labour law rules are not capable of hindering trade between States. According to the second, national labour law rules are capable of hindering trade—they may, for example, be regarded as having a "chilling effect on cross-border service providers"[25]—but are justified. Only if the second interpretation is correct will Community level action be required in order to remove a barrier to free movement.

Choosing between the two interpretations is not an easy task. The Court gives away no clues. To my mind, the answer must depend on the test employed by the Court to determine whether a national labour law rule is capable of hindering trade. It seems clear that the burden of cumulative or conflicting labour law rules is capable of *affecting* market access,[26] but that it is not capable of *preventing* such access.[27] Access remains possible so long as mobile factors are willing to adjust to the host Member State's labour law regime.

Thus, Community legislation will only be required in the social policy field in order to eliminate barriers to free movement if the *affecting* market access test is preferred. The *preventing* market access test provides few, if any, opportunities for Community intervention, quite simply because where that test is used, it is only exceptional labour law rules which are held to be capable of hindering trade. Even the *affecting* market access test provides only a limited competence for the EU. Under the affecting market access test, all differences between the labour laws of the Member State will be capable of hindering trade. Community legislation must, therefore, aim to eliminate these differences. Where the EU adopts minimum standards and allows the Member States to impose their own, more stringent, rules on imported as well as on domestic factors of production, it will not succeed in eliminating barriers to free movement. Only Community legislation which eliminates the differences between the laws of the Member States, or which, perhaps on the basis of the mutual recognition principle, obliges Member States not to impose their legislation on imported factors of production, will be capable of successfully eliminating barriers to free movement. Thus, although the affecting market access test provides competence for the EU to legislate on the basis of the integrationist rationale, it does not open up opportunities for a flexible Community level social policy, able to have "regard to the conditions and technical rules obtaining in each of the Member

---

[24] See further the Posted Workers Directive 96/71/EC, [1997] OJ L18/1.

[25] P Davies, "Posted Workers: Single Market or Protection of National Labour Law Systems?", (1997) 34 *CMLRev* 571 at 586.

[26] G Wolff, "The Commission's Programme for Company Law Harmonisation: The Winding Road to a Uniform European Company Law?" in M Andenas and S Kenyon-Slade (eds), *EC Financial Market Regulation and Company Law* (London, Sweet and Maxwell, 1993) 22.

[27] An example of a national rule which would be caught by the "preventing market access" test, is the state monopoly considered by the European Court in Case C–41/90 *Hofner* v. *Macrotron* [1991] ECR I–1979.

States".[28] If the Community institutions were serious about eliminating all barriers to free movement which were capable of affecting market access, Community level action in the social field would afford Member States far less flexibility than it typically does.

However, the fact that Community social legislation affords choices to Member States does not necessarily indicate that it is solely "concerned with the protective insulation of national regimes and the political stability of the nation-state".[29] The integrationist rationale is broad enough to encompass flexible action at the Community level. In order to investigate the possibilities which exist, it is necessary to look beyond the elimination of barriers to free movement—to the elimination of distortions of competition.

THE ELIMINATION OF DISTORTIONS OF COMPETITION

The EC Treaty claims that the maintenance of undistorted conditions of competition is essential for the establishment and functioning of the market.[30] However, there is no definition of undistorted competition in the Treaty and thus no obvious yardstick for distinguishing between differences in national regulatory regimes that are acceptable and those that amount to distortions. This section builds on two "ideologies" identified by Francis Snyder. The free trade ideology holds that " 'the distortion of competition' is defined as the restriction of free trade".[31] Adherents to this view speak in terms of "free" rather than "fair" competition,[32] and tend to rely on a neo-classical understanding of the workings of markets based on the formal equality of individuals. The second ideology, termed "the market structure and structural policy perspective", is more fearful of the consequences of free trade and lacks confidence in the workings of the "unadulterated" free market. According to this ideology, free trade "would amount to unfair competition: It would 'distort' the conditions of competition".[33] Supporters of this alternative seek to ensure that certain outcomes are realised through the workings of the market. They assume both that the economic system lends itself to "effective end-dependent rule-setting" and that "sufficient steering-knowledge is available to achieve ends related to what is considered as social justice".[34]

[28] Article 137(2) EC.

[29] Streeck, above n. 7, at 42.

[30] Article 3(g) EC.

[31] F Snyder, *New Directions in European Community Law* (London, Weidenfeld and Nicolson, 1990) 75.

[32] Both "free" and "fair" competition are referred to in the EC Treaties. The Preamble of the EC Treaty calls for "concerted action in order to guarantee steady expansion, balanced trade and fair competition"; while Article 4(1) EC, calls for the activities of the Member States and the EU to be "conducted in accordance with the principle of an open market economy with free competition".

[33] Snyder, above n.31, at 77.

[34] M Streit and W Mussler, "The Economic Constitution of the European Community—'From Rome to Maastricht' " in F Snyder, *Constitutional Dimensions of European Economic Integration* (London, Kluwer Law International, 1996) 116.

The institutions of the EU have at different times adopted one or other perspective but, frustratingly, they have failed to make the reasons for their choice of ideology explicit. I have identified no fewer than five conceptions of the distortion of competition, the first three based on the free trade ideology, and the remaining two based on a structural policy ideology, all of which appear to have influenced the Community institutions:

(1)   all differences between the laws of the Member States are capable of distorting competition;
(2)   only those differences between the laws of the Member States which do not reflect differences in productivity are capable of distorting competition;
(3)   mere differences between the laws of the Member States are not capable of distorting competition;
(4)   distortions of competition occur where standards in any Member State are unacceptably low;
(5)   the quest for competitive advantage is capable of leading to distortions of competition.

Conceptions (1), (2) and (3) are mutually incompatible. It is necessary, from the free trade perspective, to choose between them. I hope to demonstrate that (1) and (2) are unsound and that from the free trade perspective, (3) must be preferred. (4) and (5) build on (3). I evaluate the strength of the arguments for conceptions (4) and (5). It is to the extent that they are accepted that the most fruitful possibilities for a Community social policy based on the integrationist rationale exist.

THE FREE TRADE IDEOLOGY

Conception (1), which argues that all differences between the laws of the Member States distort competition, can, despite its instinctive appeal,[35] easily be rejected. Arguments in support of a level playing field, grounded on the need for equal conditions of competition, are economically incoherent.[36] Differences between the laws of the Member States result in competition between legal regimes; but why assume that this competition will be distorted? The Commission itself, albeit in the international trade context, has stated that "each state has the sovereign right to choose what labour laws it will enact and

---

[35] "Obviously, a true common market requires that enterprises should compete within it on equal terms. Equally obviously, most social costs fall directly or indirectly on enterprises, so that differences in social systems might be regarded, strictly speaking, as distortions of competition": M Shanks, "The Social Policy of the European Communities", (1977) 14 *CMLRev* 375 at 376.

[36] See B Langille, "Eight Ways to think about International Labour Standards", (1997) 31(4) *Journal of World Trade* 27 at 37–8. See also S Deakin, "Labour Law as Market Regulation: the Economic Foundations of European Social Policy" in Davies *et al*, above n. 2, at 77.

the choice made will reflect both the country's level of economic development and its political and social priorities".[37]

Conception (2), which argues that only those differences between the laws of the Member States which do not reflect differences in productivity are capable of distorting competition, was adopted by the Ohlin and Spaak reports which formed the basis of the social provisions of the EC Treaty.[38] Ohlin states that "differences in the general level of wages and social charges between different countries broadly reflect differences in productivity".[39] The Report goes on to state that adjustments in the exchange rate accurately reflect changes in relative productivity among countries.[40] This leads to the conclusion that:

> "the notion that a general harmonization of social policy is justified by reference to 'distortions of competition' brought about by differences between the labour law regimes of Member States is a delusion".[41]

Exceptionally, however, where there are "specific distortions which favour or handicap certain branches of economic activity",[42] there is a need for harmonisation in order to deal with situations in which differences in the level of social standards are not accounted for by differences in productivity.

Conception (2) relies on two, rather questionable, assumptions. First, it assumes a relationship between labour standards, productivity and the exchange rate, which does not exist.[43] Secondly, it assumes that Member States have the freedom to set their own exchange and interests rates. However, the gradual implementation of monetary union threatens the freedom of action at the national level "which the Ohlin Report considered essential if economic integration was to lead to improved living and working conditions".[44]

Conception (2), like conception (1), assumes that competition between enterprises will only be "undistorted" if enterprises compete on equal terms within a market. Conception (1) insists that enterprises must operate under the same legal regime in order for competition to be undistorted whereas conception (2) holds that competition will be undistorted only if costs per unit of output are equal. Conception (3) represents a radical departure from this approach. It argues that competitive conditions within the European market do not need to

---

[37] European Commission Communication, *The Trading System and Internationally Recognized Labour Standards* (COM(96) 402) at 6.

[38] The Ohlin Report is summarised in (1956) 74 *International Labour Review* 99. The Spaak Report is summarised in "Political and Economic Planning", (1956) *Planning*, no. 405. See also the Commission analysis in the *Explanatory Memorandum on the Proposals Concerning Certain Employment Relationships* (COM(90) 228).

[39] (1956) 74 *International Labour Review* 99 at 102.

[40] Davies, above n. 5, at 321.

[41] Deakin, above n. 36, at 92.

[42] "Political and Economic Planning", (1956) *Planning*, no. 405 at 233–4.

[43] See J Eatwell, "The Euro? It Can Save the World", *The Observer*, 22 August 1999: "Even the most casual student of the foreign exchanges should realise that, these days, the sterling exchange rate has little to do with UK competitiveness or the trade balance. Exchange rates are determined in speculative markets for financial assets".

[44] Deakin, above n. 36, at 82–3.

be equal in order for competition within the market to be undistorted. It relies on regulatory competition—the alteration of national regulation in response to the actual or expected impact of internationally mobile factors of production on national economic activity.[45] According to conception (3), so long as free movement between Member States is guaranteed, competition between legal regimes is not incompatible with the creation of the common or internal market. In fact, the harmonisation of national laws might "negate the competitive process which it was the very purpose of the principle of free movement . . . to stimulate".[46]

> "As long as undertakings have equal access to the domestic market of the State in question, in the sense of freedom to supply both goods and services, there is no reason to assume that differences in labour standards of themselves give rise to a distortion of competition."[47]

At this stage, it is instructive to reconsider the definition of the barrier to free movement. In the above quotation, Simon Deakin claims that in order for the competitive process to operate undertakings must have "equal access" to the domestic market. Thus, national rules which discriminate between undertakings from different Member States or which *prevent* market access are problematic; rules which merely *affect* market access are not. Arguments for this conception of the distortion of competition dovetail with arguments for the "preventing market access" test for barriers to free movement. Only conception (1), which states that all differences between the laws of the Member States are capable of distorting competition, sits easily with the "affecting market access" test for barriers to free movement. It should be rejected. Conception (3) and the preventing market access test are preferable, despite the fact that both reject the need for Community level action on integrationist grounds. Conception (3) sees regulatory competition as "healthy", "free" and "fair". It insists that Member States should be entitled to set their own labour standards and that there is no need for the Community institutions to intervene.

Crucially however, everything changes if a further step is taken. If one is permitted to acknowledge that regulatory competition may, under certain circumstances, be something other than "benign", a role for an integrationist Community social policy based on the elimination of distortions of competition begins to emerge.

THE STRUCTURAL POLICY IDEOLOGY

The second of Snyder's ideologies of competition distinguishes between various types of competition on the basis of their outcomes. Those that lead to positive

---

[45] J M Sun and J Pelkmans, "Regulatory Competition in the Single Market", (1995) 33 *JCMS* 67 at 68–9.

[46] Freedland, above n. 2, at 296.

[47] Deakin, above n. 36, at 74–5.

outcomes are welcomed. Those that do not are condemned as distortions. This ideology aims to ensure that those socio-political interests overlooked by the process of regulatory competition within a market are given due prominence.[48]

Conception (4) is relatively simple. It argues that distortions of competition occur where standards in any Member State are unacceptably low.[49] Where a Member State seeks to compete on the basis of unacceptably low standards the competition may be adjudged unfair, and a distortion of competition can be said to have occurred. Howse and Trebilcock put it as follows:

> "Assuming there is nothing wrongful with another country's environmental or labor policies . . . then why should a cost advantage attributable to these divergent policies not be treated like any other cost advantage, i.e. as part and parcel of comparative advantage?"[50]

Where social standards are unacceptably low, the necessary element of wrongfulness is introduced and, with it, the distortion of competition. If this conception of the distortion of competition is accepted, minimum standard-setting—not harmonisation—will be the appropriate policy response. The objective is not to eliminate the differences between the laws of the Member States but rather to ensure that standards in any Member State do not reach unacceptably low levels. This has been accepted by the Community institutions. As the Commission stated in 1994 "the establishment of a framework of basic minimum standards, which the Commission started some years ago, provides a basic bulwark against using low social standards as an instrument of unfair competition".[51]

The level at which the standards are set is of significance. European standards must be set at a low level. If minimum standards are set at too high a level, they will exclude certain types of "fair" (according to this definition) competition between States. Of course the definition of the "unacceptably low" standard will be controversial. Inspiration may be derived from the ILO, the OECD, or the Council of Europe; or the European Union might develop its own (perhaps higher and more wide-ranging) standards.

Conception (5) affords the greatest scope and indeed the most formidable challenge for Community level social policy. Under this conception distortions of competition can occur even when standards in any single Member State are not unacceptably low. Brian Langille describes the way in which the quest for competitive advantage might distort competition:

---

[48] Joerges, above n. 13, at 142.

[49] The Commission has defined social dumping, as "the gaining of unfair competitive advantage within the Community through unacceptably low social standards". Commission Green Paper, *European Social Policy—Options for the Union* (COM(93) 551) at 7. Note however that the "vogue" term "social dumping", is also associated with the phenomenon described in conception (5) below. See C Barnard, "EC 'Social' Policy" in Craig and de Burca, above n. 16, at 501–6.

[50] R Howse and M Trebilcock, "The Fair Trade/Free Trade Debate: Trade, Labor, and the Environment", (1996) 16 *International Journal of Law and Economics* 61, at 74.

[51] Commission Social Policy White Paper (COM(94) 333) at 5.

"In a world of unemployment in which investment is sought, it might well be in the interest of any one island jurisdiction to lower its optimal standards in an effort to attract the benefits of further jobs brought by investment. And it might be logical for that single jurisdiction to calculate that the loss of optimality in its labour policy would be more than compensated for by the gains in additional investment. The problem is that every other jurisdiction will see the same thing and engage in a process of lowering their labour standards as well".[52]

As a result of this process, every country's social standards might be reduced to sub-optimal levels. In such circumstances competition between legal regimes might be termed "destructive". Simon Deakin and Catherine Barnard have identified a:

"particular danger that 'social dumping' may emerge not so much in the form of large-scale movements of capital to countries with minimal regulation, but as a process which in various ways induces Member States to deregulate in the area of social policy in order to attract or retain capital investments, precipitating a destructive 'race to the bottom' ".[53]

Bernard Ryan agrees, stating that the most basic rationale for Community social policy is "to forestall 'competitive deregulation'—or, government attempts to attract trade and investment by lowering social and employment standards".[54] Pressure for competitive deregulation on the part of governments results from "the possibility that firms that are subjected by their home countries to broad social obligations may suffer disadvantages in international markets, and in response could move jobs to lower-cost regimes".[55]

Competitive pressures have *de facto* restricted the freedom to create social policy at the level of the Member State. As the internal market becomes established those pressures will continue to intensify. In its proposal for a Council Directive establishing a general framework for informing and consulting employees in the European Community, the Commission appears to recognise this. It stated that "the third stage of economic and monetary union will extend and accelerate the competitive pressures at European level" and that "this will mean that more supportive measures are needed at national level". It concluded that "action is needed at Community level to make the essential changes to the existing legal framework".[56]

The challenge for European level social policy lies in articulating a response to the threat, and it need be no more than a threat, of competitive deregulation on the part of States and of opportunistic relocation on the part of mobile

---

[52] Langille, above n. 36, at 42.

[53] S Deakin and C Barnard, "Social Policy in Search of a Role: Integration, Cohesion and Citizenship" in A Caiger and D Floudas (eds), *1992 Onwards: Lowering the Barriers Further* (Chichester, Wiley, 1996) 184.

[54] B Ryan, "Pay, Trade Union Rights and European Community Law", (1997) 13 *IJCLLIR* 305 at 317.

[55] Streeck, above n. 7, at 55.

[56] COM(98) 612, Preamble at 10.

investors. Wolfgang Streeck argues for "European-wide harmonisation of social obligations at a high level";[57] but this fails to take into account the differences between the optimal levels of social policy in the various Member States. Indeed, total harmonisation would allow "high-cost economies [to] impose certain costs on their low-cost competitors, to the detriment of the latter".[58] Minimum-standard setting, of the sort required in order to eliminate distortions of competition where standards are unacceptably low, is an insufficient policy response. Minimum standards may succeed in ruling out certain destructive options for low standard Member States. However, they cannot ensure that higher standard States do not reduce their labour standards to sub-optimal levels in an attempt to attract inward investment, and they may even encourage higher standard States to lower their standards towards the Community minimum.[59] Instead, the EU must aim:

> "to foster economic development of a particular kind by increasing the costs of certain destructive strategies or options for both undertakings and states: by obstructing downward-directed competition, and supporting dynamic modes of adjustment, the overall performance of the economy can be enhanced and the outcome of adjustment made more acceptable".[60]

CONCLUSION

The integrationist rationale for European social policy calls for the elimination of "barriers to free movement" and "distortions of competition". The definition of these terms is contested. The views of the institutions have varied over time, and, in the case of the European Court, its views seemingly vary according to whim. I would urge that the definitions of both terms must remain compatible.

The view that all differences between the labour laws of the Member States create barriers to free movement (on the grounds that they at least potentially affect market access) and distortions of competition (conception (1)) should be rejected. It is based on an unrealistic view of the competitive process and the dictates of the internal market. Moreover, while it affords Community institutions the competence to legislate in the social policy sphere, it only affords the institutions the competence to adopt rigid harmonisation measures of the sort which are neither desirable nor attainable in the labour law field.

The better view is that mere differences between Member State labour laws are not capable of distorting competition (conception (3)) or of creating barriers to free movement (they do not prevent market access). It is important to

---

[57] Streeck, above n. 7, at 55.

[58] E Whiteford, "W(h)ither Social Policy?" in J Shaw and G More (eds), *New Legal Dynamics of European Union* (Oxford, Clarendon Press, 1995) 120.

[59] Thus, the Commission's view that the establishment of a framework of basic minimum standards provides "protection against reducing social standards to gain competitiveness" is only partially correct. See COM(94) 333 at 5.

[60] Deakin, above n. 36, at 88.

stress that according to this view, the competence of the EU to adopt legislation to establish, or to improve the functioning of, the market may be non-existent. Community competence becomes securely established *only* if it can be shown both that the process of regulatory competition (potentially) produces destructive outcomes, and that the Community institutions can improve on those market-driven outcomes. Certainly, the Community institutions should only adopt legislation on the basis of the integrationist rationale if there is evidence that labour law standards in any Member State are unacceptably low or that they have been lowered to sub-optimal levels in the quest for competitive advantage. If such evidence does not exist, the EU should not take action on the basis of the integrationist rationale.

To date, the institutions have done no more than hint at an appreciation of these issues. Each of the five conceptions of the distortion of competition outlined above have received support. The Commission has shown an inclination to invoke the integrationist rationale in order to support all Community level social policy measures, whether they harmonise the laws of the Member States, lay down minimum standards, or offer Member States and/or the social partners a greater degree of flexibility. The integrationist rationale, when properly formulated, cannot lend support to such a wide range of measures. The challenge for the EU is to identify the form that its social legislation must take, specifically so as to prevent both high- and low-standard Member States from engaging in a "a war of competitive deregulation".[61]

[61] J Gray, *False Dawn: The Delusions of Global Capitalism* (London, Granta, 1998) 78.

2

Social Solidarity: A Buttress Against Internal Market Law?

TAMARA HERVEY[1]

INTRODUCTION

The European Court of Justice has observed that "Community law does not detract from the powers of the Member States to organise their social security systems".[2] However, this is not strictly the case. National welfare systems—at a time in which there is increasing interest in "private" or "market-based" models of welfare provision in the Member States[3]—are not automatically or necessarily immune from the application of Community law. Where welfare goods and services are provided through market mechanisms, Community norms of internal market and competition law[4] apply. This is illustrated by recent decisions of the European Court in its "social solidarity" rulings,[5] examined in detail in this chapter.

Social welfare policy in the European Union may be described as an area of

---

[1] Versions of this chapter were delivered at the Jean Monnet Conference, "EU Citizenship and Human Rights", Liverpool, July 1998; the SPTL subject session, "The Limits of EC Social Policy", Oxford, March 1999; the SLSA conference, Loughborough, April 1999; Newcastle Law School staff seminar, April 1999; and the ECSA conference, Pittsburgh, June 1999. I am grateful to Steve Weatherill for comments on earlier drafts: the usual disclaimer applies.

[2] Case 238/82 *Duphar* [1984] ECR 523, para. 16; Cases C–159 and C–160/91 *Poucet and Pistre* [1993] ECR I–637, para. 6; Case C–70/95 *Sodemare SA and others* v. *Regione Lombardia* [1997] ECR I–3395, para. 27; Case C–120/95 *Decker* v. *Caisse de Maladie des Employés Privés* [1998] ECR I–1831, para. 21; Case C–158/96 *Kohll* v. *Union des Caisses de Maladie* [1998] ECR I–1931, para. 17.

[3] M Rhodes and Y Mény, "Europe's Social Contract Under Stress" in M Rhodes and Y Mény (eds), *The Future of European Welfare* (Basingstoke, Macmillan, 1998); V George, "Political Ideology, Globalisation and Welfare Futures in Europe", (1998) 27 *Journal of Social Policy* 17–36; V George, "The Future of the Welfare State" and P Taylor-Gooby, "The Response of Government: Fragile Convergence?" in V George and P Taylor-Gooby (eds), *European Welfare Policy: Squaring the Welfare Circle* (London, Macmillan, 1996); P Taylor-Gooby, "Paying for Welfare: The View from Europe", (1996) 67 *PQ* 116–26; G Esping-Andersen, *Welfare States in Transition: National Adaptations in Global Economies* (London, Sage, 1996).

[4] Articles 23, 25, 28, 29, 39, 43, 49, 50, 81, 82 and 86 (ex 9, 12, 30, 34, 48, 52, 59, 60, 85, 86 and 90) EC and relevant secondary legislation.

[5] *Sodemare*, above n. 2; Case C–67/96 *Albany International BV* v. *Stichting Bedrijfspensioenfonds Textielindustrie* [1999] ECR I–5751; *Decker*, above n. 2; *Kohll*, above n. 2.

"multi-level governance",[6] in which the national or sub-national delivery of welfare provision must take its place within the EU's system of governance and socio-economic constitution. It is in the nature of the EU as an evolutionary system of governance that the influence or reach of Community law extends beyond the formal competencies granted by the EC Treaty.[7] The regulatory autonomy of the Member States has thus been constrained by the obligations on those states to fit their regulatory regimes within the provisions of Community law. This phenomenon has been observed in many fields, including for instance environmental policy,[8] labour law standards,[9] consumer policy,[10] education,[11] and even sport.[12] Hitherto however, it has been assumed that welfare policies remained largely immune from Community law,[13] and yet the changing nature of national welfare provision in the Member States will raise questions pertaining to the nature of the EU's emerging socio-economic constitution. Reform of the welfare state in the EU—a particularly intractable problem for governments of all Member States—must take place not only in the contexts of the challenges posed by changing demographics, post-industrial economies, new forms of unemployment, and the place of women in economic and social life, but also in the context of the EU's system of multi-level governance. The EU's constitutional norms may require modification in order to accommodate the values inherent in European systems of welfare provision, also known as the "European social model".

The application of Community legal norms to elements of national welfare policies opens up the possibility of private litigation, based on directly enforceable Community law, which may challenge or jeopardise the content, structure and mechanisms for provision of public welfare goods and services. The problems this might raise are discussed in the first section of this chapter. Thus, as it has done in the many fields mentioned above, the European Court must become involved in making judgments in the (multi-level) field of social welfare: the Court will in effect be required to become the guardian of the "European social

---

[6] S Leibfried and P Pierson, *European Social Policy: Between Fragmentation and Integration* (Washington, Brookings, 1995); S Leibfried and P Pierson, "Social Policy" in H Wallace and W Wallace (eds), *Policy-Making in the European Union* (Oxford, OUP, 1996).

[7] See J Weiler, "The Transformation of Europe", (1991) 100 *Yale Law Journal* 2403–83; for particular examples see the contributions to P Craig and G de Búrca, *The Evolution of EU Law* (Oxford, OUP, 1999).

[8] See, e.g., J Scott, *EC Environmental Law* (London, Longman, 1998).

[9] See, e.g., B Bercusson, *European Labour Law* (London, Butterworths, 1996).

[10] See, e.g., S Weatherill, *EC Consumer Law and Policy* (London, Longman, 1997)

[11] See, e.g., J Shaw, 'From the Margins to the Centre: Education and Training Law and Policy', in P Craig and G de Búrca (eds), *The Evolution of EU Law* (Oxford, OUP, 1999).

[12] See, e.g., S Weatherill, "Comment on Case C–415/95 *Bosman*, Judgment of the European Court of Justice of 15 December 1995" (1995) 33 *CMLRev* 99 *et seq.*

[13] Although Community law covers some discrete elements of social policy provision, notably sex discrimination in social security (see Directive 79/7/EEC, [1979] OJ L6/24; Article 141 (ex 119) EC; Directive 86/378/EEC, [1986] OJ L225/40, as amended by Directive 96/97/EC, [1997] OJ L46/20; Directive 92/85/EEC, [1992] OJ L348/1) and social security for migrant workers (Regulation 1408/71/EEC, [1971] OJ Sp. Ed. L149/2 II at 416; Regulation 574/72/EEC, [1972] OJ L74/1, as amended).

model".[14] The Court must carry out this task in the context of the existing framework of the European Union's economic constitutional law. This framework of internal market and competition law, with its focus on the "private" activity of market actors, fits poorly with new models for national provision of welfare. These new models seek to move, to some extent, from the provision of welfare goods and services through purely public agents and mechanisms, towards a mix of public and private modes of delivery. Community internal market and competition law—with its continued attempts to maintain clear linear distinctions between the public and the private—is currently ill equipped to deal with the clash of values implicit in the application of such law to national welfare systems. However, the Court appears to be attempting explicitly to address these problems, through articulation of the concept of "social solidarity". The second section of the chapter therefore examines the Court's current conceptualisation of social solidarity, concluding that, with modification, social solidarity has the potential to be an adequate means of protection for the "European social model"; a buttress against internal market law.

NATIONAL WELFARE REGIMES IN JEOPARDY?

In the context of increasing interest in various types of market models for welfare provision among governments of all Member States,[15] there is scope for increasing the application of internal market and competition law to national welfare policies. The Court's mantra, to the effect that "according to settled case law, Community law does not detract from the powers of the Member States to organise their social security systems", does not hold true. Directly effective Community internal market and competition law may be an inhospitable environment for national social welfare entitlements. This is for two main reasons.

First, because Community internal market and competition law is enforceable at the suit of individuals, particular components of national welfare

---

[14] It is beyond the scope of this chapter to consider the possibility of a legislative response from the Council and the European Parliament. However, even if the considerable political difficulties in reaching agreement in the Council of Ministers on social welfare legislation were overcome, the rulings in *Decker* and *Kohll* suggest that the enactment of EU-level coordinating legislation, designed to protect national regulatory regimes, does not totally insulate those regulatory regimes from litigation challenges based on internal market or competition law. A mechanism for coordination of national social security systems at EU level is provided in Regulation 1408/71 EEC, above n. 13, at 416. Article 22(2) of Regulation 1408/71 purports to provide that free moving patients do not have the right to claim financial support from their home Member State for treatments received in another Member State which are not available, or not publicly funded, in the home Member State. The aim of this provision was to prevent patients from circumventing waiting lists in the home Member State by claiming a Community law "right to be treated" in another Member State (see A P van der Mei, "Cross Border Access to Medical Care within the EU—Some Reflections on the Judgments in *Decker* and *Kohll*", (1998) 5 *MJ* 277–97). *Decker* and *Kohll* undermine this intention by bringing into play the fundamental Treaty provisions of Article 28(ex 30) and 49 (ex 59) EC.

[15] See references above n. 3.

provision may be the subject of opportunistic challenge before national courts.[16] Such individual litigation may reveal that some aspects of national laws and policies are inconsistent with Community law, which of course precludes national governments from pursuing those policies or maintaining in place those laws. Thus the overall structure of national welfare systems—crucial in terms of the practical economics of their operation—may be jeopardised by the "piecemeal" nature of such litigation.[17]

Secondly, and probably more importantly in practice, the dynamic of the impact and application of internal market or competition law may mean that the viability of some aspects of national social welfare policies, while not unlawful in a formal sense, comes under question. This may arise for instance from the financial drain placed on national policies by requiring non-discriminatory treatment of all citizens of the European Union (EUCs) or migrant EUC workers,[18] or because of the loss of control over supply implied by the freedom to provide and receive welfare goods and services across frontiers.[19] Control over supply is a classic mechanism for ensuring control over welfare costs in all Member States. Thus, litigation processes may constrain policy options for national or sub-national governments, not by making policies formally unlawful, but by rendering some options politically undesirable. In other words, governments of Member States of the EU no longer maintain total control over the terms on which social welfare is provided within their territory.

Building on a few examples of earlier jurisprudence,[20] the recent cases of *Sodemare*,[21] *Albany International et al*,[22] *Decker*[23] and *Kohll*[24] provide concrete examples of different pressures which Community internal market and competition law may place on national welfare systems. In these cases, the

---

[16] The European Court may hear such challenges under the Article 234 EC preliminary rulings procedure.

[17] See T Wilhelmsson, "Jack-in-the-Box Theory of European Community Law" in L Kramer, H Micklitz and K Tonner, (eds), *Law and Diffuse Interests in the European Legal Order* (Baden-Baden, Nomos, 1997). I am grateful to Steve Weatherill for drawing my attention to this reference.

[18] For instance, in the provision of educational maintenance grants to students in tertiary education; see Case 293/83 *Gravier* v. *City of Liège* [1985] ECR 593; but see also Case 152/82 *Forcheri* v. *Belgium* [1983] ECR 2323; Case 309/85 *Barra* v. *Belgium* [1988] ECR 355; Case 24/86 *Blaizot* v. *University of Liège* [1988] ECR 379; Case 39/86 *Lair* [1988] ECR 3161; Case 197/86 *Brown* v. *Secretary of State for Scotland* [1988] ECR 3205; Case C–357/89 *Raulin* v. *Minister van Onderwijsen Wetenschappen* [1992] ECR I–1027. For further discussion, see J Shaw, "From the Margins to the Centre: Education and Training Law and Policy", in Craig and de Búrca, above n. 11; J Shaw, "The Nature and Extent of 'Educational Rights' under EC Law: a Review", (1998) 20 *JSWFL* 203; T Hervey, *European Social Law and Policy* (London, Longman, 1998) ch. 6; J Shaw, "Education and the Law in the European Community", (1992) 21 *Journal of Law and Education* 415; B De Witte (ed.), *European Community Law of Education* (Baden-Baden, Nomos, 1989).

[19] For instance, if access to health care is limited through restrictive regulation of medical professional qualifications; see the discussion of *Decker*, above n. 2, and *Kohll*, above n. 2.

[20] Principally, Case C–41/90 *Höfner and Elser* [1991] ECR I–1979; *Poucet and Pistre*, above n. 2; Case C–244/94 *Fédération Française des Sociétés d'Assurance (FFSA)* [1995] ECR I–4013.

[21] See above n. 2.

[22] See above n. 5.

[23] See above n. 2.

[24] See above n. 2.

Court appears to be responding explicitly to these problems, through articulation and application of the concept of social solidarity, as a modification of the potentially deregulatory thrust of Community law.

Sodemare concerned the provision of social welfare services of a health care character in residential homes for the elderly in the region of Lombardy in Italy. The region of Lombardy subsidised (through its social welfare and health care budgets) provision of such services by licensed non-profit-making homes. As such non-profit-making homes were almost exclusively Italian, the exclusion of commercially operated homes from receipt of public funds for provision of these health care benefits was indirectly discriminatory on grounds of nationality. A Luxembourg company and its Italian subsidiaries challenged the national legislation on this basis. Questions were asked by the national court in respect of the impact of Articles 52, 58 and 59 EC[25] concerning national legislation which hampers the pursuit of business activity of a company exercising its rights of freedom of establishment in Community law, by imposing on that company the condition either that it carries out its activities on a non-economic basis, or that it takes upon itself the burden of services which should be provided at the expense of the public health service.

The Advocate General (Fennelly) was of the view that the EC Treaty rules on freedom of establishment would apply in such circumstances. Relying on earlier jurisprudence of the Court,[26] the Advocate General set forth as a general proposition of Community law that where sufficient elements of social solidarity were present, measures of national social security law would fall outside the scope of Community internal market law:

> "the existence of systems of social provision established by Member States on the basis of the principle of solidarity does not constitute, as such, an economic activity, so that any inherent consequent restriction on the free movement of goods, services or persons does not attract the application of Treaty provisions. Social solidarity envisages the inherently uncommercial act of involuntary subsidisation of one social group by another. Rules closely connected with financing such schemes are more likely to escape the reach of the Treaty provisions on establishment and services. Thus, pursuit of social objectives on the basis of solidarity may lead Member States to withdraw all or part of the operations of social security schemes from access by private economic operators."[27]

However, where only limited elements of solidarity were present, such as was the case in *Sodemare*, then Community law would apply.[28] The Court, however, did not follow its Advocate General. Rather than making a distinction between this case and the earlier cases, as the Advocate General had done, the Court simply reasserted the principle, articulated in those cases, that "Community law does not detract from the powers of the Member States to

---

[25] Articles 43, 48 and 49 (ex 52, 58 and 59) EC.
[26] *Duphar*, above n. 2, and *Poucet and Pistre*, above n. 2.
[27] *Sodemare*, above n. 2, Opinion of the Advocate General, para. 29.
[28] *FFSA*, above n. 20.

organise their social security systems".[29] For the Court, the relevant comparison was between profit-making companies established in Italy and profit-making companies established in other Member States. Here there was no discrimination.

There appears to be a contradiction in these two statements of the Court. Member States may organise their social security systems without the impact of Community law, *but only so long as they do so without the involvement of "economic operators"*. Thus it follows that if a Member State opts to keep its system of provision sufficiently "public" to satisfy the Court's definition of solidarity, then it will escape the rigours of internal market law. However, a Member State may *not* choose to "privatise" aspects of its social welfare system without subjecting its providers to competition from other Member States. Therefore, a Member State cannot operate a "privatised" social welfare policy without taking into account the possibility (or perhaps likelihood) of interaction with non-national providers. Therefore, for instance, in the UK context, if social security provision is moved onto a more private footing, as suggested in the recent Green Paper on welfare reform,[30] this will require that, unless the United Kingdom can establish a proportionate public interest justification, the "market" in the United Kingdom for social security provision is opened up to competition from providers established in other Member States, and is subject to their regulatory controls. In such circumstances, the United Kingdom will not be able to maintain regulatory control over all providers of social security benefits or services within its territory. Thus, as much as the Court may assert that "Community law does not detract from the powers of the Member States to organise their social security systems", Member States cannot be said to maintain complete control over such systems.

Sodemare illustrates the possibility of introduction of competition from providers of social welfare benefits established in *another* Member State, but the application of Community competition law in the field of social welfare may raise the possibility of increased competition from other *internal* providers. This is illustrated by *Albany International et al*,[31] concerning the Dutch system of compulsory affiliation to sectoral pension funds. Albany International (and the other litigants) were ordered to pay contributions to sectoral pension funds. They refused, on the grounds *inter alia* that their own supplementary pension scheme was more generous than the sectoral scheme. Albany took the view that the national system of compulsory affiliation breached Community competition law in a number of respects, in particular that it constituted an "abuse of a dominant position" by the sectoral pension funds, contrary to Article 86 EC.[32]

[29] *Sodemare*, above n. 2, para. 27.

[30] *New Ambitions for our Country: A New Contract for Welfare* (Cm 3805, Stationery Office, 1998).

[31] *Albany International*, above n. 5; Case C–115–7/97 *Brentjens*; Case C–219/97 *Drijvende Bokken*. [1999] ECR I–5751.

[32] Article 82 (ex 86) EC. This provides that "Any abuse by one or more undertakings of a dominant position within the common market or a substantial part of it shall be prohibited as

According to Article 90(1) EC,[33] public undertakings and "undertakings to which Member States grant special or exclusive rights" are required to comply with Community competition law. Where such an undertaking is entrusted with the provision of a "service of general economic interest", those rules apply only insofar as their application does not obstruct the performance of the particular tasks assigned to them.[34]

The Advocate General (Jacobs) rejected the contention made by the Funds, the Commission, and the governments of intervening Member States (Netherlands, France and Sweden) to the effect that there is a general exception from Community competition law for the social field.[35] The Advocate General found that, within the meaning of the competition law provisions of the EC Treaty, the sectoral pension funds constitute "undertakings", carrying out economic activities, irrespective of their social objectives, and the elements of sector-wide solidarity present within them.[36] According to the Advocate General, "the decisive factor is whether a certain activity is necessarily carried out by public entities or their agents".[37] Therefore if pension provision is made through redistribution, for instance whereby this generation's working population finances the pensions of the previous generation, this by definition is not being carried out by an "undertaking". The concept of generational solidarity implies state activity, not the "economic" activity of an undertaking. In the pension funds at issue here, there were some elements of solidarity, but not enough to deprive the funds of their economic nature.[38] On this point, the Court agreed with its Advocate General.[39] Following earlier jurisprudence,[40] the Court confirmed that organisations with sufficient elements of "solidarity" do not constitute "undertakings" under Community competition law. By contrast, the pension fund at issue here operated in accordance with the principle of

incompatible with the common market in so far as it may affect trade between Member States". The text is unchanged by the Amsterdam Treaty.

[33] Article 86 (ex 90) EC.

[34] Article 86(2) (ex 90(2)) EC. Article 86 (ex 90) provides "(1) In the case of public undertakings and undertakings to which Member States have granted special or exclusive rights, Member States shall neither enact nor maintain in force any measure contrary to the rules contained in this Treaty, in particular to those rules provided for in Article 12 and Articles 81–89. (2) Undertakings entrusted with the operation of services of general economic interest or having the character of a revenue-producing monopoly shall be subject to the rules contained in this Treaty, in particular to the rules on competition, insofar as the application of such rules does not obstruct the performance, in law or in fact, of the particular tasks assigned to them. The development of trade must not be affected to such an extent as would be contrary to the interests of the Community".

[35] *Albany*, above n. 5, Opinion of the Advocate General, para. 23. See *Höfner and Elser*, above n. 20; Case C–55/96 *Job Centre* [1997] ECR I–7119; *Poucet and Pistre*, above n. 2; *FFSA*, above n. 20.

[36] *Albany*, above n. 5, Opinion of the Advocate General, paras. 306–48, distinguishing *Poucet and Pistre*, above n. 2 and Cases C–430 and 431/93 *Van Schijndel and Van Veen* v. *Stichting Pensioenfonds voor Fysiotherapeuten* [1995] ECR I–4705; and following *FFSA*, above n. 20.

[37] *Albany*, above n. 5, Opinion of the Advocate General, para. 330.

[38] *Ibid.*, Opinion of the Advocate General, para. 343.

[39] *Ibid.*, paras. 71–87.

[40] Cited above.

capitalisation, the fund itself determined the amounts of contributions and benefits, the amounts of benefits depended on the financial results of the fund and "in the event of withdrawal from the fund, compensation considered reasonable by the Insurance Board is offered for any damage suffered by the fund, from the actuarial point of view, as a result of the withdrawal", so that, in all these respects, the fund operated in the same way as a private insurance company.[41]

Having decided that the pension funds were undertakings, the Advocate General turned to the issue of whether there was a breach of Articles 90(1) and 86 EC.[42] In view of the compulsory nature of affiliation, the pension funds held exclusive rights (in the sense of Article 90(1)) to collect and administer the contributions. The funds held the further exclusive right to decide on applications for individual exemptions. In applying Article 90(1), the Advocate General adopted what he termed the "*Corbeau*-type approach",[43] according to which Article 90(1) must be read together with Article 90(2), concerning the permissibility of conferral of exclusive rights on undertakings providing a "service of general economic interest". The pension funds did provide a service of general economic interest, that of securing supplementary pension income for a large proportion of the population. In assessing whether the exclusive rights—that is, the compulsory affiliation—are necessary to achieving the objective of providing an adequate level of protection, national courts must assess in detail all relevant economic, financial and social matters:

> "Accordingly, compulsory affiliation as such infringes Articles 90(1) and 86 only where by reason of the Netherlands' regulatory framework the funds are manifestly not in a position to satisfy demand, and where abolishing compulsory affiliation would not obstruct the performance of the services of general interest assigned to the funds".[44]

The Court's approach to the question of compatibility of the position of the funds with Community competition law left rather less discretion to the national court than that of the Advocate General. The Court confirmed that the funds occupied a "dominant position" in the sense of Article 86 EC,[45] but concluded that there was, in this case, no unjustified abuse of that dominant position. The Court did not take a "*Corbeau*-type approach", but rather examined first whether there was a breach of Article 90(1) EC, and then considered whether that breach was justified under Article 90(2) EC. The Court held that an abuse would arise "only if the undertaking in question, merely by exercising the exclusive rights granted to it, is led to abuse its dominant position, or when

---

[41] *Albany*, above n. 5, paras. 80–4.

[42] *Ibid.*, Opinion of the Advocate General, paras. 349–468.

[43] Following Case C–320/91 *Procureur du Roi* v. *Corbeau* [1993] ECR I–2533, a case concerning postal services—a subject matter not in the social security field—in which the Court held that the provision of special (postal) services could be lawfully prohibited only where the existence of those special (postal) service providers would compromise the economic basis and general equilibrium of the general (postal) service.

[44] *Albany*, above n. 5, Opinion of the Advocate General, para. 440.

[45] *Ibid.*, para. 92, following Case C–179/90 *Porto di Genova* [1991] ECR I–5889.

such rights are liable to create a situation in which that undertaking is led to commit such abuses".[46] Restrictions on competition *did* derive directly from the exclusive rights conferred on the sectoral pension fund; the system meant that, as the pension benefits available from the fund no longer met the needs of employers, employers wishing to ensure adequate benefits for their employees were required to make separate "top-up" pension arrangements. Such employers could not enjoy the administrative efficiency of comprehensive pension cover for their employees from a private insurance company. There was thus a *prima facie* breach of Article 90(1) EC. This breach was, however, *justified*, under Article 90(2) EC. The Court held that the pension scheme at issue did fulfil a "service of general economic interest" in the Netherlands pensions system,[47] and that its exclusive right (to enjoy compulsory affiliation) was necessary for the performance of that service.[48] In reaching this conclusion, the Court explicitly considered matters of social solidarity. The fund at issue displayed a high level of solidarity, including elements such as the fact that contributions did not reflect individual risks, there was an obligation to accept all workers without a medical examination, pensions continued to accrue in the event of non-payment of contributions through incapacity for work, and the amount of pensions was index-linked in order to maintain their value. Perhaps most telling is the Court's exploration of cross-generational, cross-income, cross-undertaking and activity risk subsidisation:

> "If the exclusive right of the fund to manage the supplementary pension scheme for all workers in a given sector were removed, undertakings with young employees in good health, engaged in non-dangerous activities would seek more advantageous insurance terms from private insurers. The progressive departure of 'good' risks would leave the sectoral pension fund with responsibility for an increasing share of 'bad' risks, thereby increasing the cost of pensions for workers, particularly those in small and medium-sized undertakings, with older employees engaged in dangerous activities, to which the fund could no longer offer pensions at an acceptable cost".[49]

Although the scheme at issue was held to be lawful, the Court's ruling in *Albany* confirms that, in principle, social insurance schemes may be subject to Community competition law. Thus, it is possible for undertakings administering social insurance schemes to "abuse their dominant position" in contravention of Article 82 (ex 86) EC. Such undertakings would almost certainly be granted "special or exclusive rights", as otherwise they would not be able to provide the service of universal social insurance, and thus are likely to occupy a dominant position. This is all the more likely if the relevant market is restricted to provision of social insurance of a particular type (for instance, as in *Albany*, retirement pensions), to those working in a particular Member State, or a particular economic sector within a Member State. One potential effect of the

[46] *Ibid.*, para. 93.
[47] *Ibid.*, para. 105.
[48] *Ibid.*, para. 111.
[49] *Ibid.*, para. 108.

application of Community competition law in such a case may be an increased risk of "cream-skimming" activities in pensions markets. Private pension providers must have a sufficient incentive to make a profit. Notwithstanding the possibility of profit-making through increased efficiency, there must be at least a possibility that such providers will seek to enter only the more lucrative parts of the pensions market, for instance by restricting access to lower risk groups. Governments of the Member States may impose regulatory standards on providers of such pensions, in order to counteract such behaviour. Whether these regulatory standards are justifiable will be a question of Community competition law.

In addition to the *Sodemare* situation of cross-border provision of social welfare by providers established in another Member State, Community internal market law may also have an effect on cross-border *receipt* of social welfare goods or services by individuals. This is illustrated by *Decker* and *Kohll*, involving requests to the Luxembourg social security funds for reimbursement for medical goods or treatment. In *Decker*, the issue concerned a Luxembourg national who bought, on a prescription given by an ophthalmologist established in Luxembourg, a pair of prescription spectacles from an optician established in Belgium. According to national law, treatment abroad would be reimbursed by the social security fund only where prior authorisation had been granted. That was not the case in Decker's circumstances, and so authorisation was refused. Decker challenged the refusal on the grounds that it breached Article 30 EC,[50] in that it constituted a hindrance to the free movement of goods within the internal market. The national court took the view that this case fell within Regulation 1408/71/EEC, not Article 30 EC. Article 22 of Regulation 1408/71 provides that *authorised* individuals may go to another Member State to receive medical treatment. It does not impose any duty on a Member State to grant authorisation to receive medical treatment, at the expense of the responsible Member State's public health funds, in another Member State, except in the unusual situation in which the treatment sought is not available in the responsible Member State.[51]

The European Court repeated its established formula that "according to settled case law, Community law does not detract from the powers of the Member States to organise their social security systems", citing *Sodemare*.[52] However, it went on to note that "the Member States must nevertheless comply with Community law when exercising those powers".[53] The Court found that the fact that the national rules at issue fell within Regulation 1408/71 did not

---

[50] Article 28 (ex 30) EC.

[51] See Case 117/77 *Pierek (No. 1)* [1978] ECR 825 and Case 182/78 *Pierek (No. 2)* [1979] ECR 1977. The responsible Member State is normally the state of residence of the person in receipt of the social security benefit. See further A P van der Mei, above n. 14; T Hervey, "Buy Baby: The European Union and the Regulation of Human Reproduction", (1998) 18 *OJLS* 18, 207–33, 215–16.

[52] *Decker*, above n. 2, para. 21.

[53] *Ibid.*, para. 23.

exclude the application of Article 30 EC.[54] This is in stark contrast to *Sodemare* where the rules at issue were found to be outside the scope of internal market law. Therefore, the Court had little difficulty in finding that the rules of the Luxembourg social security scheme, by requiring a prior authorisation to purchase spectacles from an optician established outside Luxembourg, but no prior authorisation to purchase spectacles from an optician established in Luxembourg, constituted a barrier to the free movement of goods, as the national rules are liable to curb the import of spectacles assembled in other Member States.[55] Moreover, with regard to Luxembourg's submission that the national rules were justified by the need to control health expenditure—an argument based on the social solidarity concept—the Court accepted that as spectacles were reimbursed only at a flat rate, the financial burden on the social security funds was the same as it would have been had the spectacles been bought in Luxembourg. In general, the risk of seriously undermining the financial balance of a national social security system could constitute a justification, but here that risk was not present.[56] The Court therefore found that the national rules requiring prior authorisation breached Articles 30 and 36 EC.

In *Kohll*, decided on the same day, the Court was faced with a very similar issue, only this time concerned with receipt of services. Kohll (a Luxembourg national) challenged the refusal of authorisation for his daughter to receive dental treatment in Trier, Germany. Kohll's doctor recommended treatment by an orthodontist established there, but the social security medical supervisors refused to authorise payment for the treatment from the social security fund. Only one orthodontist established in Luxembourg would have been able to give the treatment, thus the daughter would have had to wait much longer if she were to receive treatment there, rather than in Germany.

The text of the judgment in *Kohll* is very similar to that in *Decker*. The Court held that the "special nature of certain services does not remove them from the ambit of the fundamental principle of freedom of movement".[57] Treatment was to be provided for remuneration by an orthodontist, established in another Member State "outside any hospital [i.e. public] infrastructure".[58] Thus the application of Articles 59 and 60 EC[59] on provision of services was not excluded in this case. Luxembourg again raised as justification the need to control health expenditure. The Court accepted the argument of Mr Kohll, that he was asking for reimbursement only at the Luxembourg rate, and so application of the free movement rules presented no threat to the financial stability of the social security scheme.[60] Justification was not established.

[54] *Ibid.*, para. 25.
[55] *Ibid.*, para. 36, following Case 8/74 *Procureur du Roi* v. *Dassonville* [1974] ECR 837.
[56] *Ibid.*, paras. 39–40.
[57] *Kohll*, above n. 2, para. 20.
[58] *Ibid.*, para. 29.
[59] Articles 49 and 50 (ex 59 and 60) EC.
[60] *Kohll*, above n. 2, para. 37.

The *Decker* and *Kohll* cases establish that, provided that no direct threat is posed to the financial stability of the social security funds, individuals may receive health or welfare benefits from providers in another Member State, and require that their national social security funds meet the cost, at least at the rate at which they would be reimbursed if the benefit were received in the home Member State. Of course, this principle applies only in the case of benefits or social services provided through the mechanism of cash benefits to be spent in the market of social service providers. The principle would not apply where a Member State makes provision through publicly funded services, and health or welfare benefits are free at the point of receipt.

Two distinct pressures on national health systems may arise from the rulings. Difficulties experienced by those Member States whose nationals go elsewhere to receive medical treatment or purchase medical goods[61] are unlikely to affect a Member State where health services are not, in the main, financed through a mechanism of cash benefits. However, a Member State in which professionals have both national health service and privately funded patients[62] might find itself becoming a "host state", to which patients go to receive medical goods or services. Such host states may experience an unpredictable influx of patients. This may have an impact on national health care provision for nationals, for instance longer waiting lists. Nothing in the *Decker* or *Kohll* judgments appears to provide a mechanism by which such host states may protect the stability of their health service systems, as they may not lawfully refuse treatment to non-nationals as to do so would be discriminatory, contrary to Articles 49 (ex 59) and 12 (ex 6) EC. Moreover, a Member State that provides a higher standard of service, better value for money, or a greater choice for medical "consumers" is likely to attract more free movers to receive these services. Perhaps, for instance, Decker wanted to go to Belgium to purchase spectacles because the choice of frames and lenses was greater there. Or perhaps the amount of reimbursement would purchase a higher quality of spectacles on the Belgian market than in Luxembourg. Member States whose medical profession enjoys a high reputation may attract free movers seeking treatment. As a worst case scenario, if such pressures reached extreme levels, there might be a temptation on the part of the national authorities of those states to reduce the quality of service provided, in order to discourage such "medical tourism"; a classic "race to the bottom".

An examination of the potential effects of the principles established in these social solidarity cases illustrates that the application of Community internal market and competition law, through individual litigation, may have not insignificant effects on the organisation, financing, delivery and even content of social welfare in the Member States of the EU. The impact of internal market or competition law on social welfare provision is often regarded—in terms of "social or welfare dumping", promoting regulatory competition and "the race

---

[61] In particular, loss of control over supply as a cost containment measure.
[62] As is the case, for instance, with dental professionals in the United Kingdom.

to the bottom"—as a threat to the "European social model".[63] There are, of course, many social models among the Member States of the EU.[64] A distinctively "European" model is discernible only at a high level of abstraction. However, this does not mean that the values encapsulated in the phrase the "European social model" are not worthy of protection. The concern is that Member States may be tempted to lower their levels of social welfare provision, or alter the principles upon which social welfare provision is based, in response (*inter alia*) to the competitive pressures of the internal market on such measures. Commentators do not agree on whether the phenomenon of welfare dumping really exists.[65] However, for the purposes of this chapter, this in itself is not particularly important. What matters is that policy-makers and other institutional actors behave as if it might be a reality, and thus seek to protect "European" national welfare provision from such regulatory competition within the EU which might place the values implicit in European welfare models in jeopardy. The Court's role in this respect has focused on the concept of social solidarity.

SOCIAL SOLIDARITY TO THE RESCUE?

At least at first sight, it would seem that the Court is indeed already responding to the threat or potential threat to the "European social model" posed by the application of internal market and competition law to new modes of national social welfare provision. The Court is explicit in its discussion of the financial pressures potentially placed on national systems by the unfettered application of Community internal market or competition rules, and the consequent social

---

[63] Defined by Commissioner Flynn in a speech for the conference "Visions for European Governance", Harvard University, 2 March 1999, as follows. "The European social model spans many policy areas. Education and training. Health and welfare. Social protection. Dialogue between independent trades unions and employers. Health and safety at work. The pursuit of equality. The fight against racism and discrimination. It takes many forms—welfare systems, collective arrangements, delivery mechanisms. It has been conceived, and is still applied, in many different ways. By different agents. Under different public, private and third sector arrangements in different parts of Europe. It is a system steeped in plurality and diversity—reflecting our richness of culture, tradition and political development. All the variants reflect and respect two common and balancing principles. One is competition—the driving force behind economic progress—the other is solidarity between citizens".

[64] See T Hervey, above n. 18, at 57–61; G Esping-Andersen, *The Three Worlds of Welfare Capitalism* (Cambridge, Polity Press, 1990); N Ginsburg, *Divisions of Welfare* (London, Sage, 1992); A Cochrane, "Comparative Approaches to Social Policy" and "Looking for a European Welfare State" in A Cochrane and J Clarke (eds), *Comparing Welfare States: Britain in International Context* (London, Open University Press, 1993); R Gomà, "The Social Dimension of the European Union: a New Type of Welfare System?", (1996) 3 *JEPP* 209–30; Rhodes and Mény, above n. 3; M Ferrera, "The Four Social Europes: Between Universalism and Selectivity" in Rhodes and Mény, above n. 3.

[65] For an overview, see C Barnard, *EC Employment Law* (Chichester, Wiley, 1996) 81–7. See also H Mosley, "The Social Dimension of European Integration", (1990) 129 *International Labour Review* 147–63; M Kleinman and D Piachaud, "European Social Policy: Conceptions and Choices", (1993) 3 *JESP* 1–19; S Deakin, "Labour Law as Market Regulation" in Davies *et al*, *European Community Labour Law: Principles and Perspectives* (London, Clarendon, 1996).

dumping, regulatory competition, or "race to the bottom" considerations. The Court is using social solidarity as a means by which to articulate these arguments. However, a number of problems remain with the Court's notion of social solidarity, at least as currently conceptualised. This section of the chapter therefore examines the core elements of the current concept of social solidarity, and suggests where the Court's jurisprudence could be adjusted in order to ensure that the "European social model" remains adequately protected.

First, the Court's jurisprudence operates on the assumption that systems or bodies promoting social solidarity are not carrying out "economic" activity. It is assumed that social solidarity systems are based on social aims, not on the "economic" goal of profit-making.[66] This definition of social solidarity contains a curious elision of "economic" and "commercial" or "for-profit" activity. Subsidisation of one social group by another may not be a commercial activity, if no profits accrue to the provider. However, it may be carried out for sound economic reasons, for instance to ensure a healthy workforce. The confusion here is exacerbated by the additional assumption that private actors always operate on a commercial, for-profit basis.[67] This stark division between "commercial" or "for-profit" and social solidarity providers of welfare benefits and services is already difficult to maintain, and is likely to become more so, as social welfare systems adjust to the current circumstances in which the market has established itself as an integral provider of social welfare services.[68] The assumptions (in particular concerning patterns of employment) on which the state-funded provision of the 1950s and 1960s settlement of welfare capitalism were based, have been significantly eroded since the 1980s. These trends have led to increased interest among all western democracies, including the Member States of the EU, in "privatisation" of welfare provision, for instance by granting direct cash benefits to be spent in the market of social service providers or the contracting-out of service provision to private enterprises in competition for government social services contracts.

This state of affairs points up a second shortcoming of social solidarity as currently conceived by the Court; the assumption that direct state or public involvement in provision of benefits by means of social solidarity systems is necessary. The Court takes the view that welfare benefits provided by such systems cannot be effectively provided through private market actors. In some Member States, "third sector" voluntary or charitable organisations are traditionally key providers of social welfare benefits and services; indeed it was such providers that were at issue in *Sodemare*. These providers are neither "public" (part of the institutions of the state) nor "private" in the sense of commercial, for-profit

---

[66] Although the fact that a scheme is non-profit-making does not necessarily remove it from the scope of Community law, see *Albany*, above n. 5, para. 85.

[67] Conversely, "not-for-profit" activity does not necessarily mean activity of no commercial value; consider, for instance, Richard Branson's proposal to operate the UK national lottery on a not-for-profit basis.

[68] M Cahill, *The New Social Policy* (London, Blackwell, 1994); P Spicker, *Social Policy: Themes and Approaches* (London, Prentice Hall/Harvester Wheatsheaf, 1995).

operators. Social solidarity as currently conceived does not take sufficient account of such different mechanisms for provision of social welfare benefits, or the reorganisation of European social welfare systems to include such private or third sector actors. The "necessity" of state action is also a problematic element of the Court's current definition of social solidarity. In one sense, no state "needs" to provide any social security or social welfare measures. But all Member States of the EU do so, because that is the political choice made by their citizens. The debate is not over whether some sort of welfare provision needs to be made, but on how it should be effectively provided. Governments of Member States might argue that they "need" to provide social welfare benefits through private for-profit organs, or through charitable institutions, rather than state bodies, for instance in order to achieve value for money or to ensure that provision is financed in a situation of an ageing population. Yet it is precisely such profit-making organs that the Court seeks to expose to the provisions of Community internal market and competition law. If this leads simply to the more efficient provision of social welfare, then it cannot be objectionable. But it may be that opening up cross-border competition in social welfare provision exposes financially unprofitable (but socially necessary) elements of such provision to "cream-skimming" by private providers. Such exposure may lead to "race to the bottom" or welfare dumping pressures on European social models, if Member States seek to reduce the provision of social welfare benefits so that their national providers can compete with those from other Member States. If this were to happen, the level of social welfare provision might be reduced across the EU as a whole, or the principles upon which social welfare is provided might be altered, thus jeopardising welfare components of the European social model. The principle of social solidarity should be refined in order to guard against this.

Thirdly, the key common factor in social solidarity systems appears to be that of subsidisation,[69] either across the generations, or within one generation, for instance across social classes, or across those who are wealthy and those who are not able to meet their basic needs, or across those who are healthy and those who are not. According to the Court, subsidisation can be effected through public taxation systems, though it need not be so. However, the Court has not yet sufficiently separated out the ideas of cross-subsidisation, public or not-for-profit activity and private, commercial or for-profit activity. The Court's rulings suggest that cross-subsidisation assumes a public or not-for-profit provider. Yet many private social security or insurance schemes, operated for profit, work on precisely the basis of subsidisation by one group of another. This is particularly the case for private retirement pension schemes and private health care schemes.

---

[69] For discussion of different types of subsidisation, see L Hancher and J-L B Sierra, "Cross-Subsidization and EC Law", (1998) 35 *CMLRev* 901–45, at 905–6; G B Abbamonte, "Cross-subsidisation and Community Competition Rules: Efficient Pricing Versus Equity?", (1998) 23 *ELRev* 414–33; A Winterstein, "Nailing the Jellyfish: Social Security and Competition Law", [1999] 6 *ECLR* 324–33.

Cross-subsidisation and profit are not necessarily mutually exclusive; social solidarity as currently conceived implies that they are. Rather, the Court should concentrate, as it did in *Albany International*, on the equality of access and benefits for "good" and "bad" risks implied by cross-subsidisation in the social solidarity sense.

Fourthly, it is assumed that provision of social welfare benefits through mechanisms of cross-subsidisation, such as public taxation or mandatory social insurance, is essentially an "involuntary" act on the part of those involved, either as contributors or as recipients. It might be objected that the participation of citizens in the political process through which the policies underpinning such public collective provision of welfare are developed is implicitly *voluntary*. The idea of the "social contract", implicit in the "European social model", although perhaps under threat in the 1990s, still underpins social welfare provision in the Member States of the EU. If the Court were to develop the notion of social solidarity as part of a tentatively emerging "European social citizenship", implicitly agreed upon by EUCs, this would help to fix social solidarity as an intrinsic principle of the European system of governance.

Finally, purely in legalistic terms, the Court seems to have failed to make clear whether social solidarity is a test for whether the activities of a body fall within the scope of Community law, or whether social solidarity provides a justification or exception from Community law.[70] Indeed in *Albany International*, the Court used social solidarity for both purposes, with the result that the scheme at issue was held to have sufficient elements of social solidarity to fall within Community competition law, but at the same time sufficient elements of social solidarity to ensure its exemption under Article 90(2) EC.[71] This in itself is not a problem, although it does make it difficult to apply social solidarity in advance, in order to determine whether a particular regime is consistent with Community law. Such uncertainty might prompt increased litigation.[72]

All these objections suggest that the current concept of social solidarity may not at present be sufficiently rigorous to protect national social welfare provi-

---

[70] The outcome of litigation might be the same whichever is the case, but the issue has ramifications in terms of the reach of Community law, and in terms of which legal system applies in a particular situation. A comparison may be drawn with the debate surrounding Case C–159/90 *SPUC* v. *Grogan* [1991] ECR I–4685; see for instance D. Phelan, "Right to Life of the Unborn v. Promotion of Trade in Services: the European Court of Justice and the Normative Shaping of the European Union", (1992) 55 *MLR* 670–89.

[71] On the status of Article 86(2) (ex 90(2)) EC, see L Hancher, "Community, State, and Market" in Craig and de Búrca, above n. 7, D Edwards and M Hoskins, "Article 90: Deregulation and EC Law. Reflections arising from the XVI FIDE Conference", (1995) 32 *CMLRev* 157–86; W Sauter, *Competition Law and Industrial Policy in the EU* (Oxford, Clarendon Press, 1997) 148–53.

[72] There are clear parallels here with the difficulties faced by the Court in dealing with the opportunistic litigants in the Sunday trading cases (Case 145/88 *Torfaen BC* v. *B & Q plc* [1989] ECR 765; Case C–169/91 *Stoke on Trent and Norwich City Councils* v. *B & Q plc* [1992] ECR I–6635) which the Court sought to resolve in its controversial ruling in Cases C–267 and 268/91 *Keck and Mithouard* [1993] ECR I–6097. See N Reich, "The November Revolution of the European Court of Justice", (1994) 31 *CMLRev* 459; S. Weatherill, "After *Keck*: Some Thoughts on How to Clarify the Clarification", (1996) 33 *CMLRev* 885.

sion from internal market and competition law. However, there is ample scope for the Court to develop the concept in future jurisprudence, in order to take account of the changing face of social welfare provision in the EU, and to give adequate protection to the "European social model".

CONCLUSIONS

The matters raised by the social solidarity cases are of course one example of the more fundamental question: what kind of system of governance is to be created in the European Union?[73] Is it to be a system in which integration through the internal market and free competition is paramount? Or is it to be one in which "European" social values are respected and protected, even in cases in which they conflict with such "market" aims? If the system is to tend towards the former model and the prevention of anti-competitive behaviour by market actors, then individual rights to freedom of movement, and cross-border provision of goods and services, should be readily enforceable. Exceptions to such individual rights should be very narrowly defined. If, however, the system aims to move towards the latter model, then exercise of such individual rights must be mediated within the system through application of collective values, *inter alia* of social welfare. In that case, cases such as *Sodemare, Decker, Kohll* and *Albany International* do not present a threat to the "European social model", but rather an opportunity to promote social solidarity, as a buttress against internal market law. To achieve this aim, social solidarity needs to be more firmly "embedded in the *acquis communautaire*",[74] and more clearly articulated by the European Court in its application of Community internal market and competition law.

---

[73] A selection from the massive literature pertinent to this issue includes S Weatherill, *Law and Integration in the European Union* (Oxford, Clarendon, 1995); M P Maduro, *We, the Court: The European Court of Justice and the European Economic Constitution* (Oxford, Hart Publishing, 1998); M P Maduro, "Reforming the Market or the State?", (1997) 3 *ELJ* 55–82; C Joerges, "European Economic Law, the Nation State and the Maastricht Treaty" in R Dehousse (ed.), *Europe After Maastricht: An Ever Closer Union?* (Munich, Beck, 1994); B Bercusson *et al*, "A Manifesto for Social Europe", (1997) 3 *ELJ* 189–205.

[74] A Wiener, "The Embedded Acquis Communautaire: Transmission Belt and Prism of New Governance", (1998) 4 *ELJ* 294–315.

3

Regulating Competitive Federalism in the European Union? The Case of EU Social Policy

CATHERINE BARNARD

The founders of the European Union considered that regulatory competition between the Member States would produce the most allocatively efficient results. The EU itself would need to provide only the conditions in which this could take place. Thus social policy was a matter to be regulated by the Member States, competing with each other for the most favourable regimes. This model, reinvigorated by the inclusion of the principle of subsidiarity in the EC Treaty at Maastricht, has continued to hold considerable sway over thinking in the EU. However, the weakness of this model, due largely to the problems of market failure, has focused attention on the benefits of centralised "federal" legislation. This also has its drawbacks.

The purpose of this chapter is twofold. First, it shows that the pure model of a perfectly competitive market can never be realised in the EU. Secondly, it suggests that a Community legislative response wedded solely to the question of market failure is fraught with difficulty. It therefore argues that the justification for EU social policy must inevitably extend beyond a simple response to market failures. Once this separation occurs, then the nature, form and content of Community legislation no longer has to respond simply to an economic imperative but can, more realistically, be orientated towards social and political purposes. However, given the (largely economic) arguments in favour of decentralised legislation the chapter concludes by looking at the ways in which regulatory competition can be harnessed to centralised legislation.

COMPETITIVE FEDERALISM

The basic model

According to Tiebout's theory of a perfectly competitive market,[1] decentralisation in the production and supply of public goods (laws) by the state enables the

[1] C M Tiebout, "A Pure Theory of Local Expenditure", (1956) 64/5 *Journal of Political Economy* 416–24.

demands of the consumers for these services to be matched to their supply. If demand and supply can be brought into equilibrium then efficiency will be maximised in a Pareto sense, so that there is no rearrangement of resources (no possible change in production and consumption) such that someone can be made better off without, at the same time, making someone else worse off.[2] This efficiency is, however, dependent on perfect mobility on the part of the consumers and full autonomy on the part of the law-makers.[3] Provided these conditions are satisfied then the market will be allocatively efficient and standards in the Member States may converge spontaneously. As Sun and Pelkmans explain:[4]

> "When regulatory competition is a substitute for harmonization, internal market forces would respond to differences in national regulation. The subsequent variations in the flows of goods, services and factors would force the adversely affected Member States to react. Such an iterative process would eventually bring about a 'market-driven' regulatory convergence. Since market preferences would probably be better revealed by the dynamics of regulatory competition, than by bureaucracy driven and politicized harmonization in the Council, regulatory competition would further be a superior solution on normative economic grounds".

Thus, competition between states should produce optimal, efficient and innovative legislation (a race to the top). Various arguments have been advanced why this might be the case.[5] First, as Posner explains in the American context,[6] government by the individual states prevents the massive diseconomies of scale that would be encountered by any effort to govern so large, populous and complex a society as the USA from Washington. Secondly, state officials vie with one another to create increasingly attractive economic circumstances for their citizens, knowing that their re-election depends upon favourable comparative economic performances.[7] This is especially important in the social/labour context.[8] Thirdly, it is thought that federal law is more sus-

---

[2] G Majone, "The European Community Between Social Policy and Social Regulation", (1993) 31 *JCMS* 153, 154.

[3] S Deakin, "Two Types of Regulatory Competition: Competitive Federalism versus Reflexive Harmonisation: A Law and Economic Perspective on *Centros*", (2000) 2 *Cambridge Yearbook of European Legal Studies*, forthcoming.

[4] J Sun and J Pelkmans, "Regulatory Competition in the Single Market", (1995) 33 *JCMS* 67, 70.

[5] J Trachtmann, "International Regulatory Competition, Externalization and Jurisdiction", (1993) 34 *Harvard International Law Journal* 47, agrees and provides a useful analysis of David Charny's work and it is this which will be examined below.

[6] R Posner, "The Constitution as an Economic Document", (1987) 56 *George Washington Law Review* 4, 13–15.

[7] D Tarullo, "Federalism Issues in the United States" in A Castro, P Méhaut and J Rubery, *International Integration and Labour Market Organisation* (London, Academic Press, 1992) 101. For a discussion of the public choice versus public interest theory, see B Cheffins, *Company Law: Theory, Structure and Operations* (Oxford, Clarendon Press, 1997) 20.

[8] R J Daniels, "Should Provinces Compete? The Case for a Competitive Corporate Law Market", (1991) 36 *McGill Law Journal* 130, at 139.

ceptible than state law to the interests of *ad hoc* national coalitions[9] and special groups[10] to the detriment of resulting federal legislation.

State competition and decentralised regulation produce other advantages, notably "cultural specificity". As Charny explains, decentralisation facilitates adaptation to local conditions.[11] In the corporate context, local transaction cultures call for rules fitted to the local culture. Local decision-makers are better informed about the culture than a centralised decision-maker, and may face better incentives to accommodate the local culture. This is of particular importance in the case of "embedded" rules: namely rules that make sense because of the way they fit into other rules or practices adopted by the community. This leads to greater "voter preference satisfaction"[12] from having local concentrations of values and beliefs reflected in legislation.

Different rules also allow for localised experimentation with different forms of regulation, providing for comparative data to assist in regulatory reform and reducing the risk of widespread adoption of flawed laws. This is the classic "laboratory of democracy" theory[13] which recognises that competition is a dynamic process where trial and error is the best means for finding the best solution to complex problems.[14] This point was noted by Paul Weiler in the Canadian labour law context. He argued that:

> "The events of the 1970s have demonstrated the virtues of provincial jurisdiction and federal diversity . . . Individual provinces can try out serious innovations. Each legislature responds to different characteristics of its industries; different complexion of the workforce and its trade union allegiance; different political spectra. If a statutory experiment proves successful, it can and is emulated elsewhere in the country.[15] If it proves a mistake, it can be quickly liquidated without widespread damage".[16]

[9] Daniels, above n. 8, at 138.

[10] D Charny, "Competition among Jurisdictions in Formulating Corporate Law Rules: An American Perspective on the 'Race to the Bottom' in the European Communities", (1991) 32 *Harvard International Law Journal* 422, 440. On the other hand, J Macey and G Miller ("Toward an Interest Group Theory of Delaware Corporate Law", (1987) 65 *Texas Law Review* 469) show that Delaware law reflects an internal equilibrium among competing interest groups, in particular the Delaware bar, Delaware corporation service companies who make a living assisting out-of-state-companies in obtaining and maintaining corporate charters, and firms such as construction companies which stand to benefit in the longer term from increased state revenue.

[11] Charny, above n. 10, at 440–1.

[12] Daniels, above n. 8, at 138.

[13] Tarullo, above, n. 7, at 101.

[14] R Van den Bergh, "The Subsidiarity Principle in European Community Law: Some Insights from Law and Economics", (1994) 1 *Maastricht Journal of European and Comparative Law* 337, citing F A von Hayek, "Competition as a Discovery Process" in *New Studies in Philosophy, Politics, Economics and the History of Ideas* (Chicago, University of Chicago Press, 1978) 149.

[15] As Van den Bergh points out, above n. 14, dynamic competitive processes may produce voluntary harmonisation which may be larger than the degree of uniformity brought about by directives which, as in the case of Directive 93/104/EC on Working Time, [1993] OJ L307/18, contain derogations and opt-outs. If states choose to adapt their legislation to the superior rules of competing states a greater degree of uniformity may be reached.

[16] P Weiler, "The Virtues of Federalism in Canadian Labour Law" in F Bairstow *et al* (eds), *The Direction of Labour Policy in Canada, 25th Annual Conference, 1977* (Montreal, Industrial Relations Centre, McGill University, 1977) 58, 59 cited in Daniels, above n. 8, at 130.

Have the theoretical arguments been borne out by practice? The striking success of the American state of Delaware in attracting incorporations and reincorporations of business[17] would tend to suggest that it has. Over 40 per cent of New York stock-exchange-listed companies, and over 50 per cent of Fortune 500 companies, are incorporated in Delaware; 82 per cent of publicly traded firms that reincorporate move to Delaware[18] and 90 per cent of New York Stock Exchange-listed companies that reincorporated between 1927 and 1977 moved to Delaware.[19] It would therefore seem that competition between states to provide the most suitable "market for incorporation" has created the incentive for each state to offer the most efficient laws. Fischel concludes that Delaware's preeminence is "in all probability attributable to success in a 'climb to the top' rather than to victory in a 'race to the bottom'".[20] This produces substantial revenues from incorporation fees.[21] Winter goes further. He has argued that competition among states has worked to ensure not only the production of state corporate laws that are distinguished by their innovative and responsive nature[22] but also by their capacity to enhance shareholder welfare.[23] Because of the incentives on management to perform well[24] managers will choose to incor-

---

[17] See further C Barnard, "Social Dumping and Race to the Bottom: Some Lessons for the EU from Delaware?" (2000) 25 *ELRev.* 57.

[18] Data provided by Joseph Grundfest, SEC Commissioner, to the Council of the Corporate Law section of the Delaware State Bar Association, reprinted in Charny, above n. at 428. See also Kaouris, "Is Delaware a Haven for Incorporation?", (1995) 20 *Delaware Journal of Corporation Law* 965, 1011, who found that out of 255 surveyed companies that changed their corporate domicile between 1982 and 1994, 89 per cent reincorporated to Delaware.

[19] Dodd and Leftwich, "The Market for Corporate Charters: 'Unhealthy Competition' versus Federal Regulation" (1980) 53 *Journal of Business* 259, 263. According to Dodd and Leftwich, the states receiving the next largest numbers of changes were Connecticut, New Jersey, New York and Pennsylvania, each of which received only two changes (1.4 per cent).

[20] D Fischel, "The 'Rrace to the Bottom' Revisited: Reflections on Recent Developments in Delaware's Corporation Law", (1982) 76 *Northwestern University Law Review* 913, 920. See also F Easterbrook "The Economics of Federalism", (1983) 26 *Journal of Law and Economics* 23, 28 and F Easterbrook and D Fischel, "Voting in Corporate Law", (1983) 26 *Journal of Law and Economics* 395.

[21] Charny, above n. 10, at 431–2.

[22] D Schaffer, "Delaware's Limit on Director's Liability: How the Market for Incorporation Shapes Corporation Law", (1987) 10 *Harvard Journal of Law and Public Policy* 665, offers two examples of this: the first concerns the Revised Code of 1967, the second concerns the amendments made in response to the liability crisis created by the collapse in the directors and officers insurance market. As Schaffer explains (at 687), "The market works; corporate law is amended; and the Delaware legislature and judiciary continue to provide efficient legal rules for the conduct of American business". He also points out that Delaware increased the number of new incorporations by 28 per cent in the six months following the enactment of the amendments, and derived an additional $1.4 million in fees from the new incorporations. See also R Romano, *The Genius of American Corporate Law* (AEI Press, 1993) 240. She demonstrates that while Delaware was the first state to enact only one of the four laws under study, it adopted the other three within four to seven years from their introduction in another jurisdiction and, as a result, it outpaced the other states.

[23] R Winter, "State Law, Shareholder Protection and the Theory of Corporation", (1977) 6 *Journal of Legal Studies* 251.

[24] For example, stock option plans, risk of mergers displacing inefficient managers. Considered in L Bebchuk, "Federalism and the Corporation: the Desirable Limits on State Competition in Corporate Law", (1992) 105 *Harvard Law Review* 1437, 1445.

porate in the state where the corporation laws are most efficient from the share-holders' point of view.[25] Roberto Romano characterises this as the "genius of American corporate law".[26]

Conditions for the successful operation of the competitive federalism model

For competitive federalism to be successful, the role of the federal government is to create the legal framework and conditions in which state competition becomes possible. Therefore, as we have seen, people and capital must be able to move freely between states, and individual states must retain the autonomy necessary to produce laws. As far as free movement is concerned, the federal government must remove discrimination based on nationality,[27] allow access to the market[28] and apply the principle of mutual recognition.[29] It must have exclusive competence in this area. Otherwise, central government must not interfere with the states' capacity to produce laws. Regulatory competition therefore favours a "bottom-up" approach to subsidiarity.[30]

The EU was set up largely according to this model. The objectives of the original EEC Treaty were to create a common market consisting of free internal movement of products (goods and services) and production factors (labour and capital) with the individual states retaining almost total autonomy to regulate other issues, including social matters. The Spaak Report,[31] drawn up by the foreign ministers prior to the signing of the EEC Treaty, considered that free

---

[25] Fischel, above n. 20. As Winter (above n. 23) explains, if management chose a state whose laws were adverse to the shareholders' interests, the value of the firm's stock would decline relative to stock in a comparable firm incorporated in a state with value maximising laws, as investors would require a higher return on capital to finance the business operating under the inferior legal regime. This impact in the capital market would affect managers by threatening their jobs. Either the lower capital would attract a take-over bidder who could turn a profit by acquiring the firm and relocating it in a state with superior laws, or the firm would go bankrupt by being undercut in its product market by rivals whose cost of capital would be lower because they were incorporated in value maximising states. In either situation, in order to maintain their positions managers are compelled, by natural selection, to seek the state whose laws are most favourable to shareholders. See also R Romano, "The State Competition Debate in Corporate Law" (1987) 8 *Cardozo Law Review* 709; Arsht, "Reply to Professor Cary", (1976) 31 *Business Law* 1113; Manning, "Thinking Straight about Corporation Law Reform", (1977) 41 *Law & Contemporary Problems* 3, 15–17.

[26] Romano, above n. 22.

[27] N Reich, "Competition between Legal Orders: A New Paradigm of EC Law?", (1992) 29 *CMLRev.* 861, 866.

[28] This is a problematic concept: see Case C–267 *Keck and Mithouard* [1993] ECR I–6097; Case C–384/93 *Alpine Investments BV* v. *Minister van Financiën* [1995] ECR I–1141 and Advocate General Jacobs in Case C–412/93 *Leclerc-Siplec* v. *TF1 Publicité & M6 Publicité* [1995] ECR I–179. Weatherill, "After *Keck*: Some Thoughts on How to Clarify the Clarification" (1996) 33 *CMLRev.* 885.

[29] Sun and Pelkmans, above n. 4, at 76.

[30] N Emiliou, "Subsidiarity: An Effective Barrier against the 'Enterprises of Ambition' " (1992) 17 *ELRev.* 384 and Van den Bergh, above, n.

[31] Rapport des Chefs de Délégations, Comité Intergouvernemental, 21 April 1956, 19–20, 60–1, summarised in (1956) *Planning* no. 405. See also M Shanks, "Introductory Article: The Social Policy of the European Community", (1977) 14 *CMLRev.* 375.

movement of labour was crucial to social prosperity. It considered that free circulation of labour would, as we have seen,[32] facilitate an equalisation in the terms and conditions of competition,[33] with the result that the degree of deliberate harmonisation needed to ensure the proper working of the common market was limited. The absence of social legislation is also consistent with the principle of subsidiarity, first recognised in the social context in the Council Resolution on the 1974 Social Action Programme[34] and more thoroughly articulated at Maastricht with the inclusion of Article 5(2) (ex 3b(2)) in the EC Treaty. The role of subsidiarity was reaffirmed in the social context by the 1994 Resolution on Certain Aspects of a European Social Policy.[35] It points out that:

> "the legislation of the European Community, and the supervision thereof, as well as all other Community measures such as, for instance, programmes and recommendations, must comply with the principles of subsidiarity and proportionality, which commit all the institutions of the European Union to respect the multiplicity of economic and social traditions in the different Member States".

The literature on the economics of federalism identifies six conditions under which competition between local jurisdictions would be efficient.[36] These are:

(a)   full mobility of people and resources at little or no cost;
(b)   wide choice of destination jurisdictions to enable the citizen to have sufficient choice to make meaningful decisions about migration;
(c)   full knowledge of each jurisdictions' revenue and expenditure patterns;
(d)   resource constraints and economies of scale which result in an optimal size for any jurisdiction;
(e)   jurisdictional latitude in selection of laws (i.e. jurisdictions must not be subject to external constraints in the production of their laws); and
(f)   internalisation of costs and benefits of laws onto their direct suppliers and consumers. This means that the innovator jurisdiction must be able to prevent competitor jurisdictions from duplicating successful innovations (the "free rider" problem).

It is evident that in the European Union these conditions are far from being met. First, since there are very major costs to the mobility of citizens between Member States the risk of exit is slim. People are less likely to leave their own jurisdiction for linguistic, cultural, financial or personal reasons. Even capital

---

[32] See text to above n. 29.
[33] See above n. 4 at 78.
[34] [1974] OJ C13/1, 3: "Community social policy has an individual role to play . . . without however seeking a standard solution to all social problems or attempting to transfer to Community level any responsibilities which are assumed more effectively at other levels". See further J Addison and W S Siebert, "The Course of European-Level Market Regulation" in J Addison and W S Siebert (eds), *Labour Markets in Europe: Issues of Harmonization and Regulation* (London, Dryden Press, 1997).
[35] [1994] OJ C368/6.
[36] See Tiebout, above n. 1; Easterbrook, "Antitrust and the Economics of Federalism", (1983) 26 *Journal of Law and Economics* 23, 34, Daniels, above n. 8, at 146, and Barnard, above n. 17.

(direct investment in business operations) is unlikely to leave unless a variety of factors (market proximity, transport costs, infrastructure levels, labour costs and productivity levels) justify the move.[37] Secondly, fifteen is a small number of competing jurisdictions given the large number of regulatory questions on which each pronounces and there are many aspects of regulation in which external effects between Member States are quite significant.[38] Thirdly, state legislation is often insufficiently responsive.[39] This may be a function of "path dependency" whereby national systems become locked into particular arrangements on account of sunk costs long after it has become obvious that they are not the most efficient form available.[40] Fourthly, adequate information on all aspects of the rival jurisdiction's regulation is difficult to obtain or to assimilate. Fifthly, even free movement of goods and persons have not been fully achieved in the EU due to the existence of the express derogations contained in the EC Treaty and the Court's jurisprudence on mandatory[41] or public interest requirements[42] justifying national restrictions on free movement. In these circumstances of market failure it is unlikely that competition between jurisdictions will be effective.[43] This might justify centralised intervention to "perfect" the market. This suggests a role for the concurrent competence of the EU and the Member States; the Member States remain free to legislate in the field[44] (subject to the constitutional limits laid down in the Treaty) until the EU feels obliged to legislate due to market failure.

Another form of market failure might also justify centralised legislation, namely where competition between states is deleterious. This might occur where states are penalising the less mobile, such as workers, by reducing employment protection legislation, in order to remain attractive to the (potentially) more mobile, such as capital. This might create jobs in the short term but undermine longer term interests of the citizenry as a whole.[45] This is the basic premise of the "race to the bottom" model and this is what many allege is happening in Delaware. If the competitive federalists such as Winter and Romano are correct, then Delaware should have a legal regime which is the most efficient from the shareholders' point of view. Therefore it should have a regime that *facilitates* rather than frustrate take-overs as an important means to maximise

---

[37] This is changing: see S Lash and J Urry, *The End of Organised Capital* (Madison, University of Wisconsin Press, 1987) 101 and 306.

[38] F McGowan and P Seabright, "Regulation in the European Community" in M Bishop, J Kay and C Mayer (eds), *The Regulatory Challenge* (Oxford, OUP, 1995) 230–1; Van den Bergh, above n. 14, at 352.

[39] Sun and Pelkmans, above n. 4, at 84.

[40] S Deakin, "Integration through Law? The Law and Economics of European Social Policy" in Addison and Siebert, above n. 34, at 142.

[41] Case 120/78 *Cassis de Dijon* [1979] ECR 649.

[42] Case C–288/89 *Gouda* [1991] ECR I–4007.

[43] See further Easterbrook, above n. 36, at 25. See also D Epple and A Zelenitz, "The Implications of Competition among Jurisdictions: Does Tiebout Need Politics?", (1981) 89 *Journal of Political Economy* 1197.

[44] Van den Bergh, above n. 14, at 350 and Opinion 2/91 [1993] ECR I–1061.

[45] Tarullo, above n. 7, at 101.

shareholder value. Why then, as Bebchuk and Ferrell point out,[46] does Delaware have an anti-take-over statute?[47] This suggests that state competition is not as efficient as Winter and Romano would have us believe and may lead to a race to the bottom and not to the top. This is the view of Bill Cary, one of the leading critics of Delaware's incorporation law. He argues that Delaware, "a pygmy among the 50 states prescribes, interprets, and indeed denigrates national corporate policy as an incentive to encourage incorporation within its borders, thereby increasing its revenue".[48] Consequently, he says there is a need for uniformity in standards to prevent the application of Gresham's law.[49] Therefore, he proposed the enactment of a Federal Corporate Uniformity Act, allowing companies to incorporate in the jurisdiction of their own choosing but to remove much of the incentive to organise in Delaware or its rival states.[50]

Similar concerns about states engaging in a race to the bottom have been expressed in the EU. In the Commission's Green Paper on European Social Policy it is stated that "a commitment to high social standards and to the promotion of social progress forms an integral part of the [TEU]. A 'negative' competitiveness between Member States would lead to social dumping, to the undermining of the consensus making process . . . and to danger for the acceptability of the Union".[51] Again, in its White Paper on Social Policy,[52] the Commission states that:

> "the establishment of a framework of basic minimum standards, which the Commission started some years ago, provides a bulwark against using low social stan-

---

[46] L Bebchuk and A Ferrell, "Federalism and Take-over Law: The Race to Protect Managers From Take-overs" *NBER*, Working Paper 7232.

[47] See also M Roe, "Take-over Politics" in M Blair, *The Deal Decade* (Washington, The Brookings Institution, 1993).

[48] W Cary, "Federalism and Corporate Law: Reflections Upon Delaware", (1974) 83 *Yale Law Journal* 663, 701.

[49] Cary, above, n. 48, at 698. S Kaplan explains ("Fiduciary Responsibility in the Management of the Corporation", (1976) 31 *Business Lawyer* 883, 883), Gresham's law "alleges that the lax drives out the exacting and commands a race of leniency in corporation act provisions presently being led by Delaware".

[50] Cary, above n. 48, at 701. Subsequently, other proposals have been made for federal legislation to fill the state regulatory gap, including the Corporate Democracy Act of 1980 and the Protection of Shareholders' Rights Act 1980. See also Nader *et al*, *Taming the Giant Corporation* (New York, Norton, 1976); Folk, "Corporation Statutes: 1959–1966", (1966) *Duke Law Journal* 875; Young, "Federal Corporate Law, Federalism and the Federal Courts" (1977) 41 *Law and Contemporary Problems* (Summer 1977) 146; M Eisenberg, "The Modernisation of Corporate Law: An Essay for Bill Cary", (1983) 37 *University of Miami Law Review* 187, 188–91, 196–8, 202–9; Schwartz, "Federalism and Corporate Governance", (1984) 45 *Ohio St. Law Journal* 545; J Seligman, "The Case for Federal Minimum Corporate Law Standards", (1990) 49 *Maryland Law Review* 947, 971. See also R Karmel, "Is it Time for a Federal Corporation Law?", (1991) 57 *Brooklyn Law Review* 55; V Brudney, "Corporate Governance, Agency Costs, and the Rhetoric of Contract" (1985) 85 *Columbia Law Review* 1403.

[51] COM(93) 551 at 46. See also AG Jacob's observations in Case C–67/96 *Albany International BV v. Stichting Bedrijfspensioenfonds Textielindustrie* [1999] ECR I–5751, para.178 where he said that the "main purpose of trade unions and of the collective bargaining process is precisely to prevent employees from engaging in a 'race to the bottom' with regard to wages and working conditions".

[52] COM(94) 333.

dards as an instrument of unfair economic competition and protection against reducing social standards to gain competitiveness, and is also an expression of the political will to maintain the momentum of social progress".[53]

Race to the bottom

A race to the bottom is said to arise when, in a federal system which allows for free movement, a state unilaterally lowers its social standards[54] in an attempt to attract business[55] from other states.[56] Businesses moving in response[57] are said to be engaged in social dumping.[58] This is no longer the case of businesses moving in response to *positive* regulatory competition which, as we have seen, is the very premise of the single market[59] but in response to *negative* deregulation designed to attract capital by dismantling social protection. Faced with such deregulation by their neighbours, the states losing businesses are induced to lower, or at least relax, their own standards in order to attract capital or, as a minimum, retain existing capital. The argument goes that this jurisdictional competition creates a cycle of disadvantage from which no state eventually emerges victorious.

The reasons for this race to the bottom have long been recognised by game theorists who show how rational transactors may fail to reach welfare-maximising solutions.[60] The classic illustration of this can be found with the

---

[53] *Ibid.*, "Introduction", para. 19. See also ch. III, para. 1.

[54] It could also occur where a state fails to implement a centrally enacted standard. In the EU context this can be addressed through Article 226 (ex Article 169) enforcement proceedings and the doctrines of direct effect and state liability.

[55] B Hepple's definition of social dumping is "the export of products that owe their competitiveness to low labour standards", see "New Approaches to International Labour Regulation", (1997) 26 *ILJ* 353, 355.

[56] See K Pacqué, "Does Europe's Common Market need a 'Social Dimension'? Some Academic Thoughts on a Popular Theme" in Addison and Siebert, above n. 34, at 110.

[57] For the purposes of this chapter, social dumping does not, however, refer to the idea that producers in low cost or low labour-standard systems enjoy an inherent competitive advantage which must be countered by the imposition of a "level playing field" in labour costs. This view was rejected at the outset of the Community's existence in the Ohlin Report and in Article 136 (ex 117) EC, which embodied the perhaps optimistic assumption that labour standards would, for the most part, "level up" of their own accord once the common market was put in place. See C Barnard and S Deakin, "European Community Social Law and Policy: Evolution or Regression?", (1997) *IRJ European Annual Review* 131.

[58] Pacqué, above n. 56, at 109–10, is critical of the term "dumping", arguing that the term "dumping" in its standard economic sense means "a market supply at a price which is lower than the price at which the identical or a similar product is sold by the same producers on the exporting country's domestic market".

[59] Case C–212/97 *Centros Ltd* v. *Erhvervs- og Selskabsstyrelsen* [1999] ECR I–1459, para. 27: "[T]he fact that a national of a Member State who wishes to set up a company chooses to form it in the Member State whose rules of company law seem to him the least restrictive and to set up branches in other Member States cannot, in itself, constitute an abuse of the right of establishment".

[60] Cheffins, above n. 7, at 10–11.

famous prisoner's dilemma. Sen describes the dilemma in the following terms.[61] Two prisoners are known to be guilty of a very serious crime, but there is not enough evidence to convict them. There is, however, sufficient evidence to convict them of a minor crime. The District Attorney separates the two and tells each that they will be given the option to confess if they wish to. If both of them do confess, they will be convicted of the major crime on each other's evidence, but in view of the good behaviour shown in confessing, the District Attorney will ask for a penalty of ten years each rather than the full penalty of twenty years. If neither confesses each will be convicted only of the minor crime and get two years. If one confesses and the other does not, then the one who does confess will go free and the other will go to prison for twenty years. . . . What should the prisoners do? . . . Each prisoner sees that it is definitely in his interest to confess no matter what the other does. If the other confesses then by confessing himself this prisoner reduces his own sentence from twenty years to ten years. If the other does not confess, then by confessing he himself goes free rather than getting a two-year sentence. So each prisoner feels that no matter what the other does it is always better for him to confess. So both of them do confess guided by rational self-interest and each goes to prison for ten years. If, however, neither had confessed, both would have been in prison for only two years each. Rational choice would seem to cost each person eight additional years in prison.

Prisoner's dilemmas involve a strategic decision in which each agent makes a choice in circumstances where the reward to each depends on the reward to all and the choice of each depends on the choice of all.[62] The basic structure of the prisoners' dilemma is that the players have the choice to cooperate (keep silent) or to defect (confess) leading to the matrix shown in Figure 2.1 drawn up by Langille.[63]

Figure 2.1: The prisoner's dilemma

	I choose	*The other chooses*
(1)	Cooperation (2 years)	Cooperation (2 years)
(2)	Cooperation (20 years)	Defection (0)
(3)	Defection (0)	Cooperation (20 years)
(4)	Defection (10 years)	Defection (10 years)

Langille points out that the individual preference order of players is 3–1–4–2 but while their choice "should" be that which results in two years each (option 1), rationality operates perversely and leads them to a choice of ten years each (option 4).

---

[61] A Sen, "Behaviour and the Concept of Preference" in J Elster, *Rational Choice* (New York, NYU Press, 1986) 69.

[62] Langille, "Debates on Trade Liberalisation and Labour Standards" in Bratton *et al*, *International Regulatory Competition and Co-ordination* (New York, Clarendon Press, 1996).

[63] *Ibid.*, 483.

Richard Revesz applies this game theory to the environmental field.[64] First, he looks at an island jurisdiction where a number of firms are engaged in industrial activity which pollutes the atmosphere and causes harmful effects to the island's citizens. He says that in the absence of regulation the firms will choose the level of pollution that maximises their profits by producing goods cheaply, and will ignore the social costs resulting from their activities. State regulation will therefore enact legislation adopting optimal standards. He then contrasts this with a "competitive jurisdiction", such as a state within a federal system, whose actions are affected by the actions taken in other jurisdictions and, in turn, whose actions have effects beyond its borders, and where firms can move freely from one jurisdiction to another with no entry or exit costs. Other factors being equal, firms will try to reduce the costs of pollution control by moving to the jurisdiction that imposes the least stringent national requirements.[65] As with the island situation, while competitive jurisdictions may want to set a pollution reduction level that takes accounts of benefits to its citizens, they are aware that the location of firms can lead to the creation of jobs and thus the increases in wages and taxes. As a result the state may well consider setting standards that are less stringent than those of other jurisdictions.

Therefore, if state A initially sets its level of pollution reduction at the level that would be optimal if it were an island, state B will then consider setting less stringent standards,[66] and industrial migration will occur from state A to state B. In order to recoup some of its losses in terms of employment and tax revenues, state A then lowers its own standards. This process of adjustment and readjustment continues until an equilibrium is reached and neither side has an incentive to change its standards further. At the end of this race both states end up with equally poor standards but do not experience the out-flow or in-flow of industry. In other words, each state has the same level of activity as an island state but with lower social welfare as a result of the race.

The prisoner's dilemma and Revesz' island jurisdiction demonstrate how rational decisions of economic actors can yield inefficient or sub-optimal results. This suggests two possible alternative responses. First, the prisoners (the Member States) agree to a bilateral, legally enforceable "non-confession" Treaty to produce the optimal result[67] (Coasian bargaining).[68] In the social

---

[64] R Revesz, "Rehabilitating Interstate Competition: Rethinking the Race to the Bottom Rationale for Federal Environmental Regulation", (1992) 67 *New York University Law Review* 1254.

[65] In other words, industrial migration will occur whenever the reduction in the expected costs of complying with the environmental standards is lower than the transaction costs involved in moving.

[66] State B can then "export" the pollution (i.e. create an "externality"). This is allegedly what occurs in Delaware (lax managerial standards have an adverse impact on shareholders located elsewhere).

[67] Sen, above n. 61. See further, P Genschel and T Plümper, "Regulatory Competition and International Co-operation" (1997) 4 *Journal of European Public Policy* 626, 627.

[68] The Coase theorem (R H Coase, "The Problem of Social Cost", (1960) 3 *Journal of Law and Economics* 1) says that if there are well specified property rights, full information and low transaction costs, the efficient solution will result through bargaining between the Member States without

context this might mean an agreement between the states to adopt the optimally stringent standard thereby maximising social welfare. Therefore, if state A is seen to cut its social standards, sanctions will be imposed against it by the other Member States. Federal legislation would then not be needed. However, this might represent an unacceptable interference with state A's sovereignty; practically it may be difficult to determine whether state A has actually reduced its social standards. Therefore, this response is not feasible.

The second response would be for the states to push for the adoption of federal legislation in order to eliminate the undesirable effects of the race. If the federal legislation were to adopt standards that the states would find optimal if they were islands, the states would be precluded from competing for industry by offering less stringent standards. They would end up with optimal, rather than sub-optimally lax, standards and they would not suffer the resulting loss in social welfare; all states would be better off with federal regulation.[69] As we have seen, this is the response advocated by Cary to address the perceived problems with Delaware's corporation law. He says that:

> "A civilising jurisdiction should import lifting standards; certainly there is no justification for permitting them to deteriorate. The absurdity of this race for the bottom, with Delaware in the lead—tolerated and indeed fostered by corporate counsel—should arrest the conscience of the American bar when its current reputation is in low estate".

This discussion suggests that in the case of market failure—either due to the absence of the conditions for perfect competition or where a race to the bottom is taking place—there is a need for comprehensive (centralised) EU level legislation setting high standards, pre-empting any State legislation, to rectify suboptimal results.

CENTRALISED LEGISLATION

The basic model

Centralisation does offer various advantages. The first advantage comes from the economies of scale which may be created by establishing a single, uniform set of rules to govern a broad class of transactions.[70] The savings operate at two levels. As far as government level is concerned, the need for multiple governments incurring separate costs to produce the same legislation is reduced; the central government is providing more of the relevant public good at less of the cost.[71] As far as the trader is concerned, there are savings in terms of transaction

---

any need for further Community intervention: R Van den Bergh, "Subsidiarity as an Economic Demarcation Principle and the Emergence of European Private Law", (1998) 5 *MJ* 129, 135.

[69] Revesz, above n. 64.

[70] Bebchuk, above n. 24, at 1494, does, however, point out that given the standardisation among states around Delaware corporation law, standardisation can arise from competition and need not be imposed.

[71] Tiebout, above n. 1, at 423.

costs—namely search costs (identifying and understanding the requirements triggered by a multi-jurisdictional activity)[72] and compliance costs.[73] Secondly, the centralisation of regulatory authority enables the regulator to reduce the costs that stem from the undesirable evisceration of regulatory arbitrage: evasion, through forum-shopping, externalisation and extra-territoriality.[74] Thirdly, centralisation may be justified from the perspective of distributive—as opposed to allocative—efficiency. Regulatory competition favours those who are able to move easily—the wealthy, the fit and the educated. Traditionally, social policy (as broadly construed) has been intended to help the less mobile, the poor and the sick. As Van den Bergh points out,[75] local governments cannot carry out such policies for fear that high income residents will move to other jurisdictions. This justifies a role for central intervention.

But comprehensive state regulation in the EU poses four major problems, legal, political, practical and economic. The legal and political problem relates primarily to the strong influence of the principle of subsidiarity and the use of legal bases which provide the EU with only limited competence to act and, when it can act, empower the EU to set only minimum standards at Community level. The practical problems relate to the method of integrating very distinct systems of industrial relations. These were noted in the Council Resolution on Certain Aspects for a European Union Social Policy.[76] Stressing the diversity of the national systems, the Resolution states that it considers "unification of national systems in general by means of rigorous approximation of laws an unsuitable direction to follow as it would also reduce the chances of the disadvantaged regions in the competition for location".[77] The economic problem raises the question whether centralised regulation is necessarily more efficient than state regulation.[78] Given the problems experienced by the individual states in determining optimal regulation, how can central government be expected to produce better quality legislation which applies to a large number of disparate states when there is a lack of clear information? There is a risk that legislation produced at central level represents only the lowest common denominator upon which all the states can agree, particularly if unanimous voting is the rule. This

---

[72] These costs will be exacerbated if, in response to the stimulus of regulatory competition, national regulations are altered several times in the process of discovery.

[73] Daniels, above n. 8, at 137; Trachtmann, above n. 5, at 69–70.

[74] Trachtmann, above n. 5, at 67.

[75] Van den Bergh, above n. 14.

[76] Council Resolution of 6 December 1994 on Certain Aspects for a European Union Social Policy: a Contribution to Economic and Social Convergence in the Union, [1994] OJ C368/6.

[77] At para. 18.

[78] See the discussion by Van den Bergh, above n. 68, at 138, of Directive 93/13 on Unfair Terms in Consumer Contracts, [1993] OJ L95/29. Cheffins, above n. 7, at 15, argues that given the restrictions associated with the Pareto-standards when analysts rely on efficiency principles to justify government intervention they usually rely on the more lenient benchmark of Kaldor-Hicks efficiency whereby a legal change is efficient if, in aggregate, the benefits associated with the change exceed the costs. In such circumstances those who gain will obtain enough to compensate fully those who lose.

prompts Daniels to argue that centralised regulation can only be justified where the cost of diversity exceeds its benefits.[79] This would suggest that the EU should legislate only where there is a transnational element to the problem which cannot be regulated effectively at national level. The Directive on the establishment of European Works Councils[80] in multinational companies would be a good example of this. However, such a narrow focus fails to address the broader question of the sub-optimality of social legislation resulting from a race to the bottom.

Problems with the prisoner's dilemma model

The prisoner's dilemma model upon which, as we have seen, the race to the bottom thesis is based, is highly stylised and presupposes that there is no communication and cooperation among the parties. As Majone points out,[81] a non-cooperative game such as the prisoner's dilemma has no Pareto-efficient solution if it is played only once with the parties acting simultaneously in ignorance of each other's actions.[82] It results in the sub-optimal solution: ten years' imprisonment for the prisoners, sub-optimal legislation and no change in levels of incorporation for the states in the context of environmental law. If the game is played an indefinite number of times, however, "cheating" is no longer the dominant but inefficient strategy since a collapse of trust and cooperation carries a cost in the form of a loss of future profits. If this cost is large enough, cheating will be deterred and cooperation sustained.[83] For this to be the case the discounted value of all future gains must be larger than the short-term gain from non-cooperation.

The prisoner's dilemma model also fails to take into account moral rules of behaviour; it is based on ideas of self-centred, self-interested individual rationality. If, by contrast, each prisoner proceeded to follow the dictum of not letting the other person down irrespective of the consequences for himself, then neither person would confess and they would both get off lightly.[84] Transposing this into the EU context, moral—or more realistically political—rules of behaviour at national level, make it unacceptable in the national political debate to lower social standards significantly.

This might explain why there is little evidence of a race to the bottom actually occurring in the EU.[85] As the OECD points out, despite pressures on labour

---

[79] Daniels, above n. 8, at 140.

[80] [1994] OJ L254/64 as amended by Council Directive 97/74/EC, [1997] OJ L10/22.

[81] G Majone, *Regulating Europe* (London, Routledge, 1996) 42.

[82] Cheffins, above n. 7, at 12, citing S H Heap *et al*, *The Theory of Choice: A Critical Guide* (Oxford, Blackwell, 1992) 113–15.

[83] However, if games are repeated infinitely, cooperation does break down. See Heap, above n. 82, at 112–29 cited in Cheffins, above n. 7, at 170–1.

[84] Sen, above n. 61, at 70.

[85] For a detailed discussion of this, see Barnard, above n. 17.

standards "there is no compelling evidence that 'social dumping' has occurred so far in OECD countries".[86] This view is shared by other observers. Ross notes that:

> "there has been very little North-South social dumping in the European Union and remarkably few signs that southern EU Member States are eager to exploit their relative economic and social policy backwardness as a competitive tool. By and large, the South seems persuaded that it should cast its lot with the higher-wage, stronger welfare-state northerners".[87]

Dehousse also says that "there is no evidence that the [1992 programme] has generated any significant reallocation of resources on the part of industry. Neither has a real race to the bottom in terms of regulatory protection been noted".[88] He continues that a measure of government retreat has been noticeable in some countries but this is linked to a general rediscovery of the virtues of the market economy, rather than a mere by-product of the integration process.

This would suggest that there is no role for centralised regulation. However, although Schonfield[89] notes that "(t)he dangers of 'social dumping' have been exaggerated" he does point out that there was evidence from Germany that companies were increasingly using the possibility of relocation as a bargaining counter to achieve changes in working practices at home.[90] Thus, it would seem that despite the lack of evidence of a race to the bottom there is a *perception* that social dumping is taking place. As Easterbrook points out, movement is a fact of life but "it is hard to avoid the impression that enough of the movement is influenced—at the margin, of course—by laws and regulations that the movement itself strongly influences governments. It may take only a few searchers and movers to cause powerful responses by competing governments".[91]

Tarullo provides a telling example of this phenomenon in the USA.[92] He notes that no state enacted a significant law requiring advance notice of plant closure and mass lay-offs, despite widespread calls for such laws during the spate of closures in the mid-1970s and early 1980s. Governors of traditionally liberal states explained that although they favoured such a law they were

---

[86] OECD, "Labour Standards and Economic Integration", in *Employment Outlook 1994*, 138.

[87] G. Ross, "Assessing the Delors' Era and Social Policy" in S Leibfried and P Pierson (eds), *European Social Policy: Between Fragmentation and Integration* (Washington, Brookings Institution, 1995) 368.

[88] R. Dehousse, "Integration v. Regulation? Social Regulation in the European Community", *EUI Working Papers in Law* No. 92/93, 16. See also Majone, above n. 2, at 160: " it appears that fears of an erosion of the national welfare state as a consequence of European integration are exaggerated".

[89] Reported by Taylor, "Wage Bargaining Diversification under EU Single Market", *Financial Times*, 7 April 1997.

[90] See, e.g., the concessions made by German workers at Bosch and Daimler Benz because of threats of locating new plants abroad (see "Can Europe Compete", *Financial Times*, 28 February 1994).

[91] F Easterbrook, "Antitrust and the Economics of Federalism", (1993) 26 *Journal of Law and Economics* 23, 44, and Barnard above n. 17.

[92] See above n. 7, at 103.

reluctant to create even the *appearance* of disadvantage for employers in their own states by enacting such legislation. Therefore, he notes, where labour standards and rights do exist in the USA they are generally the product of federal legislation.[93]

In the EU the advent of EMU may serve to reinforce this perception; given the constraints imposed by the convergence criteria, Member States will lose their ability to regulate independently interest rates and exchange rates in their quest for improving their international competitiveness. The one area where they would retain their independence is in respect of the regulation—or rather deregulation—of labour standards and wages, unless transnational labour standards are put in place to discourage them from doing this.[94]

Thus, we see emerging an alternative justification for enacting centralised legislation—the need to address a *perception* of a race to the bottom. But this and the various other rationales for enacting social legislation are negative. Various commentators have argued that Community legislation can also be justified on the more positive grounds that it has an input into growth.[95] A highly trained, participative and secure workforce is a much more promising basis for economic development than a low wage, low productivity one.[96] The Commission has also taken up this theme. In its White Paper on Social Policy it says that "the pursuit of high social standards should not be seen as a cost but also as a key element in the competitive formula",[97] and again in the Medium Term Social Action Programme it talks of encouraging "high labour standards as part of competitive Europe"[98] and that social protection is a productive factor.[99] Most importantly, in its Green Paper, *Partnership for a New Organisation of*

[93] He also cites the example of the Grant Thornton Annual Study of Manufacturing in the USA (Tarullo, above n. 7, at 102), which ranks the states with an index made up of factors indicating a "favourable" business climate. While high levels of workforce skill and education, and good transportation systems, raise a state's ranking, the index is weighted more heavily towards such factors as low relative wage levels, low rates of unionisation, low unemployment insurance and workmen's compensation premiums and low taxes. He notes that there is considerable dispute about the degree to which the index accurately reflects the willingness of the business to invest in a state but there is little doubt that "states feel pressures that reflect the thinking embodied in the surveys". For equivalent studies see J Addison, C Barrett, and W S Stanley, "The Economics of Labour Market Regulation" in Addison and Siebert, above n. 34, at 82–3.

[94] OECD, above n. 86, at 164. See also Peters, "Economic and Monetary Union and Labour Markets: What to Expect?", (1995) 134 *International Labour Review* 315.

[95] See S Deakin and F Wilkinson, "Rights vs. Efficiency: the Economic Case for Transnational Labour Standards" (1994) 23 *ILJ* 289, 295–6; D Marsden, "The 'Social Dimension' as a Basis for the Single Market" in Addison and Siebert, above n. 34, at 152.

[96] B Hepple, "Law in Motion", *International Encyclopaedia of Laws* (World Law Conference, 1997) 874–5.

[97] COM(94) 333, "Introduction", para. 5. This is wholly consistent with the "essential objective" expressed in the Preamble to the EC Treaty of "the constant improvement of the living and working conditions of their peoples".

[98] *Social Europe* 1/95, 9, 18, 19. See also now the UK Government's White Paper *Fairness at Work* (1998).

[99] See the Commission Communication, *Modernising and Improving Social Protection in the EU* (COM(97) 102).

Work,[100] it argues that the cornerstone of Community competitiveness is to lie with the "flexible firm" which could offer a sound basis for fundamental organisational renewal built on "high skill, high productivity, high quality, good environmental management—and good wages".[101]

On the political level Community social legislation can be justified not only on the grounds that it has a value in its own right—that workers deserve their due share in the common market[102]—but that it is an essential component in the evolving concept of citizenship.[103] The EU sees the link between social rights and citizenship as crucial. This was demonstrated by the new section in the Amsterdam Treaty entitled "The Union and the Citizen" which includes the chapters on employment and social policy. Commentators have also recognised that for citizenship not to be "trivialised" to the point of "embarrassment"[104] it must draw on rights "scattered" across the EC Treaty, commonly citing the social provisions as a key component.[105]

The role and shape of Community legislation

If we accept that the justification for EU social legislation can no longer be confined to addressing the problem of market failure or dealing only with matters having a transnational dimension, this gives the EU greater flexibility in respect of both the form and substance of EC regulation, enabling it to ensure "the optimal economic assignment of regulatory competences in a multi-layer structure of government".[106] This has been recognised in the Commission's Green Paper on the Organisation of Work.[107] The Commission talks of the new organisation of work raising "fundamental questions concerning the balance of regulatory powers between public authorities (legislation) and the social partners (collective bargaining) and between the social partners and individual employees (individual employment contracts)". It envisages "the likely development of labour law and industrial relations from rigid and compulsory systems of statutory regulations to more open and flexible legal frameworks".[108] In the social field the EU has always allowed room for some form of diversity through the use of directives giving Member States discretion as to how they be implemented.

---

[100] COM(97) 127.

[101] *Ibid.*, para. 24. See also the Commission's Social Policy Agenda, Com(2000) 379, 7.

[102] See Pacqué, above n. 56, at 112.

[103] See further C Barnard, "EC 'Social' Policy" in P Craig and G De Búrca (eds), *The Evolution of EU Law* (Oxford, OUP, 1999).

[104] J Weiler, "European Citizenship and Human Rights" in Winter, Curtin, Kellermann and de Witte (eds), *Reforming the Treaty on European Union* (Kluwer/Asser Institute, 1996) especially 65.

[105] See, e.g., J Shaw, "The Many Pasts and Futures of Citizenship in the European Union", (1997) 22 *ELRev.* 554; N Reich, "A European Constitution for Citizens: Reflections on the Rethinking of Union and Community Law", (1997) 3 *ELJ* 131, 146–51.

[106] Sun and Pelkmans, above n. 4.

[107] COM(97) 127.

[108] COM(97) 127, paras. 43–4.

This flexibility has been increased by the use of partial harmonisation directives,[109] directives setting minimum standards, an approach endorsed by Article 118a(2) (new Article 137(2)), and directives which envisage some form of "reflexive" legislation.[110]

As far as minimum standards directives are concerned, the 1994 Council Resolution on Social Policy emphasised the importance of this approach. It said that:

> "Minimum standards constitute an appropriate instrument for achieving economic and social convergence gradually while respecting the economic capabilities of the individual Member States. They also meet the expectations of workers in the European Union and calm fears about social dismantling and social dumping in the Union".[111]

The Resolution continues by saying that the Council is convinced that a "comprehensive legislative programme" is not necessary but rather "agreement on specific fields of action in order to build up the core of minimum social standards gradually in a pragmatic and flexible manner".[112] A number of social directives have followed this approach.[113] For example, Article 15 of the Working Time Directive provides that "The Directive shall not affect Member States' right to apply or introduce laws, regulations or administrative provisions more favourable to the protection of the safety and health of workers . . .".

The advantage of this approach is that these Directives allow space for some regulatory competition, for "better rules",[114] backed up by a non-regression clause preventing Member States from using their implementation of the Directive as an excuse to lower existing standards.[115] This competition can only take place if the minimum standards are not set at too high a level. However, in *UK v. Council (Working Time)*[116] the Court of Justice explained that the phrase

---

[109] Directive 77/187/EEC, [1997] OJ L187/61, as amended by Council Directive 98/50/EC, [1998]OJ L210/88 and Council Directive 98/59/EC on Collective Redundancies, [1998] OJ L225/16 (formerly Council Directive 75/129/EEC, [1975] OJ L48/29, as amended by Council Directive 92/56/EEC, [1992] OJ L245/3 provide a good example of this. While these Directives provide a core of rights, such as the right for the transferor's employees to enjoy the same terms and conditions when transferred to the transferee, the detail of those rights and key definitions, for example, the meaning of terms "dismissal" and "worker representatives", are left to be determined by national law.

[110] See Deakin, above n. 40.

[111] At para. 10.

[112] At para. 11.

[113] Article 5 of Directive 98/59 on Collective Redundancies, [1998] OJ L225/16; Art. 7 of Directive 77/187 on Transfers of Undertakings, [1997] OJ L61/26; Art. 7 of Directive 91/533/EC on Proof of the Employment Contract, [1991] OJ L288/32; Clause 4(1) of the Framework Agreement on Parental Leave Directive 96/34/EC, [1996] OJ L145/4 as amended.

[114] Reich, above n. 27, at 890.

[115] See, e.g., Art.18(3) of Directive 93/104/EC on Working Time, [1993] OJ L307/18, Clause 4(2) of the Parental Leave Directive 96/34/EC, [1996] OJ L145/4. See further M Dougan, "Minimum Harmonisation and the Internal Market: Some Observations on the Prospects for a More Clearly Defined Relationship", (2000) 37 *CMLRev.* 853.

[116] Case C–84/94 [1996] ECR I–5755.

minimum requirements used in Article 137 (ex 118a) EC "does not limit Community action to the lowest common denominator, or even the lowest level of protection established by the Member States".[117] It added that Member States are free to adopt more stringent measures than that resulting from Community law,[118] high as that may be.[119] This would suggest that there is a reduced space for regulatory competition.

American experience shows that federal standards do tend to be truly minimal, the lowest common denominator in all labour markets in the country. Yet states are not likely to enact significantly higher standards for the same reason that they were reluctant to introduce the scheme of regulation in the first place.[120] The use of minimum standards also does not address the problem outlined above of generally sub-optimal state laws resulting from market failure or the prisoner's dilemma. As Syrpis argues in Chapter 1 above, unlike total harmonisation, the objective of minimum standards directives is not to eliminate the differences between the laws of the Member States but does at least prevent distortions of competition where standards in any Member States are unacceptably low.

Is reflexive labour law a better solution? Deakin explains that regulatory interventions are "most likely to be successful when they seek to achieve their ends not by direct prescription, but by inducing 'second-order effects' on the part of social actors". He explains that "this approach aims to 'couple' external regulation with self-regulatory processes. Reflexive law therefore has a *procedural orientation* . . . [I]t underpin[s] and encourage[s] autonomous processes of adjustment, in particular by supporting mechanisms of group representation and participation, rather than to intervene by imposing particular distributive outcomes".[121] Reflexive labour law does not seek to "perfect" the market by seeking to address market failures because it recognises that, as we have seen, information problems makes the problem of identifying "optimal" bargaining solutions extremely hazardous. Instead, it creates a space in which the social partners can experiment and adapt, negotiating better standards and—contrary to the continental legal tradition[122]—for worse. The possibility for negotiated European level collective agreements concluded by the European Social Partners, introduced by the Maastricht Social Chapter, provides an example of this phenomenon. Once negotiated, these agreements can be extended to cover

---

[117] At para. 56.

[118] See also Case C–2/97 *Società Italiana Petroli SA* v. *Borsana* [1998] ECR I–8597.

[119] As E Szyszczak notes in "The New Parameters of European Labour Law" in D O'Keeffe and P Twomey (eds), *Legal Issues of the Amsterdam Treaty* (Oxford, Hart, 1999), such high principles do not always rule the day in practice. For example, the United Kingdom was responsible for watering down the content of the Pregnant Workers' Directive 92/85/EEC, [1992] OJ L348/1, to such an extent that the Italian government abstained, claiming that the level of protection was too low for it to accept.

[120] Tarullo, above n. 7, at 104.

[121] Deakin, above n. 40.

[122] B Wedderburn, "Collective Bargaining at European Level: the Inderogability Problem", (1992) 21 *ILJ* 245.

all workers by means of a directive.[123] It is usually the (interprofessional)[124] European level social partners who are negotiating a framework collective agreement which in turn provides space for the national (interprofessional or sectoral) or subnational (enterprise, or plant) level social partners to act. Using Rogowski and Wilthagen's terminology, the directive influences centres of reflexion within other social sub-systems—the social partners.[125] The framework Directive on Parental Leave[126] provides a good example of this. It envisages two main rights: men and women workers are entitled to parental leave for at least three months on the birth or adoption of a child and workers are entitled to time off on the grounds of *force majeure* for urgent family reasons.[127] The agreement then provides, *inter alia*, that Member States and/or management and labour may specify "the conditions of access and modalities of application of this clause".[128] The proposed new information and consultation procedures provide another example.[129] The Directive lays down certain minimum requirements on the content and procedures for information and consultation.[130] However, according to Article 3(2), Member States may authorise the social partners at the appropriate level, including at undertaking level to negotiate "arrangements which are different to those" referred to in the Directive.

These examples illustrate the point recognised by Van den Bergh that "competition between legal orders requires at the same time more, and less, centralization. On the one hand Community law should organise the competition between the laws of the Member States. On the other hand, the transfer of sovereignty must remain limited to give the emergence of different legal arrangements a serious chance".[131]

Harold Laski, writing in 1939 of the forces which hindered the emergence of the welfare state, said:[132]

"Federalism . . . is insufficiently positive in character; it does not provide for sufficient rapidity of action: it inhibits the emergence of necessary standards of uniformity; it relies upon compacts and compromises which take insufficient account of the urgent

---

[123] The English version of the SPA provided for a "decision". This has been interpreted to mean any legally binding instrument, including a directive.

[124] Although see the sectoral agreement on the organisation of working time by seafarers which was negotiated under the collective route by the European Community Ship-owners' Association (ECSA) and the Federation of Transport Workers' Unions (FST) and extended by Directive 99/63/EC, [1999] OJ L167/33.

[125] R Rogowski and T Wilthagen in R Rogowski and T Wilthagen (eds), *Reflexive Labour Law* (Deventer, Kluwer, 1994) 7.

[126] Council Directive 96/34/EC, [1996] OJ L145/4.

[127] Clause 3(1).

[128] Other key matters left to the Member States and/or management and labour can be found in Articles 2(3)(a)–(f), and 2(7).

[129] Proposal for a Council Directive establishing a general framework for informing and consulting employees in the European Community (COM(98) 612).

[130] Article 4.

[131] Above n. 14, at 350.

[132] Cited in Dehousse, above n. 88.

category of time; . . . its psychological results, especially in an age of crisis, are depressing to a democracy that needs the drama of positive achievement to retain its faith".

These very arguments are equally applicable to the EU. Its continued existence depends on positive achievements which legitimise it in the eyes of its citizens. The economic mantle will never truly be shed: as Freedland points out, the evolution of Community social policy has always depended on the possibility of legitimating Community employment law in economic policy terms as well as social policy terms.[133] However, a shift away from a primary economic focus creates more flexibility for the Union and the more modern forms of legislation help to address concerns over lack of innovation and responsiveness.

---

[133] M Freedland, "Employment Policy" in P Davies, A.Lyon-Caen, S Sciarra and S Simitis (eds), *European Community Labour Law: Principles and Perspectives. Liber Amicorum Lord Wedderburn of Charlton* (Clarendon, 1996) 287.

4

The Contested Meaning of Labour Market Flexibility: Economic Theory and the Discourse of European Integration

SIMON DEAKIN and HANNAH REED*

INTRODUCTION

The debate over labour market flexibility, which began in the 1980s as an issue for national-level policy makers, has come to have an increasing influence over the direction of social and economic policy within the European Union. Concern over high levels of persistent unemployment and low levels of employment in many Member States has led many to argue that the "European social model", which is based on systems of social protection and collective employee representation, has obstructed the operation of labour markets, limiting the necessary adjustments to changes in demand, hindering innovation, and restricting job creation.[1] Highlighting the economic experiences of the United Kingdom and the USA, advocates of this viewpoint claim that employment growth in EU countries can only be achieved through the deregulation of employment legislation and the dismantling of institutional barriers to wage flexibility. While a programme of labour market deregulation has not been formally adopted at a European level, there have been growing calls for the elimination of "rigidities" in labour markets in order to widen wage differentials in places, to increase sectoral and occupational mobility within the labour force, and to encourage the use of "flexible" working patterns, all with a view to expanding overall employment levels.

If there is growing recognition that the central issue facing European policymakers is how to increase the employment rate at a time of rapidly shifting

* We are grateful to the Newton Trust for financial support, and to Catherine Barnard, Bob Hepple and Paul Skidmore for comments on earlier drafts. Responsibility for the views expressed is ours alone.

[1] J T Addison and W S Siebert, "The Social Charter of the European Community: Evolution and Controversies", (1991) 44 *Industrial and Labor Relations Review*, 597–625.

economic conditions, shaped by transnational economic integration, techno-logical developments, and changes in patterns of demand for products and ser-vices, there is nevertheless little or no consensus on the means by which this goal might be achieved. The Commission's 1998 Communication, *An Employment Agenda for the Year 2000*, used the language of deregulation in arguing for "a radical rethink of all relevant labour market systems . . . to adapt them to a world of work which will be organised differently, in which the concept of secu-rity of workers has been reformulated, focusing more on security based on employability in the labour market rather than security in a specific job".[2] But this strategy contrasts sharply with the proposals outlined in the Commission Green Paper on *Partnership for a New Organisation of Work* in 1997.[3] Here, it was argued that enhanced competitiveness and productivity in European firms could most effectively be achieved through improvements in the quality of employment and the transition to new forms of work organisation, based on high skill, high trust and high quality. The promotion of longer term and stable employment was seen as necessary to enable firms to respond to changes in product demand and to secure worker cooperation in technical development, product enhancement and general quality control.

Some commentators see in recent developments the adoption by the Community of a "Third Way" agenda which seeks to reconcile flexibility and security. Hence Wolfgang Streeck has argued that the debate over the "Third Way" is about the "search for a new balance between protection and risk, secu-rity and opportunity, collective solidarity and individual responsibility, public authority and private exchange—for a new structure of incentives that elicits additional effort to substitute for redistributable slack, enabling public policy to concentrate the scarce resources available for solidarity on those that truly can-not help themselves".[4] As part of this agenda, the European social model would be renewed through a strategy of "competitive solidarity" in which social policy interventions would be aimed at enabling individuals, sectors and, indeed, nation states to survive in an internationally competitive economy. In a similar vein, Jeff Kenner has suggested that the new Employment Title epitomises a Third Way approach under which "[h]igh levels of employment and social pro-tection are linked with competitiveness".[5]

This chapter starts from the premise that in order to facilitate informed debate on these central issues for the future development of European integra-

---

[2] *An Employment Agenda for the Year 2000: Issues and Policies* (Luxembourg, OOPEC, 1997).
[3] European Commission Green Paper, *Partnership for a New Organisation of Work* (COM(97) 127).
[4] W Streeck, "Competitive Solidarity: Rethinking the 'European Social Model'", MPIfG Working Paper 99/8 (Cologne, Max-Planck-Institut für Sozialforschung, September 1999) 3. On the influence in general of "Third Way" ideas in current EU debates, see M Pollack, "Blairism in Brussels: the 'Third Way' in Europe since Amsterdam" forthcoming in M Green Cowles and M Smith (eds), *The State of the European Union*, Volume V (New York: OUP, 2000).
[5] J Kenner, "The EC Employment Title and the 'Third Way': Making Soft Law Work?", (1999) 15 *International Journal of Comparative Labour Law and Industrial Relations* 33–60 at 51.

tion, it is necessary to clarify the different meanings which the term "flexibility" may have in the context of labour market policy. This is the focus of the second section which uses the "new institutional" economics of law to show that there are a number of theoretical positions on the role of legal and institutional mechanisms in promoting the efficient operation of labour markets. The policy implications of these positions are outlined with reference to a positive role for mechanisms of intervention at both national and transnational levels. We argue that this kind of economic analysis is not inherently antagonistic to labour market regulation, and that it is possible to envisage combinations of measures through which social justice and economic efficiency might be reconciled.

We then turn in the third section to a closer examination of the way in which labour market flexibility has entered into the discourse of social and economic policy within the Community. We focus here on two settings in which social and economic policy are closely intertwined, and in which the discourse of labour market flexibility has become particularly prominent in the construction of European integration: these are, first, the various programmes of economic convergence and stabilisation which underpin EMU, and, secondly, the employment strategy which was recently crystallised in the form of the Employment Title and associated measures. We argue, on the basis of our analysis, that a coherent alternative to neo-liberal policies, of the kind apparently promised by a "Third Way" agenda for the labour market, has yet to emerge at European level. There is a danger, instead, that the institutional arrangements for the conduct of social and economic policy (broadly conceived) within the Community are making it impossible to forge the linkages between labour standards, active labour market policy and the macro-economic framework of the kind which are needed to renew the "European social model". We therefore question whether, under present institutional conditions, the goal of Third Way advocates can be met.

THE MANY MEANINGS OF LABOUR MARKET FLEXIBILITY

Although "flexibility" has for some time been advanced as the panacea for all ills within labour markets (and beyond), the term itself is elusive, defying a watertight definition. Some analyses focus on changing patterns of demand and supply for labour; others see the issue primarily in terms of the system of regulation. These separate approaches offer radically different policy prescriptions.

Demand and supply models

The demand side: the flexible firm. The model of the "flexible firm"[6] focuses on the micro-level of labour demand, that is to say, employers' strategies with

---

[6] J Atkinson, *Flexibility, Uncertainty and Manpower Management*, IMS Report No. 89 (Brighton, Institute of Manpower Studies, 1985).

regard to the form in which labour is contracted. In particular, the emphasis is on the attempts of employers to vary labour inputs according to fluctuations in the state of external demand. Numerical flexibility allows the firm to modulate the numbers employed, while working time flexibility permits it to raise or lower hours through overtime or through variations to normal hours. Financial flexibility describes practices such as performance-related pay which link remuneration directly to output. Finally, functional flexibility refers to the multi-skilling of workers which permits them to move round between tasks and to adapt their working practices to new technological and organisational requirements.

A prediction of the "flexible firm" model was that employers would increasingly segment their workforces into a "core" of full-time staff, for whom functional flexibility was the norm, and a "periphery" of part-time, fixed-term and casual workers employed on the basis of numerical and financial flexibility. Evidence for the existence of this type of practice is disputed, but there is no doubt that the model has had a considerable influence on government policy, particularly in the United Kingdom where it was used in the 1980s and early 1990s to offer support to government measures aimed at expanding the scope of autonomy enjoyed by management at firm or company level. These included encouragement from government for the decline of multi-employer bargaining, changes to employment protection legislation which extended the period of time required to qualify for basic dismissal protection, and resistance to efforts to put the rights of part-time workers on a footing with those of full-timers. This resistance only ended when the House of Lords decided that employment protection thresholds which excluded certain part-time workers from protection contravened the principle of equal pay between men and women in the then Article 119 of the EC Treaty.[7]

The supply side: "family-friendly" policies. It is also possible to see flexibility as an issue of labour supply. From this point of view, the growth of non-standard forms of employment, such as part-time work, temporary employment and self-employment, may represent changing priorities of workers, new lifestyle choices, and responses to the changing division of labour within the household. The growth of non-standard work *may* therefore represent an enhancement of employment opportunities for groups previously discriminated against by the law's emphasis on protecting workers in the "standard" employment relationship of full-time, permanent employment, in particular women with child care and other family commitments.[8] However, commentators have pointed out that many of the non-standard jobs which have come into existence since the mid-1960s tend to be poorly paid and offer few prospects for career advancement.[9]

---

[7] R v. *Secretary of State for Employment, ex parte EOC* [1994] IRLR 176.

[8] U. Mückenberger, "Non-Standard Forms of Work and the Role of Changes in Labour and Social Security Regulation", (1989) 17 *International Journal of the Sociology of Law* 381–402.

[9] L Dickens, *Whose Flexibility? Discrimination and Equality Issues in Atypical Work* (London, Institute of Employment Rights, 1992).

Until recently, relatively few policy initiatives have succeeded in instituting flexibility of the kind which would enable individuals to move between different forms of work—in particular full-time and part-time work—in such a way as to retain the value of their "human capital" (or their investments in skills and training) and to preserve their career path. However, there is now a growing impetus for this type of supply-side flexibility. The first beginnings were made when sex discrimination legislation was used to provide the possibility of a right to move between part-time and full-time employment according to the family and other commitments of the individual workers. Employers' refusal to provide this option could be regarded as indirectly discriminatory (since it is almost invariably women workers who are adversely affected), although in Britain the courts and employment tribunals have not consistently held in favour of workers making this type of claim. Several recent EC initiatives, including the Sex Discrimination Burden of Proof Directive[10] and the Directive on Parental Leave,[11] have helped to move the law forward in this area, albeit to a limited extent (the Parental Leave Directive does not provide for leave to be *paid*).

The demand-side and supply-side conceptions of flexibility therefore point in opposite directions: the former would grant employers greater autonomy to shape personnel practices to changing market conditions, while the latter would require them to adopt "family friendly" policies which accommodate changes in the household division of labour. These conflicting pressures are evident in the 1997 Directive on Part-Time Work.[12] On one hand, Member States and the social partners are required to observe the principle of equal (or at least proportionate) treatment between part-time and full-time workers. Employers must provide information to workers on the possibility of transferring between part-time and full-time work. On the other hand, the Directive speaks to a deregulatory agenda when it calls on Member States and the social partners to identify and review potential obstacles to part-time work and, where possible, to eliminate them, subject only to the principle of non-discrimination between part-time and full-time workers.

---

[10] Council Directive 97/80/EC of 15 December 1997 on the burden of proof in cases of discrimination based on sex. See also Council Directive 98/52/EC of 13 July 1998 on the extension of Directive 97/80/EC on the burden of proof in cases of discrimination based on sex to the United Kingdom of Great Britain and Northern Ireland.

[11] Council Directive 96/34/EC on the framework agreement on parental leave concluded by UNICE, CEEP and the ETUC.

[12] Council Directive 97/81/EC of 15 December 1997 concerning the Framework Agreement on part-time work concluded by UNICE, CEEP and the ETUC, Annex: Framework Agreement on part-time work. See also Council Directive 98/23/EC of 7 April 1998 on the extension of Directive 97/81/EC on the framework agreement on part-time work concluded by UNICE, CEEP and the ETUC to the United Kingdom of Great Britain and Northern Ireland, [1998] OJ L131.

Flexibility and regulation

Deregulation and allocative efficiency. Flexibility can also be seen as a function of the system of labour market regulation in a wider sense. A view which is widely held, and which, in the United Kingdom at least, has assumed the status of a conventional wisdom across the political spectrum, is that legal and other regulations cause "rigidities" in the market; flexibility, then, is the consequence of the *absence of regulation*. More precisely, flexibility is a condition of "unregulated" markets in which the price mechanism is able to operate unimpeded. This view informs the argument that economic efficiency can be restored through deregulation. According to Professor Horst Siebert, the president of the Kiel Institute for World Economics:

> "institutional arrangements can influence the clearing function of the labour market in basically three ways: by weakening the demand for labour, making it less attractive to hire a worker by explicitly pushing up the wage costs . . . ; by distorting the labour supply; and by impairing the equilibrating function of the market mechanism (for instance, by influencing bargaining behaviour)".[13]

Elements of rigidity in the European social model are said to include centralised collective bargaining, high unionisation rates, the "tax wedge" of employment taxes and social security contributions, job protection legislation, and earnings-related unemployment benefits. The effect of such regulation is that "flexibility is prevented by institutional conditions".[14]

A crude comparison between unemployment levels in the EU Member States and those in the USA would tend to support this contention. In 1998 the American unemployment rate stood at 4.5 per cent; the average unemployment rate of the fifteen EU Member States was virtually 10 per cent.[15] However, it is widely considered that the unemployment measure is misleading as a measure of economic exclusion, since the American figures exclude a large number of the economically inactive (in particular the very large prison population).

Partly for this and other reasons, analysts have focused on differentials in employment rates. In 1998, for example, the employment rate (defined as the proportion of the working age population in employment) was just 61.1 per cent in the EU compared to around 73.8 per cent in the USA and 69.5 per cent in Japan.[16] The USA has enjoyed an apparent advantage in terms of the growth of jobs since the mid-1980s. However, it is necessary to look at population changes here; a large part of the increase in numbers in employment in the USA is caused

---

[13] H Siebert, "Labor Rigidities: at the Root of Unemployment in Europe", (1997) 11 *Journal of Economic Perspectives* 43–54.

[14] *Ibid.*, 53.

[15] OECD, *Employment Outlook* (Paris, OECD, 1999) 224, Table A.

[16] See OECD, above n. 15, at 225, Table B.

by its rapid growth in population during a period when the population of the EU Member States grew much more slowly.[17]

A more sophisticated approach is to measure flexibility in terms of the effectiveness of market mechanisms in matching supply and demand.[18] The claim that European labour markets are inflexible is based largely on the relatively limited degree of wage dispersion (or, put differently, wage inequality) in Europe compared to the USA. Wage equality is perceived to be a sign of inefficiency, since it implies that wages are only imperfectly matched to the differing qualities, capacities and endowments of individuals. Another factor is said to be the greater length of time it takes for wages in most EU systems to adjust to changes in the level of unemployment, again with the USA as a benchmark (although the empirical validity of this claim has been doubted).[19] Slow adjustment implies that wages are relatively unresponsive to shifts in the demand for labour; hence, the market mechanism is not working as it should do to bring supply and demand into line.

Together these effects can be taken to suggest that a "segmented" or "dual labour market" is in existence, in which market forces influence wages to only a very limited degree. According to one version of this theory, the unemployed and low paid are not in direct competition with those in better paid and more secure jobs. The result is increased unemployment; unemployment is ratcheted up as the low skilled are progressively excluded from access to better paid and more productive jobs. The solution lies in measures which allow for more direct and intense competition over terms and conditions by, for example, allowing employers to escape from multi-employer collective agreements, permitting "two-tier" bargaining structures with differential terms and conditions for newly-hired workers, and removing protections for the "core" workforce which insulate them from competitive pressures. The unemployed themselves can be provided with improved incentives through the elimination of earnings-related social security benefits and the tightening of benefit-disqualification rules.[20]

A difficulty with this view is that the evidence which might link particular regulatory "rigidities" to increases in unemployment is much more ambiguous than is popularly supposed.[21] For example, labour flows—the rates at which workers move in and out of employment—do not differ greatly between Europe and the USA, as they might be expected to. Moreover, within the EU, flow rates are lowest in systems which are apparently the most "flexible", such as the United Kingdom. In the USA, there is a greater degree of mobility of workers between

[17] See R Blank, "Does a Larger Social Safety Net Mean Less Labour Flexibility?" in R Freeman (ed.), *Working under Different Rules* (New York, Russell Sage Foundation, 1994).
[18] See H Siebert, above n. 13.
[19] See S Nickell, "Unemployment and Labor Market Rigidities: Europe versus North America", (1997) 11 *Journal of Economic Perspectives* 55–74.
[20] See H Siebert, above n. 13.
[21] For a particularly convincing demonstration of this point, see Nickell, above n. 19.

jobs, but this is a consequence of a much higher level of inter-regional mobility than has historically been the case in Europe.[22]

Other seemingly obvious targets of the deregulatory approach, such as the "tax wedge", look less obvious on closer inspection. The real issue here is not the extent of employment or payroll taxes, but the overall tax burden on labour which, economists remind us, should properly include consumption taxes. There is no evidence that shifting the balance of taxation away from payroll taxes to consumption makes any difference to levels of employment and unemployment. For example, it does not appear that Denmark, which has no *mandatory* payroll taxes, has achieved markedly better employment levels, over the long term, as a result, in part because extensive pension and social security contributions tend to be levied by employers as part of occupational welfare schemes.[23]

In general, employment participation rates differ very considerably across the EU Member States. The differences appear to be deep-rooted in the cultural traditions of certain Member States, rather than being a direct consequence of the system of labour market regulation. For example, the low overall employment rates of some countries (such as Spain and Italy) appear to be attributable to the relatively low participation of adult women in paid employment.[24]

Labour regulation as a response to structural imperfections in the market. Moreover, there are many variations on the theme of flexibility and regulation. The basic premise of the deregulatory approach is that in the absence of regulation, the "equilibrating mechanism" of the market will lead to an automatic adjustment of supply and demand. This is the crux of the issue; however, labour market theorists disagree on whether the labour market, if left alone, actually will function in this way. Some models predict the presence of market "imperfections" of various kinds even under conditions of pure competition. The reason for the persistence of these imperfections is that the market can only attain equilibrium under extremely unusual conditions—such as complete information and costless contracting. Economists influenced by a variety of "new institutional" approaches increasingly recognise that these conditions are rarely if ever satisfied in the case of the labour market.[25] However, there is less consensus on what to do about it, and this is where the debate is currently most intense.

---

[22] See G Alogoskoufis, C Bean, G Bertola, D Cohen, J Dolado and G Saint-Paul, *Unemployment: Choices for Europe* (London, Centre for Economic Policy Research, 1995). See also Nickell, above n. 19.

[23] Nickell above n. 19.

[24] See B Buchele and J Christensen, "Productivity, Real Wages and Worker Rights: a Cross-National Comparison", (1995) 8 *Labour* 405–22.

[25] For a fuller review of the impact of the economics of information and transaction costs on understandings of the labour market, see S Deakin and F Wilkinson, "Labour law and economic theory: a reappraisal" in G De Geest, J Seegers and R Van den Bergh (eds), *Law and Economics and the Labour Market* (Aldershot, Elgar, forthcoming).

A common theme of recent theoretical work is that norms or practices which have efficiency-enhancing effects at the micro-level may have harmful third party effects which are felt elsewhere in the system, and vice versa. This is a central finding of a body of theories known as "efficiency-wage theories". These predict that *involuntary* unemployment may result from employer strategies aimed at retaining and motivating their skilled or "core" employees. Rules (apparent rigidities) operating at workplace level for the protection of the expectations of employees, such as the loose expectation of continuing job security, may induce functional flexibility at the micro-level in the form of a greater cooperation between (core) employees and management. However, the very same rules have the effect of excluding "outsiders"—the unemployed, low paid and less highly skilled—in the sense of reducing their opportunities for entry into "primary" occupations or labour market segments. This form of exclusion is, in one sense, a "rigidity". "Rigidities" may arise, then, as a consequence of norms and practices which are privately rational for the parties immediately concerned, but which have adverse effects on third parties, or "externalities".

Some applications of this theoretical work suggest that certain regulatory rigidities may in fact be desirable. One school of thought holds that "labour market rigidities partially diversify uninsurable risks when fully contingent contracts are neither verifiable or enforceable".[26] In other words, perfectly efficient employment contracts are not achievable, because of the costs and complexity of bargaining under conditions of radical uncertainty. Regulation compensates for, or offsets, the inadequacies of private bargaining. However, the mere existence of a market imperfection is not adequate grounds for regulatory intervention, since the regulation itself may have a distorting effect, in particular where it is the product of "rent-seeking" by powerful vested interests.[27] Hence the view just expressed is qualified by the insistence that rigidities induced by regulation are "a very blunt tool for pushing market allocations nearer to an unachievable first-best".[28] Put slightly differently, labour regulation is much too blunt an instrument to be used as a means of "perfecting" the market.

This position would suggest that economic analysis does not unequivocally condemn labour standards; but nor does it provide much of an argument in their favour. According to this view, then, if there is a case to be made for labour standards, it is better made on grounds related to equity.

Labour standards and dynamic efficiency. More explicitly "institutional" approaches argue that norms and regulations "are not rigidities and constraints upon micro and macro adjustments, but they can be opportunities and advantages in order to solve the trade-off between efficiency and equity which is

---

[26] Alogoskoufis *et al*, above n. 22, at 82.
[27] G Saint-Paul, *Understanding Labour Market Institutions: A Political Economy Perspective*, CEPR Discussion Paper 1428 (London, Centre for Economic Policy Research, 1996).
[28] Alogoskoufis *et al*, above n. 22, at 84.

inherent in the wage labour contract".[29] Inherent in this approach is the suggestion that rigidities which may have short-run "disequilibrium" effects may also be the source of longer-term, so-called "dynamic" efficiencies, through stimulating technical and organisational innovation based on trust.[30]

This branch of labour economics holds to the view that there is a highly complex relationship between systems of regulation and labour market behaviour. The point was reflected in the 1997 Commission Green Paper on *Partnership for a New Organisation of Work* which argued that a normative framework for the employment relationship is not just compatible with, but is possibly a precondition of "high performance" relations at workplace level.[31] The argument is that the spread of "lean production" techniques has made management more highly dependent upon the cooperation of labour, not just in the short-term sense of meeting highly variable patterns of demand, but also, in the longer term, in adapting to new skills requirements. In this context, it has been suggested that some form of institutionalised employee representation is necessary in order for cooperative relations to be maintained.[32]

Another example of this effect is the minimum wage. By preventing firms from competing on the basis of low pay, it, in effect, gives them a choice of either going out of business or attempting to compete on the basis of better training and investment in human capital, the so-called "high road" to competitive survival. In the words of the UK Low Pay Commission, considering the possible effects of a statutory minimum wage:

> "Whatever the nature of the labour market, it is likely that a National Minimum Wage will have a greater effect on the structure of employment than on its level. Businesses which are inefficient or which produce low value-added goods may need to reorganise working practices. If the National Minimum Wage is properly enforced, business and employment are likely to transfer to more efficient firms or to those offering higher value-added products and services . . . minimum wages may cause a transfer of jobs between groups such as the substitution of more skilled for less skilled workers".[33]

From this point of view, labour standards—regulation governing both the substantive terms of the employment relationship and the procedures by which the terms and conditions are set—are an indispensable element of a productive

---

[29] R Boyer, "Labour Institutions and Economic Growth: a Survey and a 'Regulationist" Approach", (1994) 7 *Labour* 25–72, at 26.

[30] See W Sengenberger, and D Campbell (eds), *Creating Economic Opportunities: The Role of Labour Standards in Industrial Restructuring* (Geneva, International Institute for Labour Studies, 1994); S Deakin and F Wilkinson, "Rights vs. Efficiency? the Economic Case for Transnational Labour Standards", (1994) 23 *Industrial Law Journal* 289–310, and also Deakin and Wilkinson, above n. 25; D Marsden, "Deregulation or Co-operation? The Future of Europe's Labour Markets", (1995) *Labour* Special Issue, S67–91; Buchele and Christensen, above n. 24.

[31] European Commission, above n. 3.

[32] D Marsden, "Employment Policy Implications of New Management Systems", (1996) 9 *Labour* 17–61.

[33] Low Pay Commission, *The National Minimum Wage. First Report of the Low Pay Commission* (London, TSO, 1998) at 115.

economy.[34] This, in itself, does not conclude the debate about the nature and level of statutory standards, but it does suggest that both positive and negative effects of labour standards need to be taken into account at the policy level. Moreover, it implies that the idea that completely positive effects can be achieved simply by removing statutory regulation is highly misleading.

Flexibility in the production of rules: competition or coordination?

A race to the bottom? The final dimension of flexibility which we consider here refers to the process of rule-making itself. Opponents of harmonisation in the field of social policy (and elsewhere) argue that the most effective means to arrive at an efficient solution to the problem of labour standards is to put the different systems of the Member States into competition with one another, through the mechanism of the internal market. Once free movement of economic resources is guaranteed, automatic processes can come into play for the selection of efficient legal rules. *If* it is the case that systems with high labour standards enjoy, for this reason, a competitive advantage over those which rely on a lower level of minimum regulation, then under conditions of free trade we would expect resources, over time, to gravitate to the former. This is because the components of the welfare state or labour market system are "none other than an additional component of a country's competitive position as a supplier of goods and services and as a location for production".[35] Once trade is freed up, the advantages and disadvantages of a particular system are revealed for all to see. Thus "international competition in the field of the welfare state serves as a kind of process of discovery to identify which welfare state package—for whatever reason—turns out to be economically viable in practice".[36]

It is argued that harmonisation of labour standards, by contrast, would lock the Member States into a range of potentially inefficient solutions. In effect, it would foreclose the process of market discovery which is the most effective procedure for arriving at an efficient regulatory solution. Moreover, if harmonisation were to be confined to particular areas, such as social policy, on ethical grounds which were unrelated to economic considerations, distortions would follow: "why should some parameters of international competition be removed through ex ante harmonisation while others such as infrastructure, education and skills of the workforce, and environmental quality continue to determine the structure of the international division of labour"?[37]

---

[34] Deakin and Wilkinson, above n. 25.
[35] K-H Paqué, "Does Europe's Common Market Need a Social Dimension? Some Academic Thoughts on a Popular Theme" in J Addison and W S Siebert (eds), *Labour Markets in Europe: Issues of Harmonisation and Regulation* (London, Dryden, 1997) ch. 4, at 108.
[36] *Ibid.*, at 109.
[37] *Ibid.*, at 108.

We do not intend to revisit here the debate about "social dumping" and the "race to the bottom" in European social policy. Nevertheless, in the present context it may be useful to summarise some of the arguments which have been made at greater length elsewhere[38] about the relationship between harmonisation and competition in the production of labour standards. The first point to make is that harmonisation of social policy at the level of the European Community has never had uniformity, or a single welfare state model, as its goal. Directives in the social policy field tend to set minimum or basic standards below which the Member States may not go. They do not rule out higher standards being set by the Member States. In this respect, they are like labour standards operating within Member States, which generally allow for what is called *derogation in melius*, or improvements on the legally mandated standard.[39] The second point follows from the first, namely that it is not the aim of social policy intervention to achieve a parity of costs or even a "level playing field". Such an aim is plainly incompatible with the preservation of space for Member States to apply protective standards above those laid down in the relevant Directive.

What then is the economic purpose of social policy intervention? Rather than prohibiting competition over rules, it *regulates* that process, in effect giving it a steer away from the direction of a "race to the bottom". It forecloses certain options of Member States, while allowing others. For free market purists, this is not much of an improvement upon an outright prohibition. However, the key issue here is whether a completely unregulated market for social policy systems within the EU would select the most efficient available solution. There are good reasons for thinking that it would not. First, the conditions for effective competition between rule systems within the EU may not exist. Unlike in the USA, where inter-regional mobility is considerable, there is relatively little movement of labour between Member States. Capital movements are more considerable, but still limited by comparison with the USA. Under these conditions, the expectation that economic resources would flow to the most effectively functioning system would seem to be optimistic indeed.

Secondly, it is not clear that an efficient solution would necessarily emerge even under circumstances of greater mobility for capital and labour. Studies of the process of "regulatory competition" in the USA show that state legislators can be heavily influenced by lobbying activity and rent-seeking by pressure groups. Hence it is argued that Delaware's corporate law is highly receptive to the arguments of corporate managers since it is they (and not the shareholders) who decide where to incorporate the business.[40] Managerial influence is also

---

[38] See Deakin and Wilkinson, above n. 30; S Deakin, "Labour Law as Market Regulation: the Economic Foundations of Social Policy" in P Davies, A Lyon-Caen, S Sciarra and S Simitis (eds), *European Community Labour Law: Principles and Perspectives. Liber Amicorum Lord Wedderburn* (Oxford, Clarendon Press, 1997) ch. 4.

[39] Lord Wedderburn, "Inderogability, Collective Agreements and Community Law", (1992) 21 *Industrial Law Journal* 245–64.

[40] M Roe, "Takeover Politics", in M Blair (ed.), *The Deal Decade* (Washington DC, Brookings Institution, 1993) 321–80.

evident in the practices of the "right to work" states in the south and west of the USA, many of which adopted anti-union labour laws in the 1950s and 1960s in order to attract capital flows. A race to the bottom could easily result in a "low level equilibrium" where no jurisdiction felt able to take steps to raise its standards, for fear of capital flight and further "social devaluations" by its rivals.

Of course, there are limits to how far the process of "social devaluation" could go before systems exhausted the capacity for downgrading their labour standards. To that extent, the process might be said to contain the capacity for self-correction. But whether there is any point in initiating a race to the bottom on the ground that it might eventually reverse itself is another matter.

The issue of regulatory competition is important in the wider context of the debate over the European social model since it helps to clarify the appropriate role for transnational-level institutions. Some features of inter-jurisdictional competition—those which are rather crudely characterised as a "race to the top" but which may be alternatively described in terms of the benefits to be drawn from mutual learning between states—may be highly desirable. From this point of view, it should not be the aim of harmonisation to remove Member States' autonomy in the social policy field, in the manner of American-style "pre-emption" of state laws by the federal legislature. Rather, the goal of harmonisation should be actively to preserve diversity at Member State level, by ruling out the kind of destructive inter-jurisdictional competition which, in the American context, leads to Delaware-type solutions becoming universally adopted.

Labour standards, competitiveness and active labour market policy. If the "defensive" argument for transnational labour standards would see them as having a role to play in averting a mutually destructive race to the bottom, then a more constructive role would be to make a virtue out of the potential contribution of labour standards to the promotion of competitiveness based on dynamic efficiency, as explained above. This would fit together with an idea which has surfaced from time to time in European social policy without ever becoming fully accepted, namely the concept of social policy as an "input into economic development".[41]

The economic benefits of "social cohesion" operate at a number of levels. For example, the greater extent to which firms and organisations seek to compete on the basis of high quality goods and services, the wider the range of good job opportunities which are available to worker. For present purposes, we wish to stress a somewhat neglected issue, namely the links between the core of social policy—labour standards relating to individual rights and collective procedures—and the area of "active labour market policy" or, as it is sometimes called, "employment policy".

"Active labour market policy" covers a number of mechanisms aimed at improving vocational training, assisting job search and encouraging employers

---

[41] Deakin and Wilkinson, above n. 30.

to take on additional workers. It mostly takes the form of targeted public expenditure and subsidies to enterprises. As Mark Freedland has explained, at EU level the term "employment policy" has come to be used to describe "the policy agenda relating to job creation and maintenance, and the maintenance or enhancement of employment skills by means of vocational training".[42]

As such, it interacts with "social policy"—or, at least with that part of it relating to labour standards—in a number of complex ways. In contrast to the specific statutory form which is given to most interventions in the social policy field, active labour market policy is authorised only by general legislative provisions which confer broad discretionary powers upon governmental bodies. In this sense, active labour market policy is characteristic of "promotional" labour standards, the purpose of which is to promote employment growth and the reintegration of excluded groups into the labour force.[43] The point we wish to emphasise here is that the growth of active labour market policy at EU level could be seen as a natural, perhaps inevitable consequence of the decision to strengthen social policy through the adoption of the "Social Chapter". This is because of the complex economic effects, partly negative and partly positive, which the imposition of transnational labour standards may be expected to have.

As we have argued, long-run dynamic effects of labour standards, in terms of raising productivity and hence the competitiveness of industries and firms, have to be set against potentially disruptive effects in terms of the exclusion from employment of the less highly skilled and the long-term unemployed. The scale of these negative effects is hard to estimate, particularly in the light of the empirical evidence, referred to earlier, to the effect that the impact of labour standards on employment rates is often minimal.[44] However, it is because these offsetting effects of labour standards may operate to the disadvantage of certain groups that active labour market policy measures must be designed so as to interact as far as possible with interventions in the field of social policy. In Sweden, for example, a particularly extensive system of active labour market policy has been responsible for most of the post-war period in keeping unemployment at low levels,[45] in this way compensating for the effects of labour standards and wage determination polices which put firms under continuous pressure to improve productivity. In short, a "high wage, high productivity" route to competitiveness based on an extensive floor of labour standards presupposes an equally extensive range of administrative and financial measures aimed at promoting training and investment in human capital, reintegrating the unemployed into the

---

[42] M Freedland, "Employment Policy" in P Davies *et al*, above n. 38, ch. 13, at 277; see also M Freedland, "Vocational Training in EC Law and Policy—Education, Employment or Welfare?", (1996) 25 *Industrial Law Journal*, 110.

[43] See Sengenberger and Campbell, above n. 30; Deakin and Wilkinson, above n. 30; Freedland, "Employment policy", above n. 42.

[44] See in particular Nickell, above n. 19.

[45] *Ibid.*, 62.

labour market, and maintaining sustainable levels of demand for labour so as to limit "churning".

Conversely, it seems doubtful that active labour market measures can work effectively in isolation from other elements of labour market regulation. The "displacement" of workers who would otherwise be employed in regular work, and the "deadweight" effect of schemes which subsidise the employment of those who would have got jobs anyway, pose familiar problems of cost effectiveness for employment policy. Under conditions of reduced or falling demand for labour, or under circumstances where employers can hire and fire at will, a further problem is that subsidy schemes tend to result in "churning", as individuals simply move from subsidised work back into unemployment. This has been identified, for example, as a potential problem for the United Kingdom's "New Deal" scheme of subsidised employment placements, which was implemented during a period when youth unemployment was in any case falling: "a key question for the New Deal will be whether the apparently high rates of outflow into unsubsidised employment can be maintained under less favourable labour market conditions".[46] There is a case for saying, then, that rules relating to employment security and the effectiveness of macro-economic policy in stabilising employment levels play an important role in underpinning employment policy.

Thus for these various reasons, it is the *linkages* between social policy (or labour standards), employment policy (in the form of measures directed at enhancing labour market participation on the basis of investments in human capital), and macro-economic policy (the setting of general conditions for stable and sustainable economic growth) which matter. The realisation of an integrated approach to labour market regulation would represent a highly significant step in the modernisation of the European social model; the traditional core of social rights, with its emphasis on protection and compensation, would then extend to the *right to participate in the labour market on the basis of meaningful employment opportunities.*

Whether or not the strategy which we have just briefly outlined[47] can be adequately described in terms of the "Third Way" is debatable. It shares with the "Third Way" an emphasis on reconciling equity and efficiency, and on seeing social policy as having a positive role to play in maintaining competitiveness (and vice versa). However, it departs from the analyses of writers such as Streeck[48] and Giddens[49] in envisaging a positive role for labour standards and

---

[46] The source of this assessment is the *1998 Joint Employment Report* of the Council and Commission (Luxembourg, OOPEC, 1998) 34; see further section 3, below.

[47] The ideas are presented at greater length in Deakin, above n. 38; F Wilkinson and R Tarling, "Economic Functioning, Self-Sufficiency, and Full Employment" in J Michie and J Grieve-Smith (eds), *Employment and Economic Performance. Jobs, Inflation and Growth* (Oxford, OUP, 1997) ch. 4; S Deakin and K Ewing, "Inflation, Economic Performance and Employment Rights" in Michie and Grieve-Smith, above.

[48] Streeck, above n. 4.

[49] A Giddens, *The Third Way* (Cambridge, Polity Press, 1998).

macro-economic interventions in making the labour market function effectively. To that extent, the debate is as much about means as ends—in other words, it turns on whether the mechanisms proposed by Third Way thinkers are, in fact, appropriate to the goals which they are aiming to achieve. In particular, we doubt whether a conception of flexibility which sees labour standards as inevitably undesirable "rigidities", and rejects any role for a demand-orientated macro-economic policy, can succeed in maintaining social solidarity.

Extending this point, we would suggest that the feasibility of Third Way strategies at Community level is constrained by the institutional arrangements which guide economic and social policy interventions. To see how these constraints operate, we turn next to a closer examination of how the flexibility debate has been translated into the discourse of social and economic regulation in the related fields of employment policy and EMU.

TRANSLATING THEORY INTO PRACTICE: LABOUR MARKET FLEXIBILITY IN THE DISCOURSE OF EUROPEAN INTEGRATION

The idea of labour market flexibility is no longer merely a theoretical one; it has a growing role within the formal language or discourse of European construction. In this part, we focus on the uses of flexibility in the key area for the resolution of conflicts between economic and social policy objectives, namely the overlap between employment policy and EMU. We begin by identifying more precisely what is involved in the idea of a "high employment rate" which motivates current employment policy at European level, and then look in more detail at the way in which labour market flexibility has become a reference point for the achievement of this goal.

From "full" employment to a "high employment rate"

The Amsterdam Treaty adopted a number of measures including the new Title on Employment which, together, have been described as amounting to the "constitutionalisation" of employment policy.[50] Prior to 1997 there were numerous employment policy initiatives, but these were spread across several different areas of Community action—vocational and educational training, the structural funds, and resolutions of various meetings of the European Council.[51] The use of structural funds to subsidise and support training and labour mobility has a long history going back to the ECSC Readaptation Aids scheme under Article 56 of the Paris Treaty, which was used to provide financial support to workers in the coal and steel industries. The Social Fund provisions of the EC Treaty

[50] C Barnard, "The United Kingdom, the 'Social Chapter' and the Amsterdam Treaty", (1997) 26 *Industrial Law Journal* 275–82, at 281.
[51] See Freedland, above n. 42.

were also used to support active labour market measures, in particular after Council Regulations of 1988 and 1993[52] which laid out a number of objectives for the structural funds including combating long-term unemployment, facilitating the integration of young workers into the labour market, and facilitating the adaptation of workers to industrial changes and changes in production systems. The Maastricht Treaty strengthened the competence of the EU to act in relation to vocational training by inserting a new Chapter on Education, Vocational Training and Youth. In 1994 the Council used its powers under Article 127 of EC Treaty (now Article 150 of the Consolidated Version of the Treaty) to establish the LEONARDO programme of vocational training support.[53]

The idea of using the central organs of the EU to coordinate employment strategies at the level of the individual Member States only began to take shape around the time of the publication of the White Paper on *Growth, Competitiveness and Employment* in 1993.[54] The White Paper addressed the issue of the low employment rates prevailing in EU countries by comparison to Japan, the USA and the then EFTA states. In addition to making a number of proposals for the general improvement of the competitiveness within the EU, it suggested a role for large-scale public works and investments in infrastructure which, it was hoped, would stimulate job creation in the Member States. However, in the event, the Commission's budget was not increased to anything like the level needed to bring these schemes to fruition.[55]

It was at this point that attention turned instead to the articulation of a common approach to measures designed to raise the employment rate. In 1994 the Essen European Council proposed seven areas for policy initiatives from the Member States, some of which were aimed at an apparently deregulatory agenda—greater flexibility in organisational practices, reductions in indirect labour costs—while others referred to the need to target public expenditure on raising skills levels and reintegrating excluded groups into the labour market.[56] The Essen Council also established procedures for monitoring the steps taken by Member States and for exchanging information on different practices at national level. These were later extended at further European Councils, in particular the Florence Council of 1996 which approved the terms of the Commission's Confidence Pact on employment, and the Dublin Council of 1997 which issued a Declaration on Employment.

The issue was raised again during the Inter-Governmental Conference which preceded the Amsterdam Treaty, when the Swedish government proposed the inclusion of an Employment Chapter which would commit the Union to the

---

[52] Council Regulations 2052/88 and 2081/93. See Freedland, above n. 42, at 294–5.
[53] Council Decision 94/819. See Freedland, above n. 42, at 300–7.
[54] EC Bull., Suppl. 6/93.
[55] See C Barnard and S Deakin, "Social Policy in Search of a Role: Integration, Cohesion and Citizenship" in A Caiger and D Floudas (eds), *1996 Onwards. Lowering the Barriers Further* (Chichester, Wiley, 1996) ch. 10.
[56] COM(94) 333.

pursuit of "full employment", in part as a counterweight to the policy of pursuing a stable macro-economic policy through EMU. However, the British, Dutch and German governments opposed the insertion of a reference to "full" employment and succeeded in replacing it with the aim of achieving a "high level of employment". They also insisted on linking employment with the pursuit of "competitiveness". The negotiations were thrown into some confusion at almost the last minute by the election in June 1997 of the French socialist government under Lionel Jospin. The French raised again the question of using Community funds to stimulate job creation directly, through a central "growth fund", and proposed an expansionary macro-economic policy to offset what were seen as the negative effects on employment of EMU. However, these proposals were successfully resisted by the German government.[57]

The context within which the Employment Title was formulated was therefore one in which the Member States had rejected plans for a macro-economic policy aimed at achieving full employment through "demand-side" measures. This was a highly significant step. The prevailing consensus became one of support for a "stable" macro-economic policy based on meeting the convergence criteria for EMU, coupled with suggestions that Member States should take steps to implement "structural" labour market reforms aimed at enhancing competitiveness. Although the Amsterdam Treaty also achieved the incorporation of the Maastricht Agreement on Social Policy into the body of the EC Treaty,[58] thereby bringing the United Kingdom fully into the process of social policy-making, this was, by comparison, a largely symbolic and in some ways backwards-looking step, since the substance of the Agreement was very little altered. All in all, then, the Amsterdam Treaty decisively rejected an approach integrating an extension of labour standards with demand-orientated macro-economic arguments, notwithstanding the efforts of some Member States and the Commission, at least under the Delors presidency, to pursue this line.

The implications of EMU for the labour market

To appreciate the significance of the decisions taken at Amsterdam for the future of social policy and of employment (or active labour market) policy, it is necessary to consider the body of law which has grown up around procedures for the implementation of EMU. These procedures derive initially from the so-called economic convergence criteria which were laid down in the Maastricht Treaty. The convergence criteria require those Member States participating in the third stage of EMU (full monetary union leading to the single currency, the

---

[57] See A Duff (ed.), *The Treaty of Amsterdam: Text and Commentary* (London, Federal Trust, 1997) and B Moss, "The Single European Currency in National Perspective: A Community in Crisis?" in B Moss and J Michie (eds), *The Single European Currency in National Perspective: A Community in Crisis* (London, Macmillan, 1998).

[58] Now contained in Arts. 136–45 of the consolidated version of the EC Treaty.

euro) to maintain retail price inflation within certain limits, restrict national debt to 60 per cent of gross domestic product (GDP), and confine budget deficits to no more than 3 per cent of GDP. The provisions governing excessive levels of national debt and excessive budget deficits (now contained in Article 104 (ex 104c) of the EC Treaty) set up a monitoring and reporting process which, in the last resort, can result in sanctions being applied to a Member State.

In addition, Article 99 (ex 103) EC provides for the EC to issue "broad guidelines for the economic policies" of the Member States. A "multilateral surveillance procedure" is established for monitoring and reporting on the policies being followed by the Member States; it was this model, dating back to the Maastricht Treaty, that was adapted for the purposes of the new Employment Title at Amsterdam. Under Article 99(4), if a Member State's economic policies are not consistent with the broad economic policy guidelines, or if those policies "risk jeopardising the proper functioning of economic and monetary union", the Council has the power, acting on a qualified majority on the basis of a recommendation from the Commission, to make a recommendation to the Member State concerned.

These Treaty-based procedures are supplemented by the Stability and Growth Pact which was formally agreed by the Member States at the Amsterdam European Council in 1997 (having been the subject of earlier discussion and informal agreement), and which is contained in two Regulations[59] and a Council Resolution.[60] Regulation 1466/97 on the strengthening of the surveillance of the budgetary procedures and the surveillance and coordination of economic policies puts in place an "early warning system" designed to alert the Council to the possibility that a Member State participating in the third stage of EMU may be running up an excessive deficit. Regulation 1467/97 on speeding up and clarifying the implementation of the excessive deficit procedure provides, among other things, for the mode of calculation of the deposit payable by a Member State for failure to comply with its obligations to maintain budgetary stability.[61] Amplifying Article 104, it also provides that if the Member State has not rectified the situation within two years of the decision to require it to make the deposit, the deposit will be converted into a fine.[62] Here, therefore, are not only guidelines and warnings, of the kind which, as we shall see below, apply in the case of employment policy, but also sanctions for failure to comply.[63]

The Council Resolution on the Stability and Growth Pact of 17 June 1997, although not "hard law", is also highly significant for employment policy, in that it "underlines the importance of safeguarding sound government finances

---

[59] Council Regulation 1466/97, [1997] OJ L209/1 and Council Regulation 1467/97, [1997] OJ L209/7.

[60] Resolution 97/C 236/01, [1997] OJ C236/1.

[61] Regulation 1467/97, Art. 12.

[62] *Ibid.*, Art. 13.

[63] For the results of the first multilateral surveillance exercise under this provision, see European Commission, "Budgetary Surveillance in EMU", *European Economy*, Supplement A, Economic Trends, No. 3 (March 1999).

as a means to strengthening the conditions for price stability and for strong sustainable growth conducive to employment creation". Alongside this measure, the Council issued a further Resolution on Growth and Employment.[64] In language drawn directly from the debate over flexibility and deregulation, it states that:

> "it should be a priority aim to develop a skilled, trained and adaptable workforce and to make labour markets responsive to economic change. Structural reforms need to be comprehensive in scope, as opposed to limited or occasional measures, so as to address in a coherent manner the complex issue of incentives in creating and taking up a job".

To this end, the Resolution calls not just for the coordination of economic policies with the procedure laid down in the Title on Employment[65] but also, in a direct reference to social policy, for more "employment-friendly" tax and social protection systems aimed at "improving the functioning of the labour market".[66]

The implications of EMU for both employment and social policy are further spelled out in Council Recommendation 97/479 of 7 July 1997,[67] setting out the framework for the "broad economic policy guidelines" envisaged by Article 99 (ex 103) of the Treaty. The Recommendation sets as the main objectives "growth, employment and convergence", noting that the EU "must progressively achieve a high employment rate". It then identifies five areas for policy coordination: the "growth and stability-oriented macro-economic policy mix", price and exchange rate stability, sound public finances, better functioning product and services markets, and "fostering labour market reforms and investment in knowledge". As part of macro-economic policy, it is proposed that "real wage developments should be below the increase in productivity in order to strengthen the profitability of employment-creating investment". Under labour market reforms, the Recommendation identifies five areas to which priority should be given. These are "higher employment growth" through wage levels that take into account appropriate regional differences and variations in workers' qualifications; reductions in non-wage labour costs and income taxation; reform of the taxation and social protection systems; new patterns of work organisation including more flexible working time arrangements "tailored to the specific needs of firms and workers"; and adaptation of the training and education system to the need to invest in human capital, including measures aimed at "improving the employability of the unemployed".[68]

The broad economic policy guidelines, then, see flexibilisation of the labour market as a key component of economic policy aimed at achieving "high employment". Article 99 and the Stability and Growth Pact together constitute an

---

[64] Resolution 97/C 236/02, [1997] OJ C236/3.
[65] *Ibid.*, para. 6.
[66] *Ibid.*, para. 11.
[67] [1997] OJ L209/13.
[68] [1997] OJ L209/18.

attempt to lock Member States into a path of economic development based on economic convergence around tight budgetary controls and the maintenance of price stability. Labour market flexibility, in the sense of "structural reforms", is the corollary of this process. Some of these reforms, it is clear, would be deregulatory, in the sense of removing indirect labour costs through reforms to employment protection legislation and the tax-benefit system. This is evident from the economic policy guidelines which were agreed by the Council in March 1999. Here, it is argued that "the functioning of labour markets in the European Union can be improved significantly and this would make a major contribution to the reduction of high unemployment".[69] Reforms to the tax-benefit system and reviews of employment protection legislation are prominent among the guidelines issued to individual countries. Thus the version of labour market flexibility being pursued here is very largely one based on a deregulatory, neo-liberal approach.

At the same time, however, both the Stability and Growth Pact and the broad economic policy guidelines make reference to a somewhat different conception of labour flexibility. This sees social policy and, in particular, the social dialogue as playing a more affirmative role in maintaining the conditions for economic growth and competitiveness. In particular, the EMU procedures see the social dialogue as playing an important part in the formulation of wage determination policies which are compatible with employment growth. The Commission is called on to promote social dialogue at Community level "notably on macro-economic policy issues".[70] Similar language may be found in the Commission communication of 20 May 1998 on *Adapting and Promoting the Social Dialogue at Community Level*: "the incorporation of a new Employment Title in the Amsterdam Treaty and the application of these arrangements has changed the nature of the tripartite dialogue".[71]

However, on closer examination, the linkage of social dialogue to macro-economic policy is of a very particular kind. The role of social dialogue is spelled out more precisely in an important passage in the 1997 Recommendation laying down the framework for the broad economic policy guidelines, which envisages a neo-corporatist role for the social partners in tripartite, national-level dialogue over the employment consequences of EMU:

"As regards wages, which are determined by autonomous social partners according to individual countries' practices, stability-oriented monetary and budgetary policies and the impossibility of exchange rate movements within the euro area will reinforce both the conditions and the incentives for an adequate evolution. These incentives should also be strengthened by an intensified social dialogue with all relevant parties, where possible and according to prevailing traditions, at the national level. A well-functioning wage formation process is a necessary requirement for high economic growth and reduces unemployment".[72]

---

[69] Recommendation 99/570, at para. 3(3).
[70] Recommendation 97/249, para. 2(iii).
[71] COM(98) 322, at 10.
[72] Recommendation 97/249, para. 2(iii).

This reference to social dialogue can be seen in a positive light. The importance of social dialogue as a mechanism for promoting the appropriate conditions for growth has been reflected in experiences at Member State level since the early 1990s. Some Member States have a long tradition of tripartite bargaining between government and the social partners over labour costs, flexibilisation and wage growth. This tradition is strong, for example, in Italy, Spain and France. What is striking is that similar "social pacts" should have been introduced in other systems which have no such tradition. Hence, the more recent introduction of tripartite bargaining in Ireland is seen, in the view of some commentators, as playing an important role in promoting the sustained economic growth which that country has enjoyed over the past decade.[73]

However, what is lacking in the European-level discourse is any attempt to link social dialogue over wage restraint to wider support for job growth. Rather, the 1997 Recommendation is a frank recognition that the process of convergence in the third stage of EMU will place particular pressure on labour markets to provide flexibility which is no longer available to national governments through budgetary expansion or through exchange rate movements. Put most bluntly, "[I]n EMU, with a single monetary regime, the link between wages and employment will become more strict".[74] This prompts the question as to what kind of social dialogue will it be that fills the void left by the removal of national autonomy in economic policy-making? The suggestion in the Council Resolution on Growth and Employment that the social partners should "fully face their responsibilities within their respective sphere of activity",[75] coupled with the direction in the broad economic policy guidelines (noted above) that real wage levels should be pegged below increases in productivity so as to provide incentives for investment, suggests that the main role for social dialogue is to consist in suppressing wage growth. Although this idea goes back to the 1993 Delors *White Paper on Competitiveness*,[76] in the context of the White Paper it was coupled with the Commission's support for a growth-orientated macro-economic policy, which, as we saw above, now no longer forms part of the Community's approach to employment policy. Thus the *quid pro quo* for wage restraint—active measures taken by government to boost labour demand—is no longer present.

Tensions within employment policy

When we turn to employment policy, we see a somewhat more extensive role for social dialogue and, conceivably, for labour standards as parts of the emerging

[73] See R O'Donnell, "Ireland's Economic Transformation: Industrial Policy, European Integration and Social Partnership", Center for West European Studies and European Union Center, University of Pittsburgh, Working Paper No. 2, December 1998.

[74] Recommendation 99/570, para. 2.4.

[75] Resolution 97/C 236/02, para. 13.

[76] European Commission, *Growth, Competitiveness and Employment—The Challenges and Ways Forward into the 21st Century* (COM(93) 700).

employment strategy of the EU.[77] However, the shift away from the goal of "full employment" is evident throughout the process of implementing the employment strategy and this, in turn, has meant that deregulatory elements are also at the fore. Moreover, the "soft law" nature of the EU's intervention in this area, while in many ways an advantage in allowing for a decentralised approach to policy formulation and for mutual learning between Member States,[78] is less of an advantage when it comes to defining a clear role for social policy in the face of the intense pressure for economic convergence which is provided by EMU.

The leading provision of the Title on Employment is Article 125 (ex 109n) EC, by virtue of which:

"Member States and the Community shall, in accordance with the Title, work towards developing a co-ordinated strategy for employment and particularly for promoting a skilled, trained and adaptable workforce and labour markets responsive to economic change with a view to achieving the objectives defined in Article 2 of the Treaty on European Union and in Article 2 of this Treaty".

This formalised the process of coordination which was begun at the Essen Council. The main innovation in the new Title, by comparison with the procedure first established at Essen, is the process of formulating guidelines which, if they are not observed by Member States, can give rise to recommendations, in effect warnings for failure to comply with the guidelines.[79] A major difference with EMU, however, is that under the employment policy procedures, the worse that can happen to a Member State is to receive a non-binding recommendation. Under EMU, as we have seen, a Member State which fails to observe warnings issued by the Council in relation to excessive levels of national debt and excessive budget deficits may be subject to a fine. Moreover, under Article 129, the powers of the Council in the area of employment policy are explicitly stated not to extend to the power to harmonise laws and regulations of the Member States.

At the Extraordinary European Council in Luxembourg in November 1997 (the so-called Jobs Summit) it was agreed that the procedures for monitoring employment policy would be implemented ahead of the coming into force of the Amsterdam Treaty. Under what has since become known as the "Luxembourg process", the first guidelines, issued to Member States in October 1997, outlined policy areas for 1998. Member States then drew up their National Action Plans

---

[77] It is not our intention here to give a full account of the employment strategy, nor of its flanking policies in the areas of structural funds, employment aid, and the activities of the European Investment Bank; for such analyses, see J Goetschy and P Pochet, "The Treaty of Amsterdam: a New Approach to Social Affairs?", (1997) 3 *Transfer* 607–20; M Biagi, "The Implementation of the Amsterdam Treaty with regard to Employment: Co-ordination or Convergence?", (1998) 14 *International Journal of Comparative Labour Law and Industrial Relations* 325–36; J Goetschy, "The European Employment Strategy: Genesis and Development", (1999) 5 *European Journal of Industrial Relations* 117–37; J Kenner, above n. 5; P Pochet, "The New Employment Chapter of the EC Treaty", (1999) 9 *Journal of European Social Policy* 271–8; and see Erika Szyszczak in Chapter 10 below.
[78] See Biagi, above n. 77, and Kenner, above n. 5.
[79] This is the effect of Art. 128 (ex 109q) EC.

(NAPs) in the first quarter of 1998 and a preliminary assessment was made by the Commission and discussed at the Cardiff Council in June 1998. The Member States subsequently submitted their assessment of their NAPs, and these together formed the basis of the 1998 *Joint Employment Report*[80] by the Commission and Council.

The first sets of guidelines have centred on four main "pillars". Figure 4.1 indicates the relationship between pillars and guidelines as they were initially formulated in 1998 (they have since been the subject of some relatively minor amendments).

Figure 4.1: Employment pillars and guidelines, 1998

Pillars	Guidelines (numbers in brackets)
Employability	Preventive approach to reduce the inflow into long-term unemployment (1–2)
	Shifting people from dependency on welfare to work and training (3)
	Developing partnership in the provision of training and lifelong learning (4–5)
	Facilitating the transition from school to work (6–7)
Entrepreneurship	Reducing overhead and administrative costs for businesses (8)
	Promoting self-employment (9)
	Promoting job creation in the social economy and at local level (10)
	Examining ways of reducing VAT in labour-intensive sectors
Adaptability	Agreements by the social partners on modernising the organisation of work, balancing flexibility and security (13)
	Introducing more adaptable types of contracts while providing adequate levels of security (14)
	Encouraging in-house training and investment in human resources (15)
Equal opportunities	Tackling gender gaps in employment and unemployment (16)
	Reconciling work and family life (17)
	Facilitating reintegration into the labour market (18)
	Promoting the integration of people with disabilities into working life (19)

[80] See http://europa.eu.int/comm/dg05/empl&esf/empl99/joint_en.htm At the time of writing, a draft *1999 Joint Employment Report* had been issued.

Altogether, the employment guidelines are a curious mix of neo-liberal policy objectives, which stress deregulation and individual responsibility for training and labour market mobility, and neo-corporatist strategies, which envisage collective solutions to the reconciliation of flexibility and security. The *entrepreneurship* pillar appears to embody a deregulatory agenda of the kind which sees the removal of regulation and taxation as essential to providing the necessary conditions for economic growth. The *employability* pillar is more ambiguous in that it places a strong emphasis on lifelong education and training as a means of enhancing the quality of the labour supply, which implies an extensive role for state intervention. However, in stressing the obligations of individuals to enhance their skills and earning powers, it also downplays the responsibilities of employers to provide secure employment. This is in contrast to the *equal opportunities* pillar which emphasises the reconciliation of supply-side flexibility with individual employment rights in the areas of equal access to work, family-friendly policies, and the needs of people with disabilities.

We wish to focus in more detail here on the *adaptability* pillar, which has provided a focus for functional flexibility of the kind which arguably comes closest to realising the "Third Way" objective of reconciling flexibility and security. Member States are called on to initiate measures aimed at negotiation over the improvement of productivity through the reorganisation of working practices and production processes. The reduction and re-negotiation of working time, the flexible implementation of labour standards, and information and consultation over training issues have also come under this heading, and the role of social dialogue in promoting these goals has been explicitly recognised.

In this vein, the Commission's response to the 1999 NAPs noted that "[t]he adaptability pillar calls for the development of a strong partnership at all levels—European, national, sectoral, local and enterprise levels—with the aim of modernising the organisation of work and adjusting to structural change", but found that "[t]he evidence so far provided by the majority of Member States suggests that we are still quite distant from this objective". It concluded that in the United Kingdom, as well as in Portugal and Greece, "more needs to be done in involving the social partners at all levels to develop initiatives and actions in relation to work organisation".[81] Its proposals for amendments to the employment guidelines for 2000 envisage an expansion for the role of social dialogue under the adaptability pillar on the following lines:

> "The social partners are urged to agree and implement a process in order to modernise the organisation of work, including flexible working arrangements, with the aim of making undertakings productive and competitive and achieving the required balance between flexibility and security. Subjects to be covered may, for example, include training and re-training, the introduction of new technologies, new forms of work and working-time issues such as the expression of working time as an annual figure, the

---

[81] European Commission, *Commission Recommendation for Council Recommendations on the Implementation of Member States' Employment Policies* (Luxembourg, OOPEC, 1999) para. 6.

reduction of working hours, the reduction of overtime, the development of part-time working, and access to training and career breaks".[82]

Similar views have been expressed in related policy developments. In particular, the Commission Communication of 25 November 1998 *Modernising the Organisation of Work—A Positive Approach to Change*, which followed on from its earlier Green Paper on *Partnership for a New Organisation of Work*, argued that:

> "The overriding objectives of the EU are *competitiveness* and *employment*. In this context there is considerable agreement that improvements in *productivity*, through a better organisation of work, are necessary if individual enterprises are to improve their competitive position and if the Community is to achieve its objectives. In addition, a positive approach to reconciling the needs of firms for *flexibility* and the needs of workers for *security* in change, is essential".[83]

Similarly, the *Report of the High Level Group on the Implications of Industrial Change*, also published late in 1998, concluded that "top-performing companies have a good social dialogue with their employees because motivated people are the vital component for commercial success".[84]

The key issue to arise from this process of clarifying and amplifying the meaning of the adaptability pillar is how far the affirmative role for social dialogue which is envisaged at the micro-level—the level at which the social partners are seen as engaging in a process of negotiation over flexibility at firm and/or sector level—is compatible with the macro-level framework for economic and social policy which has been set by EMU. One of the few attempts to link the macro and micro levels is the notion of a "European Employment Pact", which was discussed at the Vienna summit in 1998 and adopted at the Cologne summit in the following year. According to the Commission, as part of the "Employment Pact":

> "the Social Partners should continue to support the European employment strategy, notably through appropriate wage developments in line with the 1999 Broad Economic Policy Guidelines, and contribute to implementation of the Employment Guidelines, including joint initiatives to modernise the organisation of work".[85]

The greater involvement of the social partners in the negotiation of flexibility could potentially provide a *quid pro quo* for their role in maintaining wage restraint at the macro-level. But here, the institutional priority accorded to EMU over social and employment policy limits must be taken into account. The EMU process is explicit in aiming to bring about a high level of convergence in the eco-

---

[82] European Commission, *Proposal for Guidelines for Member States' Employment Policies 2000* (Luxembourg, OOPEC, 1999) 9.

[83] At para. 2.1.1 (emphasis in original).

[84] (January 1999) 300 *European Industrial Relations Review* 2.

[85] European Commission, *Community Policies in Support of Employment* (Luxembourg, OOPEC, 1999) 4.

nomic policies of the Member States[86] and is underwritten by sanctions which can, at the end of the day, be deployed against a recalcitrant Member State in order to ensure that this degree of economic convergence is maintained.

By contrast, the EU's employment strategy does not require Member States to maintain any particular level of *social convergence* as a condition of participating in the process laid down in the Employment Title (except, implicitly, to the still-limited extent envisaged by the social policy provisions of the EC Treaty and related harmonising measures). It is, of course, possible that the employment strategy may lead over time to a degree of convergence in the way in which active labour market policies are conducted.[87] But there is no guarantee that there will be convergence around a core of social rights. There is, for example, no mechanism yet in place which could require the United Kingdom to comply with the Commission's recommendation, made in the context of its review of the United Kingdom's 1999 National Action Plan, that it should "promote concrete commitments by the social partners at all appropriate levels on the modernisation of work organisation". On the contrary, the British government remains free to oppose the expansion of social dialogue through systems of employee representation along the lines suggested by the proposal for a directive on information and consultation at national level which it has successfully blocked at Community level. As long there is no institutional means by which the harmonisation of social rights can be built into the employment strategy, there is a danger that the kind of convergence to which the Employment Title will give rise is one based on the kinds of "structural adjustment" which are envisaged by EMU—or, in other words, deregulation.

CONCLUSIONS

In the words of the *Joint Employment Report* for 1998, the new institutional framework for employment policy "supports a coordinated approach to employment policy, facilitates an exchange of best practice and brings together various Community policies in order to contribute to an employment strategy".[88] However, the main driving force behind employment growth is still seen as the process of EMU: "in the longer term, the successful launch of EMU will 'lock in' sound macroeconomic policies, expectations and policy-making processes towards favouring stable high employment-creating growth in the EU".[89] Compared to this, the suggestion that "vigorous and resolute implementation of the Employment Strategy, especially the Employment Guidelines, will

---

[86] This is particularly so, of course, for Member States which are now part of the euro zone, but other Member States are also subject to the multilateral surveillance procedures and to the general obligations under Art. 99 to coordinate their economic policies. See European Commission, above n. 63.

[87] See Biagi, above n. 77.

[88] *Joint Employment Report 1998*, above n. 80, at 2.

[89] *Ibid.*

also help to bring the employment rates to previously-recorded high levels within the foreseeable future"[90] seems at the very least to be premature.

This is because of limitations which are inherent in the process established by the Employment Title. Notwithstanding the recent reforms to the European Social Fund,[91] the Commission lacks the budgetary capacity to underwrite significant active labour market expenditure in its own right. The Amsterdam Treaty confirmed that the Member States were not prepared to endorse the type of demand-side, growth-orientated strategy for job creation which was mooted by the Commission in the early 1990s.[92] Stability rather than growth is the priority of the mis-named Stability and Growth Pact.

Both employment and social policy are currently being influenced by the view which associates flexibility with "structural" reforms to the labour market, including changes to employment legislation and the tax-benefit system. Reforms to employment protection legislation and the shifting of the tax burden from employment to consumption are seen as means of eliminating "rigidities" within the labour market. In some quarters,[93] this version of flexibility is viewed as a natural corollary to the process of EMU. As national governments lose the power to adjust to changing economic conditions by modulating the exchange rate and altering the balance between taxation and public expenditure, the burden of adjustment is thrown on to the labour market, which is now required to operate with maximum flexibility in the sense of bringing wages and terms and conditions into line with changes in demand. In this scenario, the process of economic integration creates a momentum of its own for deregulation at the national level. A further impetus for this "race to the bottom" would then be provided by the entrepreneurship and employability pillars of EU employment policy, with their stress on the need to lift the burden of regulatory controls.

None of this is necessary, nor is it desirable. We argued in the first half of this chapter that there are many different versions of labour market flexibility, and that it is highly misleading to envisage a straightforward trade-off between flexibility and regulation. Labour standards may have a number of complex economic effects, some of which may enhance long-term growth and competitiveness based on high productivity. We also saw that promotional standards—active labour market policy measures aimed at raising investments in training and education and re-integrating excluded groups into employment—are an indispensable part of a comprehensive strategy aimed at reconciling continuous improvement in productivity with a high level of employment participation.

This view is reflected in the adaptability and equal opportunities pillars of the employment guidelines. However, these elements of the employment strategy

---

[90] *Joint Employment Report 1998*, above n. 80, at 9.

[91] See Erika Szyszczak in Chapter 10 below.

[92] European social and economic policy sometimes moves rapidly, but as yet the unusual conjunction of social democratic governments in virtually all the EU Member States has not produced any change of direction in this respect.

[93] For an account of these debates within the EU and the Member States, see A Robinson, "Why 'Employability' Won't Make EMU Work", in Moss and Michie, above n. 57.

are in fundamental conflict with the language of deregulation and "structural adjustment" which is found, above all, in the entrepreneurship pillar. Rather than forming a coherent whole of the kind which could represent a viable "Third Way", the employment strategy remains riven by conflicts which may yet prove to be irreconcilable.

An extensive social policy at Community level should imply an equally far-reaching employment policy. However, the missing link, at present, is the macro-economic framework. As long as the priorities of EMU remain as they are, social policy will be under threat, and there is a danger that the potential of the employment strategy will remain unfulfilled.

PART III

National Cultures, National Laws and EU Law and Policy

5

The Challenges of Europeanisation and Globalisation in the Field of Labour Relations: The Nordic Case

NIKLAS BRUUN

INTRODUCTION

There is a widespread understanding that a very significant trend in the current development of international capitalism can be described as a process of globalisation. The changes behind this process are largely the result of the increased concentration and impact of big multinational companies within the world economy. In addition the level of foreign investment and cross-investment has grown and barriers to the free movement of capital and financial services have been removed. However, elements of globalisation can also be found in cultural patterns, the behaviour of consumers, etc.

Opinions differ regarding this development. Swedish scholar Lars Magnusson distinguishes between three groups of positions in the debate.[1] According to him, the hyperglobalist position claims that globalisation represents a revolutionary transformation of the world economic and political system, and that the end of the nation state, as we know it today, is imminent. The second position is, on the other hand, sceptical about the factual relevance of the on-going changes and says that globalisation does not extend beyond the ideological dimension; in other words it is merely a tool of economic liberalism.[2] Proponents of this view claim that the economy has been global for the last century and that very little has changed. The third (middle) position, to which Magnusson himself appears to subscribe is the transformation thesis: although globalisation represents a fundamental change, nation states still have an important part to play but they must adapt with the changing situation.

There are also very different opinions about the impact of globalisation on the welfare state and national labour relations. Amongst those who oppose the

---

[1] See L Magnusson, *Den tredje industriella revolutionen* (*The Third Industrial Revolution*) (Prisma, Stockholm, 2000) 36–48.

[2] R Hyman, "National Industrial Relations Systems and Transnational Challenges: An Essay in Review", (1999) 5:1 *European Journal of Industrial Relations* 90–3. This article refers to the position of globalisation as a myth.

deregulation of the national labour market there are a broad variety of views. Defensive positions try to retain national control over the welfare state whilst others claim that this is an impossible project and that trade unions and labour relations have to become transnational and global. Yet others claim that new national policies, such as "competitive corporatism", can be the solution in a tough environment of international competition.[3]

Another line of analysis suggests that the earlier polarised debate between the global and the national has been complemented with a debate surrounding the sub-global or regional processes of internationalisation. For instance in Western Europe, the European Union forms one regional area with its own institutional framework and this framework cannot be assesssed in the framework of the nation state, nor can it be assessed in a global framework.[4]

When examining the challenges of globalisation and Europeanisation to labour relations, the most evident and easily traced developments are located on the institutional level: for example, European works councils in so called Eurocompanies, the social dialogue in the European Union, wage coordination in the Economic and Monetary Union, and so on. The indirect consequences of the results of the hardening of competition are much more difficult to assess however. One could, for instance, ask whether the deregulation of labour relations in New Zealand in the early 1990s should be seen as a national project or as a consequence of globalisation.[5] Both elements were clearly present but they are hard to separate from each other. This example explains why the following discussion on the developments in the Nordic countries focuses mainly on the consequences of Europeanisation, although it should not be forgotten that Europeanisation has to be seen as a significant element in the global process of internationalisation.

BACKGROUND: THE NORDIC LABOUR RELATIONS MODEL

Almost a decade ago, a Nordic team, of which this author was a member, concluded a research project by publishing a book entitled, *The Nordic Labour Relations Model—Labour Law and Trade Unions in the Nordic Countries—Today and Tomorrow*.[6] One of the main conclusions of the book was that when comparing the four big Nordic countries—Denmark, Finland, Norway and Sweden—with other developed market economy countries, a single, relatively

---

[3] See for instance M Rhodes, "The Future of European Welfare: A New Social Contract?" in M Rhodes and Y Mény (eds), *The Future of European Welfare* (London, Macmillan, 1998) 178–203

[4] See P Marginson, "The Eurocompany and Euro Industrial Relations", (2000) 6:1 *European Journal of Industrial Relations* 9–34.

[5] See R Harbridge (ed.), *Employment Contracts: New Zealand Experiences* (Victoria University Press, 1993).

[6] N Bruun, B Flodgren, M Halvorsen, H Hydén and R Nielsen, *The Nordic Labour Relations Model. Labour Law and Trade Unions in the Nordic Countries—Today and Tomorrow* (Aldershot, Dartmouth Publishing Company, 1992).

uniform Nordic model for regulation of the labour market emerged, (notwithstanding specific national features).[7]

The basis for this homogeneity can be found in a common Nordic institutional setting and in common structures and goals for the building of the welfare state.[8] A traditional characteristic of the Nordic bloc as a whole has been the existence of smaller income gaps than in countries of the EU and a much smaller proportion of the population living in poverty. The traditionally egalitarian nature of Nordic social policy can also be illustrated by the fact that the right to social security in the Nordic bloc has been applied to all inhabitants on an individual basis, i.e. to everyone who is permanently resident in a Nordic country, largely independent of family circumstances, citizenship or employment, while social security in most of the EU countries has been linked to employment. This means that people outside the labour market must derive their entitlement to social security from a family member who is, or has been, employed. By largely separating paid work from the entitlement to coverage under the social security system, it has thus been possible in the Nordic countries to provide all of a country's inhabitants with extensive basic security.

In addition there is generally a high proportion of women in Nordic labour forces. The public sector employs many women and the public sector is, to a significantly greater extent than in most EU countries, responsible for the administration of vital service functions (such as child care and health services). The other side of this coin is a high level of income taxation.

The trade union movement's central role and strong position has also been regarded as characteristic of the Nordic labour market. Over 80 per cent of wage-earners are unionised in Sweden, almost 80 per cent in Finland, over 70 per cent in Denmark and just under 60 per cent in Norway.[9] Comparatively speaking this union density is very high and may be attributed in part to the successful mobilisation and organisation of both private sector white collar workers and public sector employees. In these countries, with some exceptions, trade unions, by and large, have a monopoly and there are no rival organisations within employment sectors which a dissatisfied member, who wishes to leave his or her organisation, could join. Not only is the trade union movement well organised, but also from an international perspective, a uniquely high percentage of employers are also organised.

One characteristic of Nordic trade unions is that they display a high degree of centralisation and have relatively broad powers acting vigorously in a number of issues of general importance. In addition to this, the national union level—the level at which nationwide collective agreements are usually negotiated and

---

[7] See also the debate in T Kauppinen and V Köykkä (eds), *Transformation of the Nordic Industrial Relations in the European Context 1*, IIRA 4th European Regional Congress Helsinki, Finland 24–26 August 1994, Plenary 1.

[8] The following description is based on N Bruun, "The Transformation of Nordic Industrial Relations" in Kauppinen and Köykkä, above n. 7, at 15–43.

[9] These figures depend to a large extent on whether one includes retired persons, students and the unemployed.

signed—is the most important decision-making level for regulating working conditions. Moreover local level decision-making has, in the past, clearly been subordinate to the decision-making bodies of the national unions, where the demarcation lines are drawn and decisions of principle are taken.

The uniformity of the Nordic trade union movements is accentuated by the clear dominance of the Social Democratic labour movement in the biggest central labour organisations (the LO in Denmark, Norway and Sweden, and the SAK in Finland) and this dominance has also influenced trade union policy. Since the Second World War at least, trade union movements in all of the Nordic countries have worked towards cooperation rather than militancy and have in general had a positive attitude towards growth policy, productivity increases, structural rationalisation, new technology and so on. Thus fixed and stable labour market relations and reformist and consensus policies are further hallmarks of the Nordic model.

Within the framework of tripartite cooperation, Nordic trade union organisations have become well-integrated into government decision-making and their status within government apparatus has been generally accepted, thus labour market organisations have been central co-actors in the design of national labour market policy. Similarly, it has long been considered natural in the Nordic bloc for unions and employees to be central co-actors in decision-making at the company level.

Common institutional characteristics in Nordic labour relations are however by no means limited to trade unions. The labour market is subject to extensive legal regulation and the systems of collective agreement and local-level union representation are the backbone of the labour relations system. The Danish system which was developed a century ago (from the September Agreement of 1899), served as the model for this system, at least in Sweden and in Finland. In all countries we find similar historical agreements institutionalising labour relations at the national level.

I have painted the traditional picture of the Nordic labour relations model with a very broad brush in order to provide a background for the analysis of current developments. My intention in this chapter is to map the changes or tendencies for change that have occurred during the 1990s, especially as a consequence of the process of Europeanisation. The institutional framework of Europeanisation is, of course, Finnish and Swedish membership of the EU since the start of 1995 (Denmark became a member in 1973) and the arrangements for the European Economic Area dating from 1994, which create further institutional links between the EU and Norway and Iceland. The trend towards globalisation does not have a corresponding institutional background, although the Nordic countries are WTO members.

The core of the dilemma caused by the trend towards globalisation in the Nordic countries can be described in one sentence as the problem of trying to find ways in which to maintain the state as the locus of a generous welfare state, and as the promoter of cooperative labour relations and a high-trust business environment, at the same time as opening borders, liberalising markets and promoting the flow of finance and trade through channelling, constraining and legitimising market power.[10] The Nordic dilemma further consists in the adaptation of the state to the global environment where its tools and its regulatory powers are clearly under presuure to change. The challenges to the Nordic model of labour relations and the way in which these challenges have been dealt with are addressed below.

EUROPEANISATION AND GLOBALISATION FROM A NORDIC PERSPECTIVE

In the second half of the 1980s the Nordic countries saw an explosive increase in their foreign direct investments. In these years, Nordic companies were able to establish themselves abroad primarily by acquiring existing foreign companies and incorporating them in their own corporations, or by establishing cooperation with foreign partners.

This trend continued during the 1990s although as a result of Finnish and Swedish membership of the EU, there are some new features in these trends. These developments must also be seen against the backdrop of EMU and the single currency, (established at the start of 1999). The single market and the single currency have provided fresh rationales for the consolidation of integration, although European finance and industry have, like the capital markets, historically been fragmented along national lines; the euro has made it clear that pan-European consolidation is inevitable. The effects of this can be seen across Europe where a huge wave of restructuring and mergers have recently taken place. The Nordic countries are no exception in this respect.

There have been several mergers among the biggest Nordic companies and important companies have merged or initiated closer cooperation with foreign companies (for example Volvo, Saab, Astra). Another dominant feature has been the mergers of the largest Nordic countries to create units that are large enough to compete on the internal European market or even on the global market. Some examples follow: within the paper industry the well known Swedish company Stora merged with the Finnish Enso (Enso-Stora). A merger has taken place between Fazer (Finland) and Cloetta (Sweden). The biggest bank in Finland has merged with one of the biggest Swedish banks Nordbanken (Merita-Nordbanken) and *this* bank has merged with a Danish bank and is actively trying to buy up a Norwegian bank as well. In the telecommunications sector the Swedish Telia and the Norwegian Telenor attempted to merge although this merger failed in the end.

It goes without saying that such an extensive process of restructuring also has implications for the personnel involved and for their conditions and terms of

---

[10] See M Rhodes, "Defending the Social Contract. The EU between global constraints and domestic imperatives" in D Hine and H Kassim (eds), *Beyond the Market. The EU and National Social Policy* (London and New York, Routledge, 1998) 36–59.

employment. It has further consequences for how big companies act in negotiations on collective agreements and other important issues at the national level. At the same time as this, Nordic countries themselves have had to adapt institutionally and introduce EU-legislation in the field of social policy due to the fact that although the material minimum requirements in different regulations and directives are superficially relatively easy to fulfil, some structural issues related to the implementation of Community legislation have caused problems.

THE DEVELOPMENT OF NATIONAL SYSTEMS FOR COLLECTIVE BARGAINING

In not one Nordic country in the 1990s has there been a significant reduction in the level of trade union membership. Whilst no rigorously methodological studies have been made on this subject, it is nevertheless possible to say that quite the opposite has in fact occurred and that trade union affiliation has increased in some sectors. On the other hand, however, small and medium-sized companies are not exhibiting the same interest in belonging to the traditional negotiating employers' confederations.

In all of the Nordic countries the development of national systems for collective bargaining have undergone remarkable changes during the last ten years. These changes can however be described as having taken place within the traditional framework of national collective bargaining and can be summed up in four phrases:

(a)   decentralisation;
(b)   cartelisation;
(c)   fragmentation; and
(d)   direct consequences of internationalisation.

In Sweden the explicit policy goal for several important big multinational employers have been to get rid of nationwide collective agreements. These employers want to substitute such agreements with company-level collective agreements and although the ideological debate in Sweden on this issue has not resulted in the structural change demanded by them,[11] employers have been able to achieve remarkable changes within the system of collective agreements. Thus nationwide collective agreements in Sweden today are completely different to those of twenty years ago. At that time all wages and material conditions of employment were decided on a centralised level;[12] today, almost all of the important issues are decided on the local level. Currently nationwide collective agreements only set very moderate minimum standards and the procedures for resolving conflicts. Similar developments towards decentralisation have taken

---

[11] See C Törnqvist, "The Decentralization of Industrial Relations: The Swedish Case in Comparative Perspective", (1999) 5:1 *European Journal of Industrial Relations* 71–87.

[12] See R Eklund, "Deregulation of Labour Law—The Swedish Case", (1998–1999) 3 *Juridisk tidskrift* 531–51.

place in Denmark[13] and Finland,[14] although the debate in these countries has been far more pragmatic. Corresponding developments can also be traced to some extent in Norway.[15]

Another common feature in Swedish and Finnish labour law is the ability of sectoral labour market organisations to derogate from mandatory provisions in the labour legislation, if the derogation is agreed upon in a nationwide collective agreement. Statutory derogation clauses of this kind, giving the parties increased flexibility, are not rare and the main reason why derogatory powers are placed at the nationwide sectoral organisation level is to ensure a strong counterpart to employers' representatives during negotiations. Such derogation clauses in legislation might, in the future, have an impact on preserving the centralised level on which collective agreements are concluded.

The development towards *cartelisation* is also evident in the Nordic countries. There are several examples of mergers between trade unions or employers' organisations and there are many reason for this. A larger organisation is more cost efficient and has more bargaining power. Different business sectors also occupy different positions on the international market thus one particular sector of industry is likely to have common interests and derive greater advantages from conducting its international negotiations jointly. The public sector is in quite another position. In fact the cartelisation of the private sector is leading to a situation where different groups of labour market organisations act together and take over some of the functions that were earlier performed by the national central confederations (for instance the LO and the SAF in Sweden).[16]

The significant mergers of big companies on the Nordic level might, in the future, result in Nordic trade union cartels. It is well known for example, that the central unions in the paper industry in Finland and Sweden have conducted negotiations on achieving a common base for defending their members interests in both countries and that there is a strong opinion within these unions in favour of forming a common Nordic union. A similar situation in the banking sector might also lead to a need for Nordic trade union mergers or other cooperation arrangements.

The growing tendency towards the use of atypical work and temporary workforces supplied by employment agencies, in some cases even the use of outsourcing and so-called self-employed employees, raise additional problems for traditional collective agreements. Tendencies in this direction can be

[13] See S Scheuer, "Denmark: A Less Regulated Model" in A Ferner and R Hyman (eds), *Changing Industrial Relations in Europe* (Oxford, Blackwell, 1998) 146–70.

[14] See K Lilja, "Finland: Continuity and Modest Moves Towards Company-level Corporatism" in Ferner and Hyman, above n. 13, at 171–89.

[15] See J E Dølvik and T A Stokke, "Norway: The Revival of Centralized Concertation" in Ferner and Hyman, above n.13, at 118–45.

[16] The Swedish development is described by B Nyström, "Nya samarbetsavtal på den svenska arbetsmarknaden—eller skärpt lagstiftning om medling och stridsåtgärder" in M-L Andreasen, J Kristiansen and R Nielsen (eds), *Septemberforliget 100 år* (Copenhagen, Jurist- og Økonomforbundets Forlag, 1999) 279–98.

summarised as a process of *fragmentation*. The question here is whether efforts should be made to regulate these special forms of work through collective agreements and how that could be done. This is a topical issue, at least in Finland and Sweden, and views on how these phenomena should be regulated differ to a large extent between employers and trade unions.

It is obvious that there are several direct effects of the internationalised economy on national collective bargaining; it is very clear that even the basic materials for negotiations have become international so that, for example, for metal industry or electronic companies, competition with other countries in terms of productivity, labour costs and wage incrementals is of central importance. The European trade union movement is trying in different ways to promote wage coordination and the Nordic trade unions are, in principle, in favour of such measures.

THE ROLE OF THE STATE

Internationalisation has usually been identified as one of the factors undermining the traditional Nordic neo-corporatism, described in the introductory notes as a traditional feature of Nordic labour relations.

The relationship between internationalisation and the role of the state is, however, not very easy to come to terms with as it seems to depend on many factors. The attitude among the social partners is of course important. In this respect there is a significant difference in policy between Swedish employers compared with the policy of Danish, Finnish and Norwegian employers. In Finland the central incomes policy has been able to continue during the period of EU membership and the central parties have also been able to agree on some of the measures relating to Finnish membership of EMU. Social or competitive corporatism is well and alive in Finland. In Denmark also there is institutionalised cooperation between the central labour market parties on issues relating to Community legislation. In other respects too, the central labour market organisations clearly want to continue cooperation within the framework of a neo-corporatist structure. The same appears to be true for Norway.

As early as 1990 in Sweden however, the central employers' confederation withdrew from many tripartite bodies and there has been no change in policy since then. On the other hand, the tradition of very autonomous wage negotiations by the labour market parties in Sweden has been a reason for anxiety for the government which is concerned about how to keep the control of wage formation in Sweden in the new EMU internal market regime. New legislation introduced in 1999, increasing the powers of a national mediator, solved this problem in many respects.[17] Additional proposals from the Commission on

---

[17] See the Committee on Mediation and Wage Formation, SOU 1998:41 (Stockholm, 1998). The Committee's report contains a summary in English.

Mediation and Wage Formation went further, although the government backed out from restricting the labour peace obligation and from introducing a principle of proportionality restricting industrial action. The labour market parties conducted negotiations on this issue but they failed to reach an agreement. The description of the situation in Sweden is not complete without mentioning, however, that relations between labour market parties on a sectoral level work quite well in many respects. A remarkable achievement in this area was an agreement which took place in 1997 within the industrial sector in which the most central industry federations on both sides participated.[18]

STRUCTURAL TENSION

Europeanisation not only influences Nordic labour relations in various economic respects, but the impact is also clearly felt within labour law. The reason for this is self-evident; the fragmented but extensive Community social policy legal regime has to be implemented or incorporated into the Nordic labour law systems. Although there are generally few major problems for the Nordic countries in fulfilling the minimum requirements set out by Community law, there are some structural tensions between Nordic traditions and the general EU pattern of social policy regulation, which essentially, with some minor exceptions, is based on labour law traditions in continental and southern Europe. The main tensions worth mentioning in this respect are easiest to trace in Denmark and Sweden. First, the importance and autonomy of the collective bargaining system in these countries can lead to tensions concerning the form in which Community legislation might be implemented on a national level. The traditional structure of the collective bargaining system with an extensive freedom to resort to collective action when there is an interest dispute (no collective agreement in force) might also be difficult to fit in with the law-based less autonomous European tradition. Furthermore the Nordic labour law tradition, emphasising collective rights, might easily come into conflict with the individualistic approach of both Community law and the conventions of the Council of Europe, the European Convention on Human Rights (1950) and the European Social Charter (1961).

Implementation of Directives through collective agreements

EU integration and the growing importance of Community labour law have focused attention on the question of the continuing role and status of the collective agreement as a regulator of conditions of employment. The background to this issue is that in all the Nordic countries, collective agreements are the main instrument for regulating terms and conditions in the labour market, and

---

[18] See Nyström, above n. 16.

EU discussions have for a long time centered largely on whether or not the Nordic countries are able to fulfil the regulatory requirements set out in EC directives through their own national collective agreements. The background to this problem is that Article 249 (ex 189) EC provides that Member States may choose their own "form and methods" for achieving the desired results set out in any given directive. Despite this wording, the European Court of Justice has repeatedly affirmed that collective agreements are not an adequate means of realising an EC directive unless the regulations laid down in the agreements are so comprehensive as to protect all the individual employees concerned. Where this is not the case, the Member State is deemed to have failed to meet its obligation to ensure compliance with the directive in all respects. However, so-called semi-dispositive legislation can, of course, be introduced. This will mean that the legislation is secondary and comes into effect only in cases where the social partners have not regulated the issue in a collective agreement in a way which complies with Community requirements.

In both Denmark and Sweden the role of the collective agreement has been discussed in an official exchange of views with EU authorities, especially with the former European Commissioner Padraig O'Flynn.[19] In an exchange of letters that took place before the second Danish referendum on the Maastricht Treaty and before the Swedish referendum on EU Membership, Commissioner Flynn stated that the Maastricht Social Protocol indicates that membership will not require a change of Swedish and Danish practice in labour market issues. The legal significance of this exchange of views has been a matter of debate. It has clearly had the consequence that the Commission has taken account of Nordic traditions when proposing legislation. On the other hand it cannot change the fundamental requirements of Community law on implementation measures.

This issue is likely to come to the fore again in the near future. In November 1999 the Commission noted that in Denmark the Working Time Directive[20] (93/104/EC) had not been implemented by legislation, but by collective agreements.[21] This meant that the full implementation of the minimum standard as prescribed in the Directive had not been achieved. Furthermore, some recent studies indicate that the coverage of Danish collective agreements is lower than generally claimed.[22] The issue is however highly politically controversial in Denmark where the prevailing opinion is opposed to intervention by EU authorities in the Danish system.

---

[19] For further details see N Bruun in Kauppinen and Köykkä, above n. 7, at 21–5.
[20]]1993] OJ L307/18.
[21] See K Ahlberg, *EU & Arbetsrätt* 4/1999 at 5.
[22] See especially S Scheuer, *Faelles aftale eller egen kontrakt i arbejdslivet. Udbredelsen af kollektive overenskomster, faglig organisering og skriftlige ansaettelsesbeviser blandt privatansatte* (Copenhagen, Nytt fra Samfundsvidenskaberne, 1996).

The freedom to take collective action

The wide coverage of Nordic collective agreements has traditionally been achieved by using pressure from the trade union side. Unorganised employers have been forced either to join the employers' union or to sign a separate collective agreement containing the central terms and conditions in the nationwide agreement in that sector.

During the last two years the Nordic countries have been faced with the challenge of implementing EC Directive 96/71/EC on the posting of workers in the framework of provision of services.[23] The time limit for national implementation of this Directive expired in December 1999 but for Denmark and Sweden the Directive raised a fundamental problem.[24] The Directive demands that these countries regulate the level of minimum wages for posted workers; in the cases of these countries, the level of minimum wages are set in the collective agreements. There are however, no general obligations at the national level for small companies, not belonging to an employers' union, to follow the collective agreement. The usual case is that if these small companies begin to grow they are approached by the trade unions, which have the power to force them to sign a collective agreement and if they are not willing to do this, they are likely to face some type of industrial action. During the preparatory work on the Directive on posting of workers, due account was taken of the Nordic problem. The Directive therefore prescribes that the minimum wages that a posted worker should be entitled to can also be regulated in a nationwide collective agreement entered into by the representative social partners.

So far so good. The Swedish and Danish implementing measures on posted workers do not contain any explicit provision concerning the obligation of the employer of posted workers to pay wages according to the minimum requirements in the national sectoral collective agreement, however. Why is that so? The reason is that the Swedish and Danish authorities did not want to introduce a so-called *erga omnes* system through the back door. According to the Directive, companies which are posting workers cannot be treated in a less favourable way than national companies. If we were to create an explicit obligation for foreign companies to pay wages according to Swedish or Danish collective agreements we would also have to extend this obligation to all national companies that are not bound by any collective agreement. In Sweden and Denmark there is, in a sense, an inherent, indirect obligation to adhere to the collective agreement, but this obligation is not based on law, but on factual behaviour and conduct within the labour market system. Therefore the Swedish Act implementing the Directive on posted workers concerning wages only prescribes that:

---

[23] [1997] OJ L18/1.
[24] For Finland and Norway the situation is easier because their national systems are capable of creating an "*erga omnes*" effect.

(a)   information shall be given on the content of the terms and working conditions that shall be applied in Sweden;

(b)   general rules on freedom of association and right to negotiations are to be applied.

The specific Nordic freedom to collective action encompasses the situation where the workers in a specific company themselves are not so keen on taking action. We could, for instance, think of a situation where five workers are posted for half a year in Sweden. They might be quite satisfied with their working conditions, although they do not fulfil Swedish standards. In this situation it is normal practice for the nationwide trade union to declare a blockade or a boycott of the company concerned. This action can also be supported by transport workers, which will mean that none of the needed raw materials are delivered to the company. This kind of action, normally, very effectively leads to the conclusion of a collective agreement.

According to the Swedish Co-Determination Act industrial action is permissible during the life of the collective agreement especially in the following instances:[25]

(a)   it aims at regulating matters which have not been regulated in the collective agreement;

(b)   it is intended as a sympathetic or solidarity action in support of primary legal industrial action (or in support of the demand for concluding an agreement);

(c)   it is a debt-collection blockade, i.e. a blockade to enforce payment of undisputed and due demands for wages or other remuneration for work performed.

The Nordic practice of solidarity-based industrial action has no real counterpart in continental Europe.[26] Therefore it is no surprise that the employers have asked for restrictions in this freedom. With the evolving system of European industrial relations one could however claim that there is a need for a minimum space for transnational solidarity action in all Member States. The Nordic experiences could be of considerable help when framing this space.

Collectivism versus individualism

Within the Nordic labour relations tradition, the impact of constitutional aspects have usually been seen as limited. Labour law has to a large extent been

---

[25] For more details, see S Edlund and B Nyström, *Developments in Swedish Labour Law* (Stockholm, The Swedish Institute, 1988).

[26] See N Bruun and B Veneziani, "The Right or Freedom to Transnational Industrial Action in the European Union", in Report by the ETUI Research Network on transnational trade union rights, *A Legal Framework for European Industrial Relations* (Brussels, ETUI, 1999).

regarded as a private law system in which the parties to the collective agreements play the major part. Therefore there is a clear tension between the interpretation of the European Convention of Human Rights (1950) on one hand and the Swedish and Danish labour relations traditions on the other.

Article 11 of the ECHR governs the right to association; the European Court for Human Rights in Strasbourg has gradually begun to interpret this provision as offering both the right to belong to a trade union (positive right) and the right to remain outside (negative right). The prevailing traditional view in both Sweden and Denmark has been that the negative right of association is not encompassed by the principle of freedom of association. Furthermore it has been somewhat unclear to what extent the right of association can also offer protection to the interests that employees seek to promote by forming associations. Could it be argued that the ECHR regulates the right to bargain collectively and the right to take industrial action in order to promote collective demands? The practice of the Court of Human Rights, so far, has been to rule that the right to strike is not guaranteed by Article 11. What is protected according to that Court, is the right to represent the members in an effective way and it feels that this can also be done in other ways than through strikes. However the Court has not specified which these ways are.

The Swedish case of *Gustafsson* concerned the question of whether an employer's right to freedom of association also covered the right to remain outside the collective bargaining system.[27] Gustafsson, who owned a small summer restaurant, refused to sign a collective agreement with the Hotel and Restaurant Workers' Union. He refused to negotiate with the trade union and also refused to sign a separate collective agreement (*hängavtal*). The trade union reacted with a blockade and boycott of Gustafsson's restaurant, trying to cut off all supplies and deliveries. Gustafsson felt that this action contravened the ECHR and demanded that the Swedish government should forbid the action. The government responded by saying that it had no right to intervene and that the conflict should be resolved in court. The case was heard in a national court and all of Gustafsson's demands were rejected. Gustafsson then turned to the authorities of the Council of Europe and later to the Court of Human Rights, but lost the case here too. The Court ruled that the positive right of association comprises a right to defend the interests of the members through collective bargaining and the conclusion of collective agreements. Being exposed to pressure to sign an affiliated collective agreement does not violate the employer's negative freedom of association. The Court noted that the obligations placed by the articles on freedom of association in the ECHR on the parties can also be extended to apply to treatment, which is of relevance to the collective agreement system, but only if such treatment clearly encroaches upon the freedom of association itself. Gustafsson later tried to have his case reheard on the grounds that he believed

---

[27] See European Court of Human Rights, Judgment 18/1995/524/610, *Gustafsson* v. *Sweden*, Strasbourg, 25 April 1996.

the judgment to be based on incorrect information presented by the Swedish Government. This demand was rejected by a vote of 16 to 1.

To summarise, we can thus say that the Court of Human Rights has, in certain respects, interpreted the ECHR in an extensive way (the negative right of association), and in other respects in a restrictive way, and that generally it strongly emphasises individual factors which have led to a tension between the interpretation of the ECHR and some elements of traditional Nordic labour relations.

Within the field of sex discrimination concerning pay, the Nordic practice of collective bargaining on one hand and the individual assessment of pay on the other have been difficult to combine. In the Swedish Labour Court the rulings have usually given priority to the national system of collective bargaining[28] and the court has backed down when it has been asked to assess whether different work can be of "equal value". However, when faced with a reference from a Swedish Labour Court regarding the interpretation of Article 141 EC, in the light of an alleged difference in pay between midwives and clinical technicians, the Court of Justice saw no reason to highlight any possible tensions between the individual right to non-discrimination and the legitimacy of agreements that representative organisations have concluded.[29]

EUROPEAN WORKS COUNCILS

The clearest institutional indication of the Europeanisation of labour relations is the institutional form of worker participation within European multinational corporations (MNCs) and European Work Councils. Directive 94/45/EC[30] grants employee representatives from the countries of the EU and EEA the right to be informed and consulted by the central management of large MNCs. This Directive has been implemented in all the Nordic countries. The Directive offers some advantages to those MNCs which concluded agreements before 22 September 1996. They are then exempted from several obligatory requirements in the Directive and are able to conclude an Article 13 agreement.

The Nordic countries have a long tradition of joint consultation and cooperation at workplace and company level. In accordance with this we expected to find many Article 13 agreements in Nordic MNCs. When we conducted a study on this, we did indeed find many such agreements.[31] On the other hand, a relatively large number of the Nordic agreements clearly fell below the rights contained in the Directive. We explained this by referring to the necessity of unions

---

[28] See the Swedish Labour Court (AD) 1996:41.

[29] See for instance Case C–236/98 *Jämställdhetsombudsmannen* v. *Örebrolänslandsting*, judgment of 3 March 2000.

[30] [1994] OJ L254/61.

[31] See H Knudsen and N Bruun, "European Works Councils in the Nordic Countries: An Opportunity and a Challenge for Trade Unionism", (1998) 4:2 *European Journal of Industrial Relations* 131–55.

to give concessions in order to get agreements and also by way of reference to the decentralised means of concluding the agreements. The main conclusion, however, from the study was that there is a clear tension between "group corporatism", that is cooperation within the MNCs, compared with traditional national trade union cooperation and the nationwide collective bargaining system. Here is an opportunity but also a great challenge for Nordic trade unionism.

CONCLUSION

From a Nordic perspective we can state that the post-war labour relations system was clearly very focused on the nation state. In my opinion we do not need, however, to ask whether the process of Europeanisation and globalisation is a reality or a myth.[32] The many factors that indicate that Nordic reality is influenced by this process are convincing enough.

The impact of the trends towards globalisation and Europeanisation is not straight forward however. The influence of, and the challenges made by, these trends are channelled through the institutions and frameworks of the Nordic model and the results represent a form of new "competitive corporatism" with some in-built constraints, especially in Sweden. The trend of Europeanisation also runs in both ways, as Nordic traditions of high trust industrial relations and a good cooperative spirt between the labour market parties are evidently attractive to the EU institutions.

The institutional frameworks of Nordic labour relations have not undergone any radical changes during the last years of the twentieth century, although important changes, as presented above, have taken place. The popular support for the Nordic welfare state is also still quite strong and scepticisism towards globalisation and Europeanisation can be traced in the strong political support for groups representing different kinds of euroscepticism (especially in Denmark and Sweden).

The present situation is characterised by a strong tendency towards globalisation and Europeanisation on one hand and on the other, strong support for preserving the Nordic model of labour relations. There is an obvious tension between these trends. This tension tends to create a very defensive attitude towards Europeanisation, and this defensiveness can be traced in efforts to avoid most kinds of legal and institutional intervention in the national labour relations system from the European level. These efforts can, however, be counter-productive; non-regulation at a European level might result in market regulation that might undermine the basis of Nordic labour relations. Therefore a more strategic and proactive approach is needed.

[32] See R Hyman, above n. 2, at 89–110.

The problem with the Nordic national labour relations system and internationalisation is, however, that a significant number of members, especially in the national trade unions, continue to regard the labour relations system as a national system. International elements are seen more as a threat which we should try to get rid of, than as inevitable consequences of new developments which we have to handle and live with in the future. In parallel, the employers' side also prefers market regulation and non-interference from the European level in labour relations.

My prediction, therefore, is that the development towards the, in my opinion necessary, internationalised European industrial relations system will not take place smoothly. I do not think that the necessary consciousness for change will develop without some experience of crises and turbulence, which will make the general opinion in Europe more favourable towards international cooperation and international solutions on the labour market in order to preserve some elements of a social dimension in the globalised and Europeanised Nordic countries.

6

Community Sex Discrimination Law in the National Courts: A Legal Cultural Comparison

CHLOE J WALLACE

Member State courts have a crucial role in the implementation of Community social law and policy. The doctrine of the supremacy of Community law means that it is the job of national courts to apply Community law within their national legal systems; the role of the European Court of Justice is limited to assisting them by answering interpretative questions. Consequently, the dialogue between Member State courts and the European Court plays an important part in the way in which rules and policies are interpreted and implemented in Member States. Kilpatrick has argued that national courts can be seen as existing within Community organisational structures; they can be seen as Community institutions and treated accordingly. For this reason, much of the process of integration of law can be seen as a process of mediation, between the European Court and national courts, of how law should be done.[1] The results of that mediation have a significant effect on the application of Community law within Member States.

The notion that different courts have different ways of seeing how law should be done can be related to much contemporary comparative law work on the question of legal cultures and, more specifically, the way in which the existence of different legal cultures has an impact on the harmonisation of law in Europe and, ultimately, on European integration as a whole.[2] If, as Gessner has argued, Europe is the region in the world with the most variation in legal cultural characteristics,[3] then any mediation amongst national courts, or between national courts and the European Court, on the question of how law should be done, and how legal rules and policies should be approached, interpreted and applied, must necessarily involve meetings and potential clashes of legal cultures. These

---

[1] C Kilpatrick, "Community or Communities of Courts in European Integration? Sex Equality Dialogues Between UK Courts and the ECJ", (1998) 4 *ELJ* 121.
[2] See in particular, P Legrand, "European Legal Systems are Not Converging", (1996) 45 *ICLQ* 52.
[3] V Gessner, "Global Legal Interaction and Legal Cultures", (1994) 7 *RJ* 132.

meetings of cultures must be considered to be of crucial importance in the process of integration.

This point becomes particularly relevant in areas, such as social policy, which give a broad field of operation to national courts. This is, of course, not to argue that the question of legal culture has no relevance in economic or trade law. However, because social policy inevitably involves the implementation of rules within a Member State, rather than at a supranational level, and leads to much litigation in national courts, it is a fertile ground for examining the relationship between legal culture and European integration.

Doctrines developed by the European Court have been aimed towards the goal of involving national courts in the process of the enforcement of Community law and, consequently, in the process of European integration. Weiler has argued that the genius of the doctrines of direct effect and supremacy lies in the fact that they give national courts and, as a result, nationals them-selves, the power to enforce Community law against Member States, in the same way as the courts in the USA have the power to enforce the Constitution against the constituent states and the federal government.[4] However, a key problem that arises from this argument is that of the role of the courts and, particularly, their perception of their own role. Do they see themselves as central instruments in the goal of European integration? The question can be asked on two levels. First, is it reasonable to expect a national court, which has specific roles to play within its own legal system, to take on an extra role, that of Community enforcer, and to give that role priority when dealing with Community law? Secondly, even if a national court is prepared to take on that role, is it possible for it to do so, given the web of cultural expectations in which it operates? It is on this second problem I intend to focus.

I argue that the different cultural constructs in which national courts operate are reflected in the differing degrees of enthusiasm with which national courts approach the possibility of dialogue with the European Court and their own role as enforcers of Community law. This proposition will be discussed with particular reference to a comparative study of the implementation in France and England and Wales[5] of Community sex discrimination law, which analyses that implementation in the contexts of English and French legal culture, and exam-ples from that study will be given. It is dangerous to draw general conclusions about the matter from a specific study. A range of other factors may well be

---

[4] J Weiler, "The Transformation of Europe", (1991) 100 *Yale Law Journal* 2403.

[5] It should perhaps be made clear here that the reference to England and Wales rather than the United Kingdom is deliberate. When discussing legal culture, note must be taken of the existence of separate legal systems in Scotland and Northern Ireland, and, in particular, of the different roots and traditions of those systems, leading, potentially, to the development of distinct legal cultures. This, of course, conflicts with the fact that labour law is generally seen as national, UK law and is not different in England, Scotland and Northern Ireland and that, consequently, what is being dis-cussed is UK law as a whole, and not just English law. Pedantic as it may seem, however, in com-parative law terms the distinction must be made.

involved. However, this chapter will indicate some of the issues which need to be considered.

First, however, an understanding of the broad concept of legal culture used in this chapter must be offered. It will then be argued that the different legal cultures in England and France have led to clearly different perceptions within those legal systems of the role and power of the courts, and, consequently, their ability to impose Community law on the rest of the system. Finally, the question as to whether or not these legal cultural differences are reflected in the level of dialogue with the European Court and compliance with Community law will be addressed. I will suggest that, on the evidence, legal culture can be seen as a significant, although not a unique, factor in the effectiveness of a national court in its role as enforcer of Community law.

LEGAL CULTURE

The terminology of legal culture has been in use for about thirty years. At its inception, it was principally a product of the determination of some scholars to move legal studies away from an analytical study of a normative system, and towards interaction with other disciplines, notably sociology and anthropology.[6] In more recent years, questions have been posed as to the suitability of the terminology of legal culture in sociological and socio-legal analysis.[7] However, at the same time, the notion has gained some currency in the area of comparative law, and it is in this context that this chapter situates itself.[8]

The approach to legal culture taken here draws much from the anthropological work of Clifford Geertz and the hermeneutic philosophy of Hans-Georg Gadamer.[9] Culture is seen as part of the context in which individuals interpret what goes on around them. It is fundamentally linked to Heidegger's notion of "Understanding" and Gadamer's concept of a horizon—that which is an essential part of oneself which one brings to a text or event and which conditions the interpretation of that text or event. Part of that horizon, according to Geertz, is socially established, because of the individual's membership of different communities or social groups, and that part of the horizon is what we call culture. This approach to culture can be applied in the legal field. It is assumed,

---

[6] A prime mover in this field was Lawrence Friedman; see for example, "Legal Culture and Social Development", (1969) 4 *Law & Soc. Rev* 29; "Some Thoughts on Comparative Legal Culture" in D S Clark (ed.), *Comparative and Private International Law—Essays in Honour of John Henry Merryman* (Berlin, Durcher u-Humblot, 1990). See also Gessner, above n. 3, for application of this approach in the European field.

[7] See in particular, R Cotterrell, "The Concept of Legal Culture" in D Nelken (ed.), *Comparing Legal Cultures* (Aldershot, Dartmouth, 1997).

[8] See Legrand, above n. 2. For discussion of the difference between the socio-legal studies and the comparative law approach, see Legrand's review of Nelken's "Comparing Legal Cultures", (1997) 56 *CLJ* 646.

[9] C Geertz, *The Interpretation of Cultures* (London, Fontana, 1993); H-G Gadamer, *Truth and Method* (J Weinsheimer and D G Marshall (trans.), London, Sheed and Ward, 1989).

following Dworkin, that interpretation is a fundamental part of legal activity.[10] All lawyers have a background, an Understanding, which they bring to their interpretations of legal situations. Part of that background is established by the legal community of the particular jurisdiction in which the lawyer is working. It is mainly transmitted by means of legal education, but elements such as social links and professional practice also have a role to play. All lawyers are part of a particular legal culture and thus all lawyers work and think within the context of that culture.

A number of points need to be made about the nature of legal culture. First, legal culture is not static. It is in a constant state of flux. Gadamer argued that horizons, when confronted with new ideas and situations, have a tendency to change and develop in order to take account of those new ideas and situations. He refers to this phenomenon as a fusion of horizons. Consequently, while litigation or legislation is affected by the legal culture of the system, it can in turn have an effect on that legal culture. Thus, in so far as litigation or legislation is affected by social, political or economic factors or other cultural factors, legal culture will also be affected by those factors. As a result, legal cultural attitudes can and do change quite considerably over time. This facet of legal culture has particular relevance to the relationship between Community and national law, as the two legal orders are in almost constant confrontation and fusion. The potential which this creates to lead to changes in national legal cultures will be highlighted later in the chapter.

Legal cultures are also often contradictory and contain within them sub-cultures. As Walt Whitman might have said, being large, they contain multitudes.[11] The view of legal culture outlined above should not be taken as suggesting that, in any legal system, there is only one way of doing things. There is, rather, a range of ways of doing things, and the particular way in which things are done is, to a greater or lesser extent, dependent on the individual or individuals making the decision. However, it is argued that legal cultures contain within them broad themes which are generally accepted and which can be seen to be operating within those legal systems. It is with these themes that I am concerned.

Finally, the impact which legal culture is said to have is not causal, but rather contextual. The criticisms which have been made in socio-legal terms of the notion of legal culture have, to a great extent, been responses to arguments that a causal relationship can be found between legal culture and legal developments. That relationship is not admitted in this chapter, and care has been taken not to suggest that there is, or can be, a cause-effect relationship between legal culture and specific applications of Community norms. Rather, because those applications take place in the context of a legal culture they may, and often do, reflect legal cultural characteristics. Often, however, other factors, such as gov-

---

[10] R Dworkin, *Law's Empire* (London, Fontana, 1991).

[11] "Do I contradict myself? Very well then I contradict myself (I am large, I contain multitudes)": Walt Whitman, *Leaves of Grass*, "Song of Myself", section 51.

ernment policy or social attitudes, can be identified as having an equal, if not greater, impact on the application of Community norms.

Legal culture, thus, is seen as that part of the horizon which is brought by members of a particular legal community to their understanding of texts, behaviours and situations and which is conditioned by the values, attitudes and beliefs common to and developed within that legal community. It is now necessary to apply this rather abstract theory to the concrete question of how the role of the courts, in France and England, is perceived by the legal community and, more specifically, by the judiciary themselves. This perception constitutes a key distinction between French and English legal culture. It should be emphasised that what is to follow deals with the perception of the role, rather than any objective statement of the role itself.[12] Differences of perception, however, have relevance in the context of the role of the courts as enforcers of Community law as they relate to the question of whether the legal culture allows for a national judge to take on that role.

NATIONAL PERCEPTIONS OF THE ROLE OF THE JUDGE

England

One of the characteristic elements of English legal culture is the dominance of common law within the system. Other factors have been important; the prevalence of positivist legal thinking in jurisprudential circles and the increasing pre-eminence of statute law are both equally characteristic of English legal thinking. However, the continuing emphasis on common law thinking is particularly apparent in the context of the judicial role. An important aspect of common law thinking is a reliance on consensus, rather than authority, to give power to legal propositions.[13] This reliance is evident in a number of areas, but particularly so in the characteristic form of the doctrine of precedent and the powerful role which this doctrine gives to the English judiciary.

Bryce referred to English judges as "the legal intelligence of the nation" and argued that they were figureheads, representing the will of the people in the shaping of non-legislative law.[14] They can be seen as the most important figures in the common law view of a legal system. Traditionally, common law judges have not been seen as creators of legal rules. The "declaratory" theory of law states that judges "discover" the correct rule of law by dipping into what

---

[12] It can be argued that, in fact, the role and the approach of English and French judges have much in common. See for discussion, J Bell, "English and French Law—Not So Different?", (1995) 48 *CLP* 63.

[13] See B Simpson, "The Common Law and Legal Theory" in W Twining (ed.), *Legal Theory and Common Law* (Oxford, Blackwell, 1986).

[14] J Bryce, "Methods of Law Making in Rome and in England" in *Studies in History and Jurisprudence, Vol II* (Oxford, Oxford University Press, 1901).

Goodrich refers to as a collective narrative memory of the law.[15] In 1612, Davies wrote that

> "[law reports] are but comments and interpretations of the common law, which text was never written but hath ever been preserved in the memory of man, though no man's memory can reach the original thereof".[16]

This view was supported in the present century by C K Allen, who stated, while discussing the doctrine of precedent, that "the judge follows binding authority only if and because it is a true statement of the law".[17] In this context, the doctrine of precedent can be seen as a way of establishing what the law has been thought to be, and of representing the collective view of the judiciary as to the content of the law.

However, since the 1960s, there has been a move towards the acceptance of judge-made law. Since that time, to a greater or lesser extent, the power of judges to make law has been acknowledged, maintained and exercised.[18] In the main, modern English judges are willing, and often very happy, to accept their law-making responsibility and thus their pre-eminent position within the English legal system. Indeed, it can be argued that the English judge has been, in recent years, empowered. One example of this trend is the acceptance by the House of Lords of the doctrine of supremacy of Community law and their consequent power to disapply UK legislation in favour of Community law.[19] Another example can perhaps be found with the passing of the Human Rights Act 1998, which incorporates the European Convention on Human Rights into UK law and extends the powers of the judiciary to review executive acts and to comment on the compatibility of legislation with the ECHR.

This view of the role of the judge has changed the role and perception of the doctrine of precedent. Precedent is seen less as a means of finding out what the law might be, and more a way in which we, as students and practitioners of the law, can discover the specific content of the legal rules the judges have laid down. We discover, the judges create.

English judges, therefore, have a recognised power to make law. A second relevant factor in their self-perception is an acceptance of the role of policy, rather than just legal rules and principles, in their law-making responsibilities. They are generally willing to accept that their decisions have implications beyond the specific facts of the case before them and, consequently, that policy considerations must be borne in mind when taking those decisions. This is particularly in evidence in the law of negligence. The role of public policy has always been

---

[15] P Goodrich, *Languages of Law* (London, Weidenfeld and Nicholson, 1990).

[16] Cited in C P Rodgers, "Humanism, History and the Common Law", (1985) 6 *JLH* 129.

[17] C K Allen, *Law in the Making* (Oxford, Clarendon, 1964).

[18] See Lord Reid, "The Judge as Law Maker", (1972) 12 *JPTL* 22; A Lester "English Judges as Law Makers", [1993] *PL* 269.

[19] *R v. Secretary of State for Transport, ex parte Factortame* [1991] AC 603.

recognised in the context of the question as to where a duty of care is owed.[20] In
Alcock v. *Chief Constable of South Yorkshire*, for example, it was stated that
the final determinants of liability were common sense, reasonableness, policy
and standards of value and justice, rather than any strict test.[21] The relevance of
public policy has also been acknowledged by judges writing extra-judicially.
Lord Reid stated that when making decisions, judges should "have regard to
common sense, legal principle and public policy in that order".[22] Lord Steyn, in
discussing the expansion of judicial power in the field of administrative law,
stated that ". . . judges cannot avoid considering policy issues in the process of
reviewing allegations of abuse of ministerial powers".[23]

France

English judges, then, regard themselves, and are regarded, as law-makers and
policy actors; as creative and active members of the legal community. The same
cannot be said of their French counterparts. The French judge is seen as the
junior partner in the threefold structure of the state; less important than both
the legislator and the executive bodies.[24] However, as the authority charged
with the application of law within society, the judge has a great deal of responsibility. Consequently, she has been described as "a colossus with clay feet".[25]
Her paradoxical role is illustrated by two articles of the French Civil Code.
Article 4 states: "Le juge qui refusera de juger, sous prétexte du silence, de
l'obscurité ou de l'insuffisance de la loi, pourra être poursuivi comme coupable
de déni de justice". A judge must judge, even if there are no laws, *stricto sensu*,
to apply. This would appear to force judges as a body to create law of their own,
if they are not to judge in an arbitrary fashion.

Article 5, on the other hand, states: "il est défendu aux juges de prononcer par
voie de disposition générale et réglementaire sur les causes qui leur sont
soumises". This seems to suggest that a judge is not permitted to create law, in
the sense that any judgments she makes must be restricted to the specific case
under judgment and should not be held to be applicable in future cases. Thus,
while, according to Article 5, judges cannot create law, they are required, under
the terms of Article 4, to play the role of the legislator in particular cases, without being able to take advantage of previous decisions taken by their colleagues
in similar circumstances.

[20] See for example, *Anns* v. *London Borough of Merton* [1978] AC 728 and *Caparo Industries* v.
Dickman [1990] 2 AC 605. The latter case is generally said to overrule the former but both contain
reference to the need to consider policy matters in deciding whether a duty of care exists.
[21] [1992] 1 AC 310.
[22] Lord Reid, above n. 18.
[23] J Steyn, "Does Legal Formalism Hold Sway in England?", (1996) *CLP* 43, at 51.
[24] See R J Cummins, "The General Principles of Law, Separation of Powers and Theories of
Judicial Decision in France", (1986) 35 *ICLQ* 594.
[25] R Perrot, "The Judge: The Extent and Limit of his Role in Civil Matters", (1976) *Tulane LR*
495.

The prohibition on judicial law-making runs deep within the French legal culture. Garapon and Salas sum the situation up well when they state that: "en France, en effet, on désire l'Etat de droit, mais on ne croit pas qu'il sera le fait des juges".[26] The idea of the judiciary exceeding their power, known as the *"gouvernement des juges"*, is still perceived within the French legal system as a danger to be avoided. It is, however, rather unclear exactly what the notion of the *"gouvernement des juges"* is. Nevertheless, what is clear is that it is perceived as a negative thing and is used as a threat, particularly in the context of the "spectre" of increased constitutional control of the legislature.[27]

The French legal system portrays an image of the judge as a faceless bureaucrat, who applies, automatically, the law laid down by the legislator to the cases before her. She has no role of law-making, no interpretative powers, and no role of policy implementation or creation. This image does not, however, correspond with reality. Given the paradoxical relationship between Articles 4 and 5 of the Civil Code, French judges are often forced to make law, even if they are not supposed to. Indeed, the role of case law as a source of law is now widely recognised within French legal circles. It is seen either as a formal source of law[28] or as having psychological or sociological influence.[29] Further, French judges do refer to precedent in that they refer, in their deliberations, to previous decisions which may, particularly if they are from a higher court, be considered to be persuasive.[30]

However, this does not mean that the ideal view is irrelevant. Lasser has argued that there exist two views of the judicial role in French legal culture; the formal, idealistic view, and the informal view, which corresponds more closely with reality.[31] He argues, moreover, that the formal view should not be dismissed as a fiction with no substance, but that it should be viewed as equally worthy of study as the informal view, because it conditions the way French lawyers see the law and the legal system.

The relationship between the ideal and the real view of the judicial role has important consequences. The ideal view of the judicial role means that judicial opinions are collegiate and impersonal, and that judicial decisions do not have complex reasoning process behind them and are limited to a formal, syllogistic statement of the law which has been applied, to the facts which have been found and to the consequent result. As Dawson points out, this means that the public accountability of the judge is reduced. It cannot be denied that judges do make

---

[26] A Garapon and D Salas, *La République Pénalisée* (Paris, Hachette, 1996) 46.

[27] See M H Davis, "A Government of Judges: A Historical Re-view", (1987) 35 *AJCL* 559.

[28] For an early expression of this view, see J Maury, "Observations sur la jurisprudence en tant que source de droit" in *Le Droit Privé Français au milieu du Xxe siècle: Etudes Offertes à Georges Ripert* (Paris, Librarie Générale de Droit et de Jurisprudence, 1950).

[29] See J Carbonnier, *Droit Civil: Introduction* (Paris, PUF, 1990).

[30] See C Grzegorczyk and M Troper, 'Precedent in France' in D N MacCormick and R S Summers (eds), *Interpreting Precedents: a Comparative Study* (Aldershot, Dartmouth, 1997).

[31] M Lasser, "Judicial (Self-)Portraits: Judicial Discourse in the French Legal System", (1995) 104 *YLJ* 1325.

discretionary choices, based on their interpretation of the facts, of the law or of underlying policy or principle.[32] However, the anonymity and abstract nature of their published decisions makes it impossible to offer a really coherent criticism of decisions. Judges are able to hide behind a cloak of anonymity and this can give them far more freedom than a common law judge, who produces a lengthy and personalised opinion which can be scrutinised by all.

DIALOGUE WITH THE EUROPEAN COURT: THE IMPACT OF LEGAL CULTURE

Significant differences exist, therefore, between the view of the role of the judge in English legal culture and in French legal culture, and these differences are reflected in the different powers and responsibilities which judges explicitly adopt. English judges are happy to acknowledge their law-making power and also their power in implementing and even making policy decisions which are related to the law. French judges, while indisputably having a law-making power, and probably also a policy-making and implementation power, are far less willing to acknowledge that power. This fact would appear to have important consequences for the subject matter of this chapter; the ability of the French and English courts to take on the role of Community law enforcer which has been conferred upon them by the European Court. It could perhaps be surmised, from the above analysis, that English judges would be willing and able to take on that role. Indeed, it is not a coincidence that one of the significant factors in the recent empowerment of the English judiciary has been their acceptance, in the *Factortame* decision, of their role of enforcer of Community law within the United Kingdom.[33] It could equally be surmised that while French judges may take Community law and policy into consideration, they are less happy about doing so and less happy about acknowledging that they are doing anything other than applying the law in force.

The rest of this chapter will be devoted to a discussion as to whether or not those surmises are, in fact, reflected in the true role of French and English courts in the process of the implementation of Community sex discrimination law and the consequences which that may have for the effectiveness of Community law in England and France. The first point of discussion must be the willingness of national courts to engage in dialogue with the European Court about sex discrimination law, principally by making Article 234 EC references. However, the fact of the dialogue in itself, while necessary, is not sufficient. Consequently, the effectiveness of that dialogue in ensuring compliance with Community law will also be considered.

The differences between English and French courts in terms of references on sex discrimination matters are stark. Kilpatrick points out that although equality issues produce a relatively low level of litigation within Member States,

---

[32] J P Dawson, *The Oracles of the Law* (Westwood, Conn., Greenwood Press, 1978).
[33] See above n. 19.

they result in a larger number of Article 234 EC references than any other social policy issue. This may reflect the advanced state of the development of Community sex equality law. The United Kingdom has a high level of sex equality litigation within its own courts, and a correspondingly high number of cases are referred to the European Court. This has resulted in a long dialogue between the UK courts and the European Court regarding the way in which Community sex equality law should be applied and enforced. France, on the other hand, has a much lower rate of equality litigation generally. Only four sex equality cases have ever been referred by the French courts to the European Court under Article 234 EC; two cases were referred by the Tribunaux de Police, a rough equivalent of a magistrates court,[34] one by the Tribunal des Prud'hommes, or labour court[35] and only one has been referred by the Cour de Cassation, the highest French court.[36] Previously, the Cour had been requested to refer cases, but declined to do so.[37]

Therefore, in the area of sex discrimination law there does seem to be more substantial dialogue between the English courts and the European Court than between the French courts and the European Court. This fact, in itself, may reflect the differences in legal culture. English courts see themselves as having acquired an active role in choosing to enforce Community law over and above previously stated national law and as they regard this role as new to them, they may be more willing to ask for advice on how best to do it. French courts, on the other hand, are more likely to see their role as passively applying stated law, as it always has been. The Cour de Cassation, in particular, has never worked within a mechanism where there is access to advice from elsewhere concerning its application of the law, and, if it perceives that this position has not changed, it may be unwilling to change its practice and ask the European Court for that advice.

However, the fact that dialogue takes place is only one factor to be considered. A more important question concerns the fruitfulness of that dialogue; whether the courts follow the decisions, and whether the existence of dialogue makes an appreciable difference to the effective enforcement of Community law in English and French courts.

Two cases, the *Duchemin*[38] decision and the *Thibault*[39] decision, are illustra-

---

[34] Case C–345/89 *Stoekel* [1991] ECR I–4047; Case C–158/91 *Levy* [1993] ECR I–4287. Both cases concerned the prohibition within French law of nightwork for women.

[35] Case C–218/98 *Abdoulaye* v. *Renault SA* (judgment of 16 September 1999).

[36] Case C–136/95 *CNAVTS* v. *Thibault* [1998] ECR I–2011. The fact that the lower courts can be seen to be far more willing to refer cases to the European Court than the Cour de Cassation can, perhaps, be explained with reference to Alter's theory of inter-court competition. Alter argues that lower courts throughout the Member States are more willing to apply Community law because it enhances their influence and authority, whereas higher courts are more reluctant to use Community law because it detracts from their own influence and authority. See Karen J Alter, "The European Court's Political Power", (1996) 19 *West European Politics* 458.

[37] See for example, *Marrie* Cass Crim 27 June 1995 *JCP édE* 1996 767.

[38] Cass Soc 30 March 1994 *Bull civ* 1994 No 117.

[39] Cass Soc 28 March 1995, reported in [1995] DS 1036.

tive in the French context. Both cases concerned identical facts; the withholding of promotion, on grounds of absence, from women in public service who had taken maternity leave during a particular year. In the *Duchemin* decision, the Cour de Cassation held that there had been no discrimination and made no reference to the extensive case law of the European Court on pregnancy discrimination. In *Thibault*, on the other hand, which was heard a year later, reference was made to the Equal Treatment Directive and the case was referred to the European Court.[40] The European Court held that there had been direct discrimination. When the case went back to the Cour de Cassation, the interpretation of the Court of Justice was apparently accepted without a murmur.[41]

There is no indication in the decision as to why the Cour de Cassation chose to treat *Thibault* as a case based on Community norms. The tenor of the judgment is that the court is passively applying the applicable law but this, however, demonstrates the paradoxical position of the French judiciary. They are, in fact, choosing whether or not to apply French or Community law and were initially refusing to enforce Community law against the French public service. That refusal, however, was never made explicit and was never justified. At some point, a decision was made within the Cour de Cassation to enter into a dialogue with the European Court. Again, that decision was never made explicit and was never justified. Once it was taken, the Cour de Cassation appears to be passively applying applicable law once again, but this time, it is applying different law. The Community norms are finally being enforced.

A similar point can be made with respect to the latest case from the French courts to appear before the European Court, the *Abdoulaye* decision.[42] This case concerned a collective agreement which provided, *inter alia*, that women should receive a fixed payment on the birth or adoption of a child, above and beyond the pay that they received while on maternity leave. The case was referred by the Labour Court to the European Court, which held that, as the payment was designed to offset professional disadvantages which women suffer from when they take maternity leave, it could be justified under Community law.

However, three years previously, the Cour de Cassation had ruled, regarding exactly the same provision in a collective agreement involving the same employer, that French equal pay provisions did not allow for this kind of discriminatory payment. The Cour de Cassation, it appears, did not think it necessary to refer this question to the European Court and ended up making a ruling which was directly contrary to that of the European Court.[43] It is yet to be seen how the French courts, and in particular the Cour de Cassation, will react to *Abdoulaye*. The evidence of the *Thibault* case suggests that the

---

[40] Directive no. 76/207. See above n. 34.
[41] Cass Soc 16 July 1998, reported in [1998] DS 97.
[42] See above n. 33.
[43] *Renault SA* v. *Chevalier et autres* Cass Soc 8 October 1996, decision no. 3578.

reference will lead to the bringing into line of the French courts as they change their view of the applicable law to be applied.

A further example of the problems which a failure to enter into dialogue with the European Court can bring can be seen in the non-application, within the French legal system, of the concept of indirect discrimination.[44] A typical case is that of *Marrie*.[45] In this case it was argued that legislation forbidding Sunday working was indirectly discriminatory since the majority of workers who preferred to work on a Sunday were women. While the Cour de Cassation recognised that there exists, under Community law, a category of indirect discrimination, it held that the law under question could not possibly be discriminatory because it is intended to benefit workers. It is not clear whether the Cour referred to European Court decisions in its decision-making process although it is known that the applicants asked for the question to be referred to the European Court and that that request was denied, on the grounds that the situation was *acte clair*.

This situation can be compared with the interpretation of indirect discrimination in the English courts. In contrast to their French counterparts, English courts have been happy to refer questions as to the meaning of indirect discrimination to the European Court. The biggest gap in compliance in English law on the matter of indirect discrimination lies not in the approach of the courts, but in the approach of the legislator. Section 1(1)(b) of the Equal Pay Act 1970 states that there is discrimination if an employer applies a requirement or condition which is such that the proportion of one sex who can comply with it is considerably smaller than the proportion of the other sex. The European Court, in *Enderby* v. *Frenchay Health Authority* declared that this aspect of English law was contrary to Community law.[46] There should be no need for a requirement or condition; all that is needed is a pay differential between a male-dominated group and a female-dominated group. *Enderby* was settled before it was returned to the English courts, and, in any event, it would seem that it is impossible to construe section 1(1)(b) so as to make it consistent with the European Court's judgment. Thus, following the ruling in *Marleasing*,[47] the English courts would not be required to enforce Community law in this situation.[48]

This suggests that a positive attitude and approach of the national court towards the European Court and the existence of a dialogue between national courts and the Court is not sufficient to ensure the complete compliance of the Member State with Community law. Legislative intervention may also be necessary. However, in other cases, an active dialogue between the national court and the European Court can have a positive effect in ensuring compliance. The

---

[44] For more detailed discussion of the lack of implementation in France of the notion of indirect discrimination, see C J Wallace, "European Integration and Legal Culture: Indirect Sex Discrimination in the French Legal System", (1999) 19 *LS* 397.

[45] See above n. 35.

[46] Case C–127/92 [1993] ECR I–5535.

[47] Case C–106/89 [1990] ECR I–4135.

[48] For judicial confirmation of this, see *Bhudi* v. *IMI Refiners* [1994] IRLR 204.

development of the law on pregnancy discrimination within the English legal system provides an excellent example of this.

The approaches of the English courts and of the European Court to the vexed question of how to deal with discrimination on grounds of pregnancy have, in the past, differed sharply. The English courts originally took the view that, in order to decide whether a woman had been discriminated against on the ground of her pregnancy, the industrial tribunal should try to find analogous circumstances which could apply to a man and which could be used for the purposes of comparison.[49] The European Court, on the other hand, stated that any unfavourable treatment on the grounds of pregnancy constituted direct discrimination under Directive 76/207, without the need for a male comparator.[50] The two approaches clashed head-on in a seminal case, *Webb* v. *EMO Air Cargo*.[51] The English courts initially held their ground but the House of Lords finally referred the case to the European Court, which emphasised that pregnancy is not comparable to illness. If the reason for the dismissal, or by analogy any other unfair treatment, was in any way related to the pregnancy, then it should be considered to be on the grounds of pregnancy and thus directly discriminatory. Any need for a hypothetical male comparator was rejected.

The House of Lords seemed initially unwilling to apply the decision and consequently tried to restrict its future application to situations with fixed term contracts.[52] However, later decisions in the lower courts accepted the *Webb* decision with more enthusiasm.[53] The restriction to fixed term contracts was rejected by the Employment Appeal Tribunal, in *Caruana* v. *Manchester Airport plc*, stating that *Webb* sets down a firmly and broadly stated general rule which must be followed in all circumstances.[54] The rejection in *Webb* of a hypothetical male comparator was accepted by the EAT in *O'Neill* v. *Governors of St Thomas More School*.[55] In this case, a teacher at a Roman Catholic school was dismissed because she was pregnant and it was widely and publicly known that the father of her child was a Roman Catholic priest. The EAT rejected any attempt by the school to show a comparison with a hypothetical male teacher who had impregnated a nun and held that the dismissal, being on the grounds of pregnancy, was therefore on the grounds of sex and unlawful.

What can be seen through these cases is that the English courts, and in particular the Employment Appeal Tribunal, seem to have embraced their role as enforcers of Community law and have chosen to apply what the European Court says, over and above previous English law. What is particularly interesting about this is that in doing so, they have adopted a different method of

---

[49] *Hayes* v. *Malleable Working Men's Club* [1985] ICR 703.
[50] Case 177/88 *Dekker* v. *Stichting Vormingscentrum voor Jong Volwassenen* [1990] ECR 3941.
[51] Case C–32/93 [1994] ECR I–3567.
[52] [1993] ICR 175.
[53] Again, this fact would appear to bear out Alter's inter-court competition theory, above n. 36.
[54] [1996] IRLR 375.
[55] [1997] ICR 33. See *Berrisford* v. *Woodard Schools* [1991] ICR 564 for a similar case, decided before *Webb*, which was overruled in *O'Neill*.

deciding cases to that which is traditionally adopted by the English judiciary and dominant in English legal culture. One of the characteristics of English judicial decision-making, and a consequence of the doctrine of precedent, has been a tendency to rely on case-by-case reasoning, and the emergence of very specific rules which relate closely to the fact situations of the cases from which the rules are distilled.[56] This type of reasoning was prevalent in the pre-*Webb* cases; in *Hayes*, the EAT stated that there is no such thing as pregnancy per se, only pregnancy in the specific facts of the case, and thus all those facts are relevant in order for a decision to be made. The application of rigid rules was particularly rejected in the field of social and employment law; in the EAT's decision in *Webb*, Wood J stated that: "the four industrial members . . . feel that sound industrial relations usually depend more on the maintenance of a balance rather than the rigid application of absolutes".[57] Yet, barely six years later, in *Caruana*, the same tribunal was arguing that the European Court had set down a firmly and broadly stated general rule which must be followed in all circumstances and which could not be distinguished according to particular fact situations. This represents a significant shift in approach, and one which was a clear response to the role of the English courts as enforcers of Community law and policy and to the fusion of horizons between Community and English ways of doing things. The dialogue between the English courts and the European Court had as its result the clear application of Community law in the United Kingdom.

CONCLUSION

It has been argued in this chapter that different legal cultures in England and France lead to different ways of thinking about how the law works and is created and, more specifically, to different perceptions of the role of the judiciary and the courts within a legal system. This is reflected, it is suggested, in the different ways in which French and English judges enter into dialogue with the European Court on matters of sex discrimination. It is impossible to posit direct causation between legal cultural attitudes and willingness to refer, but the different legal cultures constitute perhaps one factor which may help explain the differences between the responses of the English and French judiciary to Community sex discrimination law. As was stated earlier, it is dangerous to draw general conclusions from the specific study discussed here. Legal culture is not a sole causal factor. However, it has been shown that legal culture has a potential impact, which must be taken into consideration. Further, the specific evidence of sex discrimination dialogues suggests that, while dialogue does not inevitably lead to conformity, a lack of dialogue is quite likely to lead to non-conformity. The very fact of a refusal to enter into dialogue with the European

---

[56] See P Atiyah, *Pragmatism and Theory in English Law* (London, Stevens, 1987).
[57] [1990] ICR 442, at 451A.

Court is indicative of an unwillingness on the part of the national court to recognise that its interpretation of the law may be open to question. In *Marrie*, for example, it is clear that the Cour de Cassation believed that its own interpretation of the law was correct and that it had no need of further elucidation on the matter, despite a number of powerful arguments to the contrary. Furthermore, once the authority of the European Court has been recognised, its judgment wields considerable power over the national courts. In both *Webb*, in England, and *Thibault* in France, the national courts accepted and applied the decision of the European Court without protest, although the House of Lords did try, apparently somewhat fruitlessly, to limit its impact.

Therefore, developments in comparative law thinking and the rising importance of the discourse of legal culture in discussions of European integration must be taken seriously. If we are to identify, as surely we must, the national courts as key Community actors, the culture behind those national courts self-perception, and indeed their other legal cultural attitudes, becomes of vital relevance. Rather than assuming that the role of Community enforcer will be taken up by the national courts with enthusiasm, we must be circumspect as to the limitations of what they can and will achieve in different areas. There are many different ways of analysing the differences of approach of national courts. Political, economic and social factors all have a vital role to play in those differences. However, in this chapter I have suggested that legal cultural factors are also worthy of further examination; ingrained as they are in the national legal consciousness, they are often difficult to pin down and conceptualise but, for that very reason, they have a central and crucial role.

7

Addressing Gender in National and Community Law and Policy-making

FIONA BEVERIDGE, SUE NOTT and KYLIE STEPHEN[1]

INTRODUCTION

Community action in the social policy field raises an array of well-documented legal, institutional and policy issues. A constant struggle has been fought by EU institutions, particularly the Commission, to initiate common action by extending the remit of the European institutions beyond those areas identified as "social policy" in the EC Treaty and establishing new legal competencies.[2] The Commission, it is noted, has always been constrained by the absence of clear mandates in relation to social policy and by the lack of consensus among the Member States as to what should be done at Community level.[3] Nonetheless, the Commission, seen as a "purposeful opportunist",[4] has deployed stealth and cunning[5] to outwit the Member States until they have conceded power to EU institutions. In this, as in much else, the Commission has undoubtedly been assisted by a proliferation of Euro-interest groups which, as Cram notes, have at times been encouraged and mobilised by the Commission itself.[6] The Commission is seen as the protagonist, incrementally shaping the constitution of Europe in the field of social policy up to, and possibly beyond, the Amsterdam Treaty.[7]

One area where a great deal of progress has apparently been made is in promoting equal opportunities for women and men. The EU has been committed to securing equality between the sexes from its inception and the undertaking in

---

[1] Although Kylie Stephen now works in the Women's Unit, Cabinet Office, UK Government, the views expressed here are entirely personal and in no way represent the view of the Women's Unit.

[2] See e.g. J Shaw, "Twin-track Social Europe—the Inside Track" in D O'Keeffe and P Twomey (eds), *Legal Issues of the Maastricht Treaty* (London, Chancery, 1994) 295; E Szyszczak, "Social Policy: A Happy Ending or a Reworking of the Fairy Tale" in O'Keeffe and Twomey, above, at 313; E Vogel-Polsky, "What Future is There for a Social Europe Following the Strasbourg Summit?", (1990) 19 *ILJ* 65; P Watson, "Social Policy after Maastricht", (1993) 30 *CMLRev* 481.

[3] G Ross, 'Assessing the Delors Era and Social Policy' in S Liebfried and P Pierson (eds), *European Social Policy: Between Fragmentation and Integration* (Washington, Brookings Institute, 1995).

[4] L Cram, *Policy-Making in the EU* (London, Routledge, 1997).

[5] *Ibid.*, ch. 2; Ross, above n. 3.

[6] Cram, above n. 4, ch. 5.

[7] N Burrows, "Opting in to the Opt-out", (1997) *Web Law Journal*.

Article 141 (ex 119) EC, to guarantee equal pay for equal work. Since that time there has been a steady stream of hard and soft law measures, such as the equality directives and the Equal Opportunities Action Programmes. The entry into force on 1 May 1999 of the Amsterdam Treaty takes the whole process a stage further, by making the commitment that "the Community shall aim to eliminate inequalities, and to promote equality, between men and women".

But to act effectively in the social policy sphere, the Commission needs more than a formal legal capacity and political support from the Member States. The Commission also depends on the political and legal institutions of Member States to give effect to Community policies and to implement Community legal norms, where appropriate. As has been stated "the very existence of the Community depends upon the immediate and unquestioned validity and application of its law in all Member States".[8] Thus national parliaments and executives are expected to take whatever steps are necessary within their own constitutional framework—to enact laws, to give effect to regulations or to achieve conformity with treaty obligations—to ensure that compliance with EU legal obligations is achieved.[9] National courts are expected to protect rights derived from Community obligations and to provide adequate remedies in the event that these rights are breached.[10] Executive agencies, non-governmental bodies and local authorities may be called upon from time to time to "make it happen" on the ground in the way the EU institutions have determined that it should.

The ability of national political and legal institutions and processes to respond, to absorb and give effect to EU norms will differ from policy area to policy area. In this chapter the focus is on those national and Community policies which are intended to promote equality between the sexes. The pursuit of equality between the sexes is well-established as a social goal in all EU Member States. However, understandings about the core meanings to be attached to the concept of equality and the ways in which it is best pursued are affected by historic and contemporary national influences. Moreover these are not fixed, but are regularly revised and renewed. The purpose of this chapter is to examine the extent to which the efforts of the EU to promote equality have produced a common approach among Member States. Alternatively, has national diversity in the shape of different levels of national commitment to equality between the sexes as well as discrete national applications of equality strategies given a distinctive national "reading" to the EU's equality policies? If this is so, then the question is whether success for the EU in promoting equality depends on a common approach among Member States, or whether it is compatible with national diversity in applying such policies.

---

[8] H Schepel, 'Legal Pluralism in the European Union' in P Fitzpatrick and J H Bergeron (eds), *Europe's Other: European Law between Modernity and Postmodernity* (Brookfield VT, Ashgate, 1998) 47 at 51.

[9] Case 58/81 *Commission v. Luxembourg* [1982] ECR 2175; Case 16/69 *Commission v. Belgium* [1970] ECR 237.

[10] I Maher, "National Courts as European Community Courts", (1994) 14 *Legal Studies* 226.

In order to explore these issues, reference will be made in the course of this chapter to the results of an EU-funded research project, under the programme for Targeted Socio-Economic Research, entitled *Predicting the Impact of Policy*. One of its aims was to evaluate the influence that EU equality policies had on the national practice of a cross-section of Member States, namely Ireland, Portugal, Spain, Sweden and the United Kingdom.[11]

PROMOTING EQUALITY BETWEEN THE SEXES AT NATIONAL LEVEL

The struggle for equality between the sexes is a long-standing one, dating back in many Member States to the nineteenth century. As a result of this a variety of strategies has been formulated over the years to promote equality. Each represents an understanding of what amounts to equality and they are not necessarily compatible one with another. It is as if there have been waves or generations of equality strategies, each of which offers a different perspective on how best to secure equality between the sexes. Whilst the existence of not one but numerous equality strategies is well-understood, certain consequences follow which are less well-appreciated, particularly when evaluating the influence that Community equality policies have on national practice. The diversity which exists at national level on how best to eliminate inequality produces a corresponding diversity in the extent of the progress made by individual Member States towards equality. Hence Community equality policies are directed towards very different national contexts.

Some Member States, such as Sweden, regard themselves as being in the vanguard of the fight to eliminate inequality. This perception at times leads such states to regard Community law as rather irrelevant, seeking mainly to establish minimum standards for less enlightened states. Thus such states can be seen to be largely unaffected by Community law in matters of equality policy; indeed they may continue to seek improvement in their national policies with a view to commending new solutions and approaches to other Member States, via future Community laws and policies.

For other EU Member States, such as the United Kingdom, the struggle for equality predates their membership of the EU. Yet the strategies chosen prior to their Community membership with which to pursue equality goals may have persisted and evolved since they became Member States and may therefore continue to influence their response to Community norms. For yet other Member States, such as Spain and Portugal who have not long emerged from a period of political repression, equality between the sexes is a very new item on their political agendas. Sometimes the legal and political processes operating in these states appear resistant to substantive change; thus there may be a significant gap between formal legal commitments and "law in action".

[11] TSER: Targeted socio-economic research under the EC Commission Fourth Framework Programme. For more details of the project see http://www.liv.ac.uk/~scooper/pip.html

Apart from differential rates of progress toward equality within Member States, different Member States employ different legal and non-legal strategies to fight inequality, use different notions of equality, and distribute the burdens (and benefits) of pursuing equality policies differently. Moreover as Member States are "not all singing from the same hymn sheet" and may not have any intention of doing so in the foreseeable future, equality policy has an important national dimension. The manner in which a particular equality strategy is acted on is determined by the national context in which it operates. The attempts of the EU to harmonise equality law may, therefore, be thwarted by this fact.

STRATEGIES FOR PROMOTING EQUALITY BETWEEN THE SEXES

A variety of strategies is used for promoting equality between the sexes. First there are rights-based strategies, which commonly take the form of a guarantee of equality or equal treatment and are frequently found in a state's constitution. In Portugal the constitution has nine articles dealing with gender equality.[12] It is, however, not unusual for a guarantee of equality to extend beyond sex equality and embrace other circumstances when discrimination might occur.[13] The influence which such guarantees of equality exert depends on a variety of factors. These include the status of the constitution and whether or not it permits laws to be challenged on the grounds that they are in breach of the constitution. In Ireland, for example, laws in breach of the constitutional guarantee of equality (Article 40(1)) can be declared unconstitutional. Equally crucial is the interpretation that is given to any such guarantee of equality. In Spain it is asserted that the constitution's provisions on equality have been interpreted in a very constructive fashion so as to establish the notion of indirect discrimination and modify the burden of proof.[14] Finally the presence of conflicting provisions within the constitution can result in a situation where a guarantee of equality is overridden. In Ireland a proposed legislative measure designed to strengthen the Irish equality legislation was held to be in conflict with other provisions of the Irish constitution.[15] Of all the EU's Member States, only the United Kingdom has no constitutional provision on equality, though to a degree this gap has been filled by recourse in the courts to provisions of Community law.[16]

---

[12] Article 9, for example, imposes a duty on the state to promote equality between men and women whilst Art. 26 establishes the right to legal protection against discrimination.

[13] In the Netherlands, for example, Art. 1 of the Constitution states that discrimination "on the grounds of religion, creed, political faith, race, sex, or on any other ground is not permitted".

[14] See F Arranz, B Quintanilla and C Velázquez, "Making Women Count in Spain" in F Beveridge, S Nott and K Stephen (eds), *Making Women Count* (Aldershot, Ashgate, 2000).

[15] In the Matter of Article 26 of the Constitution and In the Matter of the Employment Equality Bill, 1996, Supreme Court 15 May 1997, unreported.

[16] See further F Beveridge, S Nott and K Stephen, "Making Women Count in the UK" in Beveridge, Nott and Stephen, above n. 14.

A second and very commonly used strategy for tackling inequality is to enact anti-discrimination legislation. In Sweden, for example, the Equal Opportunities Act 1991 contains not only prohibitions against discrimination but also active measures to promote equality. The definition of the kinds of behaviour which constitute sex discrimination is crucial. If the anti-discrimination legislation simply deals with situations where a woman is openly treated less favourably than a man or is paid less than a man for performing the same work then its impact will be extremely limited. Anti-discrimination legislation needs to address covert discrimination. It needs to acknowledge that what appear to be gender neutral conditions regarding the qualities looked for in a potential employee can discriminate against women and have no objective justification. It needs to go beyond the façade of job descriptions to enquire whether the work done by a woman is of equal value to that performed by a man. Anti-discrimination legislation needs to be revised and amended to address new challenges.

There are, however, problems associated with the use of anti-discrimination legislation. Its impact is often limited since it is used primarily to tackle discrimination in the workplace. Furthermore the insistence in some Member States, such as the United Kingdom and Ireland, on making comparisons in their legislation between how men and women are treated, can lead to difficulties when dealing with situations such as the dismissal of a pregnant worker.[17]

The manner in which the anti-discrimination legislation is enforced is equally important. This depends on the legal and political landscape of the state in question. In countries such as the United Kingdom, an individual who believes that she has been the target of sex discrimination will be expected to take legal action against the alleged offender. The difficulties associated with litigation in this field and the overall limitations of reliance on individual litigation as an enforcement strategy are well-known: the costs of litigation discourage potential claimants, the technicality of the legislation may make the outcome uncertain and the adversarial nature of proceedings imposes a further psychological barrier to legal action.[18] Yet in the United Kingdom there is as yet no other effective strategy in place to ensure that employers or service-providers abide by anti-discrimination legislation. In other countries such as Sweden, a more collectivist approach is preferred. The social partners (that is employers, trade unions and government) work together to eliminate discrimination and employers are required to adopt equality plans designed to promote equality within the workplace. The Equality Ombudsman plays a central role in enforcing and monitoring compliance with equality laws. Litigation is very rare and, where it does occur, will often be taken on an employee's behalf by the Ombudsman or her trade union. Yet there is evidence to suggest that employers often fail to put an

[17] See A Morris, "Workers First, Women Second?" in A. Morris and T O'Donnell (eds), *Feminist Perspectives on Employment Law* (London, Cavendish, 1999) 193.

[18] See e.g. A Leonard, *Judging Inequality: The Effectiveness of the Industrial Tribunal System in Sex Discrimination and Equal Pay Cases* (London, Cobden Trust, 1987).

equality plan in place until a spot check by the Equality Ombudsman forces them to take action; and this presents difficulties as the Ombudsman is said to be under-resourced.[19]

A third strategy used to promote equality is the use of positive action or positive discrimination programmes. The purpose of such programmes is to set up schemes which allow women access to employment or other areas within society where they are not well represented. Positive action is associated with low key initiatives such as the setting of numerical targets in Ireland in order to increase the numbers of women in government[20] or the use of training schemes in the United Kingdom designed to encourage women into occupations where men predominate.[21] Positive discrimination refers to more radical schemes such as the creation of all women shortlists by the Labour Party in the United Kingdom when choosing candidates for the 1997 general election[22] or making it obligatory for employment to be offered to women in certain circumstances.[23]

One of the most common pitfalls associated with positive discrimination is that in certain circumstances, the action proposed may itself be in breach of anti-discrimination legislation.[24] In addition, positive action programmes are generally not obligatory and it is left to the discretion of employers whether they choose to initiate such schemes.[25] As a consequence such programmes are often regarded as "add-ons" and there is a lack of interest in supporting them as well as little evidence that they contribute to the promotion of gender equality.

A final strategy employed against gender inequality is mainstreaming. This is defined as:

> " the (re)organisation, improvement, development and evaluation of policy processes, so that a gender equality perspective is incorporated in all policies at all levels and at all stages, by the actors normally involved in policy-making".[26]

Mainstreaming is examined further in the final part of this chapter. In the meantime it can be noted that mainstreaming, on the face of it at least, reflects the feminist perspective that gender inequality is deep-rooted and pervasive and is embedded in legal, social, economic and political structures, and in culture and psychology. As a concept, mainstreaming has the potential to tackle the structural causes of discrimination in a systematic and meaningful way and to promote a pluralistic and inclusive meaning of equality.

---

[19] M Gillberg, *Predicting the Impact of Policy: Country Report, Sweden* (Liverpool, Feminist Legal Research Unit, 1999) 28.

[20] M Donnelly, S Mullally and O Smith, *Predicting the Impact of Policy: Country Report, Ireland* (Liverpool, Feminist Legal Research Unit, 1999) 62.

[21] Sex Discrimination Act 1975, s. 48.

[22] This policy was, however, dropped after a ruling that it discriminated unlawfully against men: *Jepson and Dyas Elliott* v. *The Labour Party* [1996] IRLR 116.

[23] For examples of such schemes see Case C–450/93 *Kalanke* v. *Freie Hansestadt Bremen* [1995] ECR I–3051.

[24] See e.g. the *Jepson* and *Kalanke* cases, above nn. 22 and 23.

[25] See e.g. in the United Kingdom, Sex Discrimination Act 1975, s. 48.

[26] Council of Europe, *Final Report of the Group of Experts on Mainstreaming* (Strasbourg, Council of Europe, 1998) 14.

A variety of mechanisms are required to ensure that each of these equality strategies is developed and monitored. This is the role of what is sometimes called "women's policy machinery". This term describes "any structure established by government with its main purpose being the betterment of women's social status".[27] A range of bodies could fall within this description. In Portugal, for example, the women's policy machinery includes the Commission for Parity, Equal Opportunities and Family (a committee of the legislative assembly), the Commission for Equality and Women's Rights (a government body which commissions research, provides training and proposes legislative changes) and the Commission for Equality at Work and in Employment (a body which promotes equality in the workplace).[28]

Certain issues have, however, to be addressed if women's policy machinery is to improve women's status in society. These bodies need access to government and in particular access to the process of policy-making so that they can represent women's views and communicate their needs. In Portugal, the Commission for Equality and Women's Rights is meant to scrutinise proposed laws or policies for their potential impact on men and women. In reality, however, neither the government nor the legislature cooperate in order to make this possible.[29] Bodies of this nature also need adequate resources if they are to perform the tasks assigned to them. The United Kingdom's Equal Opportunities Commission could, with an increased budget, provide more help to litigants. In addition, where several such bodies exist, there needs to be a clear demarcation of responsibility. Otherwise, as experience in Portugal has shown, these bodies may find themselves fighting one another for resources and influence or certain tasks might not be performed since they are regarded as someone else's responsibility.[30]

In conclusion it is apparent that Member States have taken basic equality strategies and have adapted them to reflect the value they place on promoting equality between the sexes and their own institutional, legal and political landscape. The practical effect of this is that diversity reigns at the national level.

PROMOTING EQUALITY BETWEEN THE SEXES IN THE EUROPEAN UNION

It has been suggested that there was a happy coincidence between the re-emergence of feminism in the 1960s and 1970s and the growth of the European Community.[31] It is certainly the case that from its inception the EU has promoted laws and policies to eradicate inequality. In doing so it too has taken

[27] D M Stetson and A Mazur (eds), *Comparative State Feminism* (London, Sage, 1995) 3.
[28] J Casqueira Cardoso, *Predicting the Impact of Policy: Country Report, Portugal* (Liverpool, Feminist Legal Research Unit, 1999).
[29] *Ibid.*
[30] See J Casqueira Cardoso, "Making Women Count in Portugal" in Beveridge, Nott and Stephen, above n. 14.
[31] M Buckley and M Anderson (eds), *Women, Equality and Europe* (London, Macmillan, 1988).

basic equality strategies, namely anti-discrimination measures, positive action, mainstreaming and rights-based strategies, and produced its own Community measures. Such measures are just as much influenced by the priority placed by the EU on promoting equality and its institutional, legal and political landscape, as any national measures are.

The early Community measures to promote equality were anti-discrimination measures, such as Article 141 (ex 119) EC and the Equal Pay and Equal Treatment Directives (which remain in force unaltered),[32] based on a concept of equality that required men and women to receive equal treatment. The way in which these measures have been interpreted by the European Court has demonstrated just how constructively the notion of equal treatment can be deployed. The term "pay" has been given a generous definition[33] and this has enabled the concept of equal treatment to be applied to a far wider range of employment-related payments than might first have been thought to be the case. The notion of direct discrimination has been used to protect pregnant workers[34] whilst indirect discrimination has proved particularly helpful in relation to part-time employees, the majority of whom are women.[35]

However, the weaknesses of equal treatment as a means of securing gender equality in the EU have also become apparent over the years. The European Court has refused to use the notion of equal treatment to address women's caring role in the home, with the result that equal treatment in the workplace is no more than an illusion.[36] The rhetoric of equal treatment has at times been used by men to their advantage and to the disadvantage of women. In the context of occupational pensions and the *Barber* case[37] this has produced short-term gains for men and long-term losses for both men and women.[38] *Barber* and the cases that followed this decision also illustrate the European Court's willingness to subordinate the notion of equal treatment to larger economic considerations.[39]

EU anti-discrimination initiatives have the very real advantage of being legally binding on Member States, yet there is evidence to show that the way in which Member States choose to enforce these measures within their own legal

---

[32] Directive 75/117/EEC, [1975] OJ L45/19 and Directive 76/7/EEC, [1976] OJ L39/40.

[33] See e.g. Case 12/81 *Garland* v. *British Rail* [1982] ECR 359; Case C–262/88 *Barber* v. *Guardian Royal Exchange Assurance Group* [1990] ECR I–1989.

[34] Case 177/78 *Dekker* v. *Stichting Vormingscentrum voor Jonge Volwassen* [1990] ECR I–3941; Case C–32/93 *Webb* v. *EMO Air Cargo (UK) Ltd.* [1994] ECR I–3567.

[35] Case 96/80 *Jenkins* v. *Kingsgate (Clothing Productions) Ltd.* [1981] ECR 911.

[36] K Scheiwe, "EC Law's Unequal Treatment of the Family: The Case Law of the European Court of Justice on Rules Prohibiting Discrimination on Grounds of Sex and Nationality", (1994) 4 *Social and Legal Studies* 243; G More, " 'Equal Treatment' of the Sexes in European Community Law: What Does 'Equal' Mean?", (1993) 1 *Feminist Legal Studies* 45.

[37] *Barber*, above n. 33.

[38] This is as a consequence of levelling down. For example in the United Kingdom, the age at which a state pension is payable will rise to 65 for women (to match that for men) in the name of equal treatment.

[39] In Case C–408/92 *Smith and others* v. *Avdel Systems Ltd* [1994] ECR I–4435 the European Court ruled that the practice of "levelling down" (bringing the age at which women may claim their pensions into line with that of men) was legitimate.

and political landscape can substantially reduce their effectiveness. In some Member States where there is a tradition of individual litigation, the concepts of direct effect of Community law and references to the European Court have allowed individuals and equal opportunities agencies to use the EU anti-discrimination measures to challenge national laws. In other Member States where there is no such tradition, the extent to which the EU's anti-discrimination legislation has been acted upon cannot be policed in that manner. The very fact that so small a group of Member States is responsible for the majority of references to the European Court shows how few Member States actively use the Community's own enforcement machinery to make national gains.

In addition, a reference by another Member State to the European Court which produces positive results for women does not apparently lead to equal opportunities agencies in other Member States asking what benefits they can extract. There is no evidence, for example, that when equal treatment in respect of occupational pensions became an issue in the EU, this was used at national level to highlight other examples of unequal treatment in respect of pensions.

Over the years, the EU has supplemented its anti-discrimination legislation with positive action initiatives. More recently, mainstreaming has become a part of the EU's equal opportunities strategy.[40] The EU's deployment of these alternative strategies is very welcome since they embody a notion of equality that sets out to tackle the biological and cultural differences experienced by women. Rather than requiring that women be treated no differently from men, they target the differences between men and women's lives and try to address such differences in a positive fashion. These policies concentrate on eliminating gender inequality rather than inequality based on sex.

The positive impact of these alternative strategies has, however, been reduced by the EU's own legal and political landscape. In the first place they have been put in place using soft law measures such as action programmes and Commission communications. Whilst the reason for this may be the lack of an EC Treaty basis for such initiatives or the difficulty of securing agreement among Member States, there is nothing to force Member States to act on them. The situation is complicated by the fact that soft law measures can be "trumped" by anti-discrimination legislation or by EC Treaty articles.

In addition to this, the competing definitions of equality represented by different equality strategies have proved problematic for the European Court. As the *Kalanke* decision[41] demonstrated, the notion of equality embedded in a positive action strategy may directly contradict the anti-discrimination notion of equality. Faced with the outcry which followed its ruling in *Kalanke*, the

---

[40] See, for example, the Commission's Fourth Action Programme on Equal Opportunities for Woman and Men (Council Decision 95/593/EC, [1995] OJ L335/37) and the Commission's Communication, *Incorporating Equal Opportunities for Women and Men into All Community Policies and Activities* COM(97) final, 21.2.96.

[41] *Kalanke*, above n. 23.

European Court was forced to reassess the situation in *Marschall*[42] and to make some very fine (and unedifying) distinctions between acceptable and unacceptable positive action strategies. The inclusion of an article in the Amsterdam Treaty specifically dealing with this issue may not, it is suggested, have resolved this dilemma.[43]

The strategy of mainstreaming embraces yet another view of (in)equality, or of the sources of inequality, but this throws up further contradictions. It can be argued, for instance, that if equality is everyone's concern, the existence of specific equal opportunities machinery is no longer necessary. It was proposed for example, in the name of mainstreaming, to de-neutralise the European Parliament's Committee on Women's Rights. This would mean that women would no longer be able to sit on it *and* on other European Parliament committees whose work interested them. It was argued that, as with environmental issues, mainstreaming demanded that equal opportunities became every committee's business.[44] Although this may be an isolated example there is an obvious need for a clear and consistent understanding of what is meant by mainstreaming so that actions such as these are not taken in its name. Mainstreaming is meant to complement existing equality strategies not replace them.[45]

Finally, with the conclusion of the Amsterdam Treaty the EU has set out the terms of its commitment to equality in a fashion, it could be argued, which is the equivalent of those constitutional guarantees of equality which so many Member States possess. In doing this, the EU no longer restricts itself to opposing discrimination based on sex, nor does it limit its attack on discrimination to the employment sphere. Commentators point to the fact that this commitment to equality in the Amsterdam Treaty is situated firmly "within the context of the European model of socio-economic policy";[46] a fact which has, in the past, caused European institutions such as the European Court and the Commission to strike a balance between the principle of equality and the realities of the business world. There is speculation that as the EU expands and as globalisation makes its impact felt, the willingness of the EU to adopt a progressive attitude towards equality will come under increasing pressure:

> "Will it be possible for Europe to retain a European model of social development, including progressive equal opportunities policies, when faced with pressures for the relaxation of social protection in order to become more 'competitive', or less 'protectionist'? To the extent that it will become difficult to retain such standards in isolation, will Europe be forced to import lower standards, or will we be able to export our higher standards?"[47]

---

[42] Case C–409/95 *Marschall* v. *Land Nordrhein-Westfalen* [1997] ECR I–6363.

[43] C McCrudden "The Legal Approach to Equal Opportunities in Europe: Past, Present and Future", (1998) 3 *International Journal of Discrimination and the Law* 193 at 204.

[44] *Women of Europe*, May/June 1999. The proposal appears to have been abandoned.

[45] European Commission Communication, *Incorporating Equal Opportunities for Women and Men into all Community Policies and Activities*, above n. 40.

[46] McCrudden, above n. 43, at 204.

[47] *Ibid.*, at 204–5.

Certain equal opportunities strategies may be especially susceptible to these developments. Mainstreaming, for example, demands that all policies are assessed for their potential impact on gender equality. Yet mainstreaming will undoubtedly suffer if the adverse effects which it exposes are ignored in the name of allowing the EU to compete more effectively with other nations and trading organisations. In particular, the emphasis in Article 138 EC on consulting the social partners on social policy initiatives may cause equal opportunities initiatives to be blocked because of their perceived adverse impact on jobs or on the ability of European businesses to compete with the rest of the world.

There is also the question of whether the promotion of equal opportunities between the sexes will suffer as a result of the inclusion in the Amsterdam Treaty of the commitment to eradicate other forms of inequality based on "racial or ethnic origin, religion or belief, disability, age or sexual orientation" (Article 13). Will a battle for resources result and a discrimination hierarchy develop, as is said to be the case in some Member States?[48] In particular, will the equality strategies need to be modified depending on the form of discrimination being tackled? Serious doubts have been expressed by some commentators about the suitability of using the procedures for tackling gender inequality to deal with inequality based on disability or race.[49]

As is apparent, the EU has over the years adopted a variety of measures designed to eliminate gender inequality. Moreover the EU legal system, with the doctrine of supremacy of Community law and the mechanisms of direct effect, indirect effect and state liability, holds out the promise that legal action can be taken to secure compliance with the common approach iterated in the formal legal sources.

Yet despite its achievements the Commission has often been forced to compromise and the substance of Community social policy is the subject of constant and vigorous debate; it is criticised for its very modest aims and is often spoken of as representing a set of minimum rights rather than aspirational standards. This was explicit, for example, in the case of the Pregnant Workers Directive where Member States were specifically forbidden to level down their national provisions to what the Directive required.[50] The explanation behind the very limited targets that Community social policy sets itself, may be the insistence by some Member States that social policy should be subordinate to the EU's economic goals.

The European Court is also seen as having a key role to play in relation to social policy. It can claim credit for enforcing social policy by providing

---

[48] This was said to have happened in the United Kingdom in relation to PAFT (Policy Appraisal and Fair Treatment), the equality-proofing guidelines which operated in Northern Ireland. See T Hadden, B Rainey and G Mcgreevy, "Equal but not Separate", (1998) 12 *Fortnight* 371. The targets covered included age, ethnic origin, gender, religious belief, disability and sexual orientation. PAFT was said, however, to focus only on religion and gender with any regularity.

[49] M Verloo, "Making Women Count in the Netherlands" in Beveridge, Nott and Stephen, above n. 14.

[50] Directive 92/85/EEC, [1992] OJ L348/1, Art. 1(3).

concrete mechanisms through which the adherence of reluctant Member States can be secured.[51] Its interpretation of that policy is regarded by some as positive and constructive when compared with national courts. Others, however, accuse the European Court of adopting stereotypical attitudes toward women.[52]

EU EQUALITY POLICIES AND THE NATIONAL ENVIRONMENT

This array of legal instruments, and the national measures which they have spawned, create an appearance of similarity between the equality laws of the Member States, an impression of harmonisation, and the area within which this harmonisation has occurred has gradually been deepened[53] and widened.[54] However, appearances can be deceptive. The "common approach" may not be "common" at all in the sense of reflecting shared values and legal cultures of the Member States. Thus in reality, Community equality laws and policies often mix "bottom up" and "top down" elements, or are legal transplants which draw on the experiences of individual Member States, of other international organisations or of other regions in the world such as North America. In the most recent, and in future, expansions of EU membership, new Member States have been required to adapt to the EU's equal opportunities policies as a complete package without having had the chance to shape them.

The translation of Community equality policies into the national environments of Member States raises a number of complex issues. National environments play a key part in shaping an individual state's response to Community equality policy, and hence the effectiveness of that policy within that particular state. Imelda Maher argues[55] that the ability of national political and legal institutions to perform this role effectively is dependent on the existing links between law and social processes within that state and may be variable in time and place:

"as a social system, law looks for stability in its responses to its environment . . . Where a new norm is introduced which may disturb those links, that norm will be shaped by existing links and may be modified in practice if not in form . . . the ability of the existing system to accommodate [it] in particular in the light of existing linkages and coupling, may necessarily transform the Community norm and in extreme cases may

---

[51] For instance, the concept of direct effect. See for example Case 26/62 *Van Gend en Loos* v. *Nederlandse Administratie deer Belastingen* [1963] ECR 1; Case 41/74 *Van Duyn* v. *Home Office* [1974] ECR 1337.

[52] See e.g. S Fredman, "European Community Discrimination Law: A Critique", (1992) 21 *ILJ* 125; D. Muffat-Jeandet, "The Proposed Pregnancy and Maternity Directive", (1991) 20 *ILJ* 76.

[53] Relatively recent directives include those on the burden of proof and on parental leave.

[54] For instance there is a requirement that equal opportunities be promoted in the allocation of the Structural Funds and the European Social Fund: see for example Council Regulation 1260/99 on the Structural Funds 2000–2006.

[55] I Maher, "Community Law in the National Legal Order: A Systems Analysis", (1998) 36 *JCMS* 237.

result in an inability to accommodate the change at all if it would lead to disorder and even disintegration of the system".[56]

Similarly for national courts faced with applying/interpreting a Community norm:

"[i]t may be difficult if not impossible to ignore embedded legal networks in favour of a more recent Community norm where the new norm may destabilise the system. The differing priorities of the European Court and national courts reflect the position of the institutions within the legal system. Both are interpreting law through observation of their environment, and their accommodation of changes in that environment is shaped by the proximity of the institution to either the Community or national orders".[57]

Hence the effectiveness of Community equality norms depends very much on the fit between them and the national policy environment into which they have been imported.

It is not clear what impact Community equality policies have in the Member States. Where there are binding legal obligations, for instance in the form of directives or European Court judgments, Member States have on the whole been prepared to comply, sooner or later.[58] However, formal compliance with the letter of the law cannot be equated with convergence between Member States' laws and policies. Member States may be able to point to the existence of anti-discrimination legislation and to identify national practices that on their face satisfy the demands of Community law, whether hard or soft. But beneath the surface the impact of these national "implementing" measures on Member States' gender equality policies may vary widely, depending on the national legal and political climate.[59] While Community policy does provide a lever for citizens of Member States trying to make gains, there is no evidence that the existence of Community equal opportunities initiatives will transform the situation in those Member States which give equal opportunities a low priority.

An analysis of the degree to which EU policy has been assimilated into the legal and political landscapes of the Member States provides evidence of this. It is beyond the scope of this chapter to assess how Member States have reacted to a host of specific Community equal opportunities initiatives. Instead it will concentrate on the policy of mainstreaming. Mainstreaming has been chosen because it is a relatively new strategy and one on which the EU has seemingly led the way. There seems a strong possibility, therefore, that this is an occasion

---

[56] *Ibid.*, 245–6.

[57] *Ibid.*, 244–5.

[58] Though in many instances resort to the European Court has been necessary to secure the compliance of a Member State, there have been few cases of outright rejection of Community law. See, however, the United Kingdom's tardiness in accepting the prohibition on pregnancy dismissal in relation to the armed forces.

[59] See further F Beveridge, "Same Song—Different Tunes: a Lesson in Harmony Singing?' in Beveridge, Nott and Stephen, above n. 14.

where the EU could ensure a common approach among its Member States. In practice, however, this is not the case.

As has been pointed out, the term "mainstreaming" is used in two ways. It is used to describe a strategy for promoting equality, as well as a set of tools for appraising and monitoring policies for their positive and negative effects on equal opportunities.[60] If it *is* useful for the elimination of inequality to be able to evaluate policies for their gender impact, clearly there must be the methods and tools to do this.

In order to work well as a strategy and a policy tool, mainstreaming requires certain factors to be present.[61] Since it involves a commitment to take account of gender "in all policies at all levels and at all stages" it requires political commitment at the highest level (down to the lowest) to ensure that this promise is acted upon. Money has to be devoted to collecting data and commissioning research to enable conclusions to be drawn regarding the possible effect of a particular policy on women. Personnel have to be trained to be aware of the gender implications of their actions, rather than it being assumed that this is an intuitive process. Decisions additionally have to be made on the range of policies that will be audited for their impact on women and also when such exercises will take place. Mainstreaming could be confined to central government policy-making or it might be extended to local authorities and non-departmental public bodies, but if it is to succeed, it needs to be an open process which encourages groups and organisations with gender expertise to participate in assessing gender impact, and must spell out with some degree of precision how adverse impact is to be determined. It is also a process that needs to be monitored. There needs to be an agency which considers whether the predictions, which have been made regarding a policy's gender impact, were accurate. Finally there needs to be transparency surrounding the mainstreaming procedure so that those outside government can be reassured that mainstreaming is having the desired results.[62]

Mainstreaming did not originate with the EU. The concept was developed by international organisations such as the United Nations in the context of international development programmes.[63] The EU's commitment to mainstreaming

---

[60] C Booth, "Gender Mainstreaming in the European Union. Toward a New Conception and Practice of Equal Opportunities", *ESCR Seminar Series: The Interface Between Public Policy and Gender Equality* (Sheffield, Centre for Regional Economic and Social Research, Sheffield Hallam University, 1999).

[61] S Nott, "Mainstreaming Equal Opportunities: Succeeding when all Else has Failed" in Morris and O'Donnell, above n. 17, at 203.

[62] See further *Predicting the Impact of Policy: A Gender Impact Assessment Mechanism for Assessing the Probable Impact of Policy Initiatives on Women* (Liverpool, Feminist Legal Research Unit, 1999).

[63] S Nott, above n. 61.

can, it is said, be traced back to the Third Equal Opportunities Action Programme which acknowledged the need to integrate equality into the Community's economic and structural policies.[64] The Fourth Action Programme is explicit in its commitment to mainstreaming[65] and is supplemented by a Commission Communication on incorporating equal opportunities for women and men into all Community policies and activities.[66] This document envisages mainstreaming as being pursued at both EU and at Member State levels, developing "a European approach to equality which is both pluralistic and humanistic and which constitutes the basis for action both in the Community and in the rest of the world".[67] While the bulk of the document is concerned with areas which fall squarely within EC competencies and where a formal Community role has already been established (employment, the labour market, women entrepreneurs and assisting spouses, education and training and development aid), it also acknowledges that there is room for improvement in a number of other areas such as violence against women, women refugees, the trafficking of persons (specifically sexual tourism and trafficking in relation to prostitution), the recognition of judgments in the field of family law and the legal security of family members who are third country nationals. Clearly in relation to many of these fields the Commission can only urge a mainstreaming approach on the Member States, on whose cooperation it is almost entirely dependent:

> "[T]he progressive implementation of these guidelines calls for a significant increase in co-operation within the Commission's departments and strengthening of the partnership with the Member States and the various players and organisations concerned".[68]

The Member States' reaction to the mainstreaming initiative is far from consistent. Some states already possessed a procedure or a set of tools which could loosely be described as a mainstreaming procedure. For example in the United Kingdom, two procedures known as Policy Appraisal and Fair Treatment (PAFT) and Policy Appraisal for Equal Treatment (PAET) had been used from the 1980s onwards to assess policies for their impact on a range of target groups including women. These procedures have subsequently become identified with mainstreaming, though arguably they lack many of the essential features of this strategy.[69] Recent constitutional changes in the United Kingdom have served to ensure that mainstreaming takes a different form in different contexts: the

---

[64] European Commission, *Equal Opportunities for Men and Women—the Third Medium Term Action Programme (1991–1995)* (COM(90) 449).

[65] European Commission, *Fourth Medium-Term Community Action Programme on Equal Opportunities for Women and Men (1996–2000)* (COM(95) 381).

[66] See above n. 40.

[67] *Ibid.*, 2.

[68] *Ibid.*, 21.

[69] For a critique see F Beveridge, S Nott and K Stephen, *Predicting the Impact of Policy: Country Report, United Kingdom* (Liverpool, Feminist Legal Research Unit, 1999) 72–81 and references cited therein.

PAFT Guidelines in Northern Ireland assumed the status of a statutory duty under the Northern Ireland Act 1998[70] and a significant emphasis on community involvement has been developed there. In Scotland and Wales the establishment of new Assemblies has dominated the political process and it is within this democratic context that shape has been given to the concept of mainstreaming. By contrast, there has been little change in Whitehall and mainstreaming initiatives have been largely confined to the executive and bureaucratic arms of the state. Among local authorities in the United Kingdom, mainstreaming approaches have had a very varied reception and there is little or no central coordination of local authorities in this matter. Nevertheless, throughout the United Kingdom there is a tendency to address gender alongside other inequalities and to emphasise the importance of participation in decision-making, user-involvement and consultation.

In Ireland there is a tendency to address mainstreaming in the context of the development of inclusionary politics through a "partnership" approach, embracing the community and voluntary sectors. Efforts to introduce gender-proofing in policy development are closely allied to the development of poverty-proofing procedures, producing a distinct focus on social exclusion.[71] This produces a proclivity towards the development of single institutions to handle discrimination whether arising from gender, race, ethnic origin, religion, sexual orientation, disability or age, these "equal opportunities" agencies being supplemented with specialised bodies addressing phenomena such as unemployment, poverty or social exclusion.

Other Member States such as Sweden and the Netherlands have moved towards privileging gender discrimination, recognising it as being of a fundamental nature which has ramifications in all other fields and, like the EU itself, accord gender discrimination policies priority status.[72] The development of effective policies is seen as an expert task requiring specialist knowledge and a sound understanding of the pathology of gender discrimination, so that the particular policies developed are not regarded as transferable to other forms of discrimination. Mainstreaming policies in these countries have focused on the development of gender impact assessment tools[73] and on the development of appropriate expert resources.

---

[70] See further C McCrudden, "Mainstreaming Equality in the Governance of Northern Ireland", (1999) 22 *Fordham International Law Journal* 1702.

[71] See further Government of Ireland, *Partnership 2000 for Inclusion, Employment and Competitiveness* (Dublin, Government Stationery Office, 1996); M Donnelly, S Mullally and O Smith, "Making Women Count in Ireland", in Beveridge, Nott and Stephen, above n. 14; S Mullally, *Guidelines for Gender Proofing Within the Context of the Structural Funds* (Dublin, Department of Justice, Equality and Law Reform, 1999).

[72] In both of these states, formal guarantees of equality (for example in the Constitution and in employment law) which address discrimination of grounds of race, sex, religion etc. have been supplemented by the development of commitments in the policy-making sphere which have this effect.

[73] Such as the Dutch Emancipation Impact Assessment (EER) instrument and the Swedish Directive 1994:124 (requiring that the investigations and reports which precede legislative proposals include analysis of the gender impacts of the proposed measures) and JAMKOM, a project to

In Member States such as Spain and Portugal, however, mainstreaming has by comparison hardly left the drawing board. Each of these states has adopted a plan or policy statement which apparently commits them to mainstreaming but there are as yet no procedures in place to give effect to this commitment. Thus in Spain the Third Equal Opportunities Plan 1997–2000[74] aims as one of its ten objectives:

> "to integrate the dimension of equal opportunities into the policies of the public administration and institutions and to foster co-operation with both Non-Governmental Organisations and international organisations by mobilising all policies to attain equality".[75]

However, no specific mechanisms, tools, monitoring or review procedures have been established to achieve this.[76] Similarly in Portugal, the Global Plan for Equal Opportunities[77] has the single general objective of integrating the principle of equal opportunities between men and women into all economic, social and cultural policies, coupled with specific objectives in key areas, but there is both an unwillingness among key bodies to take responsibility for implementation and assessment of the Plan and a general lack of cooperation between the relevant actors.[78]

This review demonstrates that the responses of Member States to the mainstreaming initiative have varied enormously. Levels of political support for this concept differ across the Member States and this has played an extremely crucial role in determining the effectiveness of measures taken in the name of mainstreaming. In addition, Member States' responses have been shaped by both fixed and fluid features of the national political and legal landscapes into which the mainstreaming concept was projected; where this concept could be harnessed to on-going gender policy-making initiatives or even to wider constitutional reforms this has been done in a somewhat unplanned and opportunistic fashion. By contrast, in Member States where gender policies were already suffering from lack of support, new developments have been low-key and have had little impact.

Furthermore most Member States appear not to have explored at any length the strategy that underlies mainstreaming and sought to put that into practice; instead they have harnessed mainstreaming, and responsibility for mainstreaming, to some existing feature of their legal or political landscape, thus replicating

---

develop and disseminate means for the promotion of equal opportunities among local governments: see respectively M Verloo, "Making Women Count in the Netherlands" in Beveridge, Nott and Stephen, above n. 14, and M Verloo and C Roggeband, "Gender Impact Assessment: The Development of a New Instrument in the Netherlands", (1996) 14(1) *Impact Assessment* 3; M Gillberg, "Making Women Count in Sweden" in Beveridge, Nott and Stephen, above n. 14.

[74] Instituto de la Mujer, *III Plan para la Igualdad de Oportunidades entre Mujeres y Hombres 1997–2000* (Madrid, Instituto de la Mujer, 1997).

[75] *Ibid.*, 11.

[76] Arranz, Quintanilla and Velazquez in Beveridge, Nott and Stephen, above n. 14.

[77] Resolution 49/97 of the Council of Ministers of 6 March 1997.

[78] Casqueira Cardoso in Beveridge, Nott and Stephen, above n. 14.

the pre-existing diversity in equality structures and policies. The EU, for its part, lacks the legal machinery to force Member States to adopt "best practice". So the impact of what could be a very important and productive initiative is blunted from the very outset.

IMPLICATIONS

The remaining question is whether the diversity between Member States' equality laws and policies matters. Diversity in this context may be a virtue. In the first place, legal rules aimed at the furtherance of a shared goal such as gender equality may work more effectively where there is a good policy "fit" with existing policy structures. Verloo, for instance, demonstrates that the Dutch gender impact assessment measure (EER) built on and fitted in with existing Dutch understandings about the causes of gender inequality. She argues that a more simplistic approach was appropriate in Flanders where officials would be starting from a much lower base in terms of understandings and familiarity with gender issues.[79] Thus whereas the intellectual fiction of "equality" may be capable of being addressed and developed at the somewhat abstract and remote level of EU law-making, real inequalities may be better tackled through diverse, differentiated and localised strategies:

> "There can be no single meaning of sex equality, because there is no single determination of women, as of course there is not of men . . . The first duty of the feminist legal thinker is not to pronounce on sex equality, or perceived inadequate approximations to it, but radically to destabilise any pretended determination of the idea, in practice or in reality".[80]

Diversity can also be presented as more democratic than legal unity or homogeneity, in that it permits locally-made choices and preferences to determine the shape and content of norms. Here, pluralism is presented as a facet of subsidiarity, which in turn is an element of democracy. Soft law, which appears to enhance (or preserve) the scope for diversity among Member States, has been positively endorsed in this context by the Member States themselves.[81] But these observations raise questions about the objectives of EU equality laws and policies. By its own description, Community law privileges equality norms as fundamental and of central importance. Community law establishes certain "core" values in relation to equality but the precise shape given to these depends on the social and political context in the Member State in question and on the methods

---

[79] Verloo and Roggeband, above n. 73.

[80] I Ward, "Beyond Sex Equality: The Limits of Sex Equality Law in the New Europe" in T Hervey and D O'Keeffe (eds), *Sex Equality Law in the European Union* (Chichester, Wiley, 1996) 369 at 372.

[81] Conclusions of the Presidency, Edinburgh European Council, 11–12 December 1992, Part A, Annex 1. Summit; see further F Beveridge and S Nott, "A Hard Look at Soft Law" in C Harlow and P Craig (eds), *Law-Making in the European Union* (London, Kluwer, 1998) 285 at 294–5.

chosen for implementation. The diversity between the laws of different Member States would be acceptable if it merely reflected some hierarchical division between the "core" and "penumbra" of equality norms. But many would deny that a fundamental norm should permit of such diversity. In this connection it is noteworthy that the European Court has extended the "harmonisation" of equality laws beyond the substance of these norms to matters concerning their enforceability and remedies, indicating arguably that the European Court does not accept such a distinction. In support of the view that such a distinction is unacceptable, it can be observed that a significant factor producing diversity between Member States' responses to EU equality measures is the role played by powerful interest groups in the policy-making processes in different states.

Diversity is also questionable if the legitimacy of Community equality law is seen to rest on the harmonisation and uniformity of Member States' equality laws. It would be wrong to conclude from the developments on equality law in the Amsterdam Treaty that debates over the legitimacy and the role of the EU in relation to equality, or in relation to social law more generally, can be laid to rest. Recognising that the entrenched opposition of the United Kingdom to the further development of EU social policy may have allowed other Member States to engage in a great deal of "cheap talk",[82] the removal of that opposition can be anticipated to give rise to a degree of reticence and caution on the part of some Member States. Indeed, under EMU many Member States will be obliged to keep a close eye on monetary and fiscal disciplines, and will perceive this to be intrinsically opposed to further developments in the social field.

In addition, political support for future developments in Community equality law might dissipate if the issue of diversity, or differential impact, rose to prominence. Whilst it seems unlikely that equality policies would ever produce the sort of legal and political battle which has been fought in relation to the safety of beef and beef products, that dispute is a salutary reminder of the importance of even-handedness in the enforcement of Community law, and of the political importance of an underlying notion of reciprocity in Member State obligations. Transforming the narrative of social policy from a market to a citizenship-based notion is unlikely to have much impact at the state level, at which such matters are raised.

Thus, from an EU perspective, it is possible to see both merit and demerit in diversity, just as it is possible to accept much of it as inevitable. The tolerable level of diversity will always be the subject of debate and may vary over time. However, an alternative reading of the diversity between Member States' equality policies is that it is evidence of the existence of legal pluralism—that is, the coexistence of several legal systems at the same moment. Two features of equality law in particular are evident. One is that neither the EU nor the Member States has a monopoly on the legal concept of gender equality, nor a monopoly

---

[82] P Lange, "The Politics of the Social Dimension" in A Sbragia (ed.), *Euro-Politics: Institutions and Policy-Making in the 'New' European Community* (Washington, Brookings Institution, 1992); Cram, above n. 4, at 58–60.

of competence on the adoption of gender equality laws and policies. Therefore the separate systems of the EU and the Member States are perhaps inevitably locked in a struggle to impose logic and coherence in the field of gender equality, not only in the concepts of equality adopted but also in the mechanisms employed to implement them.

The second feature is that both the EU and the Member States are participants in a wider global equality forum and are influenced by a range of sources emanating both from within and outside their respective borders. As the earlier discussion on mainstreaming illustrates, both the EU and the Member States are engaged in the business of modelling and repeating formulae learned elsewhere. Equality law conforms to Boaventura de Sousa Santos' description of postmodern law as "explicitly liquid, ephemeral, ever negotiable, and renegotiable, in sum, disposable".[83]

If these observations are accurate, it is difficult to see that denying the existence of legal pluralism in Community equality law will serve any purpose. In its development of mainstreaming policy, the European Commission itself has been perhaps unexpectedly explicit in its acknowledgement of a diversity of influences on that policy.[84] Moreover the most comprehensive self-descriptions of the responses of many states to the mainstreaming initiative to date can be found not in any EU source, but in the responses prepared for the United Nations on implementation of the Beijing Declaration and Platform for Action.[85] Against this background, the diversity of Member States' responses to mainstreaming, and to Community equality laws and policies more generally, may be less problematic than at first sight. Indeed the "decentring" of Community political law-making in readings of EU equality law and policy may, as Harm Schepel suggests,[86] contribute to our understanding of European social law and of the wider process of European integration.

---

[83] B de Sousa Santos, "The Post-modern Transition: Law and Politics" in A Sarat and T R Kearns (eds), *The Fate of Law* (University of Michigan Press, Ann Arbor, 1991).

[84] See for instance the references to *Global Platform for Action* (adopted at the Fourth World Conference on Women in Beijing 1995) in the Commission's Communication on mainstreaming (see above n. 40), its *Guide to Gender Impact Assessment* and its *Annual Report on Equal Opportunities for Women and Men in the European Union, 1998* (COM(99) 106). Another document regularly referred to by the Commission is the Council of Europe's *Gender Mainstreaming: Conceptual Framework, Methodology and Presentation of Good Practices; Final Report of Activities of the Group of Specialists on Mainstreaming* (EG-S-MS (98) 2) (Strasbourg, Council of Europe, May 1998).

[85] See e.g. in Ireland, Department of Equality and Law Reform, *UN Fourth World Conference on Women: First Report on Implementation of the Platform for Action* (Dublin, Stationery Office, 1996); in the Netherlands, Ministry of Social Affairs and Employment, *Second Report of the Netherlands to the UN Committee for the Elimination of all Forms of Discrimination Against Women (CEDAW)* (The Hague, Ministry of Social Affairs and Employment, 1999).

[86] H Schepel, "Legal Pluralism in the European Union" in P Fitzpatrick and J H Bergeron (eds), *Europe's Other: European Law between Modernity and Postmodernity* (Brookfield VT, Ashgate, 1998) 47 at 59–60.

PART IV

Strategies for Equality, Employment and Employment Equity

8

Equality and Diversity: Anti-discrimination Law after Amsterdam

MARK BELL[1]

One of the more significant innovations in the Amsterdam Treaty which came into force in May 1999 was the insertion of a new provision in the EC Treaty, Article 13, which states:

"Without prejudice to the other provisions of this Treaty and within the limits of the powers conferred by it upon the Community, the Council, acting unanimously on a proposal from the Commission and after consulting the European Parliament, may take appropriate action to combat discrimination based on sex, racial or ethnic origin, religion or belief, disability, age or sexual orientation".

This addressed an enduring weakness in Community anti-discrimination law—the limitation of its remit to discrimination on grounds of EU nationality and sex. Indeed, given the lengthy debates in the past over possible alternative Treaty bases for combating discrimination,[2] Article 13 is a breath of fresh air for anti-discrimination law, moving the discussion onto the substantive questions surrounding how the EU can effectively contribute to the promotion of equal treatment. Moreover, Article 13 not only opens many possibilities for new action, it also holds the potential to change the nature of the existing law in this field.

Flowing from the nature of the EC Treaty, nationality and sex discrimination were dealt with quite separately, both in legislation and at the European Court of Justice.[3] In contrast, Article 13 brings together a range of different grounds of discrimination. This suggests a shift in emphasis towards common

[1] Many thanks to Gisella Gori and Madeleine de Leeuw for generous assistance in the preparation of this chapter. All responsibility for any errors, factual or otherwise, of course lies with the author.

[2] For a summary of the options discussed, see D Curtin and M Geurts, "Race Discrimination and the European Union Anno 1996: from Rhetoric to Legal Remedy?", (1996) 14 *Netherlands Quarterly of Human Rights* 147 at 154 *et seq*. Also, A Clapham and J Weiler, "Human Dignity shall be Inviolable: the Human Rights of Gays and Lesbians in the EC Legal Order", (1992) Vol. III, Book 2, *Collected Courses in the Academy of European Law* 237 at 265 *et seq*.

[3] With regard to the case law of the European Court, one may highlight the different definitions of indirect discrimination which emerged between nationality and sex discrimination. See R Allen, "Article 13 and the Search for Equality in Europe: an Overview" in Europaforum Wien (eds), *Anti-discrimination: the Way Forward* (Wien, Europaforum, 1999) 18.

anti-discrimination provisions across different grounds. Already, this has been labelled the *horizontal* approach to anti-discrimination law, whilst retaining separate legislative instruments for individual grounds is now referred to as the *vertical* approach.[4] This dichotomy between horizontal and vertical strategies has emerged as the primary choice facing the EU as it begins to elaborate a new body of anti-discrimination law. This chapter considers the arguments for and against the two approaches, both at the theoretical and the pragmatic levels. Before entering this debate though, it is worth considering further the exact message emanating from the Amsterdam Treaty.

THE DIRECTION OF THE FOUNDING TREATIES

The text of Article 13 certainly indicates a horizontal approach. Indeed, one could even make the argument that Article 13 obliges this approach. The article only allows for actions to "combat discrimination", whereas measures which extend protection against certain grounds of discrimination, but not others, may be regarded as creating discrimination in the law.[5] At the same time, it is questionable whether the European Court would accept such a rigorous interpretation of the article. This would considerably constrain the discretion accorded to the Council in adopting legislation, and would create tension with the explicit provision elsewhere in the EC Treaty for specific measures against sexual discrimination in employment.[6] Arguably, the adoption of measures against racial discrimination, but not, say, age discrimination, does not actually make the situation for age discrimination any worse than it was before. Indeed, such a measure can be seen as helping to address the needs of those who are affected by age discrimination but who also happen to be members of ethnic minority communities.

At the very least, Article 13 still suggests a preference for a horizontal approach, albeit not a mandatory obligation. This preference is, however, not reaffirmed elsewhere in the treaties.[7] Indeed, separate provisions are retained in the EC Treaty in respect of nationality and sex discrimination, as well as additional provisions on racism in the Treaty on European Union. Specifically, discrimination against other EU citizens by reason of nationality remains the subject of the strongest measures—Article 12 EC provides a directly effective right to non-discrimination on grounds of nationality, providing this falls within the scope of application of the EC Treaty. Moreover, the European

---

[4] For example, B Niven, "Combating Discrimination—What Types of Community Action?" in Europaforum Wien (eds), *Article 13—Anti-Discrimination: the Way Forward* (Wien, Europaforum, 1999) 31. See also in the same volume, A Pelinka, "Discrimination Grounds and Discriminatory Practices. Horizontal and Vertical Issues within the Scope of Article 13" at 49.

[5] Thanks to Elspeth Guild for suggesting this possible interpretation.

[6] Articles 137(1) and 141 EC.

[7] G More, "The Principle of Equal Treatment: from Market Unifier to Fundamental Right?" in P Craig and G de Búrca (eds), *The Evolution of EU Law* (Oxford, OUP, 1999) 547.

Court has substantially pushed back this "scope" threshold, making this a more broadly enforceable right than ever before.[8]

With regard to sex discrimination, its inclusion in Article 13 is reinforced by two specific legislative competences for combating discrimination in employment (Articles 137(1) and 141 EC). Of these, the more detailed Article 141 is perhaps the most interesting as this includes treaty protection for positive action initiatives.[9] This constitutional protection is not found in the treaties for any other category of discrimination. Furthermore, the basic legal competences are augmented by the addition of a second paragraph to Article 3 EC, stating: "in all the activities referred to in this Article, the Community shall aim to eliminate inequalities, and to promote equality, between men and women". As Article 3 EC lists all the principal policy fields of the EU, the effect of this provision is to give a treaty foundation for "mainstreaming" consideration of sex equality into all areas of EU policy-making.

Finally, in respect of racial discrimination, additional attention is found in the terms of the EU Treaty, where Article 29 EC states that "preventing and combating racism and xenophobia" is to be one of the Union's key objectives in guaranteeing "an area of freedom, security and justice". To this end, the Council may now deploy the range of new instruments available following the restructuring of the third pillar.[10] The most potent of these seems to be the "framework decision" which binds the Member States "as to the objective to be achieved but shall leave to the national authorities the choice of form and methods".[11] This approximates to an EC directive, but with the significant caveat that a framework decision "shall not entail direct effect".[12]

None of the other grounds in Article 13 (religion or belief, age, disability, sexual orientation) receive specific attention elsewhere in the treaties.[13] Overall, the Amsterdam Treaty provides conflicting signals on the future direction of anti-discrimination law. Article 13 may be correctly highlighted as proposing a horizontal approach based around common measures to tackle all types of

---

[8] See C–85/96 *Martínez Sala* v. *Freistaat Bayern* [1998] ECR I–2691, C–274/96 *Bickel and Franz* [1998] ECR I–7637. The implications of the decision in *Sala* are discussed further in S Fries and J Shaw, "Citizenship of the Union: First Steps in the European Court of Justice", (1998) 4 *European Public Law* 533. For a reaffirmation by the Court that some limits to the scope of Article 12 do still apply, see C–430/97 *Johannes* v. *Johannes*, judgment of 10 June 1999.

[9] Article 141(4) EC provides that "with a view to ensuring full equality in practice between men and women in working life, the principle of equal treatment shall not prevent any Member State from maintaining or adopting measures providing for specific advantages in order to make it easier for the under-represented sex to pursue a vocational activity or to prevent or compensate for disadvantages in professional careers".

[10] Title VI on Police and Judicial Cooperation on Criminal Matters. See generally, J Monar, "Justice and Home Affairs in the Treaty of Amsterdam: Reform at the Price of Fragmentation", (1998) 23 *European Law Review* 320.

[11] Article 34(2)(b) EC.

[12] *Ibid.*

[13] A slight exception may be disability discrimination which is the subject of Declaration 22 attached to the Amsterdam Treaty. This requires the institutions to take the needs of disabled persons into account when preparing internal market legislation.

discrimination. Yet, a wider view of the amended treaties tends more to confirm a continuation of the existing approach, where individual grounds of discrimination are subject to specific legislation providing different levels of protection.

This uncertain picture has fed through to the Commission's initial proposals for action under Article 13. Two legislative initiatives have been submitted. First, there is a "Proposal for a Council directive establishing a general framework directive for equal treatment in employment and occupation".[14] This aims to prohibit employment discrimination on the grounds of racial or ethnic origin, religion or belief, age, disability or sexual orientation. Secondly, there is a "proposal for a Council directive implementing equal treatment between persons irrespective of racial or ethnic origin".[15] This has the objective of forbidding racial discrimination in employment, social protection and social security, education, access to and supply of goods and services. On one hand, the general framework directive is horizontal in nature as it levels out the pre-existing hierarchy in EC law through extending non-discrimination rights in employment beyond sex and nationality to all remaining Article 13 grounds. On the other, the anti-racism directive is vertical in nature as it would elevate race discrimination to a level of legal protection approaching that which currently applies to nationality discrimination. It is the inherent tension between the two proposals which demonstrates the nature of the choices facing the EU. Once again, the question arises as to the legitimacy of singling out one ground of discrimination for special attention and legal protection.

EQUALITY, FUNDAMENTAL RIGHTS AND EU CITIZENSHIP

The theoretical underpinning of Article 13 seems to be a combination of guaranteeing fundamental rights and promoting the evolution of European citizenship. In both streams of thought, the principle of equality is central.

The right to non-discrimination is a very widely recognised core element of any set of fundamental rights, whether it is in national constitutions, or in international human rights instruments.[16] This has been reinforced by the jurisprudence of the European Court which has affirmed the fundamental nature of the right to non-discrimination and equal treatment.[17] A useful starting point is Article 1 of the Universal Declaration of Human Rights which provides that "all human beings are born free and equal in dignity and rights".[18] This concept of

---

[14] COM(99) 565.

[15] COM(99) 566. "Adopted: Council Directive 2000/43, [2000] OJ L 180/22."

[16] C Barnard, "P v. S: Kite Flying or a New Constitutional Approach" in A Dashwood and S O'Leary, *The Principle of Equal Treatment in European Community Law* (London, Sweet & Maxwell, 1997) 67–8.

[17] C–149/77 *Defrenne* v. *SABENA (III)* [1978] ECR 1365, paras. 26–7; C–13/94 *P* v. *S and Cornwall County Council* [1996] ECR I–2143, para. 19.

[18] S Parmar, "The Treaty of Amsterdam" in ILGA-Europe, *After Amsterdam: Sexual Orientation and the European Union* (Brussels, ILGA-Europe, 1999) 21.

equality and dignity for all is reflected in the very broad prohibitions on discrimination in the European Convention on Human Rights (ECHR),[19] the International Covenant on Civil and Political Rights[20] and the International Covenant on Economic, Social and Cultural Rights.[21] These conventions lean towards a horizontal approach to combating discrimination, based on the principle of equal protection of the law.

Nonetheless, vertical instruments may also be found in human rights law, such as the International Covenant for the Elimination of Racial Discrimination or the Convention on the Elimination of All Forms of Discrimination against Women. This combination of horizontal and vertical instruments forms a pattern whereby the fundamental texts establish a basic right to non-discrimination applied to all grounds, which is then supplemented by more detailed rules in respect of specific grounds. Similarly, within the law of the ECHR, there has been some vertical development. Article 14 provides the general, horizontal entitlement to non-discrimination in the exercise of the rights guaranteed by the ECHR. However, the European Court of Human Rights has built upon this by establishing that for certain grounds, namely sex[22] and nationality,[23] only "very weighty reasons" can justify such discrimination. In this way, one can trace how the horizontal right has been established for all grounds of discrimination in Article 14 of the ECHR, but this has not prevented the Court of Human Rights from pushing ahead with specific grounds therein and raising them to a higher level of scrutiny.[24]

A strong conception of citizenship depends on the creation of a sense of solidarity amongst citizens. Where solidarity collapses, sub-groups of citizens begin to believe that their interests may be better addressed apart from the rest of the citizenry. Indeed, European citizenship is all about building links and fostering trust between the citizens of the Member States, which will thereby strengthen the foundations of European integration and avoid the risk of a return to national separatism.[25] Equal protection of the law is an essential ingredient in upholding inter-citizen solidarity. It is this need for equal treatment which explains the importance attached by the EU to combating nationality discrimination. It has consistently been recognised that the full realisation of the right to free movement depends on individuals and businesses being able to exercise these rights on a non-discriminatory basis, and more generally in a context of

---

[19] Article 14.

[20] Article 26.

[21] Article 2(2).

[22] *Abdulaziz, Cabales and Balkandali* v. *United Kingdom* (1985) 7 EHRR 471.

[23] *Gaygusuz* v. *Austria*, judgment of 16 September 1996, Reports of Judgments and Decisions 1996-IV.

[24] This echoes some aspects of equal protection law in the USA, see further, E Gerstmann, *The Constitutional Underclass—Gays, Lesbians, and the Failure of Class-Based Equal Protection* (Chicago, University of Chicago Press, 1999).

[25] J Shaw, "The Interpretation of European Union Citizenship", (1998) 61 *Modern Law Review* 293 at 295; G de Búrca, "The Language of Rights and European Integration" in J Shaw and G More, *New Legal Dynamics of European Union* (Oxford, Clarendon Press, 1995) 42–3.

"freedom and dignity".[26] More recently though, there has been a greater appreciation that nationality is not the only element of solidarity needed to support integration. Equally, the integrity of the EU is damaged where other sub-groups of citizens feel alienated from the integration process. This has perhaps been clearest in respect of ethnic minority communities in the 1990s; the perception of the EU creating a "Fortress Europe" underlined a sense that the EU had little positive to offer ethnic minorities.[27]

In a direct fashion, the priority the Commission has placed on early and extensive action against racism seems to be a response to the alienation generated by restrictive immigration and asylum policies. At the same time, separating the different grounds for discrimination may perpetuate the cycle of exclusion. If racism is now to be raised to the inner circle of anti-discrimination law, then what message does this send to the individuals affected by the grounds not addressed? The danger is that the sense of being outside the integration project is shifted to the disabled, the young and the old, religious minorities, or gays and lesbians. Moreover, the vertical strategy fails to confront the overlapping nature of discriminatory grounds. Combating racism may enhance the commitment of some ethnic minorities to European integration, but if discrimination on grounds of third country nationality is not simultaneously addressed, then for many individuals the exclusion remains. Similarly, sex equality law, however limited in practice, gave women a stake in European integration—a reason to believe that the EU was dealing with issues relevant to their personal situations. Yet, for migrant women or lesbians, the experience was different and the loyalty generated obviously weaker.[28]

In a more precise context, enhancing the right to free movement requires a broader view of combating discrimination. This was first indicated by the Commission in its 1994 White Paper on European social policy: "the Union must act to provide a guarantee for all people against the fear of discrimination if it is to make a reality of free movement".[29] Since then, this logic has received gradual support from the European Court, within the more general context of the link between exercising free movement rights and guaranteeing basic human rights protection. This was most explicitly advocated in the Opinion of Advocate-General Jacobs in *Konstantinidis*:

---

[26] Preamble, Regulation 1612/68 on free movement for workers within the Community, [1968] OJ LII/475.

[27] J King, "Ethnic Minorities and Multilateral European Institutions" in A Hargreaves and J Leaman (eds), *Racism, Ethnicity and Politics in Contemporary Europe* (Aldershot, Edward Elgar, 1995) 181 *et seq.*

[28] A Subhan (ed.), *Confronting the Fortress—Black and Migrant Women in the European Union*, Working Paper: Women's Rights Series, E-2 External Study (Brussels, European Women's Lobby and European Parliament, 1995); S Andermahr, "Subjects or Citizens? Lesbians in the New Europe" in A Ward, J Gregory and N Yuval-Davis (eds), *Women and Citizenship in Europe—Borders, Rights and Duties: Women's Differing Identities in a Europe of Contested Boundaries* (Stoke-on-Trent, Trentham Books, 1992) 116.

[29] European Commission, *European Social Policy—a Way Forward for the Union: a White Paper* (COM(94) 333) 52.

"a Community national who goes to another Member State as a worker or self-employed person . . . is in addition entitled to assume that, wherever he goes to earn his living in the European Community, he will be treated in accordance with a common code of fundamental values, in particular those laid down in the European Convention on Human Rights".[30]

Whilst the Court did not develop the point in its judgment in that case, the more recent decision in *Calfa*[31] seems to echo the views of Jacobs. In *Calfa*, an Italian tourist in Crete was found guilty of the possession and use of prohibited drugs, and was sentenced to three months imprisonment and a life-time ban on entering Greece. Ms Calfa challenged the ban on entry to Greece on the basis that it was in conflict with her right to free movement for the receipt of services. Significantly, the Court acknowledged that:

"although in principle criminal legislation is a matter for which the Member States are responsible, the Court has consistently held that Community law sets certain limits to their power, and such legislation may not restrict the fundamental freedoms guaranteed by Community law".[32]

The willingness of the Court to imply a general duty for all Member States to respect human rights in the criminal law domain marks a clear step in the direction of Jacobs' proposition that all EU citizens should be able to depend upon respect for a basic set of rights wherever they move in the EU.

The connection with anti-discrimination lies in the centrality of combating discrimination to the idea of an EU citizen's portable charter of fundamental rights. The right to non-discrimination on grounds of nationality has already been established as a right across borders. The next stage appears to be the horizontal extension of the non-discrimination right to the full range of Article 13 grounds. All of the Article 13 grounds can impact upon free movement. For instance, a disabled person living in a state where transport and buildings are required to be accessible will be deterred from moving to a state where weaker legal obligations mean their mobility would be reduced, or made considerably more challenging. Alternatively, a gay worker in Sweden who enjoys the legal recognition of his partnership as being on an equal footing with marriage, will face a return to legal inequality if he moves to work in a state where registered partnership for same-sex couples does not exist. Indeed, a case including precisely these circumstances is pending appeal before the European Court.[33] This logic also underpins the Commission's 1998 proposal for an amendment to Regulation 1612/68 on the free movement of workers. In particular, the draft new Article 1a would provide: "Within the scope of this Regulation, all discrimination on grounds of sex, racial or ethnic origin, religion, belief, disability,

---

[30] Opinion of Advocate-General Jacobs, C–168/91 *Konstantinidis* [1993] ECR I–1191, para. 46.
[31] Case C–348/96 *Donatella Calfa* [1999] ECR I–11.
[32] *Ibid.*, para. 17. See also C–274/96 *Bickel and Franz* [1998] ECR I–7637, para. 17.
[33] T–264/97 *D* v. *Council* [1999] ECR II-1; on appeal: C–122/99 P.
[34] Proposal for a European Parliament and Council Regulation amending Council Regulation 1612/68 on the freedom of movement for workers within the Community, [1998] OJ C344/9.

age or sexual orientation shall be prohibited".[34] Implicit is the recognition that despite the overarching importance of combating nationality discrimination, there also needs to be an eye to other forms of discrimination which may hinder free movement.

Finally, the tide in favour of broad-based human rights protection looks certain to derive further support from the forthcoming EU Charter of Fundamental Rights. The initial decision to prepare this document was taken at the Cologne European Council in June 1999.[35] Specifically, a group containing representatives from the Member States, the European Parliament, national parliaments and the Commission has been charged with preparing a draft Charter for adoption by the European Council in December 2000.[36] What remains uncertain is the legal status of this Charter. The intention of the Council seems to be to establish the Charter as an initially non-binding document, akin to the 1989 Community Charter of Fundamental Social Rights for Workers.[37] The option of incorporating the Charter into the founding treaties could then be considered at a later stage. However, the fact that the preparation of the Charter coincides with the 2000 Intergovernmental Conference at least provides the opportunity for the Member States to proceed directly to an appropriate treaty amendment. Irrespective of the final nature of the Charter, there can be no doubt that equality rights should form a central element of the Charter. The various sources upon which the drafters may draw—the ECHR, international human rights instruments, national constitutions and the existing EU treaties—all contain a foundation for enshrining a general commitment to equality and non-discrimination in the new Charter.[38]

BALANCING IDEALS WITH POLITICAL REALITIES

The previous section focused on the principled arguments which, on the whole, are more supportive of a *horizontal* approach to anti-discrimination. Indeed, most of the arguments in favour of a *vertical* approach are grounded in pragmatism rather than principle. First, it is commonly suggested that separate rules result in more effective and more precise legislation. Secondly, it is argued that specific legislation will make it easier to reach political agreement, most especially in the context of the need to find unanimity in the Council of Ministers. The two arms of the argument will be dealt with separately.

---

[35] Presidency Conclusions, Cologne European Council, 3–4 June 1999, Annex IV: European Council decision on the drawing up of a charter of fundamental rights of the European Union. Press Release: Vienna, 4 June 1999, Nr. 150/99 (Presse).

[36] Presidency Conclusions, Tampere European Council, 15–16 October 1999, Annex. Press Release: Tampere, 16 October 1999, Nr. 200/99.

[37] Text appears in *Social Europe* 1/90 at 46–50.

[38] European Commission, *Affirming Fundamental Rights in the European Union—Time to Act*, Report of the Expert Group on Fundamental Rights, DG Employment and Social Affairs (Luxembourg, OOPEC, 1999) 23–5.

Making legislation precise and effective

A frequently cited reason for retaining separate legislation for the different grounds of discrimination is the *complexity* involved in drafting a single legislative framework. For instance, the Starting Line (a coalition of NGOs working against racism) proposed that the EU adopt a directive to forbid racial and religious discrimination. In their explanatory memorandum, the group justify the decision to exclude the other grounds in Article 13 on the basis that "it would be very difficult to draft a blanket directive dealing with all these types of discrimination; such a directive would have to be highly complicated and full of exceptions for specific cases".[39]

Underlying the complexity argument is the belief that substantive differences exist between the different grounds of discrimination and, as a result, these require different legislative frameworks. Certainly, each ground of discrimination appears to have its specific aspects. For people with disabilities, effectively combating discrimination requires the acceptance of an obligation on the employer to take all reasonable measures to accommodate the worker. At the same time, there also needs to be a focus on employee mobility and improving the facilities available to give disabled workers access to the workplace. In this context, tackling discriminatory barriers in the area of transport is often integral to enhancing employment opportunities.[40] Parallels may be drawn with religious discrimination where active accommodation may also be necessary to make equal treatment real in practice. For example, this could include accommodating special dietary requirements in workplace canteens, or flexible holiday arrangements for certain religious festivals.

Reflecting certain specific situations, the range of suitable policy measures also varies according to the ground of discrimination. Positive action is an obvious example of a policy tool which may not be appropriate for all grounds of discrimination. On one hand, there are many examples of positive action programmes in respect of gender and ethnic discrimination. Indeed, in both instances, the use of positive action has received EU-level approval.[41] However, the application of the same techniques to other grounds may encounter greater challenges. In particular, discrimination on grounds of sexual orientation is one area where there seems only a limited space for positive action. Goals and timetables for the recruitment of lesbians, or gay-only training programmes

[39] Starting Line Group, *Proposals for Legislative Measures to Combat Racism and to Promote Equal Rights in the European Union* (London, Commission for Racial Equality, 1998) 19.

[40] This was the subject of a proposed directive by the Commission from 1990: "Proposal for a Council directive on minimum requirements to improve the mobility and the safe transport to work of workers with reduced mobility" (COM(90) 588).

[41] See Council Recommendation 84/635/EEC on the promotion of positive action for women, [1984] OJ L331/34; UNICE, ETUC and CEEP, "Joint Declaration on the Prevention of Racial Discrimination and Xenophobia and Promotion of Equal Treatment at the Workplace" (1995), reproduced in European Commission, *The European Institutions in the Fight against Racism: Selected Texts* (Luxembourg, OOPEC, 1997).

seem inappropriate, if only because of the inherent barriers to identifying how many lesbians and gay men an employer already employs, or how many they should aim to employ in the future.

Finally, legislating for the exceptions to the ban on discrimination is another contentious area where differences emerge between the various grounds. The exceptions provided in the 1976 Equal Treatment Directive can be summarised as relating to where sex is a genuine occupational qualification,[42] pregnancy/maternity measures,[43] and positive action.[44] As indicated above, positive action exceptions may not be applicable to all grounds of discrimination. Pregnancy is an obvious example of a ground-specific exception. Whilst the remaining ground of "genuine occupational qualification" more easily applies to any of the Article 13 grounds, there are other issues not appropriate to sex discrimination which will have to be dealt with in any future, broader instrument. For instance, when discussing religious discrimination, there may be pressure to provide an exception for discrimination against religious groups advocating violence or engaging in criminal activities.[45]

One of the most sensitive questions is likely to be the status of religious employers. In national law debates, religious organisations have often argued that the freedom of religion should imply a right for them to choose whether or not to employ persons based on the compatibility of the individual's personal *mores* with their fundamental principles. As a result, several national anti-discrimination statutes (for example in Ireland,[46] the Netherlands,[47] Denmark and Sweden[48]) have provided exceptions for religious organisations from the general requirements. For example, in Denmark, section 6(1) of the 1996 Law Against Discrimination in the Labour Market states that the provisions forbidding discrimination: "shall not apply to an employer whose enterprise has the express object of promoting a particular political or religious opinion, unless this is in conflict with European Community law".[49] The claims of religious organisa-

---

[42] Directive no. 76/207. Article 2(2).

[43] Article 2(3).

[44] Article 2(4).

[45] An interesting comparison lies in the Fair Employment and Treatment (Northern Ireland) Order 1998, No. 3162 (NS. 21) which forbids discrimination on grounds of religion or political opinion. Article 4 states "in this Order any reference to a person's political opinion does not include an opinion which consists of or includes approval or acceptance of the use of violence for political ends connected with the affairs of Northern Ireland, including the use of violence for the purpose of putting the public or any section of the public in fear".

[46] Employment Equality Act 1998, s. 37, see K Rose, "Ireland" in ILGA-Europe (eds), *Equality for Lesbians and Gay Men: a Relevant Issue in the Civil and Social Dialogue* (Brussels, ILGA-Europe, 1998) 61.

[47] General Equal Treatment Act 1994, s. 3, provides that the Act does not apply to "legal relations within religious communities and independent sections thereof and within other associations of a spiritual nature".

[48] See *Euroletter* (e-mail edition), No. 68, March 1999. Available at <http://www.steff.suite.dk/eurolet.htm>, 15.9.99.

[49] Lov om forbud mod forskelsbehandling på arbejdsmarkedet m.v.; 12 juni 1996, Lovtidende Afdeling, Nr. 459, at 2526–7. Many thanks to Kim Jensen of the Danish National Association for Gays and Lesbians (LBL) for supplying me with an English translation of the law.

tions are likely to be further strengthened by Declaration 11 to the Amsterdam Treaty, which states, "the European Union respects and does not prejudice the status under law of churches and religious associations or communities in the Member States".

Taking a broader perspective, this section has been designed to illustrate the true complexity involved in drafting a horizontal anti-discrimination directive, especially if this addresses a range of areas, such as employment, education and access to goods and services. On the one hand, it is a mistake to regard this as an impossible task—legislation in several Member States has tackled a wide range of discrimination grounds, proving that it can be achieved. However, the states concerned appear to have made a choice between highly detailed legislation (Ireland and the Netherlands), or very general rules (*inter alia*, Denmark, Finland[50] and Luxembourg).[51] In these cases, there seems to be a certain trade-off between clarity and effectiveness. Highly precise laws may be more rigorous, but just as equally, they are less transparent to citizens and employers.[52]

At the EU level, it must be accepted that very detailed legislation will be difficult to achieve. The principle of subsidiarity leans towards providing discretion to the Member States where possible, and the choice of a directive also requires flexibility in implementation. Indeed, in explaining its initial proposals under Article 13, the Commission emphasises that the proposals only "intend to set a limited number of requirements based on a number of general principles, allowing Member States considerable discretion in how they choose to implement them".[53] Accordingly, the approach taken in the framework draft directive on employment discrimination avoids being overwhelmed by complexity through keeping its provisions general in nature. (Explanation: the Commission reissued the draft directive *with* a specific exception for religious employers).

Indeed, only two grounds of discrimination receive specific attention in the terms of the draft directive—disability and age. In relation to the former, an obligation on employers to make reasonable accommodation for persons with disabilities is included in draft Article 2(4).[54] It is, though, the treatment of age discrimination which perhaps best typifies the limits of a horizontal approach. Whilst age discrimination in employment is forbidden in Article 2 of the draft directive, Article 5 of the proposal then provides a *non-exhaustive* list of

---

[50] See R Hiltunen, "Finland" in ILGA-Europe, above n. 46.

[51] Loi du 19 juillet 1997 complétant le code pénal en modifiant l'incrimination du racisme et en portant incrimination du révisionnisme et d'autres agissements fondés sur des discriminations illégales (Journal Officiel du Grand-Duché de Luxembourg, A-No. 54, at 1680, 7 août 1997).

[52] For example, see the Irish Law Reform Commission's criticism of the Employment Equality Act for its lack of clarity; *Irish Times*, 6 August 1999, "Commission Hopes to Free Law of Anachronisms".

[53] European Commission Communication, *Certain Community Measures to Combat Discrimination* (COM(99) 564) at 11.

[54] "In order to guarantee respect of the principle of equal treatment for persons with disabilities, reasonable accommodation shall be provided, where needed, to enable such persons to have access to, participate in, or advance in employment, unless this requirement creates an undue hardship."

instances where direct discrimination on grounds of age may be justified.[55] Indeed, the exceptions are so broad that the network on ageing issues, Eurolink Age, has described the proposal as in fact seeking "to legalise age discrimination".[56] Overall, the proposals confirm that, at least at the EU level, a horizontal approach may produce broadly applicable legislation, but this will curtail the ability of the legislator to address in depth issues specific to a particular ground of discrimination.

Reaching political accord in the Council

In ideal circumstances, choices on the nature and form of new anti-discrimination legislation would be made purely on the basis of the relative merits of the various options open to the EU. However, a significant determinant will undoubtedly be the question of political acceptability—what is most likely to secure the unanimous support necessary for approval by the Council.

To date, the accepted wisdom seems to be that a vertical directive against racism stands a greater chance of success in the Council, at least in respect of the areas of discrimination outside the employment field.[57] Supporting this view is the more positive attitude in recent years of the Council to initiatives against racism. Both the approval of the establishment of the Monitoring Centre on Racism[58] and the Council's support for the 1997 Year against Racism initiative[59] provide some evidence to suggest there is a willingness on the part of the Member States to see the EU take a larger role in this area. The flip-side of this perspective is the assumption that the Council is not willing to accept anti-discrimination initiatives which address the full range of Article 13 grounds. However, given the proposal for the general framework directive, it seems it is only in the non-employment field that the Commission believes the Council could not accept horizontal measures against discrimination.

Certainly, a horizontal directive will make agreement more difficult by increasing the complexity of the issues at stake. Nonetheless, the experience of the 1996/97 Intergovernmental Conference negotiations which led to the Amsterdam Treaty demonstrates that when confronted with a broad anti-discrimination package, there will be pressure on the Member States not to delete less popular grounds, such as religion or sexual orientation. One of the lessons of Article 13 was the ability of more controversial grounds of discrimination to make unexpected progress through seeking inclusion in a broad

[55] European Commission, above n. 14, at 21.

[56] Eurolink Age, "Commission Package Seeks to Legalise Age Discrimination", Press Release, 30 November 1999.

[57] European Commission, above n. 53, at 8.

[58] Regulation 1035/97 establishing a European Monitoring Centre for Racism and Xenophobia, [1997] OJ L151.

[59] Resolution of the Council and the Representatives of the Governments of the Member States, meeting within the Council concerning the European Year against Racism (1997), [1996] OJ C237/1.

anti-discrimination instrument. Similarly, a horizontal approach seems to be the only short or medium-term prospect for securing a wide-ranging ban on discrimination.

Finally, it is important not to overlook the positive reasons in terms of efficiency for a horizontal approach. Member States are naturally concerned to avoid too much "red tape" overburdening firms with bureaucracy. To this end, Article 137(2) EC stresses that social legislation "shall avoid imposing administrative, financial and legal constraints in a way which would hold back the creation and development of small and medium-sized undertakings". On the face of it, this may seem to reinforce a cautious approach to Article 13, dealing with one ground at a time. However, national law experience increasingly indicates a preference for the horizontal approach, precisely because it provides greater clarity and simplicity for employers. The vertical approach inevitably results in different rules for different grounds of discrimination, and even different regulatory bodies. In the United Kingdom, a good example of a vertical approach to anti-discrimination law, employers have expressed the view that separate rules and institutions are "counter-productive and confusing".[60] This also underpins the 1999 amalgamation of anti-discrimination agencies into a single Equality Commission in Northern Ireland.[61]

CONCLUSIONS

The choices made at the outset of the implementation of Article 13 seem likely to shape its direction for many years to come. It is worth recalling that the existing hierarchy in EU anti-discrimination law is one of the principal reasons why Article 13 was felt to be necessary in the first place. Its whole *raison d'être* is surely to reduce the disparities in the level of legal protection accorded to different grounds of discrimination. At the theoretical level, it seems difficult to justify why one form of discrimination deserves greater protection in law than another. The terms of the Covenant on Civil and Political Rights are relevant here; Article 26 requires the signatories to ensure that the law guarantees "to all persons equal and effective protection against discrimination on any ground". Achieving the balance between *equal* and *effective* protection is the main challenge now confronting the European Union. Indeed, the Commission itself has acknowledged the dilemma:

> "Discrimination on different grounds can have similar features and can be combated in similar ways, and the experience built up over many years in combating discrimination on some grounds can be used to the benefit of other grounds. However, each

[60] Commission for Racial Equality, "Confused Companies Seek Equality Law Reform", *Connections* (Summer 1999) at 4.

[61] See B Fitzpatrick, "The Fair Employment and Equal Treatment (Northern Ireland) Order 1998, The Northern Ireland Act 1998", (1999) 28 *Industrial Law Journal* 336.

ground for discrimination has specific characteristics which are not necessarily shared with all other grounds".[62]

Getting the initial approach correct is crucial, not only for the success of the legislation, but also for the overall development of a stronger sense of European citizenship. Effective legislation undoubtedly requires a certain level of specificity in order to meet the particular needs of each ground of discrimination. What needs to be distinguished is a common level of protection from common legislation. Separate, vertical legislation does not automatically entail a hierarchy of discrimination norms. Providing that all grounds enjoy legislative protection, and that the terms of these laws are comparable, though not identical, then *equal* protection may truly be assured. The examples drawn from international law demonstrate how general prohibitions on discrimination have been, in due course, followed on by more specific rules. Similarly, a better starting point for the European Union could be a series of horizontal directives, setting out basic rules forbidding discrimination in the various areas within its competence—such as employment, education and access to goods and services. Having established a common foundation of protection, future measures could then pursue a vertical strategy, fleshing out the basic ban on discrimination and tailoring the law to the individual needs of each ground of discrimination. This mix of measures would stand a better chance of ensuring that EU anti-discrimination law is both equal and effective.

---

[62] European Commission, "Call for Proposals, VP/1999/016", [1999] OJ C191/14, para. II. 2.

9

Affirmative Action and the European Court of Justice: A Critical Analysis

SANDRA FREDMAN

It is becoming increasingly clear that, in order to be effective, anti-discrimination policies must reach beyond legal prohibitions and incorporate positive measures. Hence the growing emphasis on gender mainstreaming at EU level. But is it permissible to go beyond promotion and encouragement, and institute policies which openly discriminate in favour of the disadvantaged group? Official support for reverse discrimination is becoming more common among Member States such as Germany, Austria, Spain, Finland, Norway and Sweden. In addition, the Commission has committed itself to measures to achieve balanced participation of men and women in decision-making, including proposals for quotas of women members. This mirrors developments in the US, which has a long tradition of positive discrimination in allocation of federal contracts, employment and other areas. Yet such programmes appear to offend against basic principles of equality. Much of the century has been spent convincing judges and legislators that race and gender are irrelevant and their use in the allocation of benefits or rights is invidious. How then can it be legitimate to permit such use for purportedly remedial purposes? The US Supreme Court has dealt with a string of cases on the constitutionality of reverse discrimination, and the European Court of Justice has already had to face four challenges of affirmative action policies by aggrieved men who argue that they have been subjected to detrimental treatment solely because of their gender.[1] Several more cases are waiting in the wings. Controversies are likely to be further fuelled by new provisions in the Amsterdam Treaty, which includes a newly worded provision for positive action[2] and introduces a wide-ranging power to legislate in respect of discrimination on grounds such as race, religion and sexual orientation.[3]

In this chapter, I argue that affirmative action needs to be assessed from two perspectives: its coherence and its effectiveness. In the first section, I consider

---

[1] Case C–450/93 *Kalanke* v. *Bremen* [1995] ECR I–3051; Case C–490/95 *Marschall* v. *Land Nordrhein-Westfalen* [1997] ECR I–6363; Case C–158/97 *Badeck* v. *Hessischer Ministerpräsident*, judgment of 28 March 2000, Case C–407/98 *Abrahamsson*, judgment of 6 July 2000.

[2] Article 141(4) EC.

[3] Article 13 EC.

arguments for the coherence of affirmative action, concluding that a substantive view of equality provides a sound theoretical basis for affirmative action. In the light of these arguments, I turn in the second section to a critical assessment of the case law of the European Court and the US Supreme Court. The ferocity of the controversy over its theoretical legitimacy has, however, meant that little attention is paid to explicating the aims of affirmative action. In the third section, therefore, I examine the effectiveness of affirmative action. I conclude that affirmative action has both a legitimate and a useful role to play in decreasing disadvantage and social exclusion, but that this role is limited and must not be a substitute for a more thoroughgoing and radical programme of structural change.

LEGITIMACY[4]

The argument against reverse discrimination is, on the face of it, clear and compelling. As the US Supreme Court Justice Powell declared in the famous *Bakke* case: "The guarantee of equal protection cannot mean one thing when applied to one individual and something else when applied to an individual of another colour".[5] Equality is, as this dictum emphasises, irrefutably symmetrical. Nor does it matter that reverse discrimination is intended to be remedial. There is, according to Justice Thomas, a moral and constitutional equivalence between laws designed to subjugate a race and those that distribute benefits on the basis of race.[6] Symmetry is reinforced by a strong appeal to individual rather than group justice. There can, on this view, be no "creditor or debtor race".[7] Finally, it is argued, reverse discrimination offends against basic constitutional principles of state neutrality and the rule of law. As Abram puts it: "Without doing violence to the principles of equality before the law and neutral decision-making, we simply cannot interpret our laws to support both colour blindness for some citizens and colour-consciousness for others".[8]

Closer examination reveals that this critique is based on a particular conception of equality, which rests on three basic propositions. First, it assumes that justice is defined *a priori* and applies in all societies regardless of the particular distribution of benefits, historical or social context. Justice, on this view, is an objective yardstick, which stands apart from any specific historical facts. If discrimination on grounds of gender or race is unjust, it must be unjust whether it creates extra burdens on a group already disadvantaged, or whether it redis-

---

[4] These arguments are a development of earlier work: see S Fredman "Reversing Discrimination", (1997) 113 *Law Quarterly Review* 575; and S Fredman "After Kalanke and Marschall: Affirming Affirmative Action", [1998] 1 *The Cambridge Yearbook of European Legal Studies* 199.

[5] *Regents of University of California* v. *Bakke* 438 US 265 (1978).

[6] *Adarand* v. *Pena* 115 S. Ct. 2097 (1995) at 2119.

[7] Per Scalia J in *Adarand* at 2118.

[8] M Abram, "Affirmative Action: Fair Shakers and Social Engineers", (1986) 99 *Harvard Law Review* 1312 at 1319.

tributes those burdens to a previously privileged group. Equality must therefore always be symmetrical. Secondly, this critique of affirmative action assumes the primacy of the individual. Group characteristics such as sex or race must, on this view, always be disregarded in distributing benefits such as jobs or promotion; instead, individuals must be rewarded only on the basis of individual merit. Conversely, burdens should only be allocated on the basis of individual responsibility. Thus individuals may only be treated as responsible for their own actions; they should not be held accountable for more general societal wrongs. This means in particular that an individual man should not be required to compensate for historical or institutional sex discrimination by being excluded from a job or promotion for which he is well qualified. Finally, this conception of equality asserts that the state should be neutral as between citizens, favouring no-one above any other. Thus official policies giving preferential treatment to women or blacks are evidence of an impermissible partiality on the part of the state.

The surface appeal of this view has, however, been dented by the limited impact of laws based on a formal, symmetrical view of equality. The unfortunate reality is that it is women rather than men who have suffered cumulative disadvantage due to sex discrimination; blacks rather than whites who have suffered from racism. Equality laws are not ends in themselves, but a means to redress the results of a history of detrimental treatment based on sex or race. Once this is accepted, it becomes clear that to adopt a symmetrical approach, whereby unequal treatment of men is regarded as morally identical to discrimination against women, is to empty the equality principle of real social meaning. The same is true of race.

A similar argument can be mounted against the assertion of the primacy of the individual. It is true that the merit principle has played a valuable role in advancing equality of opportunity by displacing nepotism and class bias in the allocation of jobs or benefits. However, in the context of sex or race, the uncritical use of merit as a criterion for employment or promotion could perpetuate disadvantage.[9] This is because, despite the appearance of scientific objectivity, the choice of criteria for deciding merit may well reinforce existing societal discrimination or incorporate implicit discriminatory assumptions. For example, in the American case of *Griggs* v. *Duke Power*,[10] a blatantly racist selection policy was replaced by a literacy test. On the face of it, this was a racially neutral, merit-based approach. Yet, as the US Supreme Court recognised, the exclusionary effect of the test was identical to that of the explicitly racist policy, because the discrimination experienced by black people in education, housing and other aspects of society made it far more difficult for black candidates to pass the test than whites. Moreover, the skills tested were wholly unnecessary for the job, which was unskilled manual labour.

---

[9] For a valuable discussion of merit, see C McCrudden, "Merit Principles", (1998) 18 *Oxford Journal of Legal Studies* 543.
[10] 410 US 424 (1971).

Equally misleading is the reliance on a notion of individual fault, which generates an image of an "innocent" third party who is deprived of a job or other opportunity because he is white or male. A substantive view of equality suggests that the responsibility for correcting disadvantage should not be seen to rest merely with those to whom "fault" can be attributed. Instead, all who benefit from the existing structure of disadvantage should be expected to bear part of the cost of remedy. A community structured on racial or gender discrimination has conferred benefits on the dominant group as a whole. Each member of the community should, therefore, be required to bear part of the costs of correction, provided these costs are not disproportionate for the individual.

The final assumption is that the state should be neutral or impartial as between its citizens. This depicts the state as separate from society with its current set of power relations. Yet the state is no more than an emanation of the democratic process, the aim of which is to function as a conduit for or resolution of the cross-currents of social power. The modern state plays a central role in distributing benefits in society. It cannot therefore be truly neutral: if it refuses to take an active role in reducing disadvantage, it is in fact supporting the existing dominant groups in maintaining their position of superiority over groups which have suffered from discrimination and prejudice.

What then are the alternatives to a symmetrical, individualist view of equality? Two sets of arguments have been used in the case law and academic literature, one based frankly on a substantive, non-individualistic view of justice, and the second based on the more elusive concept of equal opportunity. Each will be examined in turn.

The substantive approach to reverse discrimination rejects an abstract view of justice and instead insists that justice is only meaningful in its interaction with society. Since it is impossible to deny the continuing effects of discrimination against ethnic minorities or women in society, justice necessitates an asymmetric vision. As Dworkin puts it, "The difference between a general racial classification that causes further disadvantage to those who have suffered from prejudice, and a classification framed to help them, is morally significant".[11] Similarly, the substantive approach rejects as misleading the aspirations of individualism, maintaining that the emphasis on formal equality of individuals simply ignores the extent to which opportunities are determined by individuals' social and historical status, which includes their race and gender. Not only is it impossible to define merit in the abstract; prejudicial assumptions may well permeate the appraisal of merit itself. For example, a stress on formal qualifications and work experience rather than acquired knowledge or informal experience is likely to undervalue women's skills. The fault principle is also seen to be flawed. Instead, the structural nature of discrimination means that the responsibility for correcting institutional discrimination should not lie only with those to whom fault or causality can be attributed: all members of the privileged class share the

---

[11] R Dworkin, *A Matter of Principle* (Cambridge, Mass., Harvard University Press, 1985) 314.

duty and may be expected to bear some of the cost of remedy. Finally, the substantive approach rejects the possibility of a neutral state, maintaining that a purported refusal to intervene is itself a positive statement of state support for continuing societal discrimination. Instead, the state has a duty to act positively to correct the results of such discrimination.

The approach based on "equal opportunities" is less clearly delineated. This model recognises the shallowness of the notion of formal justice, acknowledging the extent to which an individual's life chances are distorted by structural discrimination based on group membership. Instead, it is maintained that true equality cannot be achieved if individuals begin the race from different starting points. An equal opportunities approach therefore aims to equalise the starting point, accepting that this might necessitate special measures for the disadvantaged group. It is, however, at this point that the traditional notions of neutrality, symmetry and the primacy of the individual reassert themselves. Once individuals enjoy equality of opportunity, it is argued, the problem of institutional discrimination has been overcome, and fairness demands that they be treated on the basis of their individual qualities, without regard to sex or race. This model therefore specifically rejects policies which aim to correct imbalances in the workforce by quotas or targets whose aim is one of equality of outcome.

It should be noted at this point that the metaphor of equal starting points is deceptively simple. At its narrowest, equality of opportunity requires the removal of procedural obstacles to the advancement of women or minorities, but does not guarantee that this will lead to greater substantive fairness in the result.[12] Such measures might include the replacement of word of mouth recruitment by open advertising; the use of "outreach" measures encouraging groups to apply for jobs or training places, and the removal of non-job-related selection criteria. These measures remove procedural obstacles and so open up more opportunities to women, but do not guarantee that more women or minorities will in fact be in a position to take advantage of those opportunities. Those who lack the requisite qualifications as a result of past discrimination will still be unable to meet job-related criteria; women with child care responsibilities will not find it easier to take on paid work. In the famous words of US President Lyndon Johnson, it is "not enough to open the gates of opportunity. All our citizens must have the ability to walk through those gates".[13] This demands more than procedural changes; it requires substantive input such as education, training, child care and flexible working so that persons from all sections of society have a genuinely equal chance of satisfying the criteria for access to a particular social good.[14] Moreover, it does not accept uncritically the criteria themselves.

---

[12] See J Waldron in S Guest and A Milne (eds), *Equality and Discrimination* (Stuttgart, Steiner Verlag Wiesbaden, 1985) 97.

[13] Lyndon B Johnson, Address at Howard University (4 June 1965) cited in A Thernstrom, "Voting Rights, Another Affirmative Action Mess", (1996) 43 *UCLA Law Review* 2031 at n. 22.

[14] B Williams, "The Idea of Equality" in P Laslett and W G Runciman (eds), *Philosophy, Politics and Society* (Oxford, Blackwell, 2nd series, 1962) 110 at 125–6.

As Hepple argues, one is not supplying genuine equality of opportunity if one applies an unchallenged criterion of merit to people who have been deprived of the opportunity to acquire "merit".[15] A thorough-going policy of equalising opportunities thus requires a level of state intervention and resource allocation far beyond what most proponents of the equal opportunities model would envisage, including properly resourced education and training programmes, investment in child care facilities, and guarantees of flexible working opportunities available both to the mother and the father.

AFFIRMATIVE ACTION IN THE COURTS: THE EUROPEAN COURT AND THE US SUPREME COURT

The growing support for reverse discrimination has inevitably led to a spate of cases challenging the legitimacy of such policies in Community law. Faced with the need to reconcile reverse discrimination with the principle of equality embedded in Community law, the European Court has found it difficult to generate coherent and predictable principles. This is not helped by the way in which European Court decisions are constructed: instead of permitting a lively debate in the form of majority and dissenting judgments, the appearance of unanimity is achieved at the cost of compromises which are often inscrutable. Thus the two major decisions thus far, *Kalanke* and *Marschall* are difficult to reconcile with each other. Although a valiant attempt is made in *Badeck* to crystallise the resulting principles, their rationale remains elusive and their internal coherence problematic. This contrasts with the sophisticated jurisprudence of the US Supreme Court where individual judges have been able to develop their own lines of argument, often widely divergent. The result has been as complex and unpredictable as that in the EU, as shifting majorities gain the ascendancy in different cases. Nevertheless, the underlying principles are more clearly articulated and therefore present a rich source of alternative approaches to those found in Community case law. In this section, I begin by considering European Court case law, and then turn to the alternative approaches found in American law.

The first major case challenging an affirmative action policy, *Kalanke*,[16] concerned one of the mildest forms of affirmative action, namely, the "tie break" policy pursued by the City of Bremen. According to this policy, if a man and a woman with the same qualifications applied for promotion, and women were under-represented in that grade, the woman was to be given priority. The European Court struck down the policy on the grounds of the breach of the Equal Treatment Directive. Both the Advocate General and the Court situated Community law within the equal opportunities model, taking their cue from

---

[15] B Hepple, "Discrimination and Equality of Opportunity—Northern Irish Lessons", (1990) 10 *Oxford Journal of Legal Studies* 408 at 411.

[16] See *Kalanke*, above n. 1.

Article 2(4) of the Equal Treatment Directive,[17] which expressly provides for an exception to the principle of equal treatment for measures which "promote equal opportunity for men and women, in particular by removing existing inequalities which affect women's opportunities" in their access to employment, vocational training and in their working conditions. *Kalanke* highlights the two main elements of an equal opportunities approach: a recognition of the limits of formal equality or equality of treatment, allied with a strong endorsement of the primacy of the individual. Thus the Court recognised that formal equality could well perpetuate disadvantage: equal treatment of two individuals may yield results which simply reflect their different starting points. It therefore accepted the legitimacy of measures which give an advantage to women with a view to improving their ability to compete equally with men in the labour market. However, this does not authorise measures which depart from the principle of individual merit. "National rules which guarantee women absolute and unconditional priority for appointment or promotion go beyond promoting equal opportunities and overstep the limits of the exception in Article 2(4) of the Directive".[18] Advocate General Tesauro goes even further than the Court in stressing the primacy of the individual: "In the final analysis must each individual's right not to be discriminated against on grounds of sex . . . yield to the rights of the disadvantaged group, in this case, women, in order to compensate for the discrimination suffered by that group in the past?"[19] Such a formulation of the problem makes it inevitable that the answer be in the negative. The attainment of numerical equality, he concludes, violates the right of each individual to equal treatment. Also central to the decision in *Kalanke* is the attempt to draw a clear line between equality of opportunity, which is acceptable, and between equality of results, which is illegitimate. Thus stated the Court: "In so far as it seeks to achieve equal representation of men and women in all grades and levels within a department, such a system substitutes for equality of opportunity as envisaged in Article 2(4) the equality of result which is only to be arrived at by providing equality of opportunity".[20] In any event, according to Tesauro, equality of results will remain illusory unless it is a natural consequence of equal opportunity measures.

Despite its endorsement of the equal opportunities principle, the Court omits to examine what an "equal opportunities" strategy would entail. The only clues are provided by the Advocate General, who appears to regard as legitimate, measures which are superficially discriminatory but in fact aim to neutralise the effects either of specific differences between men and women, or of past discrimination, or of continuing difficulties related to women's dual role. This entails a procedural version of equal opportunities, removing specific barriers; and leaves the legitimacy of substantive equal opportunities policies unresolved.

---

[17] Directive 76/207/EEC.
[18] *Kalanke*, above, n. 1, judgment of the Court at para. 22.
[19] *Kalanke*, above, n. 1, Opinion of AG Tesauro at para. 7.
[20] *Kalanke*, above, n. 1, judgment of the Court at para. 23.

Kalanke is also problematic in that its stress on individual merit in fact fails to solve the problem before it: a situation in which both parties competing for the particular job have, by definition, equal merit. Kalanke had no greater right on the assumed facts to be selected than the woman; and there was thus no question of an "innocent" person suffering detriment on the grounds of his sex. Given that there was no difference in merit, the Court's decision that gender cannot be used to tip the balance, even if the aim is to increase the participation of women in an under-represented area, implies that only a random selection, such as spinning a coin, would be acceptable.

The result in *Kalanke* clearly flew in the face of a widening consensus on the usefulness of affirmative action policies, particularly in the public sector. The European Commission itself was faced with the need to salvage its affirmative action strategies. It did so by arguing that the Court in *Kalanke* had not rejected all preference based policies, but only those which were automatic and left no scope for consideration of individual circumstances. The individualist concerns of the Court could be met, it suggested, by an affirmative action policy which permitted exceptions for individual men. It was this approach which was tested within two years in a second affirmative action case, *Marschall*.[21] *Marschall* differed from *Kalanke* only in that the requirement that equally qualified women be preferred to men was softened by a proviso allowing exceptions if "reasons specific to another candidate predominate". Despite the strong opinion of the Attorney General, who argued that there was no relevant distinction between this policy and that in *Kalanke*, the Court upheld the plan. Thus the Court held, Article 2(4) permitted a rule which gave priority to the promotion of female candidates where there were fewer women than men in the relevant post and both female and male candidates for the post were equally qualified, as long as the priority accorded to female candidates could in principle be overridden where an objectively assessed individual criterion tilted the balance in favour of the male candidate.[22]

This conclusion, like that in *Kalanke*, attempts to combine a substantive notion of equality with a continuing commitment to the primacy of the individual. Thus the Court focuses specifically on the mandate given in Article 2(4) to move beyond formal equality to a substantive notion, reiterating its view that "Article 2(4) is specifically and exclusively designed to authorise measures which, although discriminatory in appearance, are in fact intended to eliminate or reduce actual instances of inequality which may exist in the reality of social life".[23] Indeed it goes beyond *Kalanke* in its refusal to accept at face value the objectivity of the merit principle itself. Instead, it recognises that an apparently objective, merit-based system can incorporate prejudicial assumptions: "Even where male and female candidates are equally qualified, male candidates tend to

---

[21] *Marschall*, above, n. 1.

[22] *Marschall*, above n. 1, at para. 35.

[23] *Marschall*, above n. 1, at para. 26; and see Case 312/86 *Commission* v. *France* [1988] ECR I–6315 (para. 15) and *Kalanke*, above n. 1, at para. 18.

be promoted in preference to female candidates particularly because of prejudices and stereotypes concerning the role and capacities of women in working life and the fear, for example, that women will interrupt their careers more frequently, that owing to household and family duties they will be less flexible in their working hours, or that they will be absent from work more frequently because of pregnancy, childbirth and breast-feeding".[24] Thus a measure giving preference to women candidates where men and women are equally qualified may fall within Article 2(4) if, subject to a savings clause, such a rule "may counteract the prejudicial effects on female candidates of the attitudes and behaviour described above and thus reduce actual instances of inequality which may exist in the real world".[25] However, despite this apparently robust notion of substantive equality, the Court will not give up the adherence to individuality which it evidenced so strongly in *Kalanke*. In a statement which is almost entirely devoid of reasoned support, the Court declares that a measure which guarantees absolute and unconditional priority to women goes beyond the limits of Article 2(4). By contrast, a rule which provides a guarantee of individual assessment which could override the presumption of priority to women remains within the scope of that provision.

It is difficult to see what difference such a savings clause could make in practice. A male applicant could not claim to be more meritorious than the woman competitor, since by definition, merit is equal. Nor could he rely on age, seniority or breadwinner status since, as the Court recognised, this would simply be reintroducing exclusionary or indirectly discriminatory criteria. It is possible that an alternative source of discrimination, such as race or disability, might rebut the presumption, but some further guidance would be needed to assist a court or decision-maker to balance the claims of a woman against those of other victims of discrimination. If indeed there is no way of giving meaning to this clause, then the Court is upholding a plan which does not differ in substance from that in *Kalanke*.

Moreover, the justification for the outcome in *Marschall* is limited to tie-break measures. It gives no guidance to the Court as to how to deal with measures which are not premised on equal qualification, but instead require quotas for jobs or membership of decision-making bodies. Yet it is precisely here that future challenges lie. Statistical objectives or quotas are a central part of the Commission's strategy to achieve balanced participation for men and women in decision-making.[26] Gender specific programmes to achieve a higher level of representation of women in public bodies are already in use, particularly in Germany,[27] where, in the state of Schleswig-Holstein, for example, the general

---

[24] *Marschall*, above n. 1, at para 29.

[25] *Marschall*, above n. 1, at para. 31.

[26] Medium Term Community Action Programme on Equal Opportunities for Women and Men: see *Equal Opportunities Magazine* No. 2, July 1997; and Recommendation 96/694/EC, [1996] OJ L319.

[27] All the examples of German measures are taken from N Colneric, "Making Equality Law More Effective: Lessons from the German Experience", (1996) 3 *Cardozo Women's Law Journal* 229 at 239. [Editors note: In summer 2000, Niran Celnetic was appointed as German Judge at the Court of Justice, only the second woman to be appointed as Judge.]

rule states that, where only one seat can be nominated or delegated, alternating preferences should be given to men and women. Similarly, explicit measures have been instituted to ensure that women are represented on works' and personnel councils. In Britain, the Labour Party introduced all-women short-lists in half of all winnable seats in 1993. This policy, although eventually declared unlawful,[28] was a major factor in almost trebling the number of Labour women MPs returned to Parliament after the 1997 election.[29] A similar approach is evident in respect of training. Even in Britain, in which a symmetrical approach to affirmative action in predominant, "women only" training programmes are permitted where it can be shown that women are under-represented in a trade or profession. The same is true of training schemes set aside for black or other minority workers.

To what extent then can the principles in *Marschall* be used to address differently formulated affirmative action programmes? Its first major challenge came in the form of *Badeck*,[30] a more far-reaching and sophisticated affirmative action programme than those in the two earlier cases. The case concerned an Act of Parliament of the German State of Hesse, which mandates "*Frauenförderung*" plans to remedy the under-representation of women in public offices. There are several elements to these schemes. First, more than half of the posts to be filled in a sector in which women are under-represented are to be designated for filling by women, unless it can be convincingly demonstrated that not enough women with the necessary qualifications are available. If measures are taken to abolish posts, it must be ensured that the proportion of women in the affected sector remains the same. Secondly, fixed term academic posts are to be filled with at least the same proportion of women as the proportion of women among the graduates in the discipline in question. Thirdly, in trained occupations in which women are under-represented, at least half of the available training places must be allocated to women. Fourthly, in sectors in which women are under-represented, at least as many women as men, or all the women applicants, must be called to interview if they satisfy the conditions for appointment to the post in question. Finally, at least half the members of commissions, advisory boards, boards of directors and supervisory boards, and other collective bodies should be women. Equally important is the attempt to address the difficulties, outlined above, with the merit principle. In assessing qualifications, the Hesse statute specifies that the capabilities and experience which have been acquired by looking after children or other persons requiring care must be taken into account in so far as they are of importance for the suitability of applicants. On the other hand, the family status or income of the partner may not be taken into account; nor may part-time work, leaves or delays in completing training as a result of looking after children or other dependants. Seniority, age and the

---

[28] *Jepson* v. *The Labour Party* [1996] IRLR 16.

[29] See M Eagle and J Lovenduski, *High Time or High Tide for Labour Women* (Fabian Pamphlet 585, 1998).

[30] See *Badeck*, above n. 1.

date of the last promotion may be taken in to account only in so far as they are of importance for the suitability, performance and capability of applicants. The "savings" clause is also more sophisticated than that in *Marschall*. Thus the rule of advancement of women may be overridden in five specified cases. The first two place actual parenting responsibilities ahead of gender preference, whether the input is from a man or a woman. Thus priority must be given to individuals who have taken time out of work or worked on a part-time basis in order to look after children or other dependants. The fourth and the fifth give similar recognition to other social priorities, allowing the preferential treatment rule to be overridden in order to promote disabled persons or to end a period of long-term unemployment. It is only the third which could potentially tip the balance back in favour of men, namely preference given to those who served longer than the compulsory period of military service; and even then only marginally.

The challenge to the Hesse provisions confronted the Court with two of the main aspects of the principle it had established in *Kalanke*: the primacy of the individual, and the difference between equality of opportunity and equality of results. Thus, the applicants argued, the Hesse statute contravened the merit principle by choosing candidates not because of their merits, but because of their sex. Moreover, it breached the rights of all individuals to equal opportunities at the start, by attempting to ensure results which were advantageous to a specific category of persons. The Court, however, side-stepped these principled arguments in favour of a formulaic approach. That is, having rehearsed the findings in *Kalanke* and *Marschall*, it distilled a two-part formula which it proceeded to apply to each of the elements of the case before it. The formula, representing in large part the approach in *Marschall* rather than *Kalanke*, would make a measure giving priority to women in under-represented sectors of the public service compatible with Community law if (i) it does not automatically and unconditionally give priority to women when women and men are equally qualified; and (ii) the candidatures are the subject of an objective assessment which takes into account the specific personal situations of all candidates.[31] Although the European Court held that it is for the national court to determine whether these conditions are fulfilled, it went on to use its powers to supply the national court with an interpretation of Community law so that the latter could properly determine the issue. Applying the formula to each element of the scheme, the Court held the scheme as a whole to be compatible with the Equal Treatment Directive. *A fortiori*, it would be compatible with the new affirmative action provisions contained in Article 141(4), as introduced by the Amsterdam Treaty.

This formulaic approach differs markedly from that of Advocate General Saggio, whose opinion attempts to develop some of the principles in the previous cases, and in particular reiterates the dual emphasis on substantive equality and the primacy of the individual. The reconciliation of the two, he argues, lies

---

[31] *Badeck*, above n. 1, at para. 23.

in the development of a proportionality criterion. Equal treatment, or formal equality, comes into conflict with substantive equality only if the remedial measure, in this case positive action in favour of women, is disproportionate, either in that it demands excessive sacrifices from those who do not belong to the group, or when the social reality does not justify it. Positive action could therefore be lawful provided it is proportionate in this sense. However, individual merit, in his view, remains the governing principle behind the reconciliation of equality with reverse discrimination. Provided an appointment or promotion is made on the basis of an individual's suitability and qualifications for the job, it is permissible to use sex as a secondary criterion, tilting the balance in favour of women in order to remedy an under-representation of women in a particular grade or occupation. It is only therefore permissible to institute automatic preferences for women to redress under-representation if there is an objective examination of the professional and personal profile of each candidate and there is no bar on the selection of a man if he is more suitable for the job. This is turn requires merit to be purified of discriminatory assumptions, and thereafter insists that merit is the only basis of equality in selection.

Such arguments are, however, conspicuously absent in the Court's judgment in *Badeck*. Their absence makes it difficult to deal with situations which move beyond a tie-break, and require the selection of a woman, even if she is not equally qualified with a man, in order to improve the proportion of women in a particular grade or career. This question has already been faced by the Court, in respect of a Swedish scheme, aimed at increasing the number of female professors. In that case, regulations required that a person from the under-represented sex who had the necessary qualifications should get the post even if she was less qualified than a candidate from the opposite sex, unless the difference between the applicant's qualifications and the qualifications of a candidate of the opposite sex was so great that the application of the rule would offend against common sense. In *Abrahamsson and Anderson* v. *Fogelqvist*,[32] the board of nomination at the University of Gothenburg had recommended that a man be appointed to a vacant professorship. However, the principal of the institution instead appointed a woman, claiming that the difference in merit between her and the male aspirant was not large enough to displace the presumption in favour of women. The Court concluded that the Swedish scheme infringed the principle of equal treatment. In doing so, the court made it clear that its support for substantive equality was subordinate to the primacy of the individual. It was not enough to make a selection based on the 'mere fact of belonging to the under-represented sex'.

It is thus worth looking to the sophisticated jurisprudence of the USA to discover alternate means to deal with affirmative action. The US Supreme Court has in fact been the arena of fierce struggle between judicial proponents of a symmetrical view of equality and those who advocate a more substantive posi-

---

[32] Case C–407/98, judgment of 6 July 2000.

tion. The use of affirmative action policies began in the USA as a court-ordered remedy for cases of proven past discrimination.[33] This approach was upheld by the Supreme Court,[34] and indeed extended to cases under the Equal Protection Clause of the US Constitution. The Supreme Court in these cases, having signalled a clear departure from an abstract, formal view of justice, soon began to move beyond both individualism and the idea of a neutral state. As a start, it has been accepted that court-ordered reverse discrimination need not be restricted to the victim. Non-victims may also be beneficiaries provided they are members of a group previously suffering from invidious discrimination.[35] In addition, the emphasis on both fault and merit have been weakened. Thus the Supreme Court soon began to accept voluntarily instituted affirmative action programmes, despite the lack of proven fault on the part of the employer. Instead, the focus is again on the social context in which the equality concept operates: in upholding voluntary affirmative action programmes, the Court has only required sufficient evidence of imbalances and segregation for which the employer appears responsible,[36] not proof of fault against the defendant.

This approach is exemplified in *Johnson* v. *Santa Clara*[37] which, like *Kalanke* and *Marschall*, concerned a voluntarily instituted affirmative action plan for hiring and promoting women and minorities in a context of severe under-representation of both groups in the workforce. The aim was expressly result-oriented, the target being a statistically measurable yearly improvement in hiring and promotion, so as ultimately to achieve a workforce of which about a third of jobs were held by women. The *Johnson* plan was more flexible than that of *Kalanke*, in that the sex of a qualified applicant was only a factor among several to be considered. It was also more controversial in that a woman could be promoted even if she was marginally less well qualified than a male applicant. The plan was challenged when a qualified woman was promoted ahead of a man to the position of road dispatcher, a grade in which to date none of the 238 positions had been held by a woman. The male employee, who in fact had a marginally better test score, complained of sex discrimination contrary to Title VII. The *Johnson* policy received warm judicial endorsement. Brennan J, giving judgment for the court, declared that it was no violation of Title VII to take sex into account in promoting a woman over a male employee where this was in pursuance of an affirmative action plan to remedy the under-representation of women and minorities in traditionally segregated job classifications.

Similarly, the US Supreme Court has rejected the neutral view of the state, instead upholding both the right and the responsibility of the state to use its public and market powers in remedying discrimination. Thus in *Fullilove* v. *Klutznick*[38] the Supreme Court upheld a policy setting aside 10 per cent of

---

[33]   Mandated by Title VII of the Civil Rights Act 1964.

[34]   *Franks* v. *Bowman Transportation Co.* 424 US 747, 96 S. Ct. 1251 (1975).

[35]   *US* v. *Paradise* 480 US 149 (1988), 107 S. Ct. 1053.

[36]   *United Steel Workers* v. *Weber* 442 US 193 (1979).

[37]   107 S. Ct. 1442 (1987), 480 US 616.

[38]   448 US 448 (1980); 100 S. Ct. 2758.

federal funds granted for the provision of public works to procure services from minority-owned businesses, even if the latter were not the lowest bidder. Chief Justice Burger stated specifically that in a remedial context, it was not necessary for Congress to act in a wholly colour-blind way. Indeed, substantive reverse discrimination of this sort was viewed as a necessary means to achieve equal economic opportunities.

However, recent cases in the USA have been marked by the ascendancy of a far more symmetrical approach. This is reflected in the controversies within the case law on two main issues: the "innocent" third party who is discriminated against on grounds of race or sex in the process of preferring minorities or women; and the standard of scrutiny. So far as the "innocent third party" is concerned, the Court has attempted to reach a balance (not dissimilar to that hinted at by the Advocate General in *Badeck*) whereby individuals who are not members of the target group are not expected to bear too great a burden in redressing the disadvantage of the preferred group. Thus while it is permissible to reserve jobs, promotions or training places, to which no-one has an absolute right, loss of a job (for example in a redundancy situation) has been held to be too serious a prospect to permit individual interests to be subordinated. The result has been that, except in the case of identified victims of discrimination, the vested interests of "dispreferred" workers to retain seniority rights and therefore remain in work have generally trumped the goals of achieving and maintaining a balanced workforce. The effects of this compromise are evident in *Wygant* v. *Jackson Board of Education*,[39] in which a collective agreement was struck down as contrary to the Fourteenth Amendment because it gave preferential protection against layoffs to minority employees. The result was, however, largely to undermine the effects of positive action programmes incorporating under-represented workers: such workers were the "last in" and therefore inevitably the "first out".

The second controversial issue in American case law concerns the standard of scrutiny which should be applied in affirmative action cases. The Supreme Court has a well developed jurisprudence requiring "strict scrutiny" of any classifications which burden blacks: such a classification must serve a compelling governmental interest and be narrowly tailored to achieve that aim.[40] In practice, the insistence on strict scrutiny has outlawed most racist policies or practices discriminating against blacks. This raises the question: does an equally strict standard of review apply to racial classifications which benefit blacks at the expense of whites? American case law is criss-crossed with deeply conflicting judicial statements on this point. In *Bakke*, Powell J, consistent with his symmetrical stance, was unequivocal in his rejection of the argument that strict scrutiny applies only to classifications that disadvantage discrete and insular minorities. Instead, he argued, all kinds of race-conscious criteria should be sub-

---

[39]   106 S. Ct. 1842 (1986).
[40]   *Korematsu* v. *US* [1944] 323 US 214.

ject to the "most exacting of judicial examination".[41] By contrast four judges (Brennan, White, Marshall and Blackmunn JJ), taking a substantive asymmetric view, held that a less stringent standard of review should apply to racial classifications designed to further remedial purposes than to pernicious classifications. On this view, it was sufficient for the policy to be "substantially related" to the achievement of an important government objective, a standard known as intermediate review.[42] However, the case was inconclusive on this issue since four other judges, having decided the case on statutory grounds, did not address the standard. Similarly indecisive were the later cases of *Fullilove* v. *Klutznick*[43] and *Wygant* v. *Jackson Board of Education*.[44] It was not until the 1989 case of *City of Richmond* v. *JSA Croson*[45] that the symmetrical insistence on strict scrutiny received majority support in the Supreme Court, and then only in respect of local and state policy. It remained only to apply the same standard to action by the federal government. This was done, in the face of a strong dissent, in *Adarand* v. *Pena*.[46] Ultimately therefore, the exacting standard of strict scrutiny has won the day; even at the level of the federal government, all racial classifications should now be subjected to strict scrutiny.

However, a closer examination of the judgments in *Adarand* reveals that the dispute between the asymmetric and the symmetric approaches continues despite the triumph of strict scrutiny. While O'Connor J agreed with Thomas and Scalia on the standard of strict scrutiny, in fact their interpretation of that standard differed markedly. Thomas and Scalia JJ upheld the strict standard from a strongly symmetrical and individualistic camp. However, O'Connor J, giving judgment for the court, articulated a sensitive synthesis of the difficult opposing views. She was at pains to dispute the notion that strict scrutiny is strict in theory but fatal in fact.[47] Indeed, she held, the federal government might well have a compelling interest to act on the basis of race to overcome the "persistence of both the practice and lingering effects of racial discrimination against minority groups".[48] In this respect, her approach incorporates important elements of the clearly substantive view expressed in dissent by Stevens J,[49] who rejected the strict scrutiny standard by reasserting the fundamental difference between a policy designed to perpetuate a caste system and one seeking to eliminate racial discrimination.

In most post-*Adarand* cases, the controversy has primarily occurred in respect of voting rights. The clear discrimination against blacks in the USA, effectively depriving them of the vote, led to a systematic positive action

---

[41] *Bakke*, above n. 5.
[42] *Fullilove* v. *Klutznick*, above n. 38, per Marshall J.
[43] Above n. 38.
[44] Above n. 39.
[45] 488 US 469 (1989).
[46] Above n. 6.
[47] *Adarand*, above n. 6, at 2117.
[48] Rehnquist, Kennedy and Thomas JJ all agreed.
[49] Joined by Souter, Ginsburg and Breyer JJ.

programme. This included, as a central strategy, the redrawing of electoral districts to give black voters a better opportunity to influence the outcome of elections.[50] The deliberate creation of districts with black majorities has caused deep controversy within the USA, particularly in recent years.[51] Not surprisingly, it has led to a spate of litigation,[52] in which the Supreme Court has been required to decide whether such gerrymandering is necessary to ensure that blacks have equal opportunity to elect representatives of their choice, or, whether it reinforces harmful racial stereotypes and impedes progress towards a multi-racial society. The divergence between those members of the Supreme Court who take a substantive approach and those who take a symmetrical approach emerges more clearly than ever. Thus in the 1996 case of *Shaw* v. *Hunt*,[53] the majority struck down a congressionally mandated redistricting plan on the ground that it was not narrowly tailored to serve a compelling state interest. Rehnquist J for the Court declared emphatically that all laws classifying on racial grounds are constitutionally suspect. This is true even if the reason is benign or the purpose remedial. This fiercely symmetrical approach was countered for the minority by Stevens J, who declared that the sorry state of race relations in North Carolina was sufficient reason to attempt to facilitate greater participation of blacks in the electoral process. The crucial casting vote remained that of O'Connor J, who attempted, as she did in *Adarand*, to use the strict scrutiny test in a way which was sensitive to the range of conflicting interests. Most importantly she has reaffirmed her position that strict scrutiny should not be equated with total prohibition of affirmative action. Thus she declared in *Bush* v. *Vera* that the state could indeed have a compelling interest in pursuing equality of opportunity of voters to elect representatives of their choice; and that it was possible to find means which were "narrowly tailored to those ends" by producing electoral districts which aim to produce black majorities, but which do not deviate too much from established districting principles.[54] By contrast, the strictly symmetrical judges (although concurring with O'Connor J) make it extremely difficult if not impossible to justify deliberate use of race in drawing districts.[55] At the same time, a vocal minority[56] continues to advocate a more substantive approach.

---

[50] Voting Rights Act 1965, amended in 1982 to include a "results-based" test to ascertain whether the right had been violated.

[51] See, e.g., A Thernstrom, "Voting Rights: Another Affirmative Action Mess", (1996) 43 *UCLA Law Review* 2031.

[52] *Shaw* v. *Reno* 509 US 630 (1993); *Miller* v. *Johnson* 115 S. Ct. 2431 (1995); *US* v. *Hays* 115 S. Ct. 2431 (1995); *Bush* v. *Vera* 116 S. Ct. 1941 (1996).

[53] 116 S CT 1894 (1996).

[54] *Bush*, above n. 52 at 1969–70.

[55] *Bush*, above n. 52, at 1971 per Kennedy J; at 1972–3 per Thomas and Scalia JJ.

[56] Stevens, Ginsburg and Breyer JJ.

AIMS AND EFFECTIVENESS

The discussion above has demonstrated that the principled objections to affirmative action can be plausibly repudiated. The ferocity of the controversy over its legitimacy has, however, deflected attention away from an equally problematic issue: what are its aims, and is affirmative action effective in achieving those aims? The European Court has made little progress in explicating means and ends. The *Kalanke* case simply outlaws affirmative action.[57] *Marschall*, although reaching the opposite results, avoids any sustained discussion either of which aims are legitimate and the extent to which the means must fit the ends. Although the Advocate General in *Badeck* explicitly introduces a proportionality test, he too does not suggest legitimate ends or the standard of scrutiny of the means. By contrast, the "strict scrutiny" test used by the American courts, requires a demonstration of legitimate state aims, and of means that are narrowly tailored to achieve those ends. This has forced the US Supreme Court to grapple with these questions. In the course of discussion, several aims of affirmative action have been articulated. These can be grouped under three main headings: namely, (i) the removal of discriminatory barriers or redressing past disadvantage, (ii) the representation of the interests of the previously excluded group, and (iii) the fostering of diversity and the creation of role models.

Removal of barriers and redressing past disadvantage

The use of reverse discrimination as a remedy for past discrimination is, as has been seen, well known in the USA. A closer look at the cases of both *Kalanke* and *Marschall* reveals a similar strategic impulse to remove discriminatory barriers within the German public services. Despite apparently objective eligibility standards, there are many hidden obstacles to women's advancement.[58] This is because the assessment process in the German public services normally gravitates towards uniform results. Faced with numerous equally qualified candidates, the selectors have created auxiliary selection criteria, the most prominent ones being duration of service, age and number of dependants. It is well established that all these criteria, despite being equally applicable to both men and women, in practice exclude substantially more women than men. Against this background, the tie-break provisions introduced by the City of Bremen can be seen to be part of a strategic attempt to overcome hidden barriers to women's advancement. Indeed, both the Court in *Marschall* and the Advocate General in *Badeck* were aware of this process, noting, in *Marschall*, that the "mere fact that

---

[57] See AG Jacobs' opinion in *Marschall*, above n. 1.
[58] D Schiek, "More Positive Action in Community Law", [1998] *ILJ* 155; D Schiek, "Positive Action in Community Law", [1996] *ILJ* 239.

a male candidate and a female candidate are equally qualified does not mean that they have the same chances".

Redressing past discrimination and removing present barriers are clearly legitimate state interests. More difficult, however, is the question whether the use of gender or race preferences is a means which is "narrowly tailored" to achieve those ends. On the assumption that, in the absence of barriers, there would be a random spread of men and women, and members of different ethnic groups across the labour force and government, the very fact that a group is seriously under-represented in a sphere or activity is evidence of the subtle operation of often invisible barriers. Yet could this not be dealt with by the familiar principle of indirect discrimination? Indirect discrimination expressly aims to remove apparently neutral barriers which in fact function to exclude more women than men unless they can be justified.[59] However, it has proved to be too clumsy a tool to achieve its aims. The apparently clear legislative definition of indirect discrimination in British law leaves a host of questions unanswered. Must the "requirement or condition" be an absolute bar? And what is the "proportion" a proportion of? The whole population or just a part of it, such as the working population, the establishment or other individuals with the same qualifications? Applicants seeking to prove indirect discrimination have found that the courts give varying and often unpredictable answers to these questions.[60] Equally problematic, it is left to an individual victim to initiate court proceedings and argue each of these issues. Finally, even if she can surmount all these barriers, she may find that an employer successfully shows that the criteria, despite being exclusionary, are justifiable by reference to the needs of the business.

Affirmative action resolves all of these difficulties. Instead of relying on litigation by individual victims, the employer takes the initiative. Nor is it necessary to prove that an exclusionary rule has had a disproportionate impact. Instead, it is sufficient to demonstrate a clear pattern of under-representation of women in particular grades or occupations. The complex questions above are unnecessary. Moreover, discriminatory selection criteria are unequivocally removed; by creating a presumption in favour of women in conditions of equal merit, it makes it impossible for such criteria to be reintroduced surreptitiously through subjective decision-making.

Phrased in this way, affirmative action can be legitimated as an effective means of overcoming hidden barriers. At the same time, this formulation reveals its very limited impact. Most importantly, while preference policies may change the gender or racial composition of some higher paid occupations, they do not challenge the underlying structural and institutional forces leading to the discrimination. As Young argues,[61] because affirmative action diagnoses the prob-

---

[59] Sex Discrimination Act 1975, s. 1(1)(b)(i).

[60] For a recent example see Case 167/97 *Seymour Smith* [1999] IRLR 253. For further discussion see S Fredman, *Women and the Law* (Oxford, Oxford University Press, 1997) 287–300.

[61] I M Young, *Justice and the Politics of Difference* (Princeton, NJ, Princeton University Press, 1990) 193.

lem as one of maldistribution of privileged positions, its objective is limited to the redistribution of such positions among under-represented groups. However, this narrow distributive definition of racial and gender justice leaves out the equally important issues of institutional organisation and decision-making power. The under-representation of women in higher positions in the employment ladder, both public and private, is only partially solved by inserting some women into those positions. While some women "make it to the top", the vast majority will remain in poorly-paid, low status jobs. It is not surprising that in practice, reverse discrimination is often found to do no more than favour middle class women or blacks who are already relatively privileged in society. This outcome is particularly striking in India, where it has been found that the main beneficiaries of affirmative action programmes reserving benefits for members of scheduled castes and tribes (SC/ST categories) were those who were already upwardly mobile and already had some resources. Indeed, Menski points out: "The benefits of the SC/ST category are now snatched away and appropriated by a thin elite layer of SC/ST members and their offspring, while the vast majority remain as backward and disadvantaged as ever".[62] For fundamental change to occur, the structural and institutional causes of exclusion need to be changed, including the division of labour in the home, the interaction between work in the family and work in the paid labour force, education and others. Indeed, this insight was recognised and articulated by Attorney General Tesauro in *Kalanke* when he said: "Formal numerical equality is an objective which may salve some consciences, but it will remain illusory . . . unless it goes together with measures which are genuinely destined to achieve equality . . . In the final analysis, that which is necessary above all is a substantial change in the economic, social and cultural model which is at the root of the inequalities".[63]

Representation and perspective

A more dynamic way of justifying the use of affirmative action policies is to argue that the very presence of women or minorities in higher status positions will lead to structural changes. On this argument, women or minorities in such positions will be able to represent the needs and interests of their groups in decision-making, changing both the agenda of decision-making and their outcomes. Women will, for example, be in a position to argue for maternity leave, child care and family friendly policies, thus paving the way for more women to enter these positions. This representative function is important, on this view, for both formal decision-making institutions such as legislatures or trade union executive bodies, and for informal decision-making. Managers, civil servants, judges,

---

[62] W F Menski, "The Indian Experience and its Lessons for Britain" in B Hepple and E Szyszczak (eds), *Discrimination and the Limits of Law* (London, Mansell Cassell, 1992) 300 at 330.

[63] *Kalanke*, above n. 1, at para. 28.

professionals and chief administrators make a host of decisions, all of which require that the interests of women or minorities be properly represented.

This has indeed been the rationale driving recent moves at EU level to achieve balanced participation of men and women in decision-making. At a conference in April 1999, Padraig Flynn, who was then the responsible Commissioner, emphasised that increasing the numbers of women in decision-making was crucial not only to achieve the "quantitative objective of a numerical balance of women and men" but also the "qualitative objective of improving decision-making". Citing studies which revealed that a critical mass of about 30 per cent of women was needed to "create the necessary dynamic" to allow women's concerns, needs and interests to be taken into account, he went on to declare that "the different but complementary and mutually enriching views of men and women should be reflected in all policies shaping the citizen's life".[64]

However, more support is needed to underpin the assumption that the mere presence of women will guarantee that women's interests will be articulated. As Phillips puts it, we generally reject a politics of presence in favour of a politics of ideas. "The shift from direct to representative democracy has shifted the emphasis from *who* the politicians are to *what* (policies, preferences, ideas), they represent, and in doing so has made accountability to the electorate the pre-eminent radical concern".[65] Two possible arguments could be mounted to justify the renewed emphasis on presence, but both turn out to be problematic. The first is to argue that any woman or minority will inevitably articulate the needs, interests and concerns of other women or minorities. Her presence is therefore all that is needed. This appears to be the basis of Commissioner Flynn's unhesitating assertion that women and men have different views. However, although there is some evidence that women may have a different moral sense to men,[66] modern feminists are acutely aware of the range of differing interests among women, and indeed of the potential for conflict. Attempts to construct an "essential woman" merely land up replicating the dominant ideology about women, obscuring crucial differences in class, race, sexual orientation etc. This is equally true of minority groups; the assumption that black groups share common interests merely veils deep differences based on religion, country of origin or language.

A second way of justifying the representative function of affirmative action is to accept that the mere presence of women is not sufficient, but to argue instead that women beneficiaries of affirmative action are there as genuine representatives of other women. But this in turn requires some mechanism of accountability. Our experience of the Thatcher years demonstrated clearly that a woman in power is not necessarily a representative of women's interests. Indeed, she may have achieved power partly because she was able to conform to a male ethic and

---

[64] See http://europa.eu.int/comm/dg05/index_en.htm

[65] A Phillips, *The Politics of Presence*, (Oxford, Clarendon Press, 1995) 4.

[66] See C Gilligan, *In a Different Voice* (Cambridge, Harvard University Press, 1982) especially ch. 5.

thereby suppress any belief in the importance of articulating women's concerns. There are no mechanisms for accountability in affirmative action plans in public or private employment, and even on decision-making bodies, including the legislature, women decision-makers are not cast as accountable to women constituents. Even if there was such a link, it is not clear that representation of a minority interest could make an impact on decisions. Indeed, minority representation could well consign a group to perpetual defeat.

There is, however, a third and more promising way to justify the use of affirmative action policies to improve the extent to which women's concerns are addressed. This is to argue, as Young does, that decision-making is wrongly conceived of as a process of bargaining between interests groups, each of which represents a fixed set of interests, and whose representatives are mandated to further those interests and to compromise only as a *quid pro quo*.[67] Instead, it is argued, decision-making is a result of communication and discussion based on more than egotistical impulses, but on a desire to reach a fair and reasoned result.[68] Participants are prepared to recognise others' concerns and beliefs in their own right, not just in order to wrest return favours catering for their constituents' interests. In addition, this approach does not take an abstract, impartial view of rationality, but recognises that the particular life experience of the decision-maker is reflected in his or her view. Since gender and race remain such strong determinants of a person's life experience, the overwhelming predominance of one gender or race in decision-making fora make it unlikely that the experience and perspectives of the excluded group will be articulated.[69] Indeed, a recent study in Britain demonstrated that the biggest barrier to advancement for ethnic minorities, women and disabled people within the senior Civil Service is believed to be a deeply embedded culture which acts to exclude those who are different from traditional Civil Service employees, who are generally middle class middle-aged white men.[70] On this view, it is possible to characterise women's presence as functioning to open up new perspectives on decision-making, to cast light on assumptions that the dominant group perceives as universal, and to enhance the store of "social knowledge".

Corresponding to the rejection of interest group politics is a rejection of the notion of fixed interest groups. As Young convincingly argues, groups are better understood, not as fixed categories with impermeable boundaries, but as a set of relationships between different people. Such a relational understanding replaces the notion that a group consists of members who all share the same fixed attributes and have nothing in common with members of other groups with an idea of a group as a social process of interaction in which some people have an affinity with each other. Assertion of affinity with a group may change with social context and with life changes, and members may have interests

---

[67] Young, above n. 61, at 118–19.
[68] Young, above n. 61, at 92–4.
[69] Phillips, above n. 65, at 52.
[70] *Equal Opportunities Review* No. 87 (1999) 4.

which differ from other members of the group but are similar to members of other groups.[71] This approach makes sense of the notion that women or minorities may have distinct perspectives, which the very process of exclusion negates, and therefore which need to be guaranteed a place in deliberative decision-making. But it also makes it unnecessary to conceive of women or minorities as groups with a fixed essence, or indeed to require women to perform a specific representative function. In addition, it makes sense of the view that a critical mass is needed both to reflect a diversity within the social group in question and to make the common interests more audible.

Role models and diversity

The pursuit of diversity and the provision of role models are related goals which draw on the insights discussed above in relation to the importance of minority perspectives in influencing decisions. The principle behind diversity was clearly articulated by the US Supreme Court, Powell J, in the famous *Bakke*[72] case in the context of an affirmative action plan relating to admissions of students to medical college: "An otherwise qualified medical student with a particular background—whether it be ethnic, geographic, culturally advantaged or disadvantaged—may bring to a professional school of medicine, experiences, outlook, and ideas that enrich the training of its student body and better equip its graduates to render with understanding their vital service to humanity".[73] In other words, where a group has been excluded from a particular setting, be it a workforce or an educational institution, the likelihood is that the perspectives and experiences of members of the excluded group, particularly those relating to its exclusion, will be undervalued, misunderstood or ignored by the dominant group, making it impossible for the excluded group to change its disadvantaged position. While diversity operates to change the perspectives of the dominant group, the provision of role models operates on the self perception of excluded groups, piercing stereotypes and giving them the self-confidence to move into non-traditional positions.

Both these aims have been highly controversial in American case law. In *Bakke*, Powell J considered that diversity could be a factor which might tip the balance in favour of a minority student in competition with another similar applicant. However, this did not receive explicit support from the other judgments in the case. More recently, the US Court of Appeals emphatically rejected the argument, put forward by University of Texas law school, that its policy of giving substantial preference in its admissions program to blacks and Mexican Americans was justifiable on the grounds of the educational benefits that flow

---

[71] Young, above n. 61, at 171–2.
[72] *Bakke*, above n. 5.
[73] *Bakke*, above n. 5, at 2760.

from a racially and ethnically diverse student body.[74] Taking a narrowly individualist view of affirmative action, the Court held that diversity contradicts rather than furthers the aims of equal protection. By treating minorities as a group, rather than as individuals, the judge argued, it uses racial criteria unlawfully, undercutting the goal of the Fourteenth Amendment, namely, the end of racially motivated state action. A similar trend is visible in relation to the provision of role models. Thus Powell J in *Bakke* accepted as permissible the goals of supplying more professional people for under-served communities although he did not see this (or educational diversity) as necessitating a quota system. However, in *Wygant*,[75] the defendant Board of Education argued, *inter alia*, that its policy of protecting newly-hired minority teachers against layoffs was justified by the state's duty to reduce racial discrimination by providing minority role models for minority students. This Powell J roundly rejected on the grounds that it would permit affirmative action long past the point of its remedial purpose.

The arguments in both these cases can, however, be countered. The view that using race to promote educational diversity is impermissible is based on an explicit rejection of the ways in which race (or gender) affect a person's life experience, opportunities and perspectives. According to Circuit Judge Smith: "To believe that a person's race controls his point of view is to stereotype him." Yet the same judge was prepared to accept that a university may properly favour one applicant over another because of issues such as an applicant's relationship to school alumni, whether an applicant's parents attended college or the applicant's economic and social background. As argued above, there is no need to assume that a person's race "controls" her point of view; indeed that would be wrongly to essentialise her. But this is not to say that her particular cultural, social and personal perspectives have not been influenced by her gender or her race; nor that the perspectives of the dominant group have not been similarly influenced in a way that excludes others. The rejection of the need for role models rests on a similarly tenuous base.

An immensely valuable counter is provided by the Supreme Court of Canada. As Chief Justice Dickson put it in a recent case,[76] the aim of an employment equity programme (in this case setting a quota of one woman in four new hirings until a goal of 13 per cent women in certain blue collar occupations was reached) is not to compensate past victims, but "an attempt to ensure that future applicants and workers from the affected group will not face the same insidious barriers that blocked their forebears".[77] He identified at least two ways in which such a programme is likely to be more effective than one which simply relies on equal opportunities or the proscription of intentional prejudice. First, the insistence that women be placed in non-traditional jobs allows them to prove that

---

[74] *Hopwood* v. *Texas* 78 F.3d 932 (5th Cir., 1996).
[75] See above n. 39.
[76] *Action Travail des Femmes* v. *Canadian National Railway Co* 40 D.L.R. (4th) 193.
[77] *Canadian National Railway*, above n. 76, at 213.

they really can do the job, thereby dispelling stereotypes about women's abilities. This was particularly evident in the case at hand, in which the quotas ordered by the tribunal concerned traditionally male jobs such as "brakeman" or signaller at Canadian National Railways. Secondly, an employment equity programme helps to create a "critical mass" of women in the workplace. Once a significant number of women are represented in a particular type of work, "there is a significant chance for the continuing self-correction of the system".[78] The critical mass overcomes the problem of tokenism, which would leave a few women isolated and vulnerable to sexual harassment or accusations of being imposters. It would also generate further employment of women, partly by means of the informal recruitment network and partly by reducing the stigma and anxiety associated with strange and unconventional work. Finally, a critical mass of women forces management to give women's concerns their due weight and compels personnel offices to take female applications seriously. As the Chief Justice concluded: "It is readily apparent that, in attempting to combat systemic discrimination, it is essential to look to the past patterns of discrimination and to destroy those patterns in order to prevent the same type of discrimination in the future".[79]

CONCLUSION

It has been argued above that the objections to affirmative action in principle can be seen to rest on a particular view of equality, namely one that is based on an abstract view of justice, which asserts the primacy of the individual and which assumes a neutral state. By contrast, a substantive conception of equality recognises that justice must operate within a specific social context, based on the actual patterns of exclusion and disadvantage; that it must take into account the role of groups in influencing individual's life chances, and that it must recognise that the state is necessarily partial. On such a view, a coherent justification for affirmative action can be constructed. However, this is not the end of the matter. The aims of affirmative action need closer scrutiny on the basis of a proportionality principle, which require an affirmative action policy to be narrowly tailored to meet legitimate ends. The above discussion has shown that there is a set of coherent and mutually reinforcing justifications for affirmative action. This in turn is based on a particular view both of groups and of decision-making: of groups as sets of relationships based on affinity, rather than self-contained and clearly demarcated sets of individuals; and of decision-making as a process of communication and deliberation, rather than of interest group bargaining.

At the same time, it is important to stress the limitations of affirmative action as a strategy. The introduction of new perspectives, while an important goal,

[78] *Canadian National Railway*, above n. 76, at 214.
[79] *Ibid.*, 215.

can only have a limited impact: entrenched structures are often resilient and indeed have powerful conformist pressures. Women or minorities may find themselves forced to hide their views and ignore their own needs and interests in order to ensure that their continued participation is viable. Even if they do articulate their perspectives, the process of recognition and affirmation is halting and erratic. Thus affirmative action needs to be only one part of a broad-based and radical strategy, which does more than redistribute privileged positions but refashions the institutions which continue to perpetuate exclusion.

10

The Evolving European Employment Strategy

ERIKA SZYSZCZAK[1]

"Social policy" as interpreted in the narrow guise of labour law and labour market regulation, has undergone a quiet revolution. The Amsterdam Treaty ushered in new and radical ways of thinking about social policy by developing an *employment strategy* for the EU which will have major repercussions for Member State competence in this area. It marks yet another step in the transformation of the EU from an economic community into a European polity. I use the term "quiet revolution" in the sense that lawyers have had little to say about the new processes of decision-making which will ultimately have an impact upon the way that ordinary citizens come to view the social policy of the EU.

The silence of lawyers stems not from complacency but from inadequacy. Our breath has been taken away by the sudden and rapid way in which the Commission and the Member States fast-tracked the implementation of the new Employment Chapter of the Amsterdam Treaty (Title VIII) even before the Treaty had been ratified. The new typology of acts, the acronyms, the new institutions and actors, and the new processes and outcomes that this dynamic has brought to social policy thinking adds further challenges to the traditional understanding that lawyers have of the legal and constitutional processes and structures of the EU. The emergence of a European labour law has already posed problems of definition for legal commentators. The Amsterdam Treaty adds even more challenges to the ways in which lawyers think about the conduct of research in this area.

THE BACKGROUND TO THE NEW EMPLOYMENT STRATEGY

The Amsterdam Treaty approaches employment policy from two angles: Title VIII (entitled "Employment") and Title XI (entitled "Social Policy, Education, Vocational Training and Youth"). Title XI is a horizontal consolidation of accepted judicial and political practice.[2] For the first time we have a clear, albeit

---

[1] I am indebted to Samantha Vellutti, Richard Disney and Oliver Ismail. This chapter was completed in September 1999.

[2] See E Szyszczak, "The New Parameters of European Labour Law" in D O'Keeffe and P Twomey (eds), *The Treaty of Amsterdam* (Oxford, Hart, 1999).

not altogether coherent,[3] legal base for the development of a Community social policy, with new institutional actors, the social partners, underpinned in Article 136 EC by ideas of fundamental rights.[4] In contrast Title VIII represents a vertical consolidation of a number of years of political thinking initiated by the Commission and often endorsed by the Member States through what is labelled generically as "soft law".[5] A discourse has emerged through Commission Communications,[6] Green[7] and White Papers[8] and Reports[9] which has been endorsed by the Member States through Summit Declarations,[10] and Council Resolutions.[11]

The reasons why this discourse has taken this shape can be explained as a response to two problems which have bedevilled the development of social policy since the inception of the common market in the 1950s. The first problem arose from two issues relating to the role of social policy in the EU. First, until the Amsterdam Treaty, there was a perceived lack of competence for the Community to intervene in social policy issues at the expense of Member State sovereignty.[12] Secondly, even where there was legal competence to be found, the institutions and the Member States were divided as to the role social policy should play in the development of economic integration. The second problem

---

[3] The lack of coherence is seen in the treatment of one of the fundamental pillars of EC social policy, equal treatment between the sexes. Equal treatment is dealt with in Article 137 EC which involves the social partners, the Commission and the Council in the decision-making process. The European Parliament is only involved when the social partners fail to agree on a policy and then the Article 251 EC co-decision procedure comes into play. Equal treatment is also covered in Article 141(3) EC) which involves the Commission, Council and European Parliament, again using the Article 251 EC procedure. The Economic and Social Committee is to be consulted. Equal treatment is also dealt with in Article 13 EC which has much stricter conditions to be satisfied: action can only be taken on a proposal by the Commission with the Council acting *unanimously* "within the limits of the powers conferred on it by the Community". The European Parliament is only *consulted* in this process.

[4] See S Sciarra, "From Strasbourg to Amsterdam: Prospects for the Convergence of European Social Rights Policy" in P Alston (ed.), *The EU and Human Rights* (Oxford, Oxford University Press, 1999).

[5] See S Sciarra, "The Employment Title in the Amsterdam Treaty: A Multi-Language Legal Discourse" in O'Keeffe and Twomey, above n. 2.

[6] European Commission, *A European Strategy for Encouraging Local Development and Employment Initiatives* COM(95) 273; European Commission, *Action for Employment in Europe. A Confidence Pact* (Luxembourg, OOPEC, 1996).

[7] See S Sciarra in O'Keeffe and Twomey, above n. 2.

[8] European Commission, *Growth, Competitiveness and Employment—The Challenges and Ways Forward into the 21st Century* (COM(93) 700); *European Social Policy—A Way Forward for the Union* (COM(93) 700).

[9] *Ciampi Report* 1996; Comité des Sages, *For A Europe of Civic and Social Rights* (Luxembourg, OOPEC, 1996); European Commission, *First Report on Local Development and Employment Initiatives. Lessons for Territorial and Local Employment Pacts* (Luxembourg, OOPEC, 1997).

[10] Conclusions of the Essen European Council, *Bulletin of the EU* 12-1994, 7; Conclusions of the Cannes European Council, *Bulletin of the EU* 6-1995, 10; Conclusions of the Florence European Council, *Bulletin of the EU* 6-1996, 9.

[11] Council Resolution on Prospects for a European Union Social Policy: a Contribution to Economic and Social Convergence in the Union, [1994] OJ C368/3.

[12] See R Nielsen and E Szyszczak, *The Social Dimension of the European Union* (Copenhagen, Handelshøjskolens Forlag, 1997) 16–22.

arises from the sharp division drawn in Community thinking about social policy between the "economic" and the "social" dimension of the EU and its constituent transnational and national economies, where similarly polarised views are found to varying degrees. Even where the rhetoric recognises a social dimension to the common and internal markets the "economic" and the "social" are seen as separate and competing interests.[13] The schism is seen in the publication by the Commission of two White Papers: *Growth, Competitiveness and Employment—The Challenges and Ways Forward into the 21st Century*[14] and *European Social Policy—A Way Forward For the Union*.[15] As it turns out, this schism has been instrumental in allowing a new kind of employment policy to develop and has shaped the legitimisation of that policy.

The political and economic sub-agenda for Amsterdam was established before the Intergovernmental Conference began its formal deliberations. On the agenda, three issues underpinned the radical re-thinking of social policy. The first was unemployment; not just unemployment but persistent and high levels displaying characteristics which were specific to Europe.[16] This feature hampered and frustrated national economic planning during the 1980s.[17] The second was the need to adapt to the effects of Economic and Monetary Union. The transfer of monetary and exchange rate policy from some of the Member States to the European Central Bank entailed a reassessment of what kind of policy instruments could be used by those Member States facing asymmetric shocks to their economies. The move towards EMU also entailed reconciliation between macro-economic and monetary policies. If monetary and budgetary policy was to be decided at a European level, employment policies could either be a by-product of such policies or a core element of EU-level economic policy. EMU demanded not only a synchronisation of budgetary procedures but also the emergence of a form of economic governance in matters relating to budgetary deficits, public expenditure and stability of taxation systems. The third item on the agenda was global competitiveness. The USA and Japan were held up as industrialised economies untainted with persistently high levels of unemployment and which were capable of creating new employment.[18] As we shall see, in

---

[13] For example, the Paris Communiqué 1972, *Bulletin of the EC* 10/1972, paras 6 and 9; Case 43/75 *Defrenne* v. *Sabena (No. 2)* [1976] ECR 455, para. 15.

[14] COM(93) 700.

[15] COM(94) 333.

[16] D Meulders and R Plasman, "European Economic Policies and Social Quality" in W Beck *et al.* (eds), *The Social Quality of Europe* (The Hague, Kluwer, 1997) argue that European unemployment displays a number of distinctive characteristics; high levels of unemployment, a high proportion of long-term unemployed, especially for young people and women, low exit rates from unemployment and a weak relationship between economic growth and the creation of jobs.

[17] It should be remembered that the first Social Action Programme 1974–76 (*Bulletin of the EC*, Supp. 2/74, 8) had focused upon an ambitious set of measures to achieve full and better employment in the EC. Thus the idea of *Community level* action in tackling unemployment is not new to the Amsterdam Treaty.

[18] But compare the more upbeat views of the Commission in its *Communication from the Commission to the Council, The European Parliament, The Economic and Social Committee and the Committee of the Regions: Growth and Employment in the Stability-Oriented Framework of*

the first *Joint Employment Report*[19] Japan and the USA are viewed as the natural yardsticks against which the performance of the EU and individual Member States are measured.

In terms of policy development there remains an underlying tension within the discussion of the roles for social policy and labour market regulation in the EU.[20] Given this underlying tension, "soft law" has been used in an attempt to create a Community process for directing social policy amongst the Member States on the occasions when unanimity could not be achieved under the old legal bases of Articles 100, 100a(2) and 235 EC. During the 1980s the Commission had attempted to introduce a number of legal measures which were designed to introduce flexibility into the Community labour market[21] but even after the formal involvement of the social partners and the use of qualified majority voting, excluding the United Kingdom, such measures did not find automatic favour with the Member States.[22] Thus the various Commission Communications have been interpreted by Sciarra as a "proactive" response to the lethargy of the Member States in the social arena.[23]

Underlying this political impasse was a more deep-rooted problem. While economists were able to identify the *causes* of the high levels of unemployment[24] in Europe, there was little agreement within this discipline as to the issues that political intervention should address. While "flexibility" and policy coordination solutions were possible responses, it was unclear how these could be achieved. A particularly influential analysis of the unemployment problem, often ignored in the analyses of the development of social policy in the late 1980s and 1990s, is a report commissioned by the OECD.[25] The report (which was contentious even within the OECD) identified four main causes of high unemployment and lack of job creation which centred around rigidities in the labour

---

EMU: Economic Reflections in View of the Forthcoming Guidelines (COM(98) 103). Here the Commission argues that the EU has a competitive edge over the USA and Japan in the *capacity* to create jobs as a result of the dynamic of the single market programme and EMU. The EU lags behind the USA in the creation of jobs in the service sector, not in industry.

[19] European Commission, *Employment Policies in the EU and the Member States*, *Joint Employment Report for 1998* (Luxembourg, 1999). See also draft *Joint Employment Report for 1999* (COM(99) 347).

[20] See, e.g., Council Resolution on Prospects for a European Union Social Policy: a Contribution to Economic and Social Convergence in the Union, [1994] OJ C368/3.

[21] Discussed in E Szyszczak, *Partial Unemployment* (London, Cassell/Mansell, 1999).

[22] A directive on part-time work was adopted under the old Article 118a EC, Council Directive 91/383/EEC. Two more directives have been enacted through the agreement between the social partners route: Council Directive 97/81/EC of 15 December 1997 concerning the Framework Agreement on part-time work concluded by UNICE, CEEP and the ETUC, [1998] OJ L14/9; and Council Directive 1999/70/EC of 28 June 1999 concerning the Framework Agreement on fixed-term work concluded by ETUC, UNICE and CEEP, [1999] OJ L175/43.

[23] S Sciarra, "Social Values and the Multiple Sources of European Social Law", (1995) 1 *European Law Journal* 60.

[24] Different definitions of unemployment as well as different societal and political perceptions of who should be in paid employment (for example, married women, older workers, younger workers) as well as how unemployment should be measured add to the problem.

[25] *Labour Market Flexibility. Report by a High Level Group of Experts to the Secretary General* (Paris, 1986).

market. The message[26] was that a particular strategy, combining a set of macro-economic policies designed to keep inflation and budget deficits under control alongside specific measures to improve the design of labour market interventions, was essential to solving the EU's unemployment problem.

One clear message got through; limited and *ad hoc* interventions would never have an impact on the overall level of unemployment within the EU. An overall *strategy* was necessary. The Maastricht Treaty had introduced the task of "a high level of employment and social protection" into Article 2 EC but political wrangling resulted in the proposed Chapter on employment matters being taken out of the main body of the EC Treaty and being annexed as a Protocol and Agreement. Moreover, despite optimism in some quarters,[27] the Social Policy Agreement did not introduce a broad set of Community level employment measures and there are suggestions that a number of other Member States joined the United Kingdom in rejecting the idea of Community competence for employment issues.[28]

Thus the Commission began a process of *persuading* the Member States to consider a radical and coordinated rethinking of national policies. This shift in Commission thinking is seen in the relative paucity of its ambitions in annual work programmes and Action Programmes for Social Policy[29] but more aggressively it is seen in the persuasive arguments made for a new mix of social and economic policies in the various soft law messages[30] sent out in the 1990s, although, as we have already seen, the interdependence of the two policies is not always clearly linked.

Within this discourse emerged the subtle but radical message that the search was on for the right "model" to run the European economy with a central focus upon the regulation of labour markets in such a way as to improve "flexibility". The political cradle of this was the White Paper, *Growth, Competitiveness and Employment*[31] (the "economic" policy) which explored a number of strategies and which led, in 1994, to the Essen Council drawing up five priorities around which the Member States were invited to organise their employment policies in order to stimulate job creation.[32] These were labelled "The Essen Priorities".

---

[26] See *The OECD Jobs Study: Evidence and Explanations, Parts I and II and Implementing the Strategy* (Paris, 1994).

[27] B Bercusson, "Maastricht: a Fundamental Change in European Labour Law", (1992) 23 *Industrial Relations Journal* 177.

[28] See M Binyion, "EC Voices Doubts on Social Charter" *The Times*, 27 November 1990.

[29] See H Cullen and E Campbell, "The Future of Social-Policy Making in the European Union" in P Craig and C Harlow (eds), *Lawmaking in the European Union* (London, Kluwer Law International, 1998).

[30] See Sciarra in O'Keeffe and Twomey, above n. 2.

[31] See European Commission, above n. 8.

[32] Conclusions of the Essen European Council, *Bulletin of the EU* 12/1994, 7. *Priority 1*: improving employment opportunities for the working population by promoting investment in vocational training; *Priority 2*: Increasing the employment intensiveness of growth; *Priority 3*: Reducing non-wage labour costs, particularly for non-qualified workers; *Priority 4*: Improving efficiency of employment policies by avoiding measures that negatively affect the availability for work and by replacing passive policies for active ones; *Priority 5*: Improving measures to affect groups most affected by unemployment (women, young people, older employees, long-term unemployed).

Inherent within these priorities were a number of unresolved underlying tensions. In its White Paper on Social Policy,[33] the Commission had identified two goals of social policy: tackling unemployment and social exclusion, but the Essen Priorities would seem to have overriden the twinning of these two goals which, on the face of it, might have attracted compatible policies. In addition, these goals were not compatible with the convergence criteria set for the attainment of EMU in the Maastricht Treaty.[34] Thus the need for Member States to constrain budgets and reduce public debt inevitably led to cuts, some drastic, in their public spending programmes. Meulders and Plasman[35] argue that at least three of the Essen Priorities challenged a policy addressing social exclusion: flexibilisation of work and salaries may lead to job insecurity and increase poverty, the reduction of non-salary costs is a euphemism for reducing social security contributions and Priority 4 could lead to lower unemployment compensation.

The Commission urged the Member States to take account of the Essen Priorities in their monetary convergence programmes and made proposals for decisions in the employment field.[36] The Member States reiterated the Essen objectives at subsequent Summit Meetings in Cannes in 1995[37] and Florence in 1996[38] and the catalogue of proposed measures to tackle unemployment was refined. At the Florence Summit the social partners were invited to address not only matters concerning social integration (such as training) for excluded groups but also, and significantly in the light of the recent framework agreements on part-time[39] and fixed time work,[40] to develop flexibility in working time arrangements and the organisation of work. Crucially, however, the initiatives were non-binding. It was easy for the Member States to say there was political consensus and to pay lip-service to the *goal* of tackling unemployment, but much harder to find legal instruments to turn the goal into a Community obligation. In effect, the "Essen Priorites" were not at the forefront of Member States' EMU adaptation programmes.[41]

In the Commission's ensuing medium-term Social Action Programme 1995–97[42] few legislative proposals were made[43] and the focus was instead upon

---

[33] COM(94) 333.

[34] See the old Article 109(j) EC.

[35] See above n. 16.

[36] European Commission, *Follow-up to the Essen Council on Employment* (COM(95) 74).

[37] Conclusions of the Cannes European Council, *Bulletin of the EU* 6-1995, 10.

[38] Conclusions of the Florence European Council, *Bulletin of the EU* 6-1996, 9.

[39] Council Directive 97/81/EC, [1998] OJ L14/9.

[40] Council Directive 99/70/EC of 28 June 1999 concerning the Framework Agreement on fixed-term work concluded by ETUC, UNICE and CEEP, [1999] OJ L175/43.

[41] Some of the Priorities have re-emerged post-Amsterdam in a Commission Communication, *Modernising Public Employment Services to Support the European Employment Strategy* (COM(98) 641), and in the Conclusions of the European Summit in Vienna, *Bulletin of the EC* 12-98, we see the re-emergence of social exclusion from the fifth Essen Priority. See also European Commission, *A Concerted Strategy for Modernising Social Protection* (COM(99) 347), and *Towards a Europe for All Ages—Promoting Prosperity and Intergenerational Solidarity* (COM(99) 221).

[42] COM(95) 134.

[43] After an initial era of optimism proceeding the implementation of the Commission's *Action*

the *policies* to be pursued from the (economic) White Paper, *Growth, Competitiveness and Employment*.[44] Despite the fact that this attempt at directional policy-making[45] was endorsed by Heads of State and Government, few Member States did attempt a coordinated European strategy to tackle unemployment.

Nevertheless, an emerging European-level discourse can be seen in this period. It focuses upon the rules and institutions which govern labour markets: wage differentials, earnings inequality, the structure of unemployment, the role of unemployment insurance and the role of trade unions. What is striking for the lawyer conversant with the history of social policy at the Community level, however, is that these areas are precisely the ones where Member States have historically tried to protect their sovereign rights, deliberately leaving such areas of social policy outside of Community competence[46] or insisting upon unanimity voting.[47] Title XI continues this division of sensitive and non-sensitive areas of Community intervention. This explains the structural dichotomy in the ensuing Amsterdam Treaty.

Arguably, if the EU is to take tackling labour market regulation seriously, it should maximise the competence given to it in the Amsterdam Treaty and use the two Titles to achieve complementary goals. Sciarra has suggested ways in which the emerging "soft law" discourse of tackling unemployment through labour market regulation could be translated into an effective Community employment policy.[48] For example, the regulation, and thereby the reduction, of working time could be enacted through directives using the old legal base of Article 137 (ex 118a) EC.[49] In addition to this, the recent agreements on part-time work and fixed term work[50] reveal the use of the social partners to develop legal frameworks around which issues of flexibility and employment protection rights may be explored. The complementarity of the two policies would bring with it guarantees of the "rule of law" approach, ensuring proper consultation, transparency and proper legal processes in creating legislation. Such legislation would be reviewable and capable of creating legal rights which would then be enforceable in national legal systems through the principles of direct and

Programme to Implement the Community Charter of the Fundamental Social Rights of Workers 1989 (COM(89) 568), disillusion seems to have set in. This is evident in the withdrawal of the Annex to the SAP, containing a list of Commission initiatives, after failure to gain acceptance in the Council of Ministers—even after the exclusion of the United Kingdom government in the Social Policy Protocol and Agreement introduced at Maastricht.

[44] See above n. 31.

[45] See *The European Employment Strategy: Commission Communication on Trends and Developments in Employment Systems in the European Union* (COM (95) 465).

[46] See Article 137(6) EC and B Ryan, "Pay, Trade Union Rights and European Community Law", (1997) 13/4 *The International Journal of Comparative Labour Law and Industrial Relations* 305.

[47] See Article 137(3) EC.

[48] "Social Values and the Multiple Sources of European Social Law", (1995) 1 *European Law Journal* 60.

[49] The legitimacy of such a programme was endorsed in the European Court's ruling in Case C–84/94 *United Kingdom* v. *Council* [1996] ECR I–5755.

[50] See above n. 22.

indirect effect and state liability. Such "hard law" also has a valuable role to play in identifying a clear set of social values upon which European social policy is based.

However, the major event which altered the context in which unemployment as an issue of European governance was thought about, was the election of new governments in Britain, France and Germany. These new political groupings redefined the parameters of the scope of EU competence to regulate employment matters and allowed not only the *acceptance* of EU level action but also facilitated the *integration* of employment policies with other macro-economic policies. The previous political complexion of Europe had been divided between a conservative belief in macro-economic stability and minimum employment policy, and the "old" socialist belief in wage rigidity but no macro-economic stability. Within the new agenda there was a recognition of the need to have an employment policy to avoid social exclusion combined with macro-economic stability. As we shall see, however, there is still a battle as to how to achieve the latter goals.

THE LEGAL ANALYSIS OF TITLE VIII OF THE AMSTERDAM TREATY

Duff[51] reports that Title VIII was included in the Amsterdam Treaty at the instigation of Sweden. In fact other Member States[52] shared the view that employment issues should be a matter of common concern but the stumbling block continued to be a lack of consensus on the role of employment as an EU objective and its relationship with EMU. By 1997 the Member States had differing political perspectives towards labour market regulation. Thus, the new Title VIII does not explicitly make the link between employment policy and economic policy but instead reveals an evolutionary approach to creating the links between the two policies.

Article 125 EC provides that the Member States *and the EU* shall work towards developing a coordinated strategy for employment; a particular aim of this strategy is to promote a skilled, trained and adaptable workforce, and labour markets responsive to economic change. In Article 126 EC, the sharing of competence between Member States and the EU is revealed in the requirement that Member States are to contribute towards the EU's aims by developing their employment policies in a manner which is consistent with the broad

---

[51] A Duff, *The Treaty of Amsterdam. Text and Commentary* (London, Sweet and Maxwell, Federal Trust, 1997).

[52] A broad consensus can be seen in the 1995 *Westendorp Report* which contains the idea of including employment among the shared objectives of the EU in the context of economic and monetary union: General Secretariat of the Council of the European Union, 1996 Intergovernmental Conference: *Reflection Group Report and Other References for Documentary Purposes* (1995). See also the European Commission, *Reinforcing Political Union and Preparing for Enlargement* (COM(96) 90) and European Parliament Resolution A4-0068/96 of 13 March 1996, [1996] OJ C96/77.

economic guidelines of the economic policies of the Member States and the EU as articulated in Article 99(2) EC. Moreover in Article 126(2) EC, "promoting employment" is said to be a matter of "common concern" and Member States are to coordinate their action in the Council in accordance with procedures set out in Article 128 EC.

Article 128(1) EC charges the European Council with considering the employment situation in the EU each year on the basis of an annual Joint Report drawn up by the Council and the Commission. On the basis of the Council's conclusions, guidelines are to be drawn up and Member States are to take account of these guidelines in their employment policies. The guidelines are to be adopted from a proposal from the Commission, after consulting the European Parliament, the Economic and Social Committee, the Committee of the Regions and the new Employment Committee, established in Article 130 EC. Again, the Council's guidelines must be consistent with the broad economic guidelines adopted pursuant to Article 99(2) EC.

Each Member State must provide the Council and the Commission with an annual report on the measures taken to implement its national employment policy and Article 128(4) EC provides that the Council will examine the implementation of the Member States' employment policies in the light of the guidelines after receiving the views of the Employment Committee. Then the Council, acting by *qualified majority*, on a recommendation by the Commission "May, if it considers it appropriate in the light of that examination, make recommendations to the Member States". Thus, significantly, there is now a legal basis within the Treaty for Community institutions to interfere in the national employment policies of the Member States.

Thereafter Article 128(5) EC states that, on the basis of the examination carried out under Article 128(4) EC, the Council and the Commission shall make a joint annual report to the European Council on the employment situation in the EU and the implementation of the employment guidelines. Article 129 EC goes on to set clear boundaries for Community action by stating that the Council, using the co-decision procedure and after consultation with the Economic and Social Committee and the Committee of the Regions "May adopt incentive measures designed to encourage co-operation between Member States and to support their action in the field of employment through initiatives aimed at developing exchanges of information and best practices, providing comparative analysis and advice as well as promoting innovative approaches and evaluating experiences, in particular by recourse to pilot projects". The boundaries of this competence are clearly spelt out in the Amsterdam Treaty: "Those measures shall not include harmonisation of the laws and regulations of the Member States".

Analysts of this process disagree about its significance. Whilst Sciarra finds it hard to classify Title VIII,[53] Barnard has suggested that Title VIII can be

---

[53] See above n. 30.

characterised as the "constitutionalisation" of Commission/Council soft law policies.[54] This argument, however, offers no explanation of what legal or practical consequences follow from the classification of Title VIII as a "constitutionalisation" of existing policies. Barnard's description fails to address the fact that the transition from Essen to Amsterdam was not a smooth one, or the fact that moves to include Title VIII into the Amsterdam Treaty were as a result of the *failure* of the "Essen Priorities" and the failure of the Commission's White Paper, *Competitiveness, Growth and Employment*, to resolve European economic stagnation. Thus the Amsterdam Treaty is an attempt to give employment policy a *legal framework* whereby the soft law discourse may be translated into binding normative rules.

Kenner[55] has argued that the new Employment Title of the Amsterdam Treaty together with the body of soft law measures enacted before and after the fast-tracking implementation of the Employment Chapter, represent a positive affirmation of a *policy approach* which has become associated with the "Third Way" political agenda. This suggests that *legal tools* have been used to develop a dramatic change in the political structure of European governance. The next two sections of this chapter will address the structure and process of the new employment policy for Europe.

THE (IL)LEGAL IMPLEMENTATION OF TITLE VIII

The principles of Title VIII were fast-tracked into operation using the legal basis of a Resolution adopted by the Heads of State and Government at the European Council of Amsterdam on 16 June 1997.[56] The procedure has been viewed as an emergency[57] procedure by the Heads of State and Government and was prompted by the high levels of unemployment in some of the Member States.[58] Not only did this fast-tracking establish a controversial[59] precedent but it also

---

[54] C. Barnard, "EC 'Social Policy'" in P Craig and G de Búrca (eds), *The Evolution of EU Law* (Oxford, OUP, 1999) and "The United Kingdom, the 'Social Chapter' and the Amsterdam Treaty" (1997) 27 *Industrial Law Journal* 281. See also J Kenner, "The EC Employment Title and the 'Third Way': Making Soft Law Work?", (1999) 33 *The International Journal of Comparative Law and Industrial Relations* 48.

[55] *Ibid.*

[56] Amsterdam Presidency Conclusions of 16 June 1997 (Doc. CONF 4001/97). The political acceptance of the Employment Chapter is seen in a Resolution on Employment and Growth and a Resolution on a Stability and Growth Pact, [1997] OJ C236/3 and [1997] OJ C236/1.

[57] M. Biagi, "The Implementation of the Amsterdam Treaty with Regard to Employment: Coordination or Convergence?", (1998) 14 *International Journal of Comparative Labour Law and Industrial Relations* 325.

[58] At the time of the signing of the Amsterdam Treaty, EU unemployment stood at a figure of 18 per cent. There was a wide disparity in the levels of unemployment, however, with Spain having the highest level (19 per cent) and Luxembourg the lowest level at 3.5 per cent: *Eurostat*, November 1997.

[59] M Weiss, "Ill Trattato di Amsterdam e la politica sociale", (1998) VIII *Diritto delle relazioni industriali* 7.

provided the legal and political basis for the creation of *new* procedures, principles and practices which both fleshed out and also altered, the aims and content of Title VIII even before the Amsterdam Treaty was ratified.[60]

This use of a Resolution signifies the use of a formal instrument where there is agreement in the Council outside of formal Community procedures and although the body of case law weighs heavily against recognising Resolutions of the Council and of the European Council as having legally binding effects, Klabbers[61] points out that in cases before the European Court of Justice, Member States have attempted to alter legally binding Treaty commitments by means of a Resolution.

Preceding the Amsterdam Council, the Commission set an agenda for the European Council meeting on employment which was to take place in Luxembourg in November 1997[62] by (in a manner reminiscent of its Action Plan to implement the Community Charter of Fundamental Social Rights of Workers in 1989)[63] issuing its proposals for the draft 1998 Employment Guidelines the previous month.[64] These proposals focused upon four pillars around which a *European* employment strategy was to be centred: entrepreneurship, employability, adapatability and equal opportunity. (Kenner, incidentally, argues that these are "all buzz words and phrases regularly used by 'Third Way' advocates".)[65] The Commission also singled out *objectives* which were to be adopted by the Member States and included nineteen "Guidelines" in its document. Entitled the "Jobs Summit", this meeting was the beginning of a *process* which has become officially known in subsequent Commission and Council documents and communications as the "Luxembourg Process".[66] The Commission's Guidelines for 1998 were adopted at the Council Meeting of 15 December 1997

---

[60] We should not overlook the fact that Title XI was also fast-tracked into operation before the Amsterdam Treaty was ratified. Using the legal base of Article 194 (ex 100) EC, the Works Council Directive (Council Directive 94/45/EC, [1994] OJ L254/64) and Parental Leave Directive (Council Directive 96/34/EC, [1995] OJ L145/4) were extended to the United Kingdom (Council Directive 97/75/EC, [1998] OJ L10/24 and Council Directive 97/74/EC, [1997] OJ L10/22). The United Kingdom participated in the negotiations set out in Article 4 of the Social Policy Agreement (now Article 138 EC) for implementing proposals relating to sectoral agreements on working time in the maritime and transport sectors, fixed-term contracts and worker consultation at the national level. See Szyszczak, above n. 2.

[61] J Klabbers, "Informal Instruments Before the European Court of Justice", (1994) *CMLRev* 997.

[62] Conclusions of the Extraordinary European Council on Employment, *Bulletin of the EU* 11-1997.

[63] COM(89) 568.

[64] COM(97) 497.

[65] Kenner, above n. 54, at 52.

[66] There has been continuity and consistency in this process. The 1999 Guidelines continued the 1998 Guidelines with only minimal changes: gender equality was to be streamlined through all four pillars and the number of Guidelines was increased from 19 to 21 in 1999 and to 22 in 2000: *Guidelines for the Member States' Employment Policies for 2000* (COM(99) 441). However, in the Commission Recommendation for Council Recommendations on the Implementation of Member States' Employment Policies (COM(99) 442), the Commission prioritises eight of the Guidelines. Creating priorities in this way will affect the view the Commission has of each National Action Plan.

in the form of a Resolution[67] with the Commission and the Employment Committee setting a date of 15 April 1998 for the presentation of a National Action Plan (NAP) by each Member State with an implementation report to be filed by 31 July 1998.

From a political, consensus-building, point of view, it was fortuitous that the United Kingdom assumed the Presidency of the Council in the first half of 1998. The speed at which Member States drew up their NAPs contrasts dramatically with their response to the Essen Priorities. All the NAPs were drawn up by the end of April 1998 for consideration at the European Council meeting in Cardiff in June 1998. However, there is a divergence from the wording of the Employment Chapter, since Article 128(2) expressly refers to "guidelines" which are to be taken into account when Member States draw up national employment policies. Such guidelines must be consistent with the broad principles of the *economic* guidelines drawn up in pursuance of Article 99(2) EC but instead, the Commission persuaded the Member States to draw up detailed plans conforming to the Commission employment guidelines.

Shortly after the Cardiff Summit, Doug Henderson (then Minister for Europe in the United Kingdom), argued that it was the view of the Member States at the Cardiff Summit that employment policy would remain a matter for national governments and that the Luxembourg process was seen only as one of "peer review" and "exchange of best practice".[68] Henderson also argues that there was a degree of the consensus at the Cardiff Summit in the belief that "unemployment can only be brought down sustainably if labour markets are made more flexible and government intervention is focused on increasing skills and employability."[69] This opinion is open to dispute since there were clear rifts or a "battle of the models" between the French and the German/United Kingdom's political views as to whether unemployment can and should be tackled by other policies such as job-sharing, reduction of working time measures, rather than reducing perceived rigidities and costs in the labour market. Such differences become important when we examine the Commission's assessment of the NAPs.

THE COMMISSION'S METHOD OF ASSESSING THE NAPS

As a result of the Commission's Communication of 1997, defined policy Guidelines are now in place which reveal two deliberate moves; first towards active labour market policies and secondly towards turning existing passive labour market policies into active ones. In some of the Guidelines an open attempt to move beyond pure aims to reaching concrete targets can be tied to the first differences of opinion between the Commission and the Council at the

---

[67] [1998] OJ C30/1.
[68] D Henderson, "The UK Presidency: An Insider's View", (1998) 36 *JCMS* 563 at 567.
[69] *Ibid.*

Luxembourg Summit. The Commission had proposed a five-year target employment rate of 65 per cent which would involve the creation of at least twelve million new jobs. The European Council, perhaps mindful of how political promises of "No new taxes" can become hostages at election times, opted for the lesser commitment of arriving "at a significant increase in the employment rate in Europe on a lasting basis".[70]

Nevertheless some clear and concrete targets have been set by the Commission. For example, Guidelines 1 and 2 give a commitment to tackling youth employment and to fighting long-term unemployment. The active side of such policy is that Member States *must ensure* that every unemployed young person is offered a new start in the form of training, retraining, work practice, a job or other employability measure, before reaching six months of unemployment. The transition from passive to active labour market measures is found in Guideline 3 which provides that Member States will endeavour to increase significantly the number of persons benefiting from active measures to improve their employability. Thus the consequences of these Guidelines have a definitive impact upon a number of aspects of national policy.

The Commission's Guidelines have put in place ideas similar to the use of *convergence* criteria in the second phase of EMU. At the national level Member States have lost the ability to determine unilaterally their own employment policies and must adapt other economic and political processes such as budget cycles and allocations in order to adjust to the new dynamics of Community level reporting and appraisal. Moreover their individual progress is monitored by the need to "converge" their policies. This goes much further than, and indeed is a very different concept from, the activities of the Community as set out in Article 3(i) EC[71] and the aim of Article 125 EC which states that "Member States and the Community shall, in accordance with this Title, work towards developing a *co-ordinated* strategy for employment" and also from the role allotted to the Community in Title XI, Article 137 EC, which states "With a view to achieving the objectives of Article 136 EC, the Community shall *support and complement* the activities of the Member State" (emphasis added).

MORE THAN "STATE-WATCHING"?

The fast-track implementation of the Employment Chapter suggests that the EU is doing more than just monitoring the Member States or "state-watching." The first round of NAPs produced in April 1998 showed many of them to be mere summaries of the Member States' existing practices and policies organised around the Commission's Guidelines. This is not surprising given the short

---

[70] Luxembourg Presidency Conclusions, para. 22.

[71] "the promotion of co-ordination between employment policies of the Member States with a view to enhancing their effectiveness by developing a co-ordinated strategy for employment."

amount of time that Member States were given to draw up the NAPs. [72] Nevertheless the Commission was determined not to be fobbed off. In May 1998 in a Communication, *From Guidelines to Action: the National Action Plans for Employment*,[73] in which the Commission analysed the NAPs, the Commission notes that many of the NAPs are vague and expresses regret that "the majority of NAPs had been drafted as documents to formulate general policies rather than operative instruments". More generally the Commission does make some positive observations on the Member States' commitment to multi-annual planning, the involvement of the social partners, transparency and some of the Member States' willingness to criticise their own shortcomings. The promotion of policy goals of active labour market intervention, decentralisation and modernisation of the public sector are seen *as shared goals* between the Member States which elicit the Commission's praise. The Commission is, however, critical of the lack of an integrated approach to the four pillars, the vagueness of some of the plans, the unreliability of national employment indicators and the lack of clarity about budget and resources implications. As Biagi notes,[74] best practice is singled out for praise but there is silence when Member States do not measure up to the Commission's expectations. In the draft assessment of the 1999 NAPs the Commission is bolder, naming those Member States which have not implemented the NAP to the Commission's expectations.[75]

In its preparation of the 1998 *Joint Employment Report*, the Commission tried to organise better information on the Member States by sending them questionnaires beforehand. The questionnaires were divided into two parts. The first part comprised general questions posed to all the Member States and the second part addressed specific questions to individual Member States. In their answers the Member States were asked to distinguish between initiatives launched before the drafting of the NAP, those adopted at the time of the NAP and those adopted after the NAP. The questions asked not only for clarification of the NAPs but also asked a number of the Member States to show both that the policies had been adopted and that budgetary procedures had been put in place to finance initiatives. Thus in 1998 Member States prepared *two* reports: the NAP and an implementation Report on the NAP. Again this is a departure from the strict letter of the Treaty, Article 128(3) EC, which states that only one annual report from each Member State is necessary. In 1999 the Commission demanded only one NAP.

The Commission Communication *From Guidelines to Action* represents a decisive shift in changing the mindset of the Commission and the Member States as to where competence for determining the employment policy of the EU lies.

---

[72] The Commission was more impressed with the 1999 NAPs. Commissioner Flynn announced that "in terms of presentation, articulation of priorities and quantification of resources and effort" there was an improvement, the Member States being influenced by the high standards set by France and Spain in their presentation of the 1998 NAPs COM(98) 316.

[73] COM(98) 316.

[74] See above n. 57.

[75] See above n. 73.

Member States are no longer free to determine national policy but must work within officially recognised Community Guidelines which have taken on a normative status. The Commission has gained the upper hand in defining and interpreting these Guidelines. At this juncture we might pause to reflect the contrast with the old EC Treaty and the Social Policy Agreement under which Member States had been able to stall Commission initiatives under the 1989 Action Programme to implement the Charter of Fundamental Rights of Workers.[76] This was a blow not only to the Commission's legislative power of initiative but also to the attempt, initiated by Jacques Delors, to bring a social fundamental rights discourse into Community social policy thinking. Under the Social Policy Agreement, now implemented as Article 138 EC, the Commission's power of initiative in the social policy field had been made subject to the social partners' deliberations.

A second aspect of the Communication is that it has been used by the Commission to sanction Member States' policies, albeit in a subtle way. At the original "Jobs Summit" in Luxembourg in 1997 it had been stressed that participation in the "Luxembourg Process" was voluntary and that there would be no sanctions attached to the process. The Communication and its subsequent questionnaires have, however, seen the Commission adopting a critical role, particularly with regard to highlighting the inadequacies of the Member States against the "Luxembourg criteria". In the Communication the Commission singles out only four Member States, the United Kingdom, France, Spain and Luxembourg as having adopted a preventative approach to addressing the developments and consequences of unemployment. Similarly only those Member States who had provided convincing descriptions of their policies in relation to Guideline 3 were singled out.[77] Biagi points out that the absence of reference by the Commission to a Member State in relation to a specific point was considered an implicit criticism.[78]

This might be compared to the Employment Committee's examination of each Member State in May 1998. Biagi describes the May 1998 examination of the Member States as "an exercise of significant interest" whereby "there was a kind of cross-examination among Member States". Ostensibly, the purpose was to elicit best practice and although the Employment Committee did not mention Member States individually, it did make general evaluations. Thus the practices of the Member States in the field of labour market regulation were suddenly put under the spotlight *at the European level* for scrutiny, justification and comment. The *Joint Report*,[79] produced by the European Council and Commission is more explicit. It addresses each Member State and again highlights examples

---

[76] *Social Europe* 1/90, 46. Cf. J Addison and W Siebert, *Regulating European Labour Market: More Costs Than Benefits?* (London, The Institute of Economic Affairs, 1999).
[77] Similar methodology is seen in the Commission Recommendation for Council Recommendations on the Implementation of Member States' Employment Policies (COM(99) 445).
[78] Biagi, above n. 57, at 332.
[79] See above n. 19.

of "good practice" in employment policy. The Commission has therefore assumed a lead role as censor of "bad practice" for which there is no legal basis within the EC Treaty.

THE RE-CONFIGURATION OF THE EUROPEAN EMPLOYMENT STRATEGY: TOWARDS ECONOMIC AND POLITICAL GOVERNANCE?

The "Luxembourg Process" has not evolved in isolation. Although the internal contours of the European Employment Strategy have been mapped out and refined, largely by the Commission, the inherent logic of a European Employment Strategy has come under pressure from other processes rapidly emerging in the field of economic governance of the EU. The convergence of employment policies and macro-economic policies being developed as a result of EMU in the Broad Guidelines of the Economic Policies,[80] has resulted in a re-configuration of European governance structures although the links between employment policy and the macro-economic policies were not developed fully at either the Amsterdam or Luxembourg Summits.[81] Another political process was adopted at the Cardiff Summit to create a comprehensive approach to structural reforms in services, product and capital markets; the "Cardiff Process", and it took a German initiative at the Vienna Council Meeting of December 1998 to produce a plan for closer cooperation to boost employment and economic reforms. Thus the European Pact for Employment was initiated at the Cologne Summit of June 1999; the "Cologne Process". The aim of this process is to create a new dialogue between all actors responsible for wage nego-tiations, monetary, budgetary and fiscal policies with enhanced roles for the social partners and the European Central Bank.[82] Therefore a new set of insti-tutional arrangements and structures are emerging around discussions between central bankers, finance ministers and the social partners.[83] Once again the Commission is taking a central role, not only in meshing employment policy with economic policy, but also in creating a forum for the discussion of

[80] The Broad Economic Guidelines are presented by the Commission in March of each year. They are the main instrument of collective control in the framework of the national stability plans. They contain recommendations to the Member States. The ECOFIN Council may alter these rec-ommendations and then adopts them on a provisional basis. The final European Council meeting of the first semester of the Presidency will either confirm or alter the recommendations. The ECOFIN Council of July each year adopts the final version.

[81] From the wording of the Amsterdam Treaty the employment policy has to be consistent with the aims of the EU as set out in Article 2 EC, and Member States' employment policies must be con-sistent with the broad guidelines of the economic policies of the Member States and the EU as adopted under Article 99(2) EC.

[82] Sciarra describes these processes as loose and open sequence of actions, uncertain as to when they start and how they should be completed: Sciarra in O'Keeffe and Twomey, above n. 2. The con-tinuity and consistency of the policy was continued at the EU level by the use of another special Jobs Summit in 2000.

[83] P Pochet, "The New Employment Chapter of the Amsterdam Treaty", (1999) 9 *Journal of European Social Policy* 271.

European level policies through more soft law Communications and Notes to the Economic Policy Committee. Although the independence and autonomy of the various actors is to be respected, latent issues can now appear legitimately on European-level economic governance agendas: the appropriate level of wage-bargaining, the organisation of collective bargaining, labour market reforms,[84] the appropriate level and uses of employment and social protection measures, and the modernisation of the organisation of work.[85]

SOME COMMENTS ON THE METHOD OF THE EUROPEAN EMPLOYMENT STRATEGY

Through soft law tools the Commission has created a frame of reference as well as a monitoring process for a European Employment Strategy. Soft law, which was used in the early 1990s to manage social policy pluralism, has ended the decade as the principal legal tool for coercing Member States to address labour market regulation in line with European policies.[86]

The methodology of the *Joint Report* is to look at the Member States' starting positions in their labour markets by reference to a number of key areas of labour market performance. This builds upon the earlier work of the Employment Observatory.[87] The Commission is adamant that this is only "peer review", but in relation to the 1999 NAPs, the Commission announced that there will be a greater intensification of the "peer review" process with the performance of each Member State being reviewed in greater detail by the other Member States. As the Commission points out, "This kind of peer pressure can be very effective as we saw during the convergence process leading up to the third stage of EMU".[88] Arguably this is in keeping with the "name and shame" policy and process of the single market scoreboard, where Member States' performance is held up to public scrutiny. Moreover the Commission has announced that it considers itself to be under *a legal duty*, as a result of Article 128 EC, to make recommendations to the Member States "where it is deemed appropriate and useful"[89] and in the Commission Recommendation, *Council Recommendations on the Implementation of Member States' Employment*

---

[84] See European Central Bank, *Annual Report* (Frankfurt, 1999).

[85] See *inter alia*, European Commission, *Public Investment in the Framework of Economic Strategy* (COM(98) 682); *Social Action Programme 1998–2000* (COM(98) 259); *Community Policies in Support of Employment* (COM(99) 167); *Modernising the Organisation of Work* COM(98) 592; *Modernising Public Employment Services to Support the European Employment Strategy* (COM(98) 641).

[86] Soft law has been used as a procedural tool as well as continuing the discourse on the role of an employment strategy for Europe, see European Commission, *Report from the Commission, Employment in Europe 1998* (COM(98) 666); OOPEC, *Supiot Report* (Luxembourg, 1999).

[87] Employment Observatory, *Benchmarking Employment Performance and Labour Market Policies—Final Report* 1998.

[88] http://europa.eu.int/comm/dg05/empl&esf/news/napev-en.htm

[89] *Ibid.*

Policies,[90] not one Member State escapes the Commission's intervention in its domestic policies.

In order to create a frame of reference for the European Employment Strategy, eight indicators are selected to monitor the performance of Member States in employment and unemployment. For *employment* these are: employment rate, employment growth, employment, employment gender gap. For *unemployment* these are: the unemployment rate, long-term unemployment, youth unemployment and the unemployment gender ratio. Each indicator is used to create an axis on which the performance of the Member State is measured. The individual Member State's performance is measured as a relative value against the average of the best performances for each indicator by the three best performing Member States in 1997. Thus the "three best performing Member States" represent not only a standard of reference but also an example for worse performing Member States.

The criteria are then combined to create diagrammatic indicators of the surface measure of overall performance of each Member State. Similar combined indicators have been produced to compare the performance of the USA and Japan. It is interesting to note that two of the "smaller" Member States (Austria and Finland) perform consistently better than any of the other Member States; they are followed by Sweden and Luxembourg with three "top three" rankings. The United Kingdom, Ireland and the Netherlands have two "top three" places and Germany achieves only one. Significantly France, Italy, Spain, Greece, Belgium and Portugal never feature in a "top three" ranking. The resulting analysis leads us to the creation of a league table in which the USA and Japan are in the "super league", both states performing comfortably in comparison with the "top three" EU Member States on each indicator.

Again, this kind of comparison, which results in censure, does not have a legal basis in the EC Treaty[91] and such a ranking process may be harmful, not only to coordination, but also to convergence. If the Member States are constantly evaluated by reference to the "best three" performers, the gap between those Member States that can, or want to, activate particular policies and those that cannot, will widen. Using only the Employment Chapter without thought as to how other Community-based policies, either using the structural funds or legal instruments developed under Title XI, might bring about coordination or convergence of employment policies paradoxically questions *Community competence* in the area of employment policy.

In her analysis of the two White Papers of 1993 and 1994, Sciarra argued that the Commission had prescribed a therapy, but the question remained "Who will the therapist be?"[92] The European Employment Strategy relies upon economic

---

[90] COM(99) 442.

[91] The use of the best performing Member States as a reference point or benchmark serves as a reminder of the early aspirations of the EC Treaty to seek the "constant improvement of the living and working conditions" of the people of the Member States.

[92] S Sciarra, "Social Values and the Multiple Sources of European Social Law", (1995) 1 *European Law Journal* 60 at 76.

criteria as the therapist and the dominant methodology of evaluation in the Commission's analysis of the "Luxembourg Process" is an economic one. Therefore it seems that what the EU apparently wants is for prescriptive economic criteria to point the way to the best labour market policies. This however is something which some labour economists fight shy of.[93]

A major problem seems to be that the EU does not have a clear idea of how to get from A to B in tackling labour market regulation and instead has merely provided a series of targets. The methodology of the "Luxembourg Process" gives only snap-shot glimpses of what is happening to Member States' labour markets and intra-Member State studies can tell us very little unless they are done rigorously, using longitudinal data showing how changes in labour market structure occur over time and how they are related to specific factors such as union density, minimum wages, employment subsidies etc. Even then such factors cannot stand alone; one has to look at the interactions of labour market institutions and economic outcomes. Equally the methodology needs to take counter-factuals into account. Longtitudinal studies can show the effect of labour market institutions over time, but to be *prescriptive* there needs to be an observable counter-factual. Would the Member State have done better or worse without a change in labour market institutions?[94] There is, unfortunately, no experimental laboratory where such experiments can be tried out. Economists can only provide a hypothesis with huge amounts of data and yet, even in its simplest procedures, the Commission bemoans the lack of available data from Member States.[95]

The same criticisms can be levelled at the use of "best practice" examples by the Commission and the Employment Committee. The Commission defends the use of "best practice" on the grounds that "Good ideas should always be imitated", and that by collecting together successful policy examples, there is a bridging of the "knowledge gap" whereby it can be shown that abstract ideas, when translated into national policies, can bring positive results.[96] Nevertheless, as Kahn-Freund has reminded lawyers, it is not always easy to transplant legal and institutional concepts from country-specific settings.[97]

Finally we must ask how apt comparisons with the USA and Japan are. Do we want a European social model that mirrors American and Japanese models? There has been very little democratic discussion at EU, or in some cases,

[93] See R Freeman, "War of the Models: Which Labour Market Institutions for the 21st Century?", (1998) 5 *Labour Economics* 1.
[94] An example of this kind of methodology was carried out in relation to the political arguments for and against improving the legal position of part-time work using an EU Directive; see R Disney and E Szyszczak, "Protective Legislation and Part-Time Employment in Britain", (1984) 22 *British Journal of Industrial Relations* 78.
[95] European Commission, *Report on Ways of Improving the Comparability of Statistics to Monitor and Evaluate Progress Under the European Employment Strategy* (COM(98) 572).
[96] For best practice examples see "What Can Europeans Learn from Each Other?" http://Europa.eu.int/comm/dg05/elm/summit/en/backg/examl.htm
[97] O Kahn-Freund, "On Uses and Misuses of Comparative Law", (1974) 37 *Modern Law Review* 1.

national level, of the outcome of the European Employment Strategy. The USA has had full employment but this has been a result of growth in the service sector wherein a number of jobs are low paid, reliant upon gratuities and do not have the concomitant access to social security schemes which permanent jobs have. Within the USA there are huge pay inequalities, low levels of social security (for example no national minimum wage, limited welfare benefits, and a heavy reliance on private and occupational social security and health schemes). In contrast the EU does have high unemployment but also a legacy of social solidarity *within* (but not across) Member States.[98] It also has a compressed pay structure, and crucially, its national state social security systems are in crisis.

A RESEARCH AGENDA FOR THE EUROPEAN EMPLOYMENT STRATEGY?

The purpose of this chapter has been to argue that lawyers have legal skills, which, when combined with social science skills, can contribute to the evolution of a new stage of social policy thinking in the EU. This chapter cannot provide a definitive analysis of this process since it is an embryonic and evolving one but it can establish a research agenda.

The chapter has additionally argued that the development of an employment strategy for the EU contributes to the transition of the EU from an economic community based upon particular economic freedoms and values to an emerging polity. Thus, any conclusions that a social policy analyst might draw from the development of the European Employment Strategy may have a central role to play in the definition of the EU as a polity. By looking at the structures and processes involved in developing new policies we can identify the role of key actors, gauge the legal and political relationships that are emerging *within* Member States and *between* Member States and the Community institutions. We can also look at the legal tools used to formulate, legitimate and sanction emerging policy. We can already see that the new employment policy involves a number of defined actors, new institutional arrangements, policy objectives, normative tools, regulatory and monitoring techniques, and (indirect) sanctions, all taking place within structures of *EU* economic and political governance.

In the past there has been a tendency to draw an analogy between the structure of the EU and a Russian doll,[99] or the peeling of an onion, as a means of explaining the nature of policy-making. However, such an analogy is not the best one. The essential feature of the Russian doll is the close nesting, self-containment of each doll, the same as, but smaller than the original. This anal-

---

[98] This is acknowledged in the "economic" White Paper, *Growth, Competitiveness and Employment*, above n. 8. See also Hervey's essay in Chapter 2 above on the reluctance of the European Court to make inroads into Member States' concepts of social solidarity.

[99] See G Ross, "Assessing the Delors Era and Social Policy" in S Leibfried and P Pierson, (eds), *European Social Policy Between Fragmentation and Integration* (Washington, Brookings, 1995).

ogy does not convey an adequate picture of the disparate, complicated, multi-level, multi-actor and essentially non-linear decision-making processes involved in EU social policy decision-making. If Biagi[100] is right, the Commission is attempting to engineer the convergence of European social policy law-making at national and supranational levels, but the replication of European policies at the national level is not exact, as a Russian doll analogy would lead us to believe. In the future, a major political and legal issue will be how to blend the convergence mechanisms of the European Employment Strategy with the different national models of social policy and labour market regulation, and how to reconcile both with emerging countervailing tendencies towards decentralisation and regional political autonomy in the EU as well as with new forms of power structures emerging at the transnational level.[101]

Another analogy, drawn by Sciarra,[102] regards the multiple voices in the discourse surrounding the Employment Chapter as "a very noisy tower of Babel".[103] I would like to suggest that the fast-tracked implementation of Title VIII is not so anarchic or indeed as multi-voiced as Sciarra's analogy suggests. Events to date instead hint at a monologue orchestrated by the Commission and its technical advisers; this fits more precisely into what Curtin has described as a "synoptic model of decision-making" where an exchange of data by professionals is combined with the application of pre-set scientific rules to determine a form of optimal decision-making.[104] Although a wider group of actors are involved in consultation processes these are not formalised[105] and the European Parliament appears to be side-lined in the decision-making processes of both Title VIII and Title XI.

A further challenge for legal analysis is whether soft law should be classified as "real law" given the central role it plays in the new employment policy and its spill-over effect into other policies, for example in the area of state aids.[106] However, the use of soft law processes, or as Goetschy and Pochet call them, "diplomatic style" processes (such as negotiations), are risky in terms of the

---

[100] See above n. 57.

[101] The growth in cross-border mergers between multinational companies allows new sites of economic power to determine their own social policies. There is also evidence of transnational collective bargaining practices; see P Marginson and K Sisson, "European Collective Bargaining: A Virtual Prospect?", (1998) 36 *JCMS* 505. In March 1999 the European Metalworkers' Federation adopted a solidarity pact which provides for cross-border rights for its members and trade unions affiliated to the EMF, (1999) 307 *European Industrial Relations Review and Report* 2.

[102] See above n. 7.

[103] See above n. 7, at 170.

[104] D Curtin, "Civil Society and the European Union: Opening Spaces for Deliberative Democracy?", *Collected Courses of the Academy of European Law*, vol. VII Book 1 (The Hague, Kluwer Law International, July 1999).

[105] Reading through the press releases of Council meetings we see that consultation with the social partners often takes place informally before Council meetings themselves, in the "margins of the Council" or "over lunch". See, e.g., Council of the EU Press Release 13370/97, Labour and Social Affairs Council Meeting, 15 December 1997.

[106] Although, of course, this is not new in the regulation of state aids. See A Evans, *EC Law of State Aid* (Oxford, Clarendon Press, 1997) chs 6 and 7.

consistency of diagnosis and solutions[107] and consensual solutions might be favoured over controversial solutions which may, in the long run, be more effective. The real test will be how far Commission and Council recommendations to Member States under Article 128(4) EC are followed.

Lawyers' involvement with soft law has revolved around harnessing its use as an interpretative mechanism to give more bite to the enforcement of Community law at the national level but do the Employment Guidelines, while having normative effects, give rise to individual rights? Are they enforceable by individuals, interest groups or trade unions? The Guidelines are influential in policy-making at the national level but the chances of litigation arising from them depends on the legal rules of standing at the national level. A strong argument against elevating soft law to the status of hard law is the democratic deficit that such a law-making process might create. However, a counter-argument is that given the normative consequences of such soft law,[108] its acceptance, or translation into hard law,[109] would only serve to strengthen the Commission's hand in directing EU policy while subjecting the whole process to the rule of law principle.[110] Despite this, Kenner[111] makes the point that probably the reason why the Employment Chapter has been popular is precisely because of its seemingly non-binding nature.

If we accept my initial hypothesis that the new Title VIII has assumed considerable importance[112] what are the repercussions for lawyers? One repercussion is that our conventional pastime of "Court-watching" will instead become a habit of "agenda-watching". In this, many of the tools used by lawyers in analysing the development of intergovernmental decision-making can be usefully employed. But the development of the European Employment Strategy also involves transcending EU levels of governance to analyse the formal "multi-tiered" system of governance; in particular looking at how NAPs and other national employment and fiscal strategies are drawn up. If we doubt the importance of Title VIII, we are likely to favour Sciarra's argument about individual rights enforceable in national courts. Sciarra thus describes the rights contained in Title VIII as:

> ". . . a new and vague category of non-rights: not a traditional subjective right which can give rise to a claim in a national court, no more a program for national parliaments which had attached to 'right to work' constitutional provisions the obligation

---

[107] J Goetschy and P Pochet ,"The Treaty of Amsterdam: a New Approach to Employment and Social Affairs?", (1997) 3 *Transfer* 117.

[108] Kenner, above n. 54, at 59, argues that "The Amsterdam Employment Title, and the soft law instruments used to make its provisions effective over the past two years, *represents as a collective body of rules*, a positive affirmation of a policy approach that has come to be associated with the 'Third Way' agenda" (emphasis added).

[109] Kenner makes the argument that soft law may have to be translated into binding rules as the most effective means to "turn guidelines into solid achievements". See above n. 54, at 60.

[110] Case 294/83 *Parti Ecologiste "Les Verts"* v. *European Parliament* [1986] ECR 1339.

[111] See above n. 54.

[112] *Contra* Pochet, above n. 83, at 277, who argues that there has been "a lot of procedural innovation with a rather weak content".

to legislate in order to keep those already employed in their jobs, not a right to a minimum income when unemployed, nor yet a right to be trained and educated with a view to moving into new occupations".[113]

Moreover, should legal disputes arise between Member States *inter se*, and Member States, the Commission and the European Parliament over Title VIII, the European Court will be asked to address the legality of the processes and measures used to implement it. Such rulings will improve the recognition of Community competence and economic governance in this area but issues relating to standing, rights to representation, consultation and so on in the drawing up of NAPs will continue to remain contingent upon national processes.

In addition to the above, new fora for dialogue are developing between different groupings of social partners, social ministers and civil servants at the national and Community level. These new fora, however, lack an institutional base within the EC Treaty or soft law. Thus we have seen challenges in law to the Commission's choice of which social partners to consult and involve in the formal law-making processes of what is now Article 138 EC.[114] This issue is discussed at length by Bernard in Chapter 14 below but it is worth noting here the willingness of the Court of First Instance to entertain such actions and second, by implication, the acceptance of the Commission's discretion to choose the representatives of the two sides of industry using the method of a soft law Communication.[115]

CONCLUSIONS

The European Employment Strategy has provided a platform on the European stage for the most vocal of the Member States to present their views on the best way to manage labour markets as a conduit for the management of the European economy. Goetschy and Pochet[116] question whether or not there is indeed a need for a joint approach to unemployment given the fact that unemployment has been reduced in a number of the Member States using different policy choices, and the fact that within the economic literature there are divergent views of the effectiveness of the prescriptions offered. Kenner's contention is that the new strategy is heavily biased towards "Third Way" *political* choices.[117] At the European level there is little *democratic* discussion over *policy choices*. Some of these discussions may occur at the national level but each Member State is now constrained by the *Luxembourg Process* which can be used to justify and direct policy choices. The EU has embarked on a high risk

---

[113] See above n. 7.

[114] Case T–135/96 *UEAPME* v. *Council* [1998] ECR II–2335.

[115] See W Streeck, "European Social Policy After Maastricht: The 'Social Dialogue' and Subsidiarity", (1994) 15 *Economic and Industrial Democracy* 151.

[116] Goetschy and Pochet, above n. 107.

[117] See above n. 54.

strategy and its success or failure will determine the future direction of European economic and political governance. The outcome of the "battle of the models" will set an agenda for the relationship between the "economic" and "social" which will bear the hallmark for what "social policy" means for the EU in the years to come.

PART V

Hidden Agendas: Family Formations and Human Capital Development

11

A Family Law for the European Union?

CLARE McGLYNN*

Is it possible (yet) to talk about a European Union family law? For many, the initial response to this question will be no. Such dissenters may point to the Treaties and argue that they do not provide any legal basis for the development of a family law; nor, it might be suggested, is there any direct reference to "family law" in the legislation of the EU. Indeed, the infamous judgment of the European Court of Justice in *Hofmann* might be put forward to confirm that the EU has no jurisdiction regarding the "organisation of family life".[1] There is some merit in these responses, but I argue in this chapter that the time has now come to reveal and discuss the evolving "European Union family law". Moreover, I suggest that this developing field of law and policy must become the focus of greater critical attention in order to be challenged and, where it has developed, to be subject to careful and critical scrutiny.

To date, a number of scholars have been critically engaged in evaluating the employment and construction of the concept of "the family" in Community law, revealing its partiality and consequent adverse effects for many excluded individuals and communities.[2] This chapter develops these arguments by examining a number of recent cases which serve to reinforce the traditional interpretation of "the family" fashioned and employed by the European Court. In particular, I argue that the Court has fashioned a "model European family" through its jurisprudence, principally in the field of sex equality law, which forms the basis for Community law entitlements. This analysis belies any residual suggestion that the reach of Community law is beyond "the family". At the same time as the Court has been constructing its vision of the "model European

* Many of the issues discussed in this essay were first presented at the faculty of law, University of Helsinki and I should like to thank Kevät Nousiainen, Eeva Nykänen and Anu Pylkkänen for their insightful comments and suggestions.

[1] Case 184/83 *Hofmann* v. *Barmer Ersatzkasse* [1984] ECR 3047, para. 24.

[2] See in particular Tamara Hervey, "Migrant Workers and their Families in the European Union: the Pervasive Market Ideology of Community Law" in Jo Shaw and Gillian More (eds), *New Legal Dynamics of European Union* (Oxford, Clarendon Press, 1995); Tamara Hervey and Jo Shaw, "Women, Work and Care: Women's Dual Role and Double Burden in EC Sex Equality Law", (1998) 8 *Journal of European Social Policy* 43; Kirsten Scheiwe, "EC Law's Unequal Treatment of the Family: the Case Law of the European Court of Justice on Rules Prohibiting Discrimination on the Grounds of Sex and Nationality", (1994) 3 *Social and Legal Studies* 243; Louise Ackers and Helen Stalford, "Children, Migration and Citizenship in the European Union: Intra-Community Mobility and the Status of Children in EC Law", (1999) 21 *Children and Youth Services Review* 699.

family", the second part of the chapter examines the formation of an EU "family policy" by the European Parliament, Commission and Council. This policy seeks to address "family" concerns in all areas of EU law and policy. The third part of the chapter considers these parallel developments in the context of recent proposals to harmonise private international law and create a new "European judicial area". I argue that these latter two developments may presage a common family law for the EU.

Accordingly, therefore, the terminology "EU family law" employs the concept of "family law" in its broadest sense. I use the term to encompass a range of different legal and policy fields, all of which have an impact on, construct and regulate family forms and practices, including the construction of "the model European family" in the jurisprudence of the European Court, the developing "family policy" emerging from the institutions of the European Union and recent proposals from the European Council, Commission and legal scholars for a common EU civil law. In this way, this chapter draws together a wide range of different strands of law and policy, with the aim of presenting a broadly cohesive whole, forming the field of "EU family law". The gathering together of these disparate policy areas, and their consequent analysis as a whole, is an essential process in revealing their significance and enabling future analysis of developing policy.

THE EUROPEAN COURT AND THE CONSTRUCTION OF THE "MODEL EUROPEAN FAMILY"

Despite the lack of a distinct legal basis for Community regulation of families, it is unrealistic to believe that the EU's activities will remain wholly divorced from any consideration of these issues, especially in view of its jurisdiction in the fields of free movement of persons and sex equality law. As these fields of law have developed, and questions regarding the interpretation of "family" and the nature of family life have been raised, the European Court has constructed a "model European family" in which the rights and privileges of Community law reside.[3] This privileging of particular family forms, relationships and individuals has not been achieved on a random, arbitrary basis; nor from a neutral, objective perspective. On the contrary, Community law reproduces a particular conception of the traditional "nuclear" family: that of the heterosexual married union, in which the husband is head of the family and principal breadwinner and the wife is the primary child carer. It is also a conceptualisation of family

---

[3] My focus on how Community *law* constructs "the family" does not presume that law is the sole determinant in such a process. It is without doubt that a host of societal and cultural factors impinge on constructions of "the family". Nonetheless, law in this context is an important "signifier of power" as it claims the power of definition of entitlement to rights. On this point generally, see Katherine O'Donovan, *Family Law Matters* (London, Pluto, 1993) 18–29. It is important therefore to examine law's power in constituting a particular conception of "the family" and this is ever more so at the level of the EU, with the facility to produce supranational law binding on fifteen Member States.

which reinforces the notion of children as dependants.[4] This is the "model European family" constructed by Community law.[5] This model, although mythical and imaginary, and bearing little relation to the realities of family life in the EU,[6] is nonetheless a powerful concept in Community law. The "model European family" excludes some families from rights under EU law, it privileges specific relationships and it perpetuates discrimination against both women and men. Most significantly, as the EU contemplates ever greater jurisdiction in the family field, the "model European family" potentially provides the normative foundation for the development of EU family law.

An analysis of the "model European family" may begin with the privileging of heterosexual marriage. It was in *Netherlands* v. *Reed* that the European Court considered that a "spouse", for the purpose of the grant of free movement "family rights", is to be limited to married persons, and does not therefore include cohabitees.[7] A Community law "family", therefore, entails heterosexual partnerships which are accorded the status of "family" only via marriage. Equally, whereas marriage bequeaths the status of "family", divorce appears to take it away.[8] This pattern of the Court's jurisprudence has led Isabella Moebius and Erika Szyszczak to argue that the free movement provisions are based on a "male breadwinner family model".[9] The apparent aim of Community law, therefore, is to privilege, and encourage the movement of, those families which provide the "infrastructure for men's mobility"[10], that is, the availability of a (preferably full-time) wife. This is the nuclear family model writ large at Community level: the "model European family".

This articulation of the concept of "family" in the area of free movement of persons has been entrenched in recent judgments relating to the rights of gays and lesbians under the EU's sex equality laws. In *Grant* v. *South West Trains* the European Court refused to extend the scope of Article 141 and the Equal Pay Directive to cover discrimination on the grounds of sexual orientation.[11] In

---

[4] On the construction of childhood in Community free movement law, see Ackers and Stalford, above n. 2.

[5] In presenting an argument that Community law *constructs* an idealised and mythical "family" as the "model family" of the EU, I am aware of the challenges of the constructionist approach to analysing "family law" (on which see John Dewar, "The Normal Chaos of Family Law", (1998) 61 *MLR* 467). Nonetheless, the analysis remains valuable in order to reveal the general construction of the law, even if there may be some exceptions.

[6] For a detailed examination of the nature of family forms and relationships within the EU today, see Eileen Drew, Ruth Emerek and Evelyn Mahon (eds), *Women, Work and the Family in Europe* (London, Routledge, 1998). See also the Commission's publication *The European Union and the Family* (Luxembourg, European Commission, 1994) part of the *Social Europe* series, vol. 1/94.

[7] Case 59/85 *Netherlands* v. *Reed* [1986] ECR 1283.

[8] It may be implied from Case 267/83 *Diatta* v. *Land Berlin* [1985] ECR 567 that the rights of a migrant worker's "spouse" may be extinguished on divorce. See further Louise Ackers, *Shifting Spaces—Women, Citizenship and Migration within the European Union* (Bristol, Policy Press, 1998) especially ch. 4.

[9] Isabella Moebius and Erika Szyszczak, "Of Raising Pigs and Children", (1998) 18 *YEL* 433.

[10] Scheiwe, above n. 2, at 251.

[11] Directive no. 75/117. Case C–249/96 *Grant* v. *South West Trains* [1998] IRLR 165.

doing so, the Court stated that there is a lack of consensus among Member States about whether "stable relationships between persons of the same sex may be regarded as equivalent to stable relationships between persons of the opposite sex".[12] It continued that Member States held this position "for the purpose of protecting the family".[13] Clearly, same sex partnerships do not constitute a "family", nor are they deemed worthy of the protection of Community law. The Court of First Instance relied on this expression of the limits of Community law when interpreting the scope of allowances paid to "spouses" of Community officials in *D* v. *Council*.[14] D argued that his homosexual partnership, registered under Swedish law and therefore accorded similar rights and privileges to those who marry, entitled his partner to be treated as his "spouse". The Court held that "*Community* notions of marriage and partnership exclusively address a relationship founded on civil marriage in the traditional sense of the term".[15] Thus, there now exists a *Community* concept of spouse and partner which excludes same sex partnerships.

In view of the fact that Community law privileges heterosexual partnerships legitimated by civil marriage, it is perhaps not surprising that it also reproduces traditional roles for women and men within "the family". I have argued elsewhere that this reproduction of particular familial roles is based on a dominant ideology of motherhood.[16] Briefly, this ideology constructs a normative model of women and motherhood, the foundation of which is the perceived natural, universal and unchanging nature of the maternal role, together with the presumed existence of a strong maternal instinct in *all* women.[17] This leads to the assumption that motherhood is the usual and appropriate role for women; the rightful (and actual) ambition of all "normal" women. Unsurprisingly, therefore, the mother-child relationship is privileged, it being considered as sacrosanct and pivotal to the emotional and physical well-being of the child, based on the now discredited theories of mother-infant bonding.[18] Accordingly, child care is seen to be the primary responsibility of women, and if paid employment is taken up, it should take second place to the woman's responsibilities within the home.

That this ideology is dominant in the jurisprudence of the European Court can be seen by examining a series of cases from the mid-1980s to the present day.

---

[12] *Ibid.*, para. 35. Note that this "lack of consensus" did not prevent the Court extending the Equal Treatment Directive to cover discrimination on the grounds of transsexuality, see case C–13/94 *P* v. *S and Cornwall County Council* [1996] ECR I–2143. See further Carl Stychin in Chapter 13 below.

[13] See above n. 11, para. 33.

[14] Case T–264/97 *D and Sweden* v. *Council* [1999] ECR II-1, para. 26.

[15] *Ibid.*, unofficial translation (emphasis added). This case has been appealed to the European Court, Joined Cases C–122, 125/99.

[16] "Ideologies of Motherhood in European Community Sex Equality Law" (2000) 6 *ELJ* 29.

[17] See Evelyn Nakano Glenn, "Social Constructions of Mothering: A Thematic Overview", in Nakano Glenn *et al* (eds), *Mothering: Ideology, Experience and Agency* (London, Routledge, 1994) 1.

[18] For a detailed discussion of these theories and their impact on Community law and the dominant ideology of motherhood, see above n. 16.

The cornerstone of the ideology can be traced to the cases *Commission* v. *Italy* and *Hofmann*, but it has been fortified in the recent cases of *Hill and Stapleton* and *Abdoulaye*.[19] The Court in *Commission* v. *Italy* was faced with legislation which provided women only with leave on the adoption of a child: that is, legislation based on a traditional conception of motherhood. The Court, therefore, had the opportunity to rule on whether the legislative pursuit of this vision, and the privileging of the mother-child relationship, was compatible with Community sex equality law. It held that the Italian legislation did not conflict with Community law and, moreover, that the Italian government had been motivated by a "legitimate concern" which led it "rightly" to introduce legislation attempting to assimilate the entry of adoptive and natural children into the family, especially during the "very delicate initial period".[20] The Court continued that, in these circumstances, the difference in treatment between women and men "cannot be regarded as discrimination" within the meaning of the Equal Treatment Directive.[21] Underpinning this judgment is the belief that different treatment on account of motherhood (and not biological differences regarding the capacity to give birth) does not constitute unlawful discrimination. In making this judgment, the Court reinforces sexual divisions of labour in which child care is always the responsibility of mothers, ignoring any conception that the father may also have a legitimate need and/or desire for a period of leave. Fatherhood is thereby limited, by implication, to a breadwinning role, with the assumption that a man's primary commitment and identification should be with paid work, rather than child care.[22]

This approach was followed up in *Hofmann* where the European Court upheld the grant of an optional period of maternity leave to women only. In effect, the Court accorded primacy to the role of the mother, stating that the "protection" of "pregnancy and motherhood" and the "special relationship between a woman and her child"[23] are legitimate aims of Member State and Community policy. This is the reproduction of the dominant ideology of motherhood in which the mother and child are expected to have a very close relationship and where the child is to receive constant and individualised care and attention given solely by the mother.[24] This clearly assumes that the mother has a more important role than that of the father. There is no desire to protect (or encourage) fathers, or fathers' special relationships with their children. Thus, in *Commission* v. *Italy* and

---

[19] Cases 163/82 *Commission* v. *Italian Republic* [1983] ECR 3273; *Hofmann*, above n. 1; Case C–243/95 *Hill and Stapleton* v. *The Revenue Commissioners and the Department of Finance* [1998] ECR I–3739; Case C–218/98 *Abdoulaye* v. *Renault*, [1999] IRLR 811.

[20] *Ibid.*, para. 16.

[21] See above n. 19, para. 17.

[22] On the traditional conception of fatherhood and the part this plays in limiting opportunities for women, see Richard Collier, " 'Feminising' the Workplace? Law, the 'Good Parent' and the 'Problem of Men' ", in Anne Morris and Therese O'Donnell (eds), *Feminist Perspectives on Employment Law* (London, Cavendish, 1999).

[23] See above n. 19, para. 26.

[24] See further Jan Windebank, "To What Extent Can Social Policy Challenge the Dominant Ideology of Mothering", (1996) 6 *Journal of European Social Policy* 147.

Hofmann the European Court articulated a clear vision of the role of mothers, and, by implication, of fathers, representing a judicial reinforcement of the dominant ideology of motherhood and the traditional family model.

The *Commission* v. *Italy* and *Hofmann* judgments were handed down in the mid-1980s and it might have been thought that the traditional rendering of women's and men's roles within "the family" would have given way in recent years to a more progressive and egalitarian response. However, the recent judgment in *Abdoulaye* demonstrates that such optimism is unfounded. In *Abdoulaye* the Court was asked to rule that a payment made to women "on taking maternity leave" constituted discrimination against men in view of the fact that the payment was equivalent to a child allowance to which women and men should be equally entitled. This argument was augmented by an examination of two further aspects of the company's policy, namely the fact that the payment was made to women in addition to their entitlement to maternity leave on full salary and that on the adoption of a child, the company made a payment to either the adoptive mother or father. The Court, however, upheld the payment to women only arguing that women suffer "several occupational disadvantages inherent in taking maternity leave"[25] which makes their situation not comparable with men becoming parents. As it was not possible, according to the Court, to compare the treatment of women and men, the payment to women only did not constitute a breach of the equal pay principle.

The Court has legitimated special treatment on account of motherhood, reinforcing the idea that the birth of a child is the principal responsibility of women. The appropriate comparison in *Abdoulaye* would have been women and men becoming parents. As both become parents, as both could become adoptive parents, the payment to women only would have constituted direct sex discrimination. To exclude men from a societal recognition of the significance (and financial expense) of the birth of a child is to perpetuate a traditional assumption that the birth and care of a child is a women's concern and responsibility. Not only is this a disservice to women, ensuring the continuation of outdated assumptions about their family and workplace roles, but it also means that men are not encouraged and/or helped to take up new and expanding opportunities to play a significant role in the care and upbringing of their children.[26]

In light of the above rulings regarding the nature of women and men's roles within the family, it is of great concern that the Court stated in *Hill and Stapleton* that the aim of Community policy is to "encourage and, if possible, adapt working conditions to family responsibilities" and to ensure the "[p]rotection of women within family life".[27] The crucial question here is, what constitutes the

---

[25] See above n. 19, para. 18.

[26] Furthermore, it could be argued that the judgment in *Abdoulaye* runs counter to the Court's earlier ruling in Case 312/86 *Commission* v. *France* [1988] ECR 6315 in which the Court rendered unlawful employment provisions for the "special protection" of women which included child allowances which were paid only to women.

[27] See above n. 19, para. 42. See further Clare McGlynn and Catherine Farrelly, "Equal Pay and the 'Protection of Women in Family Life'", (1999) 24 *ELRev* 202.

"family life" in need of protection? It is arguable that it is a conceptualisation captured by the "model European family", that of a heterosexual married union in which women and men pursue traditional roles regarding work and family. This is because the Court implies that it is policy to change working conditions to meet *existing* family responsibilities: as opposed to family responsibilities needing to change in order to liberate women and men. Thus, the Court assumes a static position regarding family responsibilities and merely seeks to adapt working conditions to meet that reality. Thus, although the Court goes on to state that women's "professional activities" should also be protected, this implies a workplace in which traditionally masculine modes of working continue, with adaptations only being made to enable *women* to meet "their" family commitments.

As well as a belated recognition of the need for some change, this is also a limited vision of the future. It is indeed crucially important that working conditions are modified, but they must be altered for women and men. In addition, there must be concomitant changes in the domestic responsibilities of women and men, with men assuming greater familial obligations. Thus, although the Court goes on to state that it is also Community policy to protect "men's role" in family life,[28] it appears that the role for men that is being "protected" is that which perceives men as the primary breadwinners and of fathers removed from day-to-day child care which remains the mother's responsibility. It thus suggests a preservation of the limits of men's existing involvement in the family.

I am arguing, therefore, that the Court has constructed a "model European family" which forms the normative basis for its jurisprudence when faced with interpretations of "family" and "equality" rights. This is an exclusionary and reactionary model and one which limits the dynamism of the EU as a progressive polity. It also potentially limits the effectiveness of the EU's sex equality laws and, more particularly in the context of this chapter, as jurisdiction in the family field develops, it is of great concern that it is this model of the "family" which may form the basis for an emerging EU family law and policy.

A "FAMILY POLICY" FOR THE EUROPEAN UNION

In tandem with the construction of the "model European family", the institutions of the EU, particularly the Parliament, Commission and Council, have been developing an EU "family policy" in recognition that the "family" and the intimate relationships of all individuals both have an impact on, and are affected by, EU activity.[29] The EU first began to develop a family policy in the early 1980s

---

[28] See above n. 19, para. 42.
[29] In analyses of social and public policy, a particular policy is termed a "family" policy if the "family" is the deliberate target of specific actions and the measures initiated are designed to have an impact on family resources and structures. See further Linda Hantrais and Marie-Therese Letablier, *Families and Family Policies in Europe* (London, Longman, 1996) 139.

when the European Parliament advocated the adoption of a "comprehensive family policy".[30] It suggested that such a policy should be developed by encouraging Member States to take account of the needs of families when introducing legislation and, where appropriate, harmonising policies at Community level. The Parliament also called for further research to determine the need for Community action relating to the *laws* on adoption, custody of children, rights of access to children and maintenance obligations. The Parliament reiterated its call for an "integrated family policy" in 1994, stressing the need to "adapt family *law*" at both national and European levels.[31] Most recently in 1999, the Parliament targeted its proposals for family policy on cross-border disputes, demanding a "co-ordinated mechanism among all European countries in the area of family law in order to avoid penalising children in the event of divorce between partners of different nationalities".[32] This latest proposal was made within the context of moves towards the creation of a "European judicial area", and envisages coordinated action in the field of cross-border child custody disputes, although it is not clear whether it is harmonised family laws or the greater integration of private international laws which are being recommended. Nonetheless, what characterises the views of the Parliament is the extent to which the jurisdiction of the EU in the family *law* field is considered legitimate, and the integrationist approach, i.e. the extent to which the harmonisation of laws, is recommended.

The Commission largely endorsed the approach of the Parliament in its Communication on an EU family policy,[33] and this was followed by a Council Resolution on the same theme.[34] The Community action envisaged by the Council was considerably more limited than the proposals from the Parliament and the Commission, and recommended that the exchange of information regarding family policies should be strengthened and that the "family dimension" should be taken into account when adopting policy. The Council also noted that any action at Community level would "have to be pragmatic in order to respect the special features of different national policies already created and the varying socio-economic contexts in which such policies operate". Notwithstanding the limited tenor, the conclusions are of symbolic significance as they accept the legitimacy and necessity of a role for the EU in family policy.

However, it is the grounds on which jurisdiction is assumed by the Community institutions that are of particular concern. The Commission's interest in an EU family policy springs largely from anxiety regarding changing demographics in Europe, in particular decreasing fertility rates and the problems that this poses for the "labour market", "social security systems" and the

---

[30]   Resolution on Family Policy in the EC, [1983] OJ C184/116.

[31]   Resolution on the Protection of Families and Family Units at the Close of the International Year of the Family, [1995] OJ C18/96 (emphasis added).

[32]   Resolution on the Protection of Families and Children, [1999] OJ C128/79.

[33]   European Commission Communication, *Family Policies* (COM(98) 363).

[34]   Conclusions of the Council and of the Ministers Responsible for Family Affairs, [1989] OJ C277/2.

"realisation of the single market".[35] In addition, the Commission argued that "the family" is important for the future of European society as it is "part of the economic sector, for it raises future producers and is a unit of consumption".[36] For these (largely economic) reasons, Community level action regarding "the family" is deemed necessary. National level action is apparently insufficient as national action is "relatively slow in adapting to the pace of change" in this area.[37] The Council is similarly concerned with the "demographic outlook" as it raises the considerable "question of Europe's political, economic and cultural future in the world".[38] In addition, the Council endorsed the Commission's justification for Community action as springing from the "economic role of the family", as well as its role in the care of children and "solidarity between the generations".[39] The concern is that there are not enough "Europeans" being produced in order to care for the growing elderly population and to ensure the future of Europe as a politically and economically viable polity.

The evolving EU family policy has drawn little attention from scholars of Community *law*, perhaps due to the essentially non-binding nature of the resolutions and the apparent lack of any coherent initiatives. This may begin to change as the impact of the policy begins to be felt in more and more areas of substantive law,[40] and it is important that it should. The very existence of this policy reveals, first, that family structures and practices are not beyond the reach of Community activity, despite what might be thought to be the case from a cursory glance at the Treaties and the guiding economic imperatives of the EU. Secondly, the resolutions demonstrate that there is considerable institutional support for a more coherent approach to "the family" within the EU, extending beyond mere cooperation and information exchange, to encompass changes to national family laws. Thirdly, the integrative drive of the policies can be clearly seen, particularly in the Council's concern with the future of the EU's world role. Finally, the justifications for the development of policy are largely economic and consequentialist. That is to say that the concern is with the single market and the potentially vast strains on future budgets arising from changing demographics. The development of a "family policy" is seen as a means by which to deal with those issues: family policy is not an end in itself, but a means by which to achieve the economic and political goals of the EU.[41]

---

[35] See above n. 33, para. 29.

[36] *Ibid.*, para. 37.

[37] *Ibid.*, para. 43.

[38] See above n. 34.

[39] *Ibid.*

[40] See for example the proposed directive on the right to family reunification for third country nationals, proposed by the Commission on 1 December 1999, Press Release IP/99/920, COM(99) 638.

[41] An analogy may be made with the development of the human rights jurisdiction of the EU which has been criticised as being more economistic and symbolic, than a genuine and practical attempt to improve the rights of individuals.

THE "EUROPEAN JUDICIAL AREA": A ROLE FOR FAMILY LAW?

Taken separately, the construction of the "model European family" and the promotion of an EU family policy raise many worrying questions. However, when examined together with recent moves towards the creation of a "European judicial area", they take on a new significance. Proposals for a European judicial area, and a common civil law for Europe, have been promoted by scholars and the European Parliament for many years, but have come closer to realisation since the entry into force of the Amsterdam Treaty and the Council's political agreement to take steps towards the realisation of an "area of freedom, justice and security" within the EU. The scope of this European judicial area is not yet clear, but if political statements are to be believed, it is very wide and includes the regulation of family forms and practices. In developing the field of family law in the European judicial area, it seems possible that the conceptualisation of the "model European family" and the EU's "family policy" will form an important foundation upon which policy is developed. This has potentially serious effects both in terms of the exclusionary concept of the "family" which may be employed in the emerging family law, and in relation to the potential scope of any such laws in light of the broad approach taken in the development of "family policy" thus far. The first step towards the development of a more comprehensive family law in the EU comes with the "communitarisation" of private international law.

Into the fold: harmonising private international law of the family

The Community has long played a role in the private international law arrangements of its Member States. Indeed since 1968 the Brussels Convention has regulated the jurisdiction and enforcement of judgments in civil and commercial matters, with the exception of matters relating to the "status or legal capacity of natural persons" or "rights in property arising out of a matrimonial relationship".[42] Although the Brussels Convention is an agreement between the Member States of the EU, regulated in part by the European Court, it remains an international treaty, command over which remains with national governments, including the amendment process and the right to derogate from certain provisions. Thus, the Convention merely sets the *framework* within which

---

[42] The Convention was adopted on the basis of Article 294(4) (ex 220(4)) EC. Since the signing of the Convention, it has been expanded to cover all fifteen Member States, though the implementation in each Member State varies and, in particular, a number of states have not ratified the Convention, as amended after the accession of Sweden, Finland and Austria to the Community in 1995. For details, see European Commission, Proposal for a Council Regulation on Jurisdiction and Enforcement of Judgments in Civil and Commercial Matters (COM(99) 348) para. 2.1.

national laws relating to the recognition and enforcement of foreign judgments have force.[43]

The Maastricht Treaty presaged some change in these jurisdiction and recognition procedures, with its professed desire for greater judicial cooperation.[44] However, it is the Amsterdam Treaty which brings such hopes to life and in particular enables *Community* measures to give effect to such ambitions.[45] Thus, in 1999 the Council stated that it was "determined to develop the Union as an area of freedom, security and justice" and that this objective will be placed "at the very top of the political agenda".[46] This is a project, it proclaimed, which "responds to the frequently expressed concerns of citizens and has a direct bearing on their daily lives". A "shared area of prosperity and peace" is the expressed aim, building on the already "firm commitment to freedom based on human rights, democratic institutions and the rule of law". The enjoyment of "freedom" requires a "genuine area of justice, where people can approach courts and authorities in any Member State as easily as in their own". The proposals involve greater cooperation in the criminal law and justice field, the development of common rules on asylum and immigration, together with proposals for the communitarisation of private international law. Thus, in the European area of justice, "individuals and businesses should not be prevented or discouraged from exercising their rights by the incompatibility or complexity of legal and administrative systems in the Member States".

Accordingly, the Commission has proposed a new Community Regulation on the recognition and enforcement of judgments, replacing the Brussels Convention, thereby *communitarising* the private international laws of the Member States.[47] Thus, there will be a harmonisation of central legal concepts, such as domicile, the right of initiative of amendment will rest with the Commission, the entirety of the Regulation will be binding in all Member States and enforcement will be in the hands of the Commission and European Court. The measure has been proposed in order to achieve "transparency" and to "improve and expedite the free movement of judgments in civil and commercial matters within the internal market". This in turn will contribute to the establishment of the area of "freedom, security and justice" within which the "free

---

[43] For example, concepts such as "domicile" remain determined at a national level, the Convention merely providing that it is "domicile" that is the relevant concept in specific circumstances.

[44] Title VI of the Maastricht Treaty, "Provisions on Co-operation in the Fields of Justice and Home Affairs", included as matters of common interest, "judicial co-operation in civil and criminal matters", Article K.1.

[45] Article 2 TEU commits the Member States to the objective of maintaining and developing the EU as an area of freedom, security and justice. Article 65 EC provides a legal basis for Community measures in the field of judicial cooperation in civil matters.

[46] Presidency Conclusions, Tampere European Council, 15–16 October 1999, available from the Finnish Presidency website at : http://presidency.finland.fi/frame.asp

[47] See European Commission, above n. 42. As proposed, the regulation will not apply to the United Kingdom, Ireland and Denmark which all secured opt-outs from these provisions in the Amsterdam Treaty.

movement of persons is assured and litigants can assert their rights". Finally, the measure is justified on the basis that these measures are needed to secure the "sound operation of the internal market".

Although the adoption of this measure would represent an important extension of Community competence, it does remain within the commercial field. However, the Council has given its political endorsement to the need for measures beyond the commercial field, particularly those relating to "certain judgments in the field of family litigation (for example on maintenance claims and visiting rights)".[48] It has also recommended that work begin on an instrument on the choice of law applicable not only in non-contractual obligations, but also in divorce.[49] Thus far, the Commission has proposed a *Community* Regulation on jurisdiction and the recognition and enforcement of judgments relating to the dissolution of marriage, divorce and annulment, and in matters of parental responsibility for joint children.[50] This proposal represents a significant expansion in the scope of the Community's activities. As with the communitarisation of the Brussels Convention, what was once private international law now becomes Community law. Moreover, whereas the scope of the Brussels Convention, and its proposed reform as a Community measure, continues to be concerned with commercial matters, this proposed Regulation covers matters which have hitherto remained within the sole competence of Member States. The proposed Regulation will introduce uniform standards for jurisdiction on annulment, divorce and separation and aims to facilitate the rapid and automatic recognition among Member States of judgments on these issues. It will also provide for uniform rules of jurisdiction regarding parental responsibility of children, and the recognition and enforcement of judgments relating thereto. As with the proposed reform of the Brussels Convention, this measure, being a Community Regulation, will be binding in its entirety in the Member States and will be under the authoritative interpretative jurisdiction of the European Court.

Despite this considerable expansion of jurisdiction, the justifications for the adoption of the Regulation are weak and unconvincing. It has been proposed on the basis of Article 65 EC (located in the title relating to common immigration policies and free movement of persons), and enables measures to be taken promoting "compatibility of the rules of conflicts of law and jurisdiction" which are "necessary for the proper functioning of the internal market". Not surprisingly, therefore, the Commission argues that the proposed regulation is necessary to ensure the "sound operation of the internal market" which creates a need to "recognise and enforce judgments in matrimonial matters and in matters of parental responsibility".[51] This is, however, mere assertion and fails to explain

---

[48] See above n. 46.

[49] "Priorities of the Ministry of Justice During the Finnish Presidency", 1 July 1999, at http://www.om.fi/1438.htm.

[50] COM(99) 220.

[51] See para. 1.1 of the Explanatory Memorandum accompanying the proposed regulation (COM(99) 220).

why the "sound operation" of the internal market requires uniform rules relating to the dissolution of marriage and child custody judgments. The Commission also suggests that the Regulation will represent a "fundamental stage" in the development of a European judicial area.[52] This may indeed be so, but this does not provide a justification as to why this measure in particular should be adopted. Finally, the Commission states that the introduction of European citizenship requires "additional work to be carried out in respect of certain aspects of the citizens' family life".[53] In this way, regulation of international family law is considered important not for the purpose of achieving the more efficient or equitable resolution of cross-border disputes, but for the development of the concept of European citizenship. As the measure is proposed as part of the title on free movement of workers, it might also be implied that the need to remove barriers to the free movement of workers provides a justification for this regulation.[54] Finally, an earlier version of the proposal was justified on the basis that issues of "family law" have to be faced as "part of the phenomenon of European integration".[55]

What is striking about these purported justifications is their consequentialist nature; the measures are proposed not in order to eradicate perceived problems regarding the enforcement and recognition of divorce and child custody arrangements, but in order to promote other goals such as European integration, the creation of a common judicial area, the operation of the single market and the development of European citizenship.[56] The significance of this is that if measures relating to uniform rules on recognition of divorce can be subsumed within the general aim of securing the internal market or common judicial area, there seems to be no reason why harmonisation of divorce laws could not similarly be justified. In this way, although these proposals may appear to be uncontroversial at first glance, it is the harmonisation of private international law which is being proposed, not competence regarding the legality of divorce and child custody per se. A principal note of caution must attach to possible future steps after communitarisation. These current proposals constitute the first direct Community regulation of the status of individuals, rather than just the

---

[52] *Ibid.*

[53] See above n. 51, para. 1.2.

[54] The expansion of the scope of the entitlements under Community law of workers exercising free movement rights has been premised on the need to facilitate movement by removing barriers. See Case 207/78 *Ministere Public* v. *Even* [1979] ECR 2019. It could be argued that the differences in national family laws create a barrier to free movement as families are reluctant to move to states where either their rights are not known or are less favourable in the particular circumstances.

[55] Based on Article K(3) of the Maastricht Treaty, a *Convention* on private international law, akin to the Brussels Convention, relating to marriage dissolution, was proposed in 1998. The significance of the Amsterdam Treaty is that it provides a legal basis for *Community* action. See paras. 1 and 2 of the Explanatory Report, [1998] OJ C221/27, and the proposed convention at [1998] OJ C221/1.

[56] This is perhaps due to the fact that the legal basis demands such justifications. However, this simply serves to demonstrate that "family law" proper does not clearly fall within the competence of the EU, but has to be implied from other legal bases.

rights which are accorded to them.[57] Differences of emphasis and application of the rules on recognition and enforcement between Member States will still arise, even where there are common rules of private international law, because of the different national legal and cultural traditions.[58] It is therefore readily foreseeable that in due course it may be argued that the diversity of national laws hinders the free movement of workers and the sound operation of the single market. There is an obvious means by which such "inconsistencies", lack of "transparency" and hindrance of "integration" could be eliminated; greater harmonisation of national family laws.

From uniform private international law to harmonised family laws

The experience of Nordic association in the field of family law may provide an instructive parallel to this debate. Nordic cooperation began in the late nineteenth century and arose from a belief that "harmonisation in policy and institutions was desirable".[59] In particular, the desire for greater harmonisation had a strong commercial bias and was considered necessary in order to ensure the free movement of citizens throughout the Nordic countries.[60] Likewise, it was the apparent conflicts between differing national laws, and their adverse impact on cooperation, that led to increased harmonisation, of which family laws were a crucial component. Common rules of private international law were insufficient and greater harmonisation was thought desirable. It seems clear that there existed a will to harmonise, a justification in commercial and free movement terms and that common rules of private international law were thought insufficient for the task. Although there are many reasons why the cooperation of the Nordic countries and the EU cannot properly be compared,[61] there are some obvious parallels. In this light, is it likely that the EU will progress towards uniform rules of recognition and jurisdiction in family matters and then on to greater harmonisation of national family laws?

Proposals for the harmonisation of the civil laws (including family laws) of Member States have a long pedigree and some scholars consider the convergence process to be an inevitability.[62] Inescapable convergence, of itself, appears

---

[57] That is, the difference between Community law granting certain rights to married persons, thus recognising a status, and under the new proposals, Community law determining the married or other status of persons.

[58] This can already be seen in some of the exceptions detailed in the proposed regulation relating to agreements between the Nordic states, treaties with the Holy See and the particular status of annulment in Portuguese law.

[59] David Bradley, *Family Law and Political Culture—Scandinavian Laws in Comparative Perspective* (London, Sweet and Maxwell, 1996) 29.

[60] *Ibid.*, at 31–2.

[61] In particular, the Nordic countries evidence a striking degree of homogeneity in terms of social structures, political outlook, values and legal systems which is not apparent in the EU as a whole.

[62] For example, René de Groot has suggested that "it is likely that the legal systems of the European states will form one great legal family with uniform or strongly similar rules in many

unproblematic, if indeed this is an inevitable process over which no individual or state has control. However, the movement towards greater convergence of national laws is being actively promoted by scholars through the development of doctrine, through the analysis of existing laws throughout Europe and through the demonstration of their apparent similarities. Such approaches are common in the fields of contract and tort law where scholars not only advocate common laws, but declare their existence from an analysis of present laws.[63] From these beginnings, a "regime of academic lawyers"[64] are generating proposals for a common civil code in order to eradicate the "chaotic situations" which arise from a variety of national, supranational and international laws.[65] In addition to this, the European Parliament has proposed the development of a "European Code of Private Law", suggesting in 1989 that a "start be made on the necessary preparatory work on drawing up" such a Code.[66] The Parliament later developed this idea to propose a "Common European Code of Private Law" in 1994.[67] These developments are not just concerned with developing common principles regarding common laws of tort and contract, but parallel developments regarding the development of a European criminal code also exist,[68] together amounting quite closely to a common law for Europe.

There does not yet appear to be a similar momentum regarding family laws, but this may indeed be the next step, especially in the context of the proposal of an entirely new civil code. Moreover there appears to be little reason why the scholarly projects regarding the development of common contract and tort laws should not take place regarding family laws.[69] If such developments are not

---

areas" (quoted in Pierre Legrand, "European Legal Systems are Not Converging", (1996) 45 *ICLQ* 52 at 54). Basil Markesinis has also suggested that there should be "no doubt that convergence is taking place" (quoted in Legrand *ibid.*).

[63] See generally Christian von Bar, *The Common European Law of Torts* (Oxford, Clarendon Press, 1998); Walter van Gerven, Jeremy Lever, Pierre Larouche, Christian von Bar and Genevieve Viney, *Cases and Materials and Text on National, Supranational and International Tort Law: Scope of Protection* (Oxford, Hart, 1998); Hein Kötz and Alex Flessner, *European Contract Law Volume I: Formation, Validity and the Content of Contracts; Contracts and Third Parties* (Tony Weir (trans.), Oxford, Clarendon Press, 1997); Lando Commission, *Principles of European Contract Law* (1998), referred to in Christoph Schmidt, "'Bottom-up' harmonisation of European Private Law: *Ius Commune* and Restatement" in Veijo Heiskanen and Kati Kulovesi (eds), *Function and Future of European Law—Proceedings of the International Conference on the Present State, Rationality and Direction of European Legal Integration* (Helsinki, Helsinki University Press, 1999) 81.
[64] The phraseology of Ole Lando in his review of Hein Kötz and Alex Flessner's work on European contract law (1999) 36 *CMLRev* 1106.
[65] Christoph Schmidt, above n. 63, at 77.
[66] Resolution of the European Parliament on Action to Bring into Line the Private Law of the Member States, [1989] OJ C158/400.
[67] Resolution of the European Parliament on the Harmonisation of Certain Sectors of the Private Law of the Member States, [1994] OJ C205/518.
[68] See the discussion in Kimmo Nuotio, "Should Criminal Law be Our Common European Concern?" in Heiskanen and Kulovesi, above n. 63, at 223.
[69] There are a number of comparative projects regarding the family laws of Europe (see for example Jacek Kurczewski and Mavis Maclean (eds), *Family Law and Family Policy in the New Europe* (Dartmouth, Aldershot, 1997), though as yet, the political ambition of seeking to *create* a common European family law from analysis appears to be absent.

already taking place, it is likely that the adoption of the Regulation proposing uniform recognition rules for divorce and parental responsibility may act as a spur and justification for such a task. And indeed further harmonisation is envisaged at the institutional level of the EU. The Commission has stated that the measures relating to divorce and parental responsibility represent only a "first step" which may "open the way to other texts on matters of family law and succession".[70] Furthermore the Council stated in 1999 that, in general, "[b]etter compatibility and convergence between the legal systems of Member States must be achieved".[71] In particular, it stated that there is a need for "special common procedural rules for simplified and accelerated cross-border litigation", including the adoption of a European Enforcement Order, in a number of fields, such as "maintenance claims".[72] Here the emphasis is on cross-border cases, though there is a perceived need for common procedural rules which relate to "enhanced access to law", including the taking of evidence, time limits and orders for money payment.[73] As regards substantive law, the recommendations are more modest, namely the request for an overall study on the need to approximate the substantive law of the Member States in the civil law field.[74] In this light, just as uniform rules of private international law have been proposed as necessary for the operation of the internal market, for the development of a common judicial area and as a basis for developing European citizenship, it is not inconceivable that similar justifications may be put forward for greater harmonisation of the national family laws of Member States. This may be particularly so if the measures are proposed as part of an apparently "technocratic" and therefore "apolitical" move towards greater judicial cooperation, as at present, rather than as expansive, federalising proposals to increase the competence of the EU.

Following on from the above analysis, I would suggest that the development of an EU family law may encompass the following stages. First, Community definitions of terms like "family" or "spouse" are developed alongside the fashioning of a "model European family" which forms the basis for determining Community law entitlements. Secondly, the perceived need to consider "family issues" in all aspects of EU activity is supported through the adoption of an EU "family policy". Taken together, these developments eschew any suggestion that the regulation of families lies outside of Community law and, especially in the case of the former, sets the tone for the kind of "family" law that is to be developed. The next stage moves from granting rights on the basis of an existing nationally granted status, to determining that status at Community level. Thus, the third step is the introduction of uniform rules of private international law. At present, the proposals in this field are more symbolic than substantive,

---

[70] See above n. 55, para. 1.
[71] See above n. 46, para. 5.
[72] *Ibid.*, para. 30.
[73] *Ibid.*, para. 38.
[74] *Ibid.*, paras 38–9.

but, if adopted, would create a significant precedent. From here, it is but a short (fourth) step towards proposals for, and perhaps the limited introduction of, measures to initiate greater commonality in the family laws of Member States.[75]

CHALLENGING THE DEVELOPMENT OF AN EU FAMILY LAW

My general aim in this chapter has been to reveal the evolving field of EU family law and to sound a cautionary note regarding its development. Some might argue that I am tilting at windmills. Pierre Legrand argues that a common civil code would be singularly unsuccessful due to the entrenched differences between the civil and common law traditions in the legal systems of Member States of the EU.[76] Schmidt similarly suggests that the development of a common civil code is not practical, although he generally supports greater harmonisation.[77] Furthermore, he suggests that were such a harmonisation to take place, family law is likely not to be included.[78] In the context of proposals for a common European criminal code, Kimmo Nuotio suggests that the development of such a code is similarly impractical.[79] He looks to Nordic cooperation to demonstrate that despite the homogeneity of those societies (similarities which are lacking when considering the EU as a whole), there has been no development of a common Nordic law. The same argument may be made regarding Nordic cooperation in the family law field in which, although there has been considerable harmonisation, there is no uniformity.[80]

However, impractical as the proposals for a common civil code may be, my concern is that they may yet be attempted and implemented if the political will exists. There has been no unification in Nordic family laws, despite cultural homogeneity, because national governments retain sole sovereignty in this field. In the context of a supranational organisation, with supremacy of law in some areas, and in some quarters, a zealous pursuit of European integration, attempts to harmonise are arguably more likely to succeed, even if only at the level of the legislation being adopted.[81] If this is the case, it is imperative to be alert to these possibilities now in order that such developments may be challenged: The problem is that the adoption of general principles in the area of family policy, and

---

[75] Albeit that some Member States are likely to offer many objections. In particular, as noted above, the United Kingdom, Ireland and Denmark have already secured opt-outs from measures adopted under this title of the Treaty.

[76] Pierre Legrand, "Against a European Civil Code", (1997) 60 *MLR* 44.

[77] Christoph Schmidt, above n. 63, at 79–81.

[78] Though such an exclusion is welcome, it is made on the assumption that the fields of tort and contract are "apolitical" and can therefore be harmonised legitimately: Christoph Schmidt, above n. 63, at 80.

[79] Above n. 68.

[80] David Bradley's book testifies to both the similarities and differences in the Scandinavian family laws, see above n. 59.

[81] That is, legislation being adopted even if it has little impact on the realities of family law and family life in each Member State.

even family law, are not being mooted as part of a European strategy for the modernisation of family life or the removal of traditional barriers and inequalities. Nor are harmonisation proposals being advanced on the basis of ensuring the European-wide application of the principles of equality, justice, welfare of children (even were this to be possible); or with the aim of promoting the fairer regulation of change and conflict in intimate relationships.

Hints at harmonisation are instead being proposed as part of an economistic drive to encourage the faster creation of the producers and consumers of the next generation; as part of a concern that changing patterns of family life may endanger fiscal budgets as the population gets older and younger generations are no longer able or willing to care for their elders; as part of a fear that if the birth rate is not increased, Europe may loose its footing on the international stage; and as part of a formalistic, technocratic desire for uniformity, efficiency and rationality. None of these ambitions speak to what *should be* the basis for laws which regulate families and family practices. Perhaps this is because the functions of national family laws, and the principles which govern their adoption and application, can only be fully and fairly effected at a local and individual level. Countless studies have demonstrated that even on a national scale, the uniform application of a principle of family law can have inequitable outcomes in the complex and often irreconcilable arena of family relationships.[82] Uniform application at a supranational level therefore raises frightening possibilities; adverse outcomes which are clouded when the expressed aims are not justice and fairness, but economistic, demographic and political.

In an analysis of Anglo-Australian law, John Dewar argues that family law is replete with contradictions and that it is often incoherent and chaotic.[83] He argues that this does not lead to a diagnosis of crisis, but is a perfectly normal state of affairs as family law deals with contradictory emotions, passions and values and should not be expected to conform to a theoretical rationality of clear rules. Chaos is not therefore a threat to family law, but should be expected. This approach to family law has much to commend it, but is threatened by the centripetal impulses demonstrated in Community law and EU policy. Not only is the chaotic approach threatened, but so is progressive change in the relationships of women and men and the acceptance of non-traditional families. Frances Olsen has argued that there are generally two aspects of family laws: an apologetic aspect and a utopian aspect.[84] The apologetic aspect of family law tends to justify the domination of women by men and of parents over children. In this respect, certain ideologies are used to reinforce traditional assumptions about the respective roles of women, men and children within families. The utopian

---

[82] For a recent analysis of this in English law, see Carol Smart and Bren Neale's discussion of the "welfare of the child" principle where courts appear to work *to* an abstract principle, rather than working *from* it in individual cases, thus causing unnecessary hardship: *Family Fragments?* (London, Sage, 1999), especially at 186–99.

[83] See above n. 5.

[84] Frances Olsen, "The Politics of Family Law", (1984) 2 *Law and Inequality* 1.

vision of family law is altogether more liberating. It is a conception of family law in which notions of fairness and equality are introduced and traditional assumptions are challenged. Olsen's analysis, though made over fifteen years ago, provides a salutary warning for the development of an EU family law. In the light of the discussion in the first part of this chapter, there can be little doubt that were a European family law to be built on the foundations of the "model European family", it would be clearly apologetic, with the effect of perpetuating exclusion and disadvantage.

If an EU family law is to be developed, it must surely be "utopian" in its ambition. But achieving this would be no mean feat. The European Court has constructed a clearly "apologetic" conceptualisation of families in the EU and, despite the generally progressive statements from the Commission and Parliament, Member States are generally more conservative, or "apologetic", in their approach, especially if agreement can only be reached on the lowest common denominator.[85] If a family law is developed on the present foundations of family policy and a "model European family", it will be regressive, repressive and have adverse consequences for many. For this reason alone, the evolving EU family law should be viewed with considerable scepticism. However, even if a more progressive approach were to characterise policy developments, it is far from clear that the EU requires a family law, especially one in which chaos, that is individual justice, is deemed threatening to the goals of a cohesive and rational European approach. The justifications for further development offered thus far are unconvincing and primarily aim to augment existing activities of the EU, rather than to demonstrate why advances are required in the family field. Until such time as the EU's approach to family forms and practices is more progressive and egalitarian, and even then until the justifications for European-wide action are more convincing, the further development of EU family law must be resisted.

---

[85] A recent example of this can be seen in the reservations already made regarding the proposed family reunification directive in which the Commission proposes a right to family reunification to unmarried partners, including same-sex partners, provided that the Member States treated such partnerships in the same way as married couples: see above n. 40.

12

Transferability of Educational Skills and Qualifications in the European Union: The Case of EU Migrant Children

HELEN STALFORD[1]

INTRODUCTION

The ability to transfer skills and qualifications from one country's context to another is an essential prerequisite to the operation and exercise of free movement. Since the 1970s, legislation (accompanied by a number of mobility programmes) has been developed at European level to facilitate student, graduate and professional exchange between Member States. Attention has been largely focused, however, on facilitating transferability of professional and vocational qualifications through mutual recognition policy, with relatively little policy concerned with issues of transferability at primary or secondary levels of education.

Article 47 (ex 57) EC provides the primary constitutional reference to the issue of the mutual recognition of qualifications, authorising Council ministers to issue directives for the mutual recognition of diplomas, certificates and other evidence of formal qualifications. These enable individuals to take up activities in the territory of other Member States in a number of specific professional sectors under the same conditions (as defined by the host Member State) as nationals who have completed their training under the host state's educational system.[2] Legislation governing mutual recognition of qualifications was from the outset, therefore, firmly associated with the functioning of the labour market. This association continued throughout the 1980s and early 1990s when two

---

[1] I would like to thank Louise Ackers and Ann Blair for their valuable comments on a previous draft of this chapter.

[2] Directives were implemented for example in relation to doctors: Directive 75/363 of 16 June 1975, [1975] OJ L167/14; nurses: Directive 77/453 of 27 June 1977, [1977] OJ L176/8; dentists: Directive 78/687 of 25 July 1978, [1978] OJ L233/10; veterinary surgeons: Directive 78/1027 of 18 December 1978, [1978] OJ L362/7; midwives: Directive 80/155 of 21 January 1980, [1980] OJ L33/8; and pharmacists: Directive 85/432 of 16 September 1985, [1985] OJ L253/37.

further general directives were issued to govern mutual recognition of professional qualifications.[3] Despite the accumulation of legislation and programmes governing mutual recognition and transferability of vocational and professional qualifications there is, on the whole, very little reference to purely academic qualifications, and only fleeting reference to the recognition of secondary qualifications in relation to university entrance in another Member State.[4] Any existing provision at this level operates largely within the confines of domestic policy. This is particularly problematic in relation to the children of EU migrant workers, and specifically to those children who migrate at crucial transitional points in their education; domestic systems, which cater mainly for nationals, generally fail to take into account the problems specific to children who have had to adapt to different countries' educational systems, and who are often faced with overcoming linguistic and cultural obstacles in the process. Recent research[5] highlights that, as far as migrant workers' children are concerned, the school environment provides an important arena for integration, and failure to adapt to this can serve to exacerbate the child's sense of dislocation and isolation, as well as significantly impede academic progress.

The following discussion addresses educational issues specific to these children, a category of migrants which has been largely ignored in both academic debate and policy formulation. First of all, the chapter locates the discussion in the context of the "Children and Migration" research which evaluated the impact of intra-Community migration on the social experiences and legal status of the children of EU migrant workers. It goes on to outline the existing legislation and case law relevant to the mutual recognition of qualifications and the educational status of EU migrant children,[6] and identifies the means by which existing European policy on the transferability of higher education and voca-

---

[3] Directive 89/48 of 21 December 1988 on a general system for the recognition of higher educational diplomas awarded on completion of professional education and training of at least three years' duration, [1989] OJ L16/16 followed by Directive 92/51 of 18 June 1992, [1992] OJ L209/25 on a second general system for the recognition of professional education and training to supplement Directive 89/48.

[4] The Council of Europe and UNESCO have both drawn up multilateral conventions regulating the equivalence of diplomas leading to university admission, the equivalence of university periods of study, and the academic recognition of university qualifications although these have no legally binding force. Enforcement is dependent on the goodwill of Member States. More recently, the newly drafted Bologna Declaration implements measures to ensure convergence of university diplomas across Europe: D Jobbins, "Europe Aims for Greater Student Mobility", *Times Higher Education Supplement*, 9 July 1999.

[5] The author has been involved in a three year cross-national comparative research project, funded jointly by the European Commission and the Nuffield Foundation and coordinated by Professor Louise Ackers, now of the Department of Law, University of Lancaster. The project involved partners in Greece, Sweden, Portugal and the United Kingdom and included in-depth interviews with a sample of 180 children between the ages of 11 and 19 and their EU migrant parents in the four partner countries. The research will be referred to throughout the remainder of this chapter as the "Children and Migration" research.

[6] The terms "mutual recognition" and "transferability" of qualifications will be used interchangably throughout this chapter since the former definition provides the main thrust behind most legislation in ensuring transferability.

tional training qualifications has been, and could be developed and interpreted, to extend transferability entitlement to students at secondary level. The chapter then considers the reasons behind Community reluctance to develop a more coherent strategy on issues of transferability and progression at primary and secondary level and debates the merits of implementing additional measures at EU level in this respect. A final section discusses whether harmonisation of, or further convergence between, educational qualifications across the European Union is a viable and indeed preferable option. In the process, existing models of "good practice" will be identified and reflections made as to desirable future developments in this area.

EMPIRICAL CONTEXT AND THE LEGAL AND POLICY FRAMEWORK

Regulation 1612/68[7] provides the first European legislative reference to children's education, stating in Article 12(1) that resident children of migrant workers are to be admitted to the host state's general educational and vocational training courses under the same conditions as its nationals. Article 7(2) of Regulation 1612/68, which entitles EU migrant workers to the same "social and tax advantages" as nationals, has also been applied in the context of the educational rights of EU migrant children. These articles have been broadly interpreted by the European Court of Justice to include entitlement to fees and maintenance grants.[8] Article 12 has even operated to grant children educational rights following the departure of their parents from the host country[9] and following the death of both parents.[10] In this respect, the law is developing in such a way as to view children, in some circumstances, independently from their relationship with their migrant worker parents[11] creating the potential for an increasing number of cases in which children will face their education in another Member State alone. In *Echternach and Moritz* for example, Moritz was granted the right to continue to reside in the host state in order to pursue his studies following the return of his parents to their country of origin. The Court based its decision largely on the reasoning that it would unduly disrupt the child's educational progress should he be forced to return with his parents, particularly if the move coincided with a crucial transitional stage in the child's education. Following this line of argument, it is interesting to speculate on what

---

[7] 15 October 1968, OJ Sp. Ed. 1968 L257/2 at 475 relating to the living and working conditions of migrant workers and their families, adopted on the basis of Articles 39–43 (ex 48–52) EC.

[8] Case 9/74 *Casagrande* v. *Landeshauptstadt München* [1974] ECR 773; Case 39/86 *Lair* v. *University of Hannover* [1988] ECR 3161.

[9] Joined Cases 389–90/87 *Echternach and Moritz* v. *Netherlands Minister for Education and Science* [1989] ECR 723.

[10] Case C–7/94 *Landesamt für Ausbildungsförderung Nordrhein-Westfalen* v. *Lubor Gaal* [1995] ECR I–1031.

[11] Although this remains an initial qualifying criteria. See H L Ackers and H Stalford, "Children, Migration and Citizenship in the European Union: Intra-Community Mobility and the Status of Children in EC Law", (1999) 21 *Children and Youth Services Review* 699.

might have happened if Moritz, having completed his exams in the host state, subsequently decided to return to his country of origin to rejoin his parents, and on how his "foreign" qualifications would be recognised in his country of origin to ensure him full access to further study there. Regulation 1612/68 is of little help in this respect since it does no more than guarantee "access under the same conditions as nationals".

Children and parents alike, therefore, require further assurance that once the child has been accepted into a school in the host Member State, appropriate provision is in place to enable them to progress with as little disruption to their learning as possible. Of the 180 children interviewed for the "Children and Migration" research, for instance, forty-three children had moved to another Member State with their parents which was different to the one in which they were born, thirty-seven children had undergone at least two migrations to other countries within the EU, and thirty-four children had returned to their country of origin having lived in another EU Member State for a period of time.[12] Education featured prominently in both the adults' and the children's accounts of their migration experiences with twenty-seven families asserting that the migration decision was directly influenced by considerations concerning the child's education. In nine of these cases the family attributed their decision not to move to either the perceived prejudicial effect this would have on the child's academic progress, or to uncertainty about whether or not the child's academic qualifications would be recognised in the host state, or whether or not qualifications obtained abroad would be recognised in the country to which the child anticipated a future migration. In a further seven cases, the children remained in their home country independently of their parents, often until the end of the academic year, and sometimes indefinitely to avoid any disruption which the migration might cause to their education. These figures illustrate that issues of transferability of secondary qualifications between Member States present a real and significant problem impeding mobility rather than merely a perceived legal problem having little or no impact. Furthermore, these cases illustrate that issues of transferability and progression are clearly of concern as much at primary and secondary level as at third or vocational training and professional level. Provision at European level is, therefore, necessary to accommodate the increasing trend in adults migrating with their families and to facilitate the transmission of children between different Member States.

Current provision, for instance, does not address the situation in which nationals are required to possess specific qualifications to gain access to certain systems of education, and how qualifications obtained from other Member States will be regarded. This problem is most likely to arise in relation to access to university places as there are no enforceable mechanisms in place either at EU level or in every Member State to ensure that equivalent national qualifications

---

[12] The remainder who had not migrated qualified for the purposes of the research in that at least one of their parents was an EU migrant worker from another Member State.

are recognised by the host state for initial access; access is determined instead by agreements between countries[13] and "mutual trust". Following the implementation of Directive 93/96[14] by which students are entitled to reside and study in another Member State provided they are financially independent, instances in which these agreements and the spirit of "mutual trust" will be tested is likely to increase. In the "Children and Migration" research, forty-two parents and children alike commented that they were unsure as to whether or not their final year school qualifications would be valid in the other Member States to which they had migrated or to which they anticipated migrating in the future. This highlights the need for a greater level of transparency between variable national academic requirements in order to clarify any perceived problems of transferability. The problem was particularly acute in cases where the young migrant wished to attend university in Greece where access is normally subject to passing a special national examination. In two illustrative examples, both respondents (who had migrated from France some years earlier) had already obtained their Baccalaureate[15] from a French private school in Greece which would have entitled them to attend university in France. In order to attend a Greek university, however, they were required to sit the national examination under the same conditions as nationals, despite the fact that most nationals would have received preparatory training for the examination throughout their schooling and were therefore in a highly advantageous position. Provisions preventing Member States from imposing an obligation on an individual to obtain further qualifications in the host state to support qualifications they have already obtained in a previous EU country have been implemented with regard to professional qualifications,[16] and one could argue that, by analogy, the same principle should be applied to secondary education. In this respect local authorities would be precluded from requiring young migrants to take additional exams or resit a year before they are granted access to education at the same level as that which they had attained in their country of origin, particularly if they are sufficiently competent in the language of the host state.[17]

---

[13] See above n. 4. See also Dalichow, "Academic Recognition Within the European Community", (1987) *European Journal of Education* 46.

[14] [1993] OJ L317/59.

[15] The French High School leaving certificate.

[16] See above n. 3. The first general Directive, adopted in December 1988 and effective from January 1991, covers all higher education diplomas awarded by a competent authority for all post-secondary education and training for at least three years duration or an equivalent part-time qualification, which shows that the holder is able to pursue a regulated profession in the Member States. The effect of this is that each Member State is obliged to accept that a university degree awarded in another EU country is of equivalent value to that awarded in its own country, and that migrant workers must not be submitted to any further assessment for practising a particular profession unless nationals are also subject to the same requirement. In this respect, Member States cannot covertly discriminate against migrant workers by requiring them to undergo further training unless it is justified on the basis of regulating the profession or the specific needs of that profession.

[17] Conversely, the second "supplementary" general directive referred to above (see above n. 3) concerns vocational qualifications below university diploma level. This Directive covers vocational

The problem also arises at a lower level. For example, in countries like Northern Ireland which operates a selective system of state education at secondary level, in order to determine which type of secondary school a young person can attend, the pupils are trained for and undertake an examination in their final year of primary school.[18] This presents significant problems to migrant children who have not had the opportunity to prepare for and sit this qualifying examination. In many cases, the local authorities allow them to undergo an alternative assessment in order to determine whether they are of a sufficiently high academic standard to attend grammar school. This assessment, which is generally composed of English language, grammar and arithmetic, clearly prejudices those children who, while perhaps quite able to cope with grammar school, lack confidence in speaking or writing the host language (particularly in the initial stages following migration) or are unfamiliar with this form of assessment and curriculum.

Of course, one might argue that many problems associated with gaining access to educational institutions in other Member States are as much (if not more) attributable to linguistic incompetence as they are to obtaining recognition of foreign qualifications and, in this sense, the debate shifts onto issues of progression rather than mutual recognition of qualifications and the level of European provision in place to aid progression following the transition to another country's education system. While one might maintain that issues of personal development and integration fall outside the legislative function of the EU, one could argue that problems of integration and progression at school are inextricably linked to the exercise of free movement, and, as the research has highlighted, lack of provision to aid this process potentially impedes mobility.

Directive 77/486 on the education of the children of EU migrant workers[19] supports this argument. The Directive requires Member States to implement measures to ensure that free language tuition in both the host language and mother tongue is offered to children to facilitate their initial reception in the host country and to assist them in the eventuality of their return to the country of origin. Although this refers only to compulsory education, the Directive, if properly implemented, aids the child's adjustment to a "foreign" learning environment and prevents linguistic competence from determining access to education. The Directive at least attempts to address the fact that rights attached to

---

training qualifications obtained over a two to three year duration at post-secondary or secondary level. Given the vast diversity of vocational training on offer in each Member State, individual authorities are authorised to require migrants to undertake an aptitude test or further training before they are free to exercise their profession in the host country. It is not clear why these two directives impose different obligations on Member States, particularly since they overlap with each other in many respects.

[18] The "Eleven Plus" examination. This selection procedure also operates in 5 per cent of (or 169) schools throughout England.

[19] [1978] OJ L233/1.

the free movement provisions are insufficient in themselves and that certain accompanying measures are needed to make them a practicable reality.[20]

Many families manage to overcome problems of transferability and progression by avoiding the state education system altogether and opting for private "foreign" or international schools which teach the same curriculum as the country from which they have migrated. As the Greek examples illustrate, this is still problematic for young people who decide to continue studying in Greece since the qualifications obtained in the country's private foreign schools are insufficient to gain access to state universities. Indeed, forty-five children interviewed for the children and migration project were attending or had at some point attended an international school and forty-seven children attended a "foreign" school.[21] Interestingly, a number of these private foreign schools are funded by the government of the home state as opposed to that of the host state. This signifies a fairly distorted compliance with the obligations contained in Directive 77/486 in that each Member State is, in effect, "looking after its own" in other EC countries while neglecting the needs of the young migrant population within the home country. Greece has developed a kind of compromise to this situation by establishing a number of "schools for repatriated children". These schools, which cater specifically for migrant children at both primary and secondary level who have been residing in another country for at least two years, were established in 1982 and are funded by the Greek Ministry of Education. They follow the Greek national curriculum and students who graduate from them receive an identical qualification to that awarded by state schools.[22]

EDUCATION, VOCATIONAL AND PROFESSIONAL TRAINING:
AN INCREMENTAL PROCESS

Alongside progress made by the European Court in relation to the educational rights of EU migrant children, a number of other "soft law" developments have taken place at European level. Up until the 1970s, apart from the vague,

---

[20] Implementation of the Directive across the Member States has been disappointing. See European Commission Reports COM(88) 787 at 128 and COM(94) 80. Inadequate measures to accommodate migrant children's specific learning needs has resulted in many of them having to re-sit a school year to enable them to catch up with nationals.

[21] That is, a school which teaches a curriculum and in a language different to that of the host country—for example, a Spanish school in Portugal which follows the Spanish national curriculum and where Spanish is the main teaching language.

[22] With this certificate, graduates have the option of participating either in national examinations for post-secondary studies or in the special examinations for special categories of students. The state, recognizing that some children cannot compete on equal terms with the local children due to language difficulties and a possible lack of familiarity with the Greek education system, offers them the opportunity to compete with children of similar qualifications in separate national exams which take place nationwide every September. These are for students who have attended a Greek school for no more than three years. See H L Ackers and H Stalford, *Children, Citizenship and Migration in the European Community*, Final Report for DGXXII, European Commission, chs 7 and 8 (November 1999).

derivative rights contained in Regulation 1612/68, the EU had remained respect-
fully silent on the issue of compulsory education, reserving it for the jurisdiction
of individual Member States. In 1971, however, the Council of Ministers of
Education acknowledged the need to establish a basis for cooperation in issues
concerning education and two years later, education was specified as a policy
area under the services of DGXII of the Commission together with research and
science policy.[23] A Council Resolution issued in 1974[24] set down a number of
guidelines with a view to achieving greater cooperation in the educational
domain. These included the achievement of equal opportunity to ensure open
access to all forms of education, the importance of upholding the diversity and
individual character of domestic education systems, and, with this in mind,
allowing Member States to apply any statements of objectives put forward by
the EU according to their own country context. The traditional distinction,
however, between the purely academic aspects of education (which were an
exclusively domestic concern) and its more vocational/professional nature
(which fell partly within European competence given its links with building up
the internal market) continued to be guarded. In the following decade, this conventional distinction was gradually eroded in favour of a more functional, integrated stance on educational policy which became increasingly associated with
employment and the general social policy objectives of the EU.[25] In a number of
decisions throughout the 1980s, the European Court acknowledged the correlation between formal education and vocational/professional training, viewing it
as an incremental process.[26] This was further emphasised in the Commission
White Paper on education and training which states that: "General education
must provide preparation for a vocational skill, and vocational training must
continue to develop the basic competencies provided by general education".[27]
The increasingly ill-defined distinction, therefore, between these different stages
and the formal recognition that purely academic qualifications at secondary
level are generally a condition precedent to training at vocational or professional level further supports the need for more coherent legislation governing
compulsory education.

What does distinguish European educational policy and programmes from
other aspects of vocational training, social and employment policy, however, is
the continued emphasis on cooperation rather than obligation between Member

---

[23] A Moschonas, *Education and Training in the European Union* (Aldershot, Brookfield Vt,
Ashgate, 1997) 80; J A McMahon, *Education and European Community Law* (8 European
Community Law Series, The Athlone Press, 1995) 13–14.

[24] Resolution of the Ministers of Education meeting within the Council of 6 June 1974 on
Cooperation in the Field of Education, [1974] OJ C98.

[25] Hence, both education and vocational training were placed within the activities of DGV along
with social policy.

[26] Case 293/83 *Gravier v. City of Liège* [1985] ECR 593; Case 24/86 *Blaizot v. University of Liège*
[1988] ECR 379.

[27] European Commission, *Teaching and Learning: Towards the Learning Society* (COM(95)
590). See also the Commission Green Paper on education, training and research, *The Obstacles to
Transnational Mobility* (COM(96) 462).

States, ensuring that national autonomy in this area remains intact. By way of example, in 1987 the European Community Action Scheme for Mobility of University Students (ERASMUS)[28] was established to enable students to spend periods of study in higher educational institutions of other Member States. The scheme is controlled, supervised and funded solely by the Commission, requiring all participating states to ensure the effective working of the programme by removing conflicting national law. It falls to agreements between the national authorities, however, as to the nature and content of courses to which ERASMUS students will have access.

Indeed, when education was included within the remit of Community competence following the insertion of Article 126 (now 149) into the EC Treaty, it was accompanied by a reminder of the EU's continued allegiance to the subsidiarity principle:

> "The Community shall contribute to the development of quality education by encouraging co-operation between Member States and, if necessary, by supporting and supplementing their action, while fully respecting the responsibility of the Member States for the content of the teaching and the organisation of education systems and their cultural and linguistic diversity".

Ironically, despite earlier judicial moves to conflate education with vocational training, the Maastricht Treaty amendments had the effect of actually marking the distinction between the two, not least by setting out different legislative procedures for the enactment of policy measures for each.[29] Article 149 (ex 126) EC sets out the objectives of the EU in the area of education in relation to, for example, the teaching of languages of the Member States, mobility of students and teachers and enhanced mutual recognition of qualifications. Most significantly, it extends Community competence to pre-school, primary, general secondary education and general knowledge university courses which do not equip students for a particular occupation and which are not covered by the former Article 128 EC.[30] In reality, it appears that the former Article 128 EC has merely been split up into two articles to refine the distinction between vocational training and education but without actually having the effect of extending Community competence. This is evidenced by the fact that Article 149 EC has yet to yield any concrete legislation on education. At the very most, some programmes have been established on the basis of the Article to promote student

[28] Council Decision of 15 August 1987, [1987] OJ L166/20.

[29] T Hervey elaborates on these procedures in *European Social Law and Policy* (European Community Law Series, New York, Longman, 1998) 112–14. See also P Craig and G De Búrca, *EU Law Text, Cases and Materials* (2nd edn., (Oxford, Oxford University Press, 1998) 718 for procedural changes following the Amsterdam Treaty.

[30] K Lenaerts, "Education in European Community Law after Maastricht" (1994) 31 *CMLRev* 7–41. On the other hand Article 150 (ex 127) EC includes within its remit facilitating adaptation to technological change and the promotion of cooperation between training establishments and businesses. It also obliges Member States to cooperate in "exchanges of information and experience" for example by carrying out consultations or ensuring that national training establishments are able to participate in exchange programmes.

mobility and educational exchange. The SOCRATES programme,[31] for instance, which cuts across education and vocational training issues, provides that the content of teaching and organisation of educational systems and that their "cultural and linguistic diversity" must be respected. Also supported under Article 149 is a youth exchange programme entitled "Youth for Europe" which promotes cross-national understanding and knowledge through funding research in areas affecting young Europeans' lives. Apart from these few initiatives, however, little has been adopted in the form of secondary education policy targeting children and certainly nothing relating to the transferability of qualifications for young migrants. Indeed, any existing provision is framed within the context of the free movement provisions as a means of ensuring that lack of educational provision available to migrant children will not impede (at least in theory) the exercise of free movement by the worker parent.[32] As such, little has changed since 1968 and concrete provision for EU migrant children continues to be framed within the context of their parents' rights as workers.

Having first outlined the existing legal framework relevant to the children of EU migrant workers and secondly highlighted some of the problems inherent in finding a definitional and functional distinction between compulsory education on the one hand and vocational/professional training on the other, the next section of this chapter will debate the reasons why the academic nature of educational qualifications continues to be eclipsed by policy which is led by more economic objectives.

MUTUAL RECOGNITION OF EDUCATIONAL QUALIFICATIONS: A SECONDARY
CONSIDERATION

The dominant emphasis on vocational and professional training policy, as opposed to purely academic qualifications at compulsory level, can be attributed to a number of factors. First of all, this weight of attention can be seen as the logical outcome of legal provisions prior to the Maastricht Treaty which excluded general education from Community jurisdiction. Implementing any further specific measures concerning primary or secondary level education would run the risk of seriously undermining Member State competence in this area and conflict with the principle of subsidiarity. Community legislation could only, therefore, legitimately deal with education under the umbrella of voca-

---

[31] 1995–1999. This is the main EU action programme in the area of education, covering higher education exchange (previously ERASMUS, Decision 87/327, [1987] OJ L166/20), improving language skills in schools (LINGUA, Decision 89/489, [1989] OJ L239), and Open and Distance Learning and Information Exchange (Eurydice and Arion).

[32] See Case 207/78 *Ministère Public* v. *Even and ONPTS* [1979] ECR 2019 and Case 316/85 *Centre public d'aide sociale de Courcelles* v. *Lebon* [1987] ECR 2811 in which this is referred to as the "facilitating mobility" test. In this respect therefore, the child is not the primary focus of the legislation but the parent and the functional needs of the internal market. See further Ackers and Stalford, above n. 11.

tional training[33] and work-related policy. Any ensuing legislation was drafted with the principal objective of fostering the development of a single labour market and advancing the economic capacity of the Community's human capital.[34] As such, any existing Community policy on the transferability of qualifications was aimed at serving the needs and requirements of vocational training, the ultimate aim of which was the production of a mobile, highly skilled and qualified labour force, thereby increasing productivity and enhancing international competitiveness.

While introducing provisions governing issues of transferability at compulsory level is, on the face of it, of no apparent benefit to the functional needs of the internal market, the "Children and Migration" research demonstrates that a lack of provisions aimed at the needs of the children of EU migrant workers is, in fact, a barrier to mobility. Indeed, the European Court has acknowledged this in the context of extending other free movement benefits to migrant workers' family members in its formulation of the "facilitating mobility test". Thus, in the *Even*[35] case the Court defined the material scope of Article 7(2) EC in what has become known as the "social advantages formula" to include:

> "all those [advantages] which, whether or not linked to the contract of employment, are generally granted to national workers primarily because of their objective status as workers or by virtue of their residence on national territory and the extension of which to workers who are nationals of other Member States therefore seems suitable to *facilitate their mobility* within the Community".[36]

One could argue that this principle should be applied to the children of migrant workers to justify the development of a more concrete educational policy.[37]

A further justification of the Community's non-interventionist approach is that existing European legislation relating to children's education is sufficient, particularly since the broad interpretation by the European Court of Articles 7(2) and 12 of Regulation 1612/68 has furnished young migrants with a substantial body of rights in this area. Furthermore, the prevailing assumption seems to be that situations in which individuals would need to call upon such measures are relatively rare and that existing provision is adequate for most of the cases which arise. According to John Field, this is particularly true in the

---

[33] Formerly Article 128 EC.

[34] See G Neave, *The EEC and Education* (Trentham, Trentham Books, 1984) 65 for a more in-depth analysis of the evolution of the Community approach in the field of vocational training to a more integrated approach in relation to education. Updated in R in't Veld, H-P Füssel and G Neave, (eds), *Relations Between State and Higher Education* (The Hague, Boston, Kluwer Law International, 1996) and in Lenaerts, above n. 30.

[35] See above n. 32.

[36] Emphasis added. The "facilitating mobility" approach to defining social advantages has been further supported in Case C–315/94 *Peter de Vos v. Stadt Bielefeld* [1996] ECR I–1417, para. 20 and in *Schmid v. Belgian State* [1993] ECR I–3011, para. 18.

[37] C Zilioli, "The Recognition of Diplomas and its Impact on Educational Policies" in B De Witte, (ed) *European Community Law of Education* (Baden-Baden, Nomos Verlagsgesellschaft, 1989) 64.

light of flagging migration statistics within the EU.[38] For the small number of cases which do arise, it is presumed that the local authorities concerned will deal with the situation on the particular facts of that case and in a spirit of equity and mutual trust. The "Children and Migration" research indicates, however, that while rates of migration are low in comparison to migration by third country nationals (including refugees and asylum seekers) the number of EU migrants is hardly negligible; there continues to be a great deal of movement between Member States, particularly in the wake of increasing globalisation which has created greater opportunities for individuals to work in other countries accompanied by their families. Furthermore, an increase in the number of "international" marriages and cross-national relationships has prompted a growth in migration for personal as well as work-related reasons.[39]

Thus, as economic, monetary, political and even cultural and linguistic barriers between Member States are gradually eroded, there is a growing need for provisions which will accommodate the eventuality of an increasing number of young migrants. Indeed, it is likely that many more individuals will begin moving specifically for academic purposes; the school curriculum is becoming increasingly Europe-oriented with a large number of cross-cultural exchange programmes being adopted in schools, inculcating in students from a young age a greater desire (as well as increasing opportunities) to broaden their horizons and study in other countries.[40] Furthermore, the introduction of university tuition fees in countries such as the United Kingdom may precipitate a larger attendance at foreign universities where greater financial assistance is available to students.[41] Additionally, language no longer presents the same obstacle to young people moving given the growing emphasis by schools on teaching a second modern language from a young age.

Of course, introducing legislation to ensure mutual recognition of qualifications would not offer a solution to all those who enter "foreign" education systems; language and cultural adaptation pose as much of if not a greater problem for many young people. More coherent guidelines would, however, serve to inform potential and actual migrants of their entitlements, to ease the child's transition to the new school environment, and to enable the family to make nec-

---

[38] J Field, *European Dimensions: Education, Training and the European Union* (London, J. Kingsley Publishers, 1998) 127. He attributes this decline to the rise in unemployment from the early 1970s which consequently diminished opportunities for unskilled labour. Concurrently, economic growth in Spain, Italy and subsequently Ireland reduced the income differentials between the richer and poorer nations within the EU reducing the incentive to move. Furthermore, greater affluence has also led to smaller family sizes, reducing the overall supply of young migrants.

[39] Of the 180 families interviewed for the "Children and Migration" research, 96 of them were "international" families, that is, the child's parents were of different nationalities to each other.

[40] Such as those organised by the Central Bureau for Educational Visits and Exchanges (CBEVE), based in London.

[41] In France, for instance, students can claim housing benefit from the Caisse d'Allocations Familiales et d'Allocations de Logement (CAFAL) to cover up to 40 per cent of their accommodation costs.

essary preparations prior to the migration.[42] Those most likely to benefit from a more concrete, tangible policy on mutual recognition are students who decide to return to their country of origin for further study after a period abroad, in which case, language and culture poses even less of a problem.

Having considered the possible reasons behind Europe's failure to implement legislation governing mutual recognition of secondary qualifications, the final section of this chapter will consider some alternatives to facilitate the transition of young people between different countries' educational systems.

PROPOSALS FOR THE FUTURE

One could be accused of overestimating the impact that European legislation on education could realistically have, since many of the problems which a migrant child experiences are problems of integration and progression rather than transferability, problems which are common to all children who migrate even within their own country. Furthermore, the majority of children who migrate with their parents do not experience any problems concerned with transferability of qualifications, not because these barriers do not exist, but because many of them are absorbed by the private or international school systems. International schools in particular provide a uniform curriculum across Member States which substantially eases the transition compared to cases in which the child has to adapt to different state systems and often to a new language.[43] Much can be learned from such schools and from their curricula which provide the flexibility and consistency which is so important to migrant children. The International Baccalaureate (IB), for instance, is offered by some 770 schools in more than ninety countries worldwide and in all of the countries of the EU. It is particularly appealing to young people who migrate with their parents (often to several different countries) and who wish to minimise the disruption to their studies. Given its wide availability, they can simply enrol in a school in the host state which offers the IB curriculum and take up where they left off. It is also attractive to students in their final year of study in their home country who, for a variety of reasons (such as dual nationality, bilingualism, desire to perfect a second language or in anticipation of future migrations abroad) prefer to receive an internationally recognised, multi-cultural education.

---

[42] The NARIC Network (National Academic Recognition Information Centres which arose out of the Council of Ministers of Education Resolution of 9 February 1976, [1976] OJ C38/1) is comprised of a number of centres throughout the EU which provide higher educational institutions and individuals with information concerning the validity of their academic or training qualifications in other Member States. It provides no information, however, on qualifications for access to educational institutions at secondary level.

[43] 41 per cent of those interviewed for the "Children and Migration" research had at some point attended a state school and a number of these referred to the prohibitive costs of attending international or private schools.

Proposals have been put forward for a more European version of the IB which would incorporate teaching on citizenship, politics and history from a specifically European perspective.[44] Such measures, rather than the current "mutual trust" approach, it is argued, would encourage greater inter-cultural exchange and an enhanced sense of European identity, at least if individuals were assured of the ease with which such a transition could take place. This, in turn would potentially encourage a greater number of young people to broaden their horizons by studying in another EU country or to return to their country of origin independently of their migrant parents.[45] Indeed, the desirability for a more universal curriculum is evidenced in the vast number of schools and students opting for the IB in both the state and private sector.[46]

While this appears to provide an ideal solution to mobile Europeans, such systems could be criticised for further marginalising migrant children, cocooning them in an environment which isolates them from the culture, language and people of the host state and which consequently severely hinders integration.[47] Secondly, since each national curriculum is adapted to the specific features of the society in which it is based, its cultural, historical and linguistic heritage would potentially be sacrificed to accommodate a more integrated, universal programme. This would substantially jeopardise national identity in favour of a more European one and undermine the rich diversity brought by different national systems.

Advocates of the IB and an alternative European course of study, however, expressly state that any such curriculum would remain sensitive, and indeed actively encourage the preservation of national identity. To quote Roger Peel, the Director General of the IB:

> "the IB stems from the fact that we require all students to relate first to their own national identity—their own language, literature, history and cultural heritage, no matter where in the world this may be. Beyond that, we ask that they identify with the corresponding traditions of others".[48]

---

[44] Study Group report on education and training, *Accomplishing Europe Through Education and Training*, submitted to the European Commission in December 1996. The more European IB would presumably be available as an alternative in certain schools to the national system operating in each Member State.

[45] In 1992, 8 per cent of Portuguese citizens were living in other Member States, and 78 per cent of this number were residing in France, while 35 per cent of the Danish EU migrant population were living in Sweden. Issues of transferability are clearly a concern, therefore, for those families with children, who, given the increasing prosperity of Portugal for instance, may be contemplating a return to their country of origin.

[46] More than 2,000 students per year across the EU are opting for this curriculum as opposed to the state curriculum.

[47] A number of children interviewed for the "Children and Migration" research who attended international schools had no contact with nationals of the host Member State, nor could they speak the language of the host state, despite having lived there for two or three years.

[48] Taken from IB publicity leaflet published in 1997 by the International Baccalaureate Organisation, Geneva.

Similarly, Chiara Zilioli observes of (in the context of tertiary education) the conflict between the development of a European identity and the preservation of national identity, for which education plays such a crucial role, that:

> "In European education policy, the preservation of the various European cultural identities is considered to be essential and a common policy on education should not imply a standardisation of teaching methods and university programmes . . . Equivalence of diplomas must not lead to identical curriculums".[49]

In this respect, therefore, a course of study yielding a European-wide recognised qualification should be subject to and vary according to the national context in which it is taught.

No doubt any changes in this regard will take place in the distant future and substantive measures to facilitate insertion into the state education system is still required for those who do not enter international or private foreign schools. This requires a more formal acknowledgement of the issue by placing an enforceable onus on Member States to ensure mutual recognition of qualifications rather than basing it on the tenuous assumption of "mutual trust" or allowing it to be dealt with on an ad hoc basis. Additionally, compliance with Community obligations (such as those set out in Directive 77/486) should extend beyond nationalistic measures whereby Member States are permitted to cater merely for their own nationals, and should be enforced to promote the interests and needs of all EU migrants within the territory of that Member State. This necessitates a greater level of clarity and transparency in terms of national access requirements and curriculum content which should be readily available to potential migrants.

CONCLUSION

European and domestic education policy needs to take into account not only current migration trends, but also to envisage a more integrated and mobile Community future in which more young people will be pursuing an academic route in another EU country.

The correlation between education and mobility should not be underestimated—and the legislative correlation between education and employment should not be confined to tertiary level education or vocational training. In the wake of constitutional recognition of European citizenship, and as the European Union begins to strive towards greater social as well as economic convergence, one anticipates a gradual surge in intra-Community mobility by workers, families and students alike. Education is receiving increasing recognition as a catalyst for integration and stability, most recently in the newly drafted Bologna Declaration on convergence of university diplomas across Europe:

---

[49] Zilioli, above n. 37, at 65.

"The importance of education and educational co-operation in the development and strengthening of stable, peaceful and democratic societies is universally acknowledged as paramount".[50]

Thus, the EU's involvement in the development of educational policies and mutual recognition is underpinned by the aim of promoting a sense of belonging to Europe and stressing commonality in European culture and history.[51] While provisions accommodating migrant workers in the mutual recognition of their professional and vocational qualifications have been sufficiently (although not completely) developed in anticipation of increased future mobility, concrete and clear provisions governing transferability of general educational qualifications at pre-university level remain conspicuously absent from the European social policy menu. This implies that the full breadth of European citizenship entitlement is reserved for those who can actively contribute to the economy and is not for those in secondary level education. Consequently, many young people who migrate, either independently or with their worker or carer parents, are placed in a precarious position whereby their educational progress is very much at the mercy of domestic authorities' variable and inconsistent access requirements.

---

[50] Quoted by Jobbins, above n. 4. As stated in the introductory section of this chapter, the Declaration seeks to diffuse the disparate degree structure across Europe with the aim of encouraging greater student mobility.

[51] Hervey above n. 29, at 110.

13

Consumption, Capitalism and the Citizen: Sexuality and Equality Rights Discourse in the European Union

CARL F STYCHIN

INTRODUCTION

The issue of "spousal benefits" for same sex partners has been at the forefront of lesbian and gay political and legal strategies in North America for a number of years, where it has also come to be linked to the question of same sex marriage rights. In the European arena, same sex benefits and the recognition of partnerships as a legal status akin to marriage are now assuming an important place on the political agenda in a number of different Member States. Denmark was the first country to enact same sex partnership legislation in 1989, and France is the most recent to recognise legally a range of relationship forms, both sexual and not. Not surprisingly, given the diverse ways in which sexuality is constituted across the EU, the politics of lesbian and gay relationships plays out in very different ways depending upon the national (and sub-national) context. The common EU legal order, however, has also facilitated a litigation strategy emanating from the United Kingdom, focused on sex equality rights as a legal basis for claiming the privileges which flow from the recognition of spousal-type relationships. This rights-based approach culminated in defeat before the European Court in *Grant* v. *South West Trains*.[1] The Court famously ruled that a train company's refusal to grant travel concessions to the lesbian partner of a female employee, despite a policy of granting such benefits to opposite sex partners (married or not), did not constitute discrimination based directly on the sex of the worker. Thus, it did not constitute a violation of Article 141 (ex 119) EC or the Equal Pay Directive (no. 76/207).[2] Nor did sex discrimination include discrimination on the basis of sexual orientation. The condition applied in the same way to male and female workers, and therefore could not be regarded as constituting discrimination directly based on sex.[3] Moreover, Community law

[1] Case C–249/96 [1998] ECR I–621.
[2] *Ibid.*, 646.
[3] *Ibid.*

does not regard stable relationships between two persons of the same sex as equivalent to stable relationships outside marriage between two persons of the opposite sex.[4] According to the Court, "in those circumstances, it is for the legislature alone to adopt, if appropriate, measures which may affect that position".[5] The reaction to the decision by activist and academic commentators alike was surprise and indignation, underscoring how the privileging of a rights-based activist programme as a political strategy (which, in this case, was strongly supported by the UK activist group "Stonewall") can lead to disappointing results.

The decision in *Grant* provides the point of departure for my argument in this chapter, which is grounded in an emerging discourse on the political economy of rights, sexuality and citizenship. My claim is that given the focus of European rights discourse on the market citizen, the sometimes taken-for-granted politics of European sexual citizenship rights is much in need of interrogation for its broadly political economic implications. By this I mean that I will emphasise the material, as opposed to the legal or symbolic, consequences of citizenship claims. In so doing, my aim is to question the privileging of rights discourse in sexual citizenship strategies, particularly within the European arena, because of its limitations as a vehicle for challenging underlying structural barriers to full citizenship. I advocate instead, not a sceptical approach to European politics and law, but an engagement of activism with the construction of, and participation in, democratic institutions, and a politics, not only of legal recognition, but more broadly, of recognition *and* redistribution.

THE POLITICS OF SEXUALITY RIGHTS IN A EUROPEAN CONTEXT

An analysis of the use of EU sex equality law as a tool in rights struggles importantly demands that the insights flowing from the academic commentary on the politics of rights be contextualised in the unique circumstances of the European Union. It is universally acknowledged in EU legal history that economic factors were the motivating force behind Article 141 EC; namely, the perceived need to avoid distortions in competition between member states which had differing levels of protection for sex equality rights in the workplace.[6] Subsequently, in the landmark case of *Defrenne (No. 2)*, the objectives of EU sex equality law

---

[4] Case C–249/96 [1998] ECR I–648.

[5] *Ibid.*

[6] See for example C Barnard, "The Economic Objectives of Article 119" in T Hervey and D O'Keeffe (eds), *Sex Equality Law in the European Union* (Chichester, Wiley, 1996) 321. Article 141 EC provides for equal pay for men and women, and has been supplemented by directives concerning equal pay and equal value (75/117), equal treatment in employment (76/207), equal treatment in social security (79/7), equal treatment in occupational pensions (86/378), and equal treatment for self-employed women (86/613). For an outline of the legal framework, see T Hervey and J Shaw, "Women, Work and Care: Women's Dual Role and Double Burden in EC Sex Equality Law", (1998). 8 *Journal of European Social Policy* 43 at 46–7.

were described as two-fold, embracing both the need to avoid distortions in competition, and also the desire for social progress and the improvement in the working and living conditions of the peoples of Europe.[7]

The effect of European sex equality rights in practice has been well-documented, particularly by feminist analyses which have highlighted the positive benefits of the resort to rights, but also the limitations imposed both by the structure of the rights, and the broader ideological project of the formation of an internal *market* in which rights discourse is embedded.[8] The dominant focus on formal equality and equal opportunities in the workplace has had a "revolutionary affect"[9] for some women—namely, working European women, particularly around issues such as part time work and pregnancy discrimination. And it has been through rights struggles—often by "lone women"—that these successes have been realised as a result of often protracted litigation.[10]

However, the limitations of EU sex equality law are also well known. The emphasis on "fair" competition in the marketplace, the "merit" principle, and "equal" opportunities leaves little scope for the use of rights discourse to tackle the underlying structural barriers to substantive equality, many of which result from the private sphere of the home and from impediments to full entry into the labour market, such as "the double burden of 'care' and 'work' for women".[11] This is a realm considered beyond the role of rights which, because of the ideological basis of those rights, is focused on the public sphere—the employment relation.[12] There is no recognition, for example, of voluntary work and informal care as leading to entitlements to rights such as social security.[13]

Thus, two of the many sides of rights discourse become apparent. The language of rights has meant that "the EU system can be politicised in the interests of the democratic majority",[14] but, by virtue also of the explicit ideological grounding of EU law, rights struggles are channelled into an economically liberal model tied to the atomistic individual actor freely and fairly working in the

---

[7] Case 43/75 *Defrenne* v. *Sabena (No. 2)* [1976] ECR 455.

[8] See, e.g., Barnard, above n. 6; C McGlynn, "EC Sex Equality Law: Towards a Human Rights Foundation" in Hervey and O'Keeffe, above n. 6, at 239; M Everson, "The Legacy of the Market Citizen" in J Shaw and G More (eds), *New Legal Dynamics of European Union* (Oxford, Clarendon Press, 1995) 73; C Hoskyns, *Integrating Gender: Women, Law and Politics in the European Union* (London and New York, Verso, 1996); G More, "Equality of Treatment in European Community Law: the Limits of Market Equality" in A Bottomley (ed.), *Feminist Perspectives on the Foundational Subjects of Law* (London, Cavendish, 1996) 261; Hervey and Shaw, above n. 6.

[9] Everson, above n. 8, at 209.

[10] Hoskyns, above n. 8, at 78.

[11] Hervey and Shaw, above n. 6, at 60. Recent European legislative initiatives, to some extent, can be interpreted as tackling that structural disadvantage, for example the Parental Leave Directive (no. 96/34), the Pregnancy Directive (92/85), and child care initiatives.

[12] See, for example, Case 184/83 *Ulrich Hofmann* v. *Barmer Ersatzkasse* [1984] ECR 3047 at 3075: "It is apparent . . . that the directive is not designed to settle questions concerned with the organization of the family, or to alter the division of responsibility between parents".

[13] H L Ackers, "Citizenship, Gender and Dependency in the European Union: Women and Internal Migration" in Hervey and O'Keeffe, above n. 6, at 221, 226.

[14] Hoskyns, above n. 8, at 210.

competitive labour market.[15] The potential for social change through the employment relation is certainly present (and has been achieved to some degree), but the role of rights in social change is constrained from the outset.

It is onto such a politically ambiguous terrain that actors engaged with sexual orientation struggles have sought to "graft" their claims. Such a move is practically and politically problematic, however, in several important respects. Most obviously, such a move runs into difficult questions regarding the interpretation of the words of the provision, and the fairly clear intention that Article 141 EC was not intended to cover sexual orientation discrimination. Of course, it also can be argued that if the Treaty is a central constitutional document, then it should be construed in a purposive and teleological fashion and, if Article 141 is designed to foster social progress, then a broad interpretation is justifiable.[16] The issue, according to Kenneth Armstrong, is how two central tensions in EU law are to be resolved:

> "The first is the extent to which the ECJ is willing to extend the scope of Community law beyond the domain of economic integration and to embrace the broader political dimension of laying the legal foundations for a citizenship of the EU. The second . . . is the tension between the interpretation and construction of the EC Treaty as a typical agreement between nation-states or as a constitutional text to be given meaning in the context of a process of constitution building".[17]

These core tensions suggest that a victory in *Grant* was never going to be straightforward or inevitable.

Moreover, the question of the institutional legitimacy of the European Court inevitably pushed it away from such a broad interpretation of Article 141. The inclusion of Article 13 EC as a result of the Amsterdam Treaty may suggest that this is an area for legislative, as opposed to judicial, activity. Although it remains open to speculation whether and how this enabling treaty article will be legislatively implemented in the immediate (or, indeed, longer term) future, that in itself may be a reason for the Court to exercise self-restraint. As Steve Terrett suggests, "at a time when ratification of the Amsterdam Treaty [was] by no means a certainty, the ECJ may have felt it prudent to refrain from providing ammunition to eurosceptics in the various Member States by adopting a gung-ho approach to Community legal development", an approach which might well

---

[15] See J Shaw, "Law, Gender and Internal Market" in Hervey and O'Keeffe, above n. 6, at 283. The role of rights is undoubtedly multifaceted, and my focus in this chapter is undeniably narrow. For example, rights also can be characterised as a means through which the European Court can carry on conversations with national courts, and thus rights can be understood in dialogic terms. Moreover, rights should not be singled out as the sole means by which the Court pursues legal integration. Rather, the "effect of Community law operating to the benefit of individuals extends beyond the scope of rights", creating a "multi-tiered taxonomy of juridic effects": C Hilson and T Downes, "Making Sense of Rights: Community Rights in E.C. Law", (1999) 24 *ELRev* 121.

[16] K A Armstrong, "Tales of the Community: Sexual Orientation Discrimination and EC Law", (1998) 20 *Journal of Social Welfare and Family Law* 455 at 462.

[17] *Ibid.*

have been perceived as illegitimate action on the part of the Court.[18] Indeed, the emotiveness of the combination of sexuality, rights and judicial activism has frequently resulted in claims of judicial illegitimacy in other constitutional jurisdictions and contexts.

A third problem is closely related to the institutional issue, namely, the difficulty of finding a level of uniformity in views across the Member States sufficient to warrant judicial activism. Terrett analyses this point doctrinally in terms of the way in which the European Court was asked to widen the meaning of "sex" discrimination on the basis of a general principle of law. As he argues, the essential requirement for recognising a general principle of law is "that the principle should be widely accepted by the Member States", and that it "will require some level of uniformity, albeit short of precise consensus, before it [the Court] is willing to incorporate a principle into the EC system and offer it protection at a Community level".[19] One of the explicit bases for the Court's decision was the absence of such a consensus to ground a legal principle against discrimination on the basis of a person's sexuality:

"As for the laws of the Member States, while in some of them cohabitation by two persons of the same sex is treated as equivalent to marriage, although not completely, in most of them it is treated as equivalent to a stable heterosexual relationship outside marriage only with respect to a limited number of rights, or else is not recognized in any particular way".[20]

This recognition of variation and difference in the attitudes of Member States might well be understandable in terms of the relationship of sexuality to the private sphere. Again, in terms of legitimacy, Catherine Hoskyns argues that the European Court has been of the view that "intervening in personal or domestic matters is not the function of either EC law or the Court".[21] Rather, the personal becomes associated with the national, even though the precise issue— right to equal pay—is quintessentially a public, Community law matter.[22] The alternative approach in these circumstances would be the judicial "recognition" (or, more accurately, imposition) of a principle of Community law. Arguably, that is the approach which the Court adopted in *P v. S and Cornwall County Council*, in which it took no notice of national variation in the treatment of transsexuals.[23] In interpreting that decision, Larry Backer suggests that judicial interpretation can act as a form of "normalizing harmonization",[24] in which

---

[18] S Terrett, "A Bridge Too Far? Non-Discrimination and Homosexuality in European Community Law", (1998) 4 *European Public Law* 487 at 505.

[19] *Ibid.*, 498.

[20] *Grant*, above n. 1, at 647.

[21] Hoskyns, above n. 8, at 160.

[22] On the public/private distinction in EU law, see generally G C More, " 'Equal Treatment' of the Sexes in European Community Law: What does 'Equal' Mean?", (1993) 1 *Feminist Legal Studies* 45.

[23] Case C–13/94 [1996] ECR I–2143.

[24] L C Backer, "Harmonization, Subsidiarity and Cultural Difference: An Essay on the Dynamics of Opposition Within Federative and International Legal Systems", (1997) 4 *Tulsa Journal of Comparative and International Law* 185 at 197.

"subnational cultural determinism" gives way to the discipline imposed by legal standards.[25] That tension between harmonisation and self-determination is common in rights claims around sexuality and, indeed, it can be argued that the politics of sexuality is characterised by a dialectical relationship between the local and the global.[26] This tension may well have been an important factor which motivated the Court to defer to the local, and it is a factor closely related to the issue of judicial legitimacy.

Finally, it has been argued that a central problem with this litigation strategy was, quite simply, "the facts". As is well known from the history of civil rights struggles in the United States, constitutional litigation strategies demand compelling "test cases", and Mark Bell has argued that the "justice" of the issue in *Grant* was simply not overwhelmingly compelling.[27] By contrast, a set of facts dealing with an outright, irrational dismissal from employment (as was the case in *P* v. *S*) may well have resulted in a different outcome.[28] The granting of employment "perks" may well seem to many a less than compelling *human* rights case, particularly when those perks are not granted to employees who are not in *any* sort of traditional spousal-type relationship and who thus continue to suffer this "discrimination" no matter what the result of the case.

Although Bell's point is intuitively appealing, I want to argue, by contrast, that the claim in *Grant does* fit nicely into the ideological parameters of Community law, and particularly European rights discourse, despite the fact that the claim was ultimately unsuccessful. In making this argument, I hope to illustrate how law has an often complex and contradictory role in social movement politics, and how this is exacerbated in the realm of EU law. Thus, although the facts of *Grant* may appear to lack the moral imperative of a human rights claim, that is also arguably why it fits within this paradigm of rights discourse. Indeed, it has been argued that the advantage of deploying EU law for gays and lesbians is that the economic paradigm of rights abstracts them from an obviously moral underpinning, making it easier to make claims in a morally "neutral", economically grounded language.[29] As a consequence, "successes" will be more likely. Discrimination becomes a distortion of the transnational marketplace and a barrier to free movement, and the sort of controversies which are fuelled by gay rights litigation in other constitutional jurisdictions can be avoided. In other words, the economic teleology of rights in the EU can "sanitise" the claim, making it more likely that a court will conclude that it can legit-

---

[25] *Ibid.*, 199.

[26] See P M Nardi, "The Globalization of the Gay and Lesbian Socio-Political Movement: Some Observations about Europe with a Focus on Italy", (1998) 41 *Sociological Perspectives* 567.

[27] M Bell, "Shifting Conceptions of Sexual Discrimination at the Court of Justice: from *P.* v. *S.* to *Grant* v. *SWT*", (1999) 5 *European Law Journal* 63 at 78–9.

[28] In fact, it has been argued that the European Court might still find in favour of a claimant in a sexual orientation employment recruitment or dismissal case; see C Denys, "Homosexuality: a Non-Issue in Community Law?", (1999) 24 *ELRev* 419 at 425.

[29] C A Ball, "The Making of a Transnational Capitalist Society: The Court of Justice, Social Policy, and Individual Rights Under the European Community's Legal Order", (1996) 37 *Harvard International Law Journal* 307 at 387.

imately find in the claimant's favour. Although I have argued that such an instrumental approach to rights as an activist strategy is misguided,[30] that instrumentalism does capture something of the ideology of rights discourse, in some of its forms.

In fact, the focus in *Grant* on relationships also closely fits the ideology of the "family" as it has developed in EU law. Louise Ackers and Helen Stalford have examined how the family is conceived in EU law in the context of the free movement provisions, in which a series of social rights for the families of EU migrant workers has been recognised, providing equal treatment protection in matters of employment, pay and working conditions.[31] The assumption made by the European Court is that there is a close correlation between the exercise of the right of free movement and the granting of free movement rights to family members.[32] However, Ackers and Stalford emphasise that "the rationale for the Court's incursion into areas of family policy in this area of Community law is based firmly on a conceptualisation of women and children as the non-productive appendages of male workers".[33] Moreover, only a marital relationship can be used to underpin the claim as far as the dependent partner of an EU migrant worker is concerned.[34] Thus, a "breadwinner" model of "coupledom" is assumed, in which labour mobility depends upon the ease with which the worker can move the dependent spouse with "him" when he, as a factor of production, is more highly valued in another Member State. The facts of *Grant* tap into that same ideology, in which perks are for dependants, in a model of the family based upon a breadwinner, "family" wage earner. Thus, *Grant* exemplifies a well known litigation strategy, in which test cases draw upon fact situations which are constructed so as to replicate very traditional gendered relationship patterns, albeit with a same sex twist. Replication is assumed to be the path to litigation success.

THE COMMODIFICATION OF RIGHTS AND SEXUALITIES

The tensions within the politics of *Grant* can perhaps be best illustrated through the academic debate staged between social and cultural theorists, Nancy Fraser and Judith Butler.[35] This is not the place to re-stage that debate, but suffice to say that the basic issue which divides these two theorists, who would no doubt

---

[30] See C F Stychin, *A Nation by Rights* (Philadelphia, Temple University Press, 1998) 143.

[31] H L Ackers and H Stalford, "Children, Migration and Citizenship in the European Union: Intra-Community Mobility and the Status of Children in EC Law", (1999) 21 *Children and Youth Services Review* 699.

[32] *Ibid.*, 705.

[33] *Ibid.*, 702.

[34] *Ibid.*, 708.

[35] See N Fraser, *Justice Interruptus* (New York, Routledge, 1997); J Butler, "Merely Cultural", (1998) 227 *New Left Review* 33; N Fraser, "Heterosexism, Misrecognition and Capitalism: A Response to Judith Butler", (1997) 15 (52/53) *Social Text* 279.

both describe themselves as politically progressive, is the relationship between struggles around the recognition of "sexual orientation" and wider issues of political economy and economic transformation. In the debate, this has been framed in terms of the language which Fraser has developed regarding the relationship between a politics of recognition and a politics of redistribution.[36] Fraser's point is that sexuality struggles are *essentially* about a politics of recognition, rather than about issues of redistribution in political economic terms. The two are separate struggles.

Butler, in response, has questioned the dichotomy, and has asked, pointedly, "why would a movement concerned to criticize and transform the ways in which sexuality is socially regulated not be understood as central to the functioning of political economy?"[37] That is, Butler claims that sexuality must be understood as part of the mode of production itself. She also presents examples to refute Fraser's claim that recognition and redistribution are necessarily separate. Most obviously, lesbians, as (marginalised) women as a group are likely to experience both a wage gap (an issue of economic distribution), and a lack of social recognition.[38]

The relationship between recognition and redistribution claims has now begun to be analysed explicitly in legal scholarship. Susan Boyd, for example, argues that while Fraser's sharp dichotomy is problematic for precisely the reason that she seems to forget that lesbian women are gendered, and gender is central to the mode of production, Butler's position is also troubling.[39] As Boyd notes, "it does not follow that legal recognition of non-normative sexualities (for example, same sex relationships) will necessarily, of itself, constitute a fundamental challenge to the capitalist mode of production".[40] Intuitively, given the purpose of Community rights discourse to further a market economy across national borders, it would be surprising if legal recognition in the European context would amount to such a challenge here.

In fact, the critique which Boyd offers—which is situated in the context of Canadian equality rights discourse around same sex partnership rights—is very similar to the feminist critiques of EU sex equality law. The argument in both contexts is that rights do little, if anything, to alter underlying structures which produce gender inequality, such as the role of unpaid labour in the private sphere, and barriers to entry in the workplace. Boyd argues that the nuclear family has a material role in capitalist relations of production, through a sexual division of labour and the privatisation within the nuclear family of the social costs of reproduction and care.[41] It is this same model of the nuclear family which,

---

[36] Fraser, *Justice Interruptus*, above n. 35, at 12.
[37] Butler, above n. 35, at 39.
[38] *Ibid.*, 41.
[39] S B Boyd, "Family, Law and Sexuality: Feminist Engagements", (1999) 8 *Social & Legal Studies* 369 at 375–6.
[40] *Ibid.*, 376.
[41] *Ibid.*, 376–7.

Ackers and Stalford argue, is privileged within EU legal discourse.[42] The agenda, which Boyd then advances, is one in which activists and academics should pay greater attention to whether or not that gendered economy is challenged by lesbian and gay legal struggles, or alternatively, whether the lesbian or gay subject is naturalised within the political economy through the (eventually successful) claiming of rights.[43] In this regard, it has been argued that the construction of sexual identities (and political priorities for a movement) historically has been shaped by the more privileged (in terms of social class) members of the group.[44] Thus, the question whether sexuality is integral to capitalism cannot be separated from the question of whether sexual identities are significantly constituted by, and experienced in, ways which reflect individual location within that mode of production.

Taking up Boyd's challenge to interrogate rights claims, my argument is that the *Grant* litigation provides a perfect example of such a normalisation, even though the litigation ultimately proved unsuccessful. On the immediate facts, a successful claim in *Grant* would have seen the extension of marital-type perks to "stable" same sex couples, which presumably would have marginally increased employer costs. The actual "take up" of the marital privileges no doubt would vary greatly across the EU depending upon local and corporate social attitudes towards homosexuality, the prevalence of such benefits in the cultural context at issue, and, indeed, whether there was already anti-discrimination legislation in place at national level in the EU Member State which covered this field. The wider procedural right of non-discrimination in employment in itself can be seen as a means to "perfect" the marketplace to the extent that anti-discrimination law is effective in eradicating the use of irrelevant characteristics in hiring, promotion and dismissal.

However, what is also significant, as Bell points out, is that the UK government submission in the *Grant* litigation focused on the wider implications and potential future litigation which might flow from a decision in favour of Grant.[45] In particular, state pension and social security issues may well have been at the forefront of concern. These are areas that are expensive for the state in a capitalist economy. After all, maintaining the attractiveness of the institution of marriage and marriage-like relationships requires costly social engineering. But such institutions are necessary for the maintenance of a capitalist system with a clear public/private dichotomy, in which many costs are internalised within the domestic sphere of the home.[46] Although the European Court has often been prepared to reject the appropriateness of economic justifications

---

[42] Ackers and Stalford, above n. 31, at 709.

[43] Boyd, above n. 39, at 381.

[44] See, for example, S Valocchi, "The Class-Inflected Nature of Gay Identity", (1999) 46 *Social Problems* 207.

[45] Bell, above n. 27, at 76.

[46] Boyd, above n. 39, at 377. See also Hervey and Shaw, above n. 6.

for sex discriminatory employment practices,[47] many of these decisions are themselves ideologically "loaded" (such as those concerning protective treatment of pregnant workers), and do not in themselves refute the claim of an ideological basis to the legal order centred on the public/private dichotomy.[48]

Thus, a decision in favour of Lisa Grant would have fitted very well with the ideological grounding of EC rights discourse, in terms of the nuclear family and privatised responsibility within that private sphere, and it would have furthered transnational cultural harmonisation through a common EU definition of "spouse". However, the wider implications of the decision—with the resulting social costs—would not be easily distinguishable within the "all or nothing" paradigm of formal equality in EU law. The economic costs of legally normalising the homosexual subject are greater than those of normalising the transsexual subject in *P* v. *S*, particularly when issues such as health care benefits and pension rights are considered. The scale of such costs no doubt is an inhibiting factor for the judiciary. By way of contrast, Canadian courts have found it much easier to make distinctions between cases so as to minimise the cost to the state.[49] As a result, as Claire Young argues, we now see Canadian courts developing broad definitions of "spouse" in the context of upholding private obligations (such as support), while constructing narrow definitions in the context of state pensions.[50] Had the European Court seen a way to achieve this sort of distinction, a different result might have been forthcoming.

I make this hypothesis because, on its facts, *Grant* is ideologically very attractive in terms of the underpinnings of EU law: no immediate cost to the state; a recognisable model of relationships suggesting economic dependence on a breadwinner; and the cost of the perk is a product of a contractually regulated private employment relationship. It provides a clear example of "the domestication of deviant sexualities within a safe, useful and recognisable framework",[51] while the cost of the relationship does not touch the state. At the same time, a standardised, normalised definition of "spouse" modelled on heterosexual marriage creates a level playing field across the EU (from which deviant "others" can then be excluded).

A central paradox in the use of legal discourse towards the recognition of same sex relationships thus becomes apparent. Social scientists are increasingly

---

[47] See, for example, Case C–66/96 *Handels-og Kontor funktionaerernes Forbund i Danmark* [1998] ECR I–7327 in the context of pregnancy. But see also Case C–394/96 *Brown* v. *Rentokil* [1998] ECR I–4185 and Case C–179/88 *Handels-og Kontorfunktionaerernes Forbund i Danmark* v. *Dansk Arbejdsgiverforening* [1990] ECR I–3979 (determining that pregnancy-related illness beyond the period of maternity leave is to be treated as sex-neutral).

[48] See G F Mancini and S O'Leary, "The New Frontiers of Sex Equality Law in the European Union", (1999) 24 *ELRev* 331.

[49] Compare, e.g., *M* v. *H* [1999] 2 *Supreme Court Reports* 3 (extending definition of "spouse" for purposes of spousal support law) and *Egan* v. *Canada* [1995] 2 *Supreme Court Reports* 513 (no extended definition in the context of old age security legislation).

[50] C F L Young, "Spousal Status, Pension Benefits and Tax: *Rosenberg* v. *Canada*", (1998) 6 *Canadian Labour and Employment Law Journal* 435.

[51] Boyd, above n. 39, at 377.

confirming through empirically-based research what many have long known: that lesbians and gays construct an infinite variety of ways of living—and of relationships widely defined—which not only replicate but also resist the disciplinarity of heterosexual monogamous cohabitation.[52] Yet, when legal discourse is deployed in activist struggles for social change, the engagement with law seems to require constructing relationships which replicate monogamous, heterosexual cohabitation as an "ideal" to which lesbians and gays can successfully aspire, and from which benefits then flow. These two dynamics—of resistance and discipline—appear to coexist simultaneously, although it is also important to avoid the privileging of legal discourse.

While the successful deployment of rights strategies will benefit some lesbians and gays materially, and no doubt symbolically, in terms of the affirmation of relationships (for otherwise, there would never have been litigation), the underlying economic question remains; what is the relationship between such claims—framed within the context of a sex discrimination provision—to underlying gender-based structural inequalities? More specifically, is there a necessary relationship between claims to recognition and what Butler refers to as the "holy family" of the capitalist mode of production?[53]

It does seem a reasonably general proposition that employment rights protection will have a differential impact depending upon the intersection of identities implicated in any individual case, and this point is also related to the distinction between formal and substantive equality. At this juncture, it is useful to recognise that rights discourse around sexual orientation will benefit *most* those for whom there are no other structural, identity-based impediments to the realisation of substantive equality; or, in other words, where there is no intersection of disadvantage. But there is another dynamic at work here, for all gay men (except to the extent that they are perceived to embody cross-gender characteristics) *already* benefit "from the institutions and social customs that hinder female entry into certain jobs, including traditional notions that women should be committed to domestic life and not to market labour".[54] That is, to the extent that rights discourse can eliminate irrational anti-gay animus in the workplace (and I do not want to exaggerate the extent to which law can achieve this aim), gay, childless men can benefit tremendously from patriarchal economic relations which largely privatise responsibility for the care of the young.

Meanwhile, many lesbian women *qua* women may well still face the structural barriers which are not rectifiable through a formal equality rights-based discourse of equal opportunities alone (although statistically as a group they may fare better in some economic respects than heterosexual women). Michael

---

[52] C Donovan, B Heaphy and J Weeks, "Citizenship and Same Sex Relationships", (1999) 28 *Journal of Social Policy* 689.

[53] Butler, above n. 35, at 41.

[54] M P Jacobs, "Do Gay Men have a Stake in Male Privilege?: The Political Economy of Gay Men's Contradictory Relationship to Feminism" in A Gluckman and B Reed (eds), *Homo Economics: Capitalism, Community, and Lesbian and Gay Life* (New York, Routledge, 1997) 165 at 170.

Jacobs neatly summarises a political dynamic which increasingly rings true today:

> "Gay families need not be modeled on the social norm of a two-adult household, but for gay male couples who do form a two-income household, the benefit of men's generally higher wage earnings is doubled. This amplifies income differentials by gender within the gay community and perhaps makes gay men more conscious of the economic benefits of male privilege and less comfortable with an agenda that challenges this privilege. To the extent that their efforts to integrate into their families of origin are successful as well, many gay men may no longer find the social dominance of the family particularly oppressive and thus may not respond favorably to a political rhetoric that describes it that way".[55]

In addition, for those gay male couples who do not reap the benefits of a two-income household, employment perks such as those at issue in *Grant* at least will allow them to keep pace with the heterosexual single income household. The point which this analysis drives at is that the use of sex equality laws—even if successful on its own terms—will definitely benefit some more than others (ironically, men more than women), and must be considered at best a modest part of a wider strategy of social change.

Furthermore, Jacobs' point is that many gay men may well not have a tremendous stake in a wider strategy for social and economic change, particularly if they achieve the sort of formal legal guarantees which were at issue in *Grant*. Here again, the ideology underpinning the EU integration project illustrates how the construct of citizenship—which has been widely critiqued as a limited, market-centred concept by progressive legal academics[56]—is also one which is actually advantageous in its current form to many gay men. In fact, the subject position of EU citizenship has been described as "archetypically male" because of its market-centredness, in which the citizen is imagined as enjoying the benefits of free movement unconstrained, allowing him to sell his labour to the highest bidder transnationally, and enjoying ever widening consumer choice to satisfy his wants and desires.[57] This citizen (whose primary identity is derived from paid employment) is highly atomistic and unconstrained by relationships of dependence. For many gay men, such a construct is very appealing, particularly if formal legal protection against discrimination ensures that they can exercise these citizenship rights without fear of irrational prejudice by others. Homosexuality then becomes simply, as Mariana Valverde suggests, a "lifestyle choice" and "an innocuous feature of urban consumer life" for the market citizen who can choose to consume homosexuality unconstrained—and across national borders.[58] Many gay men, in this citizenship discourse, are themselves

---

[55] *Ibid.*, 172.

[56] See generally the contributors to Shaw and More, above n. 8.

[57] Shaw, above n. 15, at 297.

[58] M Valverde, " 'The Lifestyle that Fits the Doctrine of Sexual Orientation': The Disappearing Homosexual of Human Rights Law", paper presented to the American Law and Society Association Annual Conference, Chicago, May 1999.

archetypically male; more man than most ("new") heterosexual men who are increasingly expected to prioritise their familial relationships, and to share (albeit certainly not yet equally) in child care responsibilities. Thus, European law and social policy have been subject to criticism for their "commodification of individuals" into workers (i.e., producers).[59] But homosexuality is also increasingly criticised for its own form of commodification, centred on the consumption of goods, services and, indeed, a way of life, in which "consumerism becomes the embodiment of identity".[60]

Of course, this vision of the gay male EU citizen is also dependent upon the marginalisation of traditional familial and religious discourses of homophobia; but, here again, the underlying ideology of EU law is sympathetic to such progressive change. A modernist discourse of capitalism has little room for such irrationality, which can distort competitive labour markets, and an underlying desire for cultural harmonisation demands that one should be able to cross borders freely both to produce and consume a lifestyle unconstrained by bigotry in some Member States. Historically, some lesbians and probably many more gay men have often benefited from capitalism, as the "marketplace cleared away all sorts of traditional social formations".[61] As John D'Emilio has argued, it was only when wage labour became the widespread basis by which people lived that homosexuality could become the foundation of a personal identity.[62] Thus, for example, Peter Nardi claims that in northern Italy, the pre-conditions for a lesbian and gay movement occurred only relatively recently, with the growth of urban middle class employment opportunities, economic development and personal mobility, and the growth of non-religious associations.[63] These processes no doubt will continue and accelerate throughout the EU, particularly with the likely widening of its borders eastward.

The argument underscores the idea that while capitalism has depended upon the heterosexual nuclear family to help maintain it, late capitalism can now accommodate (quite happily) a group of autonomous, unconstrained producers and consumers operating outside the traditional constraints of the nuclear family. One need only look to the "positive" attitude of many multinationals to gay consumers today for evidence of this point. It is somewhat ironic then, that within legal discourse around relationships, activists and litigants seek to discipline citizenship into something which perhaps is inevitably going to replicate the nuclear "holy family", at the same time as that "holy family" is increasingly decentred in many ways. More than anything, this irony demonstrates how legal discourse functions and constrains argumentation through the demands of

---

[59] See T Hervey, *European Social Law and Policy* (London, Longman, 1998) 204.

[60] Valocchi, above n. 44, at 220.

[61] B D Adam, J W Duyvendak and A Krouwel, "Gay and Lesbian Movements beyond Borders?" in B D Adam, J W Duyvendak and A Krouwel (eds), *The Global Emergence of Gay and Lesbian Politics* (Philadelphia, Temple University Press, 1999) 344 at 356.

[62] J D'Emilio, "Capitalism and Gay Identity" in A Snitow, C Stansell and S Thompson (eds), *Powers of Desire: The Politics of Sexuality* (New York, Monthly Review Press, 1983) 100.

[63] Nardi, above n. 26, at 579.

precedent and comparison. Finally, it suggests that Butler may underestimate the inherent conservatism of law when she suggests that same sex recognition struggles inevitably challenge the "holy family", for it is only by making one's self (or one's client) look like the (admittedly decentred) norm that "success" in instrumental terms is likely to be achieved.

CONCLUSION: FROM EQUALITY TO ACTIVE CITIZENSHIP

Given what I have suggested about the relationship between capitalism and sexuality in the face of the decline of traditional social formations, it must be tempting (at least for those gays and lesbians who are secure in their jobs), to await the "liberalising effect of time",[64] particularly given the limitations inherent in the use of rights discourse to advance social change. Why not "opt out" of law, once basic privacy rights are recognised and a libertarian approach is accepted to the criminal law regulation of sexuality (as some lesbian separatists have advocated for many years)? In answer, it is worth remembering that while we may point to the disciplinary effect of rights, and the way in which progressive politics can be ideologically channelled into principles such as formal equality, *particularly* in a legal context such as the EU, the potentialities of rights discourse also must be recalled. The problem seems to be that although it may be recognised widely that rights through law provide incomplete political strategies, the problem with rights discourse is the way in which it seduces its users into believing in its totalising potential as a political strategy.

This is particularly true in the EU context. Given the democratic deficit, the democratic potentiality of rights discourse is necessarily constrained. Thus, on the one hand, we might applaud the pleas of commentators Philip Alston and Joseph Weiler that the EU needs a general equal treatment provision and draft directive on sexual orientation discrimination[65] (which also has been called for by the European Commissioner responsible for Social Affairs and Employment).[66] Such a provision—however politically unlikely it may seem— undoubtedly would have important practical and symbolic importance. However, Alston and Weiler may well underestimate the resistance which such a provision might meet.[67] Here again, the dialectical relationship between the local and the global must be recalled. In other national contexts, rights claims around sexuality have a unique power to fuel a reaction grounded in the discourses of localism and cultural and legal self-determination.[68] Moreover, as

---

[64] J Scott, "Changing Attitudes to Sexual Morality: A Cross-National Comparison", (1998) 32 *Sociology* 815 at 839.

[65] P Alston and J H H Weiler, "An 'Ever Closer Union' in Need of a Human Rights Policy", (1998) 9 *European Journal of International Law* 658 at 717.

[66] *Stonewall News*, 7 December 1998. (<http://www.stonewall.org.uk/stonewall/cgi-bin/news.cgi?employmentcommission>).

[67] See generally Backer, above n. 24.

[68] For example, Tasmania, Alberta, Colorado, and Zimbabwe.

empirical research continues to demonstrate, "there is no monolithic Continental attitude towards sexuality in Europe",[69] and, in particular, "homosexuality generates more varied opinions across countries and more polarized responses within nations" than do other contentious issues surrounding sexuality (such as extra-marital heterosexuality).[70]

The other problem in the EU context, as Jo Shaw suggests, is that rights remain very much a "top-down" process, leaving little discursive space for the power of rights as an enabling device for social movement activism.[71] Even in Alston and Weiler's argument, rights remain "granted" from on high, rather than being perceived as the product of years of social movement mobilisation.[72] Although I have argued elsewhere that in recent years there has been some space for NGOs, such as the International Lesbian and Gay Association Europe, to intervene in European rights debates around sexuality, it remains a modest space, because the idea of European identities and transnational communities are still very much in their infancy.[73] However, as transnational communities, identities and affinities develop, there is no inherent reason why the European legal arena might not be one in which mobilisation and struggle from below could occur more widely.

In fact, one of the roles which sexuality politics might play is in seeking to expand that space of transnational politics, in an attempt to develop strategies of citizenship which go *beyond* the market towards a political and social citizenship of the European Union.[74] The EU remains an important site, and there is some evidence that a notion of "social citizenship" has increasing currency through, for example, EU funding and "soft law",[75] as well as in some recent rights-based discourse from the European Court.[76] It is an arena which should not, then, be seen as solely one for the pursuit of legal rights which can be "consumed", but instead, as having the potential to mean something "more". Indeed, NGOs such as ILGA Europe do seek to combine calls for rights and democratic participation in the EU, and this provides a useful antidote to the privileging of rights discourse.[77] It might be helpful here to imagine a floor of rights—perhaps guaranteed through EU law—which acts as a base for the development of

---

[69] E D Widmer, J Treas, and R Newcomb, "Attitudes Toward Nonmarital Sex in 24 Countries", (1998) 35 *Journal of Sex Research* 349 at 356.

[70] *Ibid.*, 352.

[71] J Shaw, "European Union Citizenship: the IGC and Beyond", (1997) 3 *European Public Law* 413 at 427.

[72] Alston and Weiler, above n. 65.

[73] See C F Stychin, "Disintegrating Sexuality: Citizenship and the European Union", in R Bellamy and A Warleigh (eds), *Citizenship and Governance in the European Union* (London, Pinter, 2001).

[74] J Shaw, "The Problem of Membership in EU Citizenship" in Z Bankowski and A Scott (eds), *The European Union and its Order, The Legal Theory of European Union* (Oxford, Blackwell, 2000).

[75] See Hervey, above n. 59, at 205.

[76] See, in particular, Case C–85/96 *Martínez Sala v. Freistaat Bayern* [1998] ECR I–2708.

[77] See International Lesbian and Gay Association Europe, *Equality for Lesbians and Gay Men: A Relevant Issue in the Civil and Social Dialogue* (Brussels, ILGA Europe, 1998).

strategies of democratic participation within the institutions of the EU (and within social movements themselves).[78]

Richard Bellamy has argued that European rights will only be made meaningful in the context of democratic political arrangements.[79] Otherwise, "rights prove too indeterminate and subject to conflicting interpretations to provide a constitutional basis for a European polity".[80] In the EU, things are "further complicated by the existence of a plurality of national political traditions",[81] and sexuality is certainly not exempt from these dynamics. Shared democratic arrangements are therefore necessary for the creation of common rights. This, I conclude, is a central limitation of litigation strategies such as *Grant*. Rights have been abstracted from any form of democratic politics and are experienced as being far removed from the individual.[82] At the same time, rights claims can appear undemocratic from the perspective of those who are members of the social group at the epicentre of the claim, to the extent that the case may not reflect what are thought to be grassroots priorities; and, furthermore, rights inevitably privilege the interests of some in the group over others.

Yet, at the same time, the experience of the *Grant* litigation, I would conversely suggest, was a valuable exercise in terms of the way in which the claim for European rights operated as, in Elizabeth Kingdom's terminology, a "heuristic device".[83] The deployment of rights discourse—and most importantly its widespread publicity, at least in the United Kingdom—drew attention, not only to sexualities and relationships, but it also placed gay *women* at the forefront of a campaign. It served an important function in drawing attention at least to the possibilities and potentialities of European citizenship claims around sexuality. In a Member State in which relatively few people are even aware that they are "citizens of the Union", the *Grant* litigation made one group aware that there was a legal arena in which the language of citizenship could be articulated on their behalf.

However, as a normative matter, rights and democratic participation must operate as two strands of a political agenda. The creation of spaces of engagement have traditionally been tried—not always successfully—at the level of

---

[78] See R Bellamy and D Castiglione, "The Communitarian Ghost in the Cosmopolitan Machine: Constitutionalism, Democracy and the Reconfiguration of Politics in the New Europe" in R Bellamy (ed.), *Constitutionalism, Democracy and Sovereignty* (Aldershot, Avebury, 1996) 111 at 122. Interestingly, the original Social Action Programme of 1974 explicitly linked the development of social rights with democratic participation, a connection which underpinned many Commission proposals, such as those on corporate governance.

[79] R Bellamy, "The Constitution of Europe: Rights or Democracy?" in R Bellamy, V Bufacchi and D Castiglione (eds), *Democracy and Constitutional Culture in the Union of Europe* (London, Lothian Foundation Press, 1995) 153.

[80] *Ibid.*

[81] *Ibid.*, 167.

[82] On the relationship between rights and deliberative democracy, see S Benhabib, "Toward a Deliberative Model of Democratic Legitimacy" in S Benhabib (ed.), *Democracy and Difference: Contesting the Boundaries of the Political* (Princeton, Princeton University Press, 1996) 67.

[83] E Kingdom, "Transforming Rights: Feminist Political Heuristics", (1996) 2 *Res Publica* 73.

local, urban government.[84] But the transnational arena should not be abandoned. The fact that transnational constructs of citizenship and "belonging" have been closely linked to the market up to now, and that many in the lesbian and especially gay male communities may have little personal interest in broadening the horizon of transnational citizenship, does not mean that this should not be struggled over, so that recognition questions might be connected to issues of redistribution, particularly in the context of a widening European Union, and in the face of the economic disparities which inevitably will be exacerbated as a result of that expansion.

[84] See generally D Cooper, *Sexing the City: Lesbian and Gay Politics within the Activist State* (London, Rivers Oram, 1994).

PART VI

Building the Normative Dimension

14

Legitimising EU Law: Is the Social Dialogue the Way Forward? Some Reflections Around the UEAPME Case

NICK BERNARD

INTRODUCTION

Without doubt, one of the most notable institutional innovations in the field of EU social law in the last decade has been the partial privatisation of the legislative process through the social dialogue.[1] The new arrangements were first introduced in the Agreement on Social Policy annexed to the Maastricht Treaty, but have been repatriated into mainstream Community law following the Amsterdam Treaty. Privatisation of the legislative process is not, however, specific to social policy. It is part of a wider phenomenon of distanciation from traditional command and control legislative edicts in favour of more flexible arrangements where key actors tend to be private agents rather than public legislators.[2] In the field of the internal market, for instance, with the so-called new approach to technical harmonisation, a large chunk of work previously understood to fall within the remit of the Community legislator was transferred to private standardisation bodies such as CEN or CENELEC; in environmental law, the Fifth Environmental Programme places great stock on voluntary action by private actors as an important mechanism to bring about desired environmental aims; more generally, the increased reliance on self-regulation at national level, both for domestic purposes and for implementation of Community law obligations, reflects this phenomenon of displacement of the (public) legislator in favour of private actors.

---

[1] The "social dialogue" has two main ingredients: first a process of consultation between the Commission and representative organisations of employers and workers; second a mechanism, in Art. 139 EC, of European-level collective bargaining between representative organisations of workers and employers (the so-called "social partners") leading to agreements susceptible to be transformed into binding EU legislation through a Council decision. This chapter is concerned exclusively with the second aspect of the social dialogue and references to the social dialogue should be read as references to the Art. 139 process exclusively.

[2] In this, Community law is mirroring comparable developments at national level.

One should be careful not to overstate the similarities between those various manifestations of involvement of private actors in the business of legislation. It needs to be acknowledged that very important differences exist between them. Nevertheless, a common thread is the increasing difficulty for legislators to master the regulatory process and bring about desired ends through traditional command and control mechanisms. Relevant factors here include the relative rigidity and cumbersome character of legislative processes, particularly at Community level. Then, there is the knowledge problem: assembling the necessary knowledge needed to regulate a particular activity effectively in a complex social system is an increasingly difficult task for a public regulator. In addition, effective regulation will usually require significant resources to be allocated to enforcement. In a climate of tight control of public spending, exacerbated by the fiscal discipline imposed by Economic and Monetary Union, such resources are hard to come by. Globalisation also adds another layer of difficulty to effective enforcement.

Devising mechanisms to incite private actors to take charge of their own regulation has obvious attractions for public policy-makers: it carries the promise, or at least the potential, of a more effective and cheaper way of reaching regulatory goals. From the perspective of those private actors, the threat of potentially more cumbersome command and control regulatory requirements may be enough of an incentive to play the game and self-regulate in the shadow of the law. Beyond regulatory efficiency issues, the involvement of private actors may also serve a legitimation function. Representative parliamentary democracy leads to an increasing alienation of a politically de-skilled mass from the elite of a professional political class.[3] Alternative mechanisms of involvement of citizens in the law-making process may counteract this deficiency.

This is an issue which has particular saliency in EU law in view of the limitations of the mechanisms of parliamentary democracy at the supranational level. National parliamentary elections enable citizens to select the government of the day and determine, however vaguely and imperfectly, the broad lines and general policy orientation of the polity for the next four or five years. However much one increases the legislative powers of the European Parliament and generalises recourse to co-decision, one cannot escape the fact that European parliamentary elections cannot fulfil that function of the parliamentary electoral process. The European Parliament certainly has a significant role to play, in a logic of checks and balances, in scrutinising legislation[4] and supervising the European Commission, a role that the crisis of Spring 1999, leading to the resignation of the Santer Commission, brought to the fore. In terms of determining the general policy orientation of the EU, the role of the European Parliament remains limited. In so far as this is not merely a conjunctural problem but a

---

[3] Cf. B Barber, *Strong Democracy—Participatory Politics for a New Age* (Berkeley, University of California Press, 1984).

[4] Indeed it is probably doing so far more effectively than many national parliaments.

structural one inherently linked to the polycentric nature of the EU,[5] participation of citizens in policy-making processes through alternatives to the mechanisms of parliamentarism assume a particular importance in the EU.

Against this background, the judgment of the Court of First Instance in the *UEAPME* case[6] deserves our attention. In the context of a judgment concerning the validity of the Parental Leave Directive,[7] the European Court recognised that the social dialogue process offered an alternative form of citizen involvement and democratic legitimation beyond the mechanisms of parliamentary democracy. The significance of the judgment, from this perspective, should not be underestimated; it is, to this author's knowledge, the first explicit judicial recognition at Community level that developing a more democratic law-making process in the EU need not necessarily mean conferring ever wider powers on the European Parliament and that other paths are also conceivable. Leaving the familiar terrain of parliamentarism, however, immediately raises the question of what framework to put in its place.

While acknowledging that the social dialogue adopts a different path to that of legitimation through parliamentary representation, the Court of First instance in *UEAPME* remains nevertheless strongly influenced by a representative model of democracy, as will be seen in the next section. Others have suggested participatory democracy as a potential basis for legitimising the social dialogue.[8] We will therefore need to consider how well the social dialogue fits under both models. Under either of them, however, we may perhaps be expecting too much from the social dialogue in terms of legitimation. Even if the social dialogue arrangements did not exist, EU social policy would not operate in a vacuum of representation of workers' and employers' interests. From this perspective, the question we will need to ask ourselves is whether the institutionalisation of the social dialogue can contribute to a more democratic process than an unstructured bazaar of interest representation. Associative democracy theory might provide a useful framework in this context.

THE *UEAPME* CASE

The *UEAPME* case took the form of a challenge to the validity of the Parental Leave Directive.[9] This Directive was the first EC implementation instrument

---

[5] See N Bernard, "Citizenship in a Polycentric Polity" in S Konstadinidis (ed.), *A People's Europe—Tuning a Concept into Content* (Aldershot, Dartmouth, 1998) 1.

[6] Case T–135/96 *UEAPME v. Council* [1998] ECR II–2335.

[7] Directive 96/34/EC of 3 June 1996 on the framework agreement on parental leave concluded by UNICE, CEEP and ETUC, [1996] OJ L145/4.

[8] Cf. S Fredman, "Social Law in the European Union: The impact of the Lawmaking Process" in P Craig and C Harlow (eds), *Lawmaking in the European Union* (London, Kluwer Law International, 1998) 386 at 408.

[9] Directive 96/34/EC of 3 June 1996 on the framework agreement on parental leave concluded by UNICE, CEEP and ETUC, [1996] OJ L145/4.

based on an agreement between the social partners following the procedure introduced by Article 4(2) of the Agreement on Social Policy, which now figures in Article 139(2) EC. The applicant in the case, UEAPME, was an association representing at European level the interests of small and medium size undertakings. UEAPME had been involved in the initial phase of consultation by the Commission in the process of framing a legislative proposal on parental leave. It had not, however, been admitted to the negotiating table for the purpose of adopting the framework agreement which the Directive implemented. Only UNICE, CEEP and ETUC took part in these negotiations and were parties to the agreement. UEAPME argued that, as a representative organisation, it had a right to participate in the negotiations, and that the breach of that right constituted a failure to observe an essential procedural requirement, affecting the validity of the Directive.

UEAPME faced a major procedural hurdle at the outset: it had to establish *locus standi* to challenge the Directive under Article 230(4) EC.[10] As those familiar with EU administrative law will know only too well, the highly restrictive case law of the European Court and Court of First Instance on *locus standi* under Article 230(4) EC makes it virtually impossible in the vast majority of cases for anybody other than a Member State or a Community institution to challenge legislative acts.[11] Without going into the many subtleties of the Article 230(4) EC case law, the basic position is that private parties do not as a rule have standing to challenge legislative acts. However, in exceptional circumstances, a private party who is able to establish that a Community legislative measure substantially affects its own private interests in a highly particularistic manner[12] may be recognised as having sufficient standing to challenge that measure. Although the Court of First Instance insisted that the Directive was a legislative act,[13] it nevertheless found that these were exceptional circumstances and that UEAPME had standing to challenge the Directive. According to the Court, notwithstanding the legislative character of the Directive, UEAPME could still have standing if it were established that it possessed specific rights that were

---

[10] Formerly Art. 173 EC.

[11] A legislative act, in this context, means a measure of general application, as distinct from an individual "decision" within the meaning of Art. 249 EC. On the distinction between general and individual measures and more generally on the issue of *locus standi* for private parties under Art. 230 EC, see P P Craig and G De Búrca, *EU Law: Text, Cases and Materials* (2nd edn., Oxford, Oxford University Press, 1998) 462, especially 466.

[12] In the language of Art. 230 EC and of the Community courts, applicants must show that the measure is of "direct and individual concern" to them. Applicants are individually concerned by a measure when the measure affects them "by reason of certain attributes peculiar to them or by reason of circumstances which differentiate them from all other persons" (see para. 69 of the judgment). It is important to note, in our context, that the requirement of *individual* concern means that harm to collective or general interests can never form a suitable basis to establish standing under Art. 230: only the *individual* interests of the applicant are relevant, although it is possible for an association to have standing for the purpose of representing the individual interests of its members (see, among many other cases, Case C–298/89 *Gibraltar* v. *Council* [1993] ECR I–3605, Joined Cases 16 and 17/62 *Producteurs de Fruits* v. *Council* [1962] ECR 471).

[13] See paras 64–7 of the judgment.

capable of infringement by the Council or Commission in the process of adopting the Directive. If that were so, the applicant's right to judicial protection of these rights might be enough to provide the necessary "direct and individual concern". While the European Court denied that any organisation could claim to have a right to be involved in the negotiations,[14] it nevertheless considered that there existed a duty on the Commission and the Council to check the representativity of the parties to the agreement before implementing that agreement by means of Community instrument. That requirement flowed from the principle of democracy which required the participation of the people in the legislative process. Normally that participation is effected, in the Community context, by means of involvement of the European Parliament. However, in so far as Parliament is excluded from the Article 139 procedure, the people must be represented by an alternative method, *in casu* through the parties to the agreement. The parties to the agreement, however, can only be regarded as representing the people if they possess between themselves sufficient cumulative representativity, hence the duty on the Commission and Council to ensure this representativity of the social partners. The Court then went on to assert that this duty was owed to those organisations not involved in the negotiations who could nevertheless claim that they should have been involved so as to ensure sufficient cumulative representativity. Thus, an organisation like UEAPME, which claimed precisely that, was entitled to judicial protection of its right to demand that the Commission and Council ensure the representativity of the social partners involved in the agreement, and could be regarded as directly and individually concerned by the Directive for these purposes.

Although superficially attractive, this tortuous reasoning is harder to sustain on closer analysis; if the Commission and the Council have a duty to check the representativity of the social partners which are parties to the agreement, it is to ensure that the people are represented in the legislative process. It is, therefore, a "public" duty, owed to the people, to all of us as citizens. It is not the correlative duty of a private right enjoyed by potential social partners excluded from the negotiations. In these circumstances, it is hard to see how UEAPME could be treated as *individually* concerned by the Directive. The right they are seeking judicial protection of, and which constitutes the starting point of the Court's analysis on standing, does not distinguish them from anybody else. It would have been far more convincing for the Court of First Instance to follow the lead of the European Court in the *Chernobyl* case[15] and recognise that decision-making in the EU has evolved in directions which could not have been contemplated when the EC Treaty was signed in 1957 and that the current evolution of the EU left a gap in the system of judicial protection in the Treaty that the Court was duty-bound to fill.[16] Article 230(4) EC is premised on a clear division

---

[14] See paras 72–80.

[15] Case C–70/88 *European Parliament* v. *Council* [1990] ECR I–2041.

[16] See also, in favour of this view, E Franssen and T J M Jacobs, "The Question of Representativity in the European Social Dialogue, (1998) 35 *CMLRev* 1295, at 1303.

between, on the one hand, the institutions of the EU as law-makers and, on other hand, private parties as *subject to* that law. Article 230(4) does not even begin to contemplate a situation where private parties are involved in the legislative process, and is wholly unsuited to provide solutions to legal problems arising out of this situation. It is therefore an even more patent gap than in the *Chernobyl* case,[17] where it would have been entirely proper for the Court to proceed on the basis of first principles rather than trying to make the case fit the Article 230(4) strait-jacket at all costs, including that of a serious distortion of the notion of individual concern.

The reasoning of the Court nevertheless has the advantage, from our perspective, of placing the issue of the democratic legitimation of the social dialogue in centre-stage: without the need for democratic legitimation, there is no duty on the Commission and Council to check the representativity of the social partners and no correlative right in UEAPME to form the basis on which to establish *locus standi*. Given the centrality of the issue in the reasoning of the Court, one might be somewhat disappointed that the Court takes no more than a short paragraph[18] to put forward its understanding of democratic requirements in the context of the Article 139 procedure. Notwithstanding this brevity, some useful indications of the Court's thinking can be gleaned from this short paragraph; in the first place, the Court adopts a procedural view of democratic legitimation; secondly, within that procedural approach, the Court opts for a representation-based model of democracy.

In very broad terms, conceptions of democracy typically build on either or both limbs of the following formula, government by the people for the people. The "for the people" element is linked to "end-oriented" democratic legitimation, where the democratic character of a mode of governance is judged by reference to its capacity to deliver certain outcomes—such as wealth, full employment, liberty or happiness—for the benefit of the people. The "by the people" element is linked to procedural democratic legitimation, where public power is exercised democratically through an uninterrupted flow of authority from the people to those nominally exercising that power. The Court is clearly concerned with the procedural aspects of the social dialogue, not its outcome.

This focus on a procedural rather than end-oriented mode of legitimation seems justified. These two elements of democratic legitimation do not stand on an equal footing. Western liberal culture privileges the procedural element: we may still be inclined to attach the "democratic" label to a relatively inefficient

---

[17] In *Chernobyl*, the European Court based its reasoning on the idea that it had not been contemplated at the time the Treaty was drafted that the European Parliament would come to fulfil such an important role in the legislative process and that, as a result, Parliament did not have the necessary standing under Art. 173 EEC (the predecessor to Art. 230 EC) to protect its legislative prerogatives. The Court thus felt justified in filling that gap and recognising a limited right of standing for Parliament specifically for the purpose of protecting its prerogatives. The solution devised by the Court was later endorsed in the Maastricht Treaty and extended to the newly-created European Central Bank, and is currently reflected in Art. 230(3) EC.

[18] At para. 89.

government which has difficulty in delivering what the people want but is backed by strong procedural legitimation; we are far less likely to regard as "democratic" a benign all-powerful ruler without procedural legitimation, however better-off citizens might be as a result of the policies pursued by the ruler. This implies that decision-making processes in the EU are unlikely to be regarded as "democratic" unless they can claim procedural legitimacy. Bringing about outcomes which enhance the well-being of EU citizens is not enough. While this may seem trite, it is nevertheless worth pointing out for two reasons: first, there is a distinct tendency among EU decision-makers to focus on outcomes so as to avoid having to face the difficult issue of procedural legitimation. This was apparent in the submissions to the Intergovernmental Conference preceding the Amsterdam Treaty, where several delegations insisted on the need for the EU to address the concerns of EU citizens regarding, *inter alia*, unemployment and the environment but had relatively little to say on reforming decision-making processes towards greater procedural democratic legitimation.[19] Secondly, in the context of the social dialogue specifically, legitimation of interest group participation in public decision-making often relies on end-oriented grounds, notably the way in which such participation leads to a more efficient realisation of public policy objectives.[20] While the "for the people" element undoubtedly constitutes an element of the democratic legitimation equation, it must not, however, totally eclipse the "by the people" element and the issue of procedural democratic legitimation.

Turning now to the second characteristic of the Court's conception of democracy that we can identify in the judgment, the representation-based model is a direct consequence of the close parallel that the Court establishes between the parliamentary process and the social dialogue; in the eyes of the Court, we are dealing here with two structurally comparable processes and in both cases, people participate in the exercise of legislative powers through representatives. In the former case, those representatives are MEPs and, in the latter, they are the social partners that are parties to the agreement. The mechanisms for designating those representatives are, of course, different. In so far as the social partners cannot claim the benefit of direct universal suffrage, additional safeguards must be put in place to ensure that they are truly representative of the people. Functionally, however, they are in a comparable position to that of MEPs.

While relying on a procedural model rather than an end-oriented one seems justified, the specific use of a representation-based model may, however, be more problematic.

---

[19] On submissions to the pre-Amsterdam Intergovernmental Conference, see G de Búrca, "The Quest for Legitimacy in the European Union", (1996) 59 *MLR* 349.

[20] Cf. D Obradovic, "Accountability of interest groups in the Union lawmaking process" in Craig and Harlow, above n. 8, at 373–81. See also P Hirst's comments on the dual conception of democracy implied in Cohen and Rogers' associative democracy theory in "Comments on 'Secondary Associations and Democratic Governance' ", (1992) 20 *Politics & Society* 473 at 474–5.

A REPRESENTATION-BASED MODEL OF DEMOCRACY?

Bercusson has vigorously attacked the judgment of the Court in *UEAPME* for establishing a parallel between the parliamentary process and the social dialogue.[21] His critique runs very deep: he rejects the very idea that the social dialogue should be seen as a legislative process. For him, the social dialogue has its roots in industrial relations and the private law realm of collective bargaining, with the consequence that public law-type norms of democratic legitimation have no place in the context of the social dialogue. While Bercusson's critique might go too far, one can nevertheless acknowledge that there are serious difficulties in adopting a representation-based approach to the social dialogue without necessarily denying the legislative character of the process.

The social dialogue and industrial relations

The centrepiece of Bercusson's argument is that the social dialogue is, at heart, a *contractual* process of collective bargaining. Agreements reached by the social partners at European level are the functional equivalent at Community level of agreements reached between the social partners at national level. Council directives implementing those agreements should be understood as a mechanism of extension *erga omnes* comparable to mechanisms of the administrative or legislative extension of collective agreements found in Member States' labour law traditions. Thus, for Bercusson, the model is that of national collective bargaining, albeit transposed in a Community context.[22] While he acknowledges that the original impetus for the social dialogue was a desire to bypass legislative deadlocks in the social field, he maintains that one should not "extrapolate" from this historical origin "to the assumption of political and legal equivalence of social dialogue and legislative processes".[23] Thus, one should not impose on the social partners and the social dialogue democratic norms premised on the legislative nature of the process and a notional equivalence between the European Parliament and the social partners.

The fundamental problem with Bercusson's thesis is hinted at by Fredman when she notes the "absence of any economic pressure, particularly in the form of industrial action or threats thereof"[24] to act as the background push for negotiations. To put it more bluntly, there is, for the time being at least, no such thing as European level industrial relations; agreements between the social partners do not have their roots in the social reality within the EU but are parasitic on the

---

[21] B Bercusson, "Democratic Legitimacy and European Labour Law", (1999) 28 *ILJ* 153.
[22] Cf.: "Specifically, the EU social dialogue is perceived as akin to another level, transnational, of collective bargaining super-imposed on national systems", above n. 21, at 164.
[23] See above n. 21.
[24] S Fredman, above n. 8, at 408.

EU legislative process. UNICE have made their position clear, they are not interested in EU-level collective bargaining. As ETUC are not in a position to force them to the negotiating table, only the prospect of legislation adopted by the normal legislative route can prompt the social partners into negotiations, the incentive for UNICE being to obtain legislation which is more favourable to its interests than would be the case for legislation adopted via the traditional channel. Under these circumstances, it is hard to see how one can argue that agreements between the social partners are anything but an alternative way of producing EU legislation. In this respect, Bercusson's adamant rejection of this view is puzzling. Describing the social dialogue as an autonomous process and the implementation of the agreement by Council decision as an EU equivalent of national legislative extensions of collective agreements, only makes sense in a purely abstracted view of the process, ignoring its dynamics. This may well be what the EU institutions and the Member States at Maastricht would have liked it to be. However, to the extent that this is so, there is a clear gap between expectations and reality, which is made all the more obvious by the fact that the alternative route to implementation via Council decision—i.e. "in accordance with the procedures and practices specific to management and labour and the Member States"—remains hypothetical.[25]

In those circumstances, one might be tempted to turn Bercusson's comment on its head and argue that one should not extrapolate from national models of collective bargaining to superficially similar epiphenomena taking place in a wholly different context.

The social dialogue as functional representative democracy

For the Court of First Instance, parliamentary representative democracy represents the point of reference for evaluating respect for democratic principles. Thus, at paragraph 88 of its judgment, the Court notes that, in the case law of the European Court, participation of the European Parliament in the legislative process "reflects at Community level the fundamental democratic principle that the people must share in the exercise of power through a representative assembly" and, to the extent that Parliament does not participate, an alternative means of involvement of the people must be provided.

If our point of reference is parliamentary representative democracy, we might be tempted to see the mechanisms provided by the social dialogue as an alternative form of representation, albeit based on a functional basis rather than a territorial one. Functional representation is not a new phenomenon in the EU legal order. Indeed, the institutional framework of the E(E)C has always included a body, the Economic and Social Committee, whose function is to

---

[25] See G Brinkmann, "Law-Making under the Social Chapter of Maastricht" in Craig and Harlow, above n. 8, at 256.

represent the "various categories of economic and social activity, in particular, representatives of producers, farmers, carriers, workers, dealers, craftsmen, professional occupations and representatives of the general public".[26] Without engaging in a deep enquiry into the merits and problems associated with functional representation, it has to be accepted that our interests and preferences as citizens might often be distributed along socio-economic lines rather than territorial ones. For instance, there will usually be greater commonality of interests on a number of issues between two farm workers in different territorial entities than between a farm worker and a lawyer within the same territorial entity. On this basis, a plausible case can be made that the decision-making system will be more reflective and responsive to these preferences if it is supplemented by functional representation rather than relying exclusively on territorial representation. The Economic and Social Committee is ill-suited to act as a vehicle for the representation and articulation of sectoral interests. Among other things, its mode of appointment, by decision of the Council, undermines its representative credentials and precludes the development of a strong popular legitimation base that would enable it to flex its political muscle and play a more significant role than the weak consultative one that it has at present. Can the social partners play that role?

A first difficulty that needs to be noted is that the range of interests represented in the social dialogue is extremely limited. The only types of interests which are recognised in the process are those of employers and employees. While there *is* an issue here that needs to be addressed, it should nevertheless not be overstated; the social dialogue is, after all, not a general law-making procedure but one which is specifically concerned with a number of issues pertaining to the labour market and the regulation of the employment relationship. To that extent, the main interests at stake are those of workers and employers. Limiting participation in the social dialogue to representation of those interests, on grounds of procedural efficiency, makes sense, even though one should then expect vigilance on the part of public authorities, and particularly the Commission, to ensure that other interests do not find themselves unduly ignored as a result of the social dialogue process.

The representativity of the partners involved in the process *vis-à-vis* workers' and employers' interests is, however, a thornier issue. The core argument of UEAPME rested on the fact that it represented a distinctive type of employers' interest that could not, UEAPME argued, be adequately represented by the employers' association which were parties to the agreement, namely UNICE and CEEP. In other words, as representatives of small and medium size enterprises (SMEs), UEAPME constituted a different "voice" to that of UNICE which, because of its broad coverage of employers of all sizes, could not adequately reflect the concerns of UEAPME members. To harness further its case, UEAPME sought to draw additional support from the requirement contained in

---

[26] Art. 257 EC.

Article 2(2) of the Agreement on Social Policy[27] that measures adopted under the Agreement should pay particular care to avoid over-burdening SMEs. Thus UEAPME was drawing from the *substantive* requirement concerning the treatment of SMEs a *procedural* implication in terms of representation of SMEs in the social dialogue process. The Court of First Instance explicitly rejected this translation of a substantive requirement into a procedural one, it stated that "Article 2(2), first subparagraph of the Agreement is a provision of substantive law, compliance with which can be sought by any interested party availing itself of the appropriate legal remedy"[28] before noting that substantive consideration had in fact been given to the situation of SMEs in the course of the negotiations.[29] On the broader issue of representation, independent of Article 2(2) of the Agreement, in so far as the framework agreement on parental leave was concerned with prescribing norms for all types of employment relationships, the Court was happy to endorse the representativity criteria developed by the Commission for these types of agreement. These are: (i) that the social partners must be cross-industry and organised at European level; (ii) that they consist of organisations which are themselves an integral and recognised part of Member States social partner structures, have the capacity to negotiate agreements and are representative of all Member States and (iii) that they have adequate structures to ensure their effective participation in implementing the Agreement on Social Policy.[30]

As noted by many, these criteria have the practical effect of conferring a monopoly over the social dialogue to UNICE, CEEP and ETUC as the only associations capable of fulfilling them. While those criteria may make sense from the perspective of making the social dialogue a viable proposition, they nevertheless remain troublesome if the objective is not just to make the social dialogue work but ensure a reasonably democratic form of governance.

If representativity is understood as essentially a function of the membership of the social partners and the organisations that are affiliated to it, representatives sitting around the negotiating table are seen as ultimately mandated by the workers and employers who are members of their respective organisations or their affiliates. An obvious difficulty here is that levels of membership, both for trade unions and employers' organisations are, in many Member States, low and what is worse, have been significantly declining over the past two decades. Thus, even if UNICE, CEEP and ETUC might claim to be the most representative organisations, their level of representativity taking the population of employees and employers as a whole remains low and therefore affects their democratic credentials.[31]

---

[27] Now Art.e 137 EC.

[28] At para. 104.

[29] See para. 105.

[30] See Commission Communication, *Concerning the Implementation of the Protocol on Social Policy* (COM(93) 600).

[31] Cf. L Betten, "The Democratic Deficit of Participatory Democracy in Community Social Policy" (1998) *ELRev* 32.

This being said, considering the low levels of participation in European elections, similar remarks could be made in relation to the European Parliament and the parliamentary representative process in the EU, so that the argument remains relative. Nevertheless, poor participation in European elections is hardly a convincing argument for an alternative system with an equally poor, if not worse, claim to ensuring representativity. Even more troublesome is the low degree of control that members have over who speaks on their behalf. While this may not be overly problematic in fairly homogenous organisations with a high degree of internal consensus, the social partners at European level are highly heterogenous umbrella groups. The quasi-monopolistic position of UNICE, CEEP and ETUC also brings an additional problem for organisations which are left out of the umbrella groupings and whose membership is therefore disenfranchised under the social dialogue system.[32]

Thus, if we assess the democratic credentials of the social dialogue through the prism of parliamentary democracy transposed to a system of functional representation, numerous difficulties arise, even though some of these difficulties need to be put in perspective with comparable difficulties within the parliamentary system at EU level itself. Such an assessment, however, may be somewhat unfair, in that the norms of parliamentary representative democracy may not constitute the proper frame of reference for assessing the democratic legitimation of the social dialogue. Some authors have suggested that participatory democracy might constitute a more appropriate framework for the social dialogue.

SOCIAL DIALOGUE AND PARTICIPATORY DEMOCRACY

Theories of participatory democracy come in many flavours, shapes and forms. In broad terms, those theories tend to start from a criticism of the mechanisms and institutions of representative democracy. At its crudest and least sophisticated, a model of representative democracy limits the input of citizens in public decision-making to the designation of representatives by means of periodic elections. Citizens do not themselves take part in the decision-making process itself. While some theorists argue that this exclusion of the "great unwashed" from decision-making is a welcome aspect of representative democracy,[33] proponents of participatory democracy would argue that the political acculturation of the masses is endogenous to, and self-reinforcing within, the institutions of representational government: the system relies on the existence of a professional political elite whose knowledge, expertise and values are quite remote from the everyday experience of the citizens they represent. The perceived distance

---

[32] Cf. the repeated refusal of ETUC to admit the French CGT, notwithstanding its status as one of the main French unions.

[33] Cf. J A Schumpeter, *Capitalism, Socialism and Democracy* (London, Allen & Unwin, 1943) 283: "The electoral mass is incapable of action other than a stampede".

between the discourse of the political elite and the everyday experience of the masses leads to apathy and disinterest in public affairs which, in a vicious circle, leads to a widening of the gulf between elite and mass and further disinterest and lack of knowledge of the latter. When citizens are barely aware of the role of their representatives in the European Parliament and show manifest disinterest in European elections, the resonance of these arguments in the Community context is patent.

Proponents of participative democracy argue for the reversal of this vicious circle into a virtuous circle of active, deliberative participation of citizens in public decision-making processes leading to a process of political re-skilling, in turn inducing greater interest and further participation in decision-making. Beyond the industrial relations and labour market regulation context of the social dialogue, the "social training" and political re-skilling aspect of participative democracy could, in principle, generate benefits from the perspective of the legitimation of EU law and institutions. The model of parliamentary representation and legitimation of government through periodical elections of representatives is the dominant model within national polities. It is mostly to this model that the great majority of citizens most naturally turn to when thinking about democracy. Given its already noted[34] inherent limitations in a polycentric polity such as the EU, acceptance of the EU by its citizens as a democratic polity entails not only the development of alternative democratic mechanisms, but also a fairly sophisticated approach to democracy capable of debunking Parliament-centered simplistic arguments about the EU's democratic deficit.

The nature of the participatory democracy agenda implies a particular concern over two issues: the level of decision-making and the form of political discourse.

Social dialogue, participatory democracy and proximate governance

Proximity is an important issue for theories of participative democracy; if a strategy of active involvement of citizens in public decision-making processes is to succeed, those processes must be sufficiently close to the citizen. The argument is put forcefully by Pateman,[35] in the context of developing an argument for democracy in the workplace: democratic practice at national level through the institutions of representative government is too remote from most people's daily life experiences to generate the sense of political efficacy necessary to establish confidence in these institutions. Democratic social training has to take place at a level which is much closer to the individual, such as the workplace.

---

[34] See above n. 5 and related text.
[35] C Pateman, *Participation and Democratic Theory* (Cambridge, Cambridge University Press, 1970).

From an EU institutional perspective, an approach in terms of participative democracy can be placed in the context of the subsidiarity principle[36] and the requirement in Article 1 of the Maastricht Treaty that decisions should be taken as closely as possible to the citizen. Proximity can be taken here in at least three related but distinct senses: in a territorial sense, proximity is associated with a logic of decentralisation and devolution of power to entities which are physically closer to citizens and more accessible to them; secondly, and more controversially, proximity may be understood as involving a bridging of the public-private divide and closer association with "civil society" structures in which citizens are voluntarily involved in decision-making processes. Thirdly, in a material rather than institutional sense, proximity may concern the subject matter of decision-making, in that citizens are more likely to get involved in issues that have a clear resonance in their daily experience.

Regarding this third dimension of the proximity issue, social law as a whole may be seen as an aspect of the "human face" of EU law. The re-birth of "Social Europe" in Community political discourse in the early to mid-1980s and the adoption of the Social Charter were very much a reaction to the rather cold and abstract welfare economics discourse underlying the single market. To be sure, the potential social consequences of the single market in themselves objectively justified an increase in awareness of the relevance of social matters at EU level. The Transfer of Undertakings Directive[37] recognises this explicitly in its preamble by linking the need for EU legislation to protect the rights of workers in the case of transfer of undertakings to the restructuring of companies engendered by the internal market. Nevertheless, the motivation for EU intervention in social matters cannot be linked exclusively to a desire to mitigate the negative social consequences of internal market liberalisation. Increasing popular acceptance of the EU by making it more relevant to its citizens was part of the equation and EU social law was to be seen as a piece in the "People's Europe" agenda.

Linking up more closely with Pateman's idea of democracy in the workplace, the participation of workers in decision-making at the level of the undertaking has been an important plank of EU social policy even though the strong opposition of some Member States has meant that results have fallen very much short of expectations. In terms of substantive law, from the ill-fated Vredeling draft Directive to the European Works Councils Directive, concerns about industrial democratisation have been present more or less throughout the existence of the E(E)C/EU. The involvement of workers' representatives in merger approval

---

[36] The link between the social dialogue and subsidiarity is made explicitly by the Commission in its Communication on the Implementation of the Protocol, see above n. 30, at para. 6c: "In conformity with the fundamental principle of subsidiarity enshrined in Article 3b there is thus recognition of a dual form of subsidiarity in the social field: on the one hand, subsidiarity regarding regulation at national and Community level; on the other hand, subsidiarity as regards the choice, at Community level, between the legislative approach and the agreement-based approach".

[37] Council Directive 77/17/EEC of 14 February 1977 on the approximation of the laws of the Member States relating to the safeguarding of employees' rights in the event of transfers of undertakings, businesses or parts of businesses, [1977] OJ L61/27.

procedures under Article 18(4) of the Merger Regulation[38] is noteworthy, even though this initiative has been somewhat torpedoed by the Court of First Instance in a surprisingly restrictive and conservative judgment.[39]

This does not mean, however, that EU developments in social law generally, should be seen as a deliberate and conscious effort towards facilitating the development of participatory government in the EU. This is patently not the case. This being said, to the extent that increased participation in decision-making is seen as a desirable end, social issues and employment rights have a rather better—although not by any means necessarily the best—grass-roots mobilising potential than, for instance, industrial standards-setting or the suitability of current institutional structures for an enlarged EU. On the importance of proximity in this sense for the social dialogue, it is worth noting this comment in the joint declaration of Commission President Jacques Santer and Social Affairs Commissioner Padraig O'Flynn when welcoming the agreement of the social partners on parental leave: "[The agreement] shows that the social dialogue at European level is able to address issues of real relevance to people's everyday lives".[40]

The relationship between participatory theory and the association of organised interests within civil society to public decision-making processes is rather tense. On the one hand, privately organised interests in the associative sector can serve at least three important purposes for a participatory agenda: private associations can be regarded as "schools of democracy" where citizens acquire the skills and psychological disposition for civic political practice. Secondly, under conditions of mass democracy, associations constitute mediating structures that can be used as a relay for citizen involvement in macro-level decision-making processes, which would otherwise be difficult to achieve directly because of scale problems. Thirdly, the private associative sector can also help to bring within the decision-making process categories of persons who are poorly represented through public processes. On the other hand, the institutionalisation and crystallisation of interests in formal structures can hamper the development of a truly deliberative search for the common good.[41] Moreover, and related, cosy relationships between public authorities and a small number of strong privileged interest groups can facilitate phenomena of regulatory capture and rent-seeking practices. Finally, imbalances in resources and organisational capability tend to accentuate power inequalities, in particular between commercial interests and more public interest-oriented organisations.[42]

Overall, the kind of civil society involvement that would fit best within a participatory logic would be that of relatively small-scale organisations at a fairly

[38] Council Regulation 4064/89/EEC of 21 December 1989 on the control of concentrations between undertakings, [1990] OJ L257/13.

[39] T–12/93 *CCE de Vittel* [1995] ECR II–1247.

[40] Cited by Obradovic , above n. 20, at 355.

[41] See discussion below on the issue of deliberative practices.

[42] On the issue of balance of interests in the social policy and social dialogue context, see W Streeck, "Neo-Voluntarism: A New European Social Policy Regime", (1995) *ELJ* 31.

localised level, in which individual citizens still have direct or near-direct access and in which the positive (from a participatory perspective) features dominate. One could envisage that sort of involvement in several areas of EU policy, such as environmental or regional development policy,[43] particularly at the implementation/monitoring/enforcement stages. The European social dialogue, however, centered as it is around a small number of peak-level associations largely detached from the grass-roots and in a virtual monopoly position, hardly fits this picture.

Social dialogue, participatory democracy and deliberation

Another potential obstacle to approaching the social dialogue from a participatory democracy perspective concerns the form of discourse used in reaching public decisions. Participatory theory stresses the importance of deliberative modes of decision-making. Deliberative decision-making can, for our present purposes, be defined as a process of discussion aimed at reaching a common position in which decision-makers are susceptible to reshaping their perceptions, views and preferences on the basis of exchanges of reasoned arguments between themselves. A key characteristic of deliberation is that it aims not merely at aggregating the pre-existing, static preferences of participants, but is geared towards the reshaping of those preferences. The "common position" that proponents of participatory democracy are looking for as a result of that reshaping, represents the "common good" or "public interest". The common good here is not meant as a Rousseauian ideal way to best satisfy the interests of the polity as a whole which, under perfect conditions of deliberation, we would be able to "discover". Rather, it should be understood as a constraint designed to exclude from the discussion arguments purely based on self-interest. Thus, if someone puts forward an argument establishing that solution X is preferable for the polity as a whole to solution Y, the deliberative constraint would force an acceptance of solution X, even if it is less satisfactory from the perspective of the participant's own interest. Even if one accepts that "public-interest" arguments may be used manipulatively as a cover for private interests, the deliberative constraint of ostensible impartiality nevertheless imposes limits not just on the form but on the substance of arguments that can be put forward.[44]

Deliberation should therefore be distinguished from other modes of collective decision-making designed as aggregative processes, such as voting or bargaining. Voting and bargaining both constitute aggregative processes because they

---

[43] See, however, P Burton's concluding comments in "Policy Networks and European Union's Structural Funds" in Konstadinidis, above n. 5, 211 at 237.

[44] On this "civilising force of hypocrisy", see J Elster, "The Market and The Forum" in J Elster and A Hylland (eds), *Foundations of Social Choice Theory* (Cambridge, Cambridge University Press, 1986) 113.

take the preferences of participants as essentially fixed and predetermined and only seek to provide the best possible combination of these interests. The aggregative principle (i.e. how one determines "the best" combination) varies with the method of aggregation; with voting, it will normally be a majoritarian principle,[45] whereas bargaining, at least in situations of equality of bargaining power between the participants, tends towards a Pareto-efficient mode of aggregation.[46] In both cases, however, the interests at stake and the objectives to be achieved from the perspective of each participant remain static throughout the process.

From a legal perspective, the deliberative model of decision-making tends to be associated with public law instruments and modes of reasoning; its instrument of choice is the archetypically public (collective) unilateral act (most conspicuously, legislative acts) and is geared towards imposing decisions based on reasoned grounds. In this latter respect, it has a close affinity with the requirement of "reasonableness" that public law imposes on public authorities. Negotiated decision-making, on the other hand, tends to borrow from the instruments and modes of reasoning of private law. Contract—institution of private law *par excellence*—is its most appropriate legal instrument, and, to the extent that we want to impose norms on the participants and the process, these tend to be designed towards ensuring the existence of a genuine consent of the parties involved. While this might go as far as trying to redress or counteract excessive imbalances in the bargaining power of the parties,[47] this does not extend to imposing requirements of rationality on outcomes, as is the case with public law decisions.[48]

From a formal perspective, the social dialogue is quite evidently based on the private law, negotiated model. The aim of the social partners is not to reach a common, unilateral "decision" but to strike a bargain. The very instrument used is that of an agreement, i.e. a contract. This being said, a degree of caution is needed here. For one thing, negotiation and deliberation are ideal types; actual decision-making happily mixes the two. Negotiated and deliberative modes of decision-making are therefore a question of degree rather than absolutes. Secondly, the dynamics of decision-making may contradict the formal format suggested by legal instruments and processes. Decision-making in the EU Council may be formally deliberative, but its dynamics give it a markedly negotiated character. As regards the participation of private interest groups in

---

[45] This is the case for ordinary simple majority voting. Different systems of voting can produce aggregation along different principles. Thus a system of voting based on congruent majorities among identified sub-sections of the electorate will tend to be oriented towards Pareto-efficient principles rather than majoritarian ones. In societies with strong internal divisions (for example Belgium or Northern Ireland), such systems of aggregation may be seen as more suitable than majoritarian ones.

[46] i.e. the best possible solution that leaves no participant worse off than the status quo.

[47] Cf. consumer law or labour law.

[48] Even if only marginally with Wednesbury-type standards of reasonableness.

public decision-making, the bringing together of associations in corporatist[49] arrangements can generate patterns of shared dependencies leading them to behave to some extent like a policy community[50] and allow for the development of more consensual and deliberative forms of dialogue. This, however, supposes a shared desire/commitment to the maintenance of those arrangements. While this might be the case in Scandinavian-type corporatism,[51] the very lukewarm enthusiasm of UNICE for the social dialogue leaves rather little room for such developments.

That we should experience difficulties in fitting the European social dialogue within a participatory democracy framework should not surprise us; under conditions of mass democracy, there is an inherent tension between allowing for the voice of citizens to be heard in the decision-making-process and designing institutions which are capable of effective decision-making. That tension may be kept at an acceptable level within a relatively homogenous polity but easily becomes difficult to manage in an heterogenous one like the EU.

To a certain extent, the outcome of the European social dialogue rather than its mechanism might be more significant for the development of a participatory democracy culture in the EU. Many labour lawyers are disappointed by the predilection in recent EU social law, and under the social dialogue in particular, for flexible solutions, leaving much to be sorted out at national, regional, industry, undertaking or plant level, instead of establishing clear, uniform rights for all workers throughout the EU. However, if we value participation of citizens in decision-making processes, there is much to be said for the flexible approach, which alone can combine the definition of broad objectives and principles, together with a meaningful participation of citizens at a level which is accessible to them. This, of course, presupposes that a participatory culture exists at the decentralised levels. However, it would be unreal in any event to expect a participatory culture to exist at EU level without a background of participatory culture within the Member States.

---

[49] Using Schmitter's definition in "Still the Century of Corporatism?" in P Schmitter and G Lehmbruch (eds), *Trends Toward Corporatist Intermediation* (London, Sage, 1979) 13–15; corporatism is "a system of interest representation in which the constituent units are organised into a limited number of singular, compulsory, non-competitive, hierarchically ordered and functionally differentiated categories recognised or licensed (if not created) by the state and granted a deliberate representational monopoly within their respective category in exchange for observing certain controls on their selection of leaders and articulation of demands and supports", to be contrasted with pluralism as "a system of interest representation in which the constituent parts are organised into an unspecified number of multiple, voluntary, competitive, non-hierarchically-ordered and self-determined (as to type or scope of interest) categories which are not specifically licensed, recognised, subsidised, created or otherwise controlled in leadership selection or interest articulation by the state and which do not exercise a monopoly of representational activity within their respective categories".

[50] For a brief overview of the idea of policy networks and policy communities, and pointers to further literature on the subject, see P Burton, above n. 43, at 214–15.

[51] On Scandinavian corporatism (and its demise) from an economic perspective, see K O Moene and M Wallerstein, "How Social Democracy Worked: Labor-Market Institutions", (1995) 23 *Politics and Society* 185.

What this means for the European social dialogue is that we should certainly avoid entertaining expectations of it representing a flagship example of democracy at work in the EU. Instead, we should recognise it as what it is, a means of structuring interest group interaction at EU level, both among themselves and between them and EU institutions. On this basis, we can set ourselves a more modest, but perhaps more useful agenda; structuring that interaction in a way that best serves democratic principles. If this is our agenda, some useful pointers might be borrowed from associative democracy theory.

SOCIAL DIALOGUE AND ASSOCIATIVE DEMOCRACY

There is something of an "if you can't beat 'em, join 'em" flavour to an argument making a case for associative democracy; given the importance of associational liberty in liberal democracies, interest groups will form and, given the dependence of public authorities on those groups[52] in order to design successfully and implement policies, groups will have an important influence on public decision-making. In so far as we cannot eliminate them or will them away, the question then becomes one of whether we can harness the power of interest groups in a way that furthers rather than hampers the satisfaction of democratic ideals. This is, in essence, the task that theories of associative democracy set themselves. In the words of Cohen and Rogers, "[t]he core idea of associative democracy is to curb faction through a deliberate politics of association while netting such group contribution to egalitarian-democratic governance. It seeks neither to abolish affirmative governance nor to insulate the state from society nor simply to open a bazaar of bargaining among more equally endowed groups. Instead, it proposes to act directly on the associative environment of public action in ways that make associations less factionalizing and more supportive of the range of egalitarian-democratic norms".[53]

In placing interest groups at the centre of the discussion of democratic legitimation, associative democracy offers the most favourable framework for developing a model of democratic legitimation for the European social dialogue. It would be beyond the scope of this chapter to present a fully developed model. What is proposed here, on a less ambitious scale, is an outline of the kind of contribution that the social dialogue could make to an associative democracy agenda as well as highlighting a number of difficulties which are inherent in the current arrangements.

As noted by many, the EU, and above all the Commission, is particularly permeable to influences from interest groups. This can be explained by the relatively small size and limited resources of the Commission which make it acutely dependent on third parties both for information but also for policy

---

[52] Notably for the purpose of collecting information.
[53] J Cohen and J Rogers, "Secondary Associations and Democratic Governance", (1992) 20 *Politics and Society* 393, at 425.

implementation. While the EC institutional set-up is premised on the Commission turning to the Member States and national administrations for these purposes, the Commission may, for fairly obvious strategic reasons, prefer to have other sources at its disposal rather than relying exclusively on the Member States. The evaluation of the democratic contribution of the social dialogue must take place against this background and prompts us to ask the question whether the social dialogue ameliorates or worsens the democratic character of decision-making compared to an unregulated "state of nature" in interest representation.

Workers' interests customarily fare less well than employers' ones in the market for interest representation. The EU is no different from other polities in this respect. Among the reasons for this, one could mention financial resources differentials, particularly in a period of falling levels of union membership and generally low levels of unionisation in some Member States, as well as the difficulty of organising and federating at pan-European level highly diverse national organisations.[54] Visser and Ebbinghaus[55] mention two additional factors: organised labour tends on the whole to be a consumer rather than producer of information and, to that extent, is comparatively less useful to the Commission than business; secondly, the compartmentalisation of the Commission into numerous Directorates General works to the disadvantage of organised labour: while there might be regular contacts between ETUC and DG V (Social Affairs), the tendency in other DGs, in particular the "economic" ones, has been to consider that social matters are better dealt with by DG V and therefore not to recognise unions as interlocutors, thereby acting as an obstacle to the mainstreaming of social issues.

The social dialogue can be seen as a partial redressing of the balance between workers' and employers' interests in the decision-making process. However, it does so only to a limited extent; its effects are limited to core social issues and it does not help the problem of the decoupling of economic and social issues resulting from the Commission's internal structures. How much workers' interests gain from the Article 139 negotiated agreement procedure as compared to engaging in consultation and discussion with the Commission on traditional legislative proposals is also open to question. The evidence from the agreement on parental leave is, in this respect, not encouraging in that the agreement is less favourable to workers than the proposal originally put forward by the Commission. To the extent that there is a redressing of the balance, this democratic "gain" also entails significant democratic "costs".

---

[54] The latter, it must be said, is a problem which is also faced on the employers' side, see L Lanzalaco, "Coping with Heterogeneity: Peak Associations of Business within and across Western European Nations" in J Greenwood *et al* (eds), *Organised Interests and the European Community* (London, Sage, 1992) 173.

[55] J Visser and B Ebbinghaus, "Making the Most of Diversity? European Integration and Transnational Organization of Labour", in Greenwood *et al*, above n. 54, 206 at 229.

First, from the perspective of accountability of the social partners, the issue of responsiveness of the social partners' hierarchy to their members —the problem of the "iron law of oligarchy"—is simply not addressed in current institutional arrangements. As Cohen and Rogers state, "[a] dense world of association may make the government more informed about, and more responsive to, the interests of group 'oligarchs' but not group members".[56] The issue is normally addressed in associative democracy theory by subordinating recognition by public authorities to the demonstration of the presence of adequate responsiveness mechanisms within the organisations concerned. The Commission, however, has refused to embark on that course and has contented itself with requiring that the social partners "consist of organizations which are themselves an integral and recognized part of Member State social partner structures and with the capacity to negotiate agreements, and which are representative of all Member States, as far as possible". This minimalist attitude of the Commission is understandable; the question is a difficult one in any system, but particularly at Community level considering the heterogeneity of social partnership structures in the Member States. One might even suggest that such an approach was perhaps unavoidable if the social dialogue was not to be killed at the outset, in that it is far from clear that the social partners would have been in a position to set up such mechanisms throughout the Member States. Be that as it may, it nevertheless undermines the democratic credentials of the social dialogue.

A second problem concerns the exclusion of certain interests from the decision-making process altogether. Here, we have to distinguish two sub-problems. One is the problem of non-inclusion of sub-constituencies within the broader classes of interests which are themselves represented. This is typically the problem posed in the *UEAPME* case itself. In its decision, the Court of First Instance noted that UNICE sought to represent all classes of employers, including SMEs. UEAPME argued, however, that UNICE, because of its all-encompassing character, was ill-placed to represent the specific concerns of SMEs. Given that there has to be a limit on the quantity of recognised interlocutors, it does not seem unreasonable to confer on an all-encompassing organisation the task of representing all interests within it rather than requiring each specific sub-interest to be singularly represented. From this perspective, the problem then collapses into the previous one, i.e. the problem of internal democracy and responsiveness within the all-encompassing organisations. The second sub-problem concerns interests other than sub-interests falling within the broader classes of interests represented, i.e. in our context, interests other than those of workers and employers. Here the problem of non-inclusiveness is potentially more serious. Where the implications of the issue under discussion have limited impact outside the workplace, the non-inclusiveness problem may be negligible. On more mixed topics with a wider social impact, such as pension entitlements or working time, the Article 139 procedure is more problematic.

---

[56] See above n. 53, at 443.

The Commission recognises that certain types of issues are not suitable for treatment under that procedure. Whether the Commission would be able to *prevent* such issues from being dealt with under that procedure is less certain, given that the Commission seems to have tied its own hands in relation to the review of agreements reached by the social partners.[57]

What is perhaps most objectionable about the Article 139 procedure is its closed nature. The problems mentioned above would not necessarily be intractable if some oil was put into the mechanism by allowing a greater degree of oversight by the EU political institutions. Had the Commission retained the faculty to review agreements reached by the social partners before proposing their transformation into EU legislation through Council decision, this would have enabled, in particular, the voices of those not involved in the negotiations to be fed into the process through consultation with the Commission on the agreement. More generally, proponents of associative democracy recognise that its legitimacy is heavily dependent on political institutions, accountable through traditional channels, retaining sufficient control of the process in order to prevent it from becoming a process of private government for private interests. Cohen and Rogers thus state that:

> "[T]he ultimate guard against independent powers, however, is the vitality of the system dispensing powers in the first place. Systems relying heavily on group-based representation should always be systems of dual, and juridically unequal, powers. Final authority should reside in encompassing territorial organizations, and both they and the electoral system that generates them should be sufficiently strong to permit exit from group representation".[58]

In national polities where corporatist arrangements benefit from a broad popular consensus, the mere fact that the legislator has the ability to modify those arrangements so as to permit exit might be enough, allowing for a more or less total hands-off approach on a day-to-day basis. The same cannot be true in the EU where institutional arrangements have a high degree of inertia, particularly when they require Treaty amendments, and a low degree of popular responsiveness. The social dialogue undoubtedly has strong formal legitimacy from this perspective, since it had to have the agreement of all Member States at Maastricht, but it can hardly be said to enjoy a significant degree of popular backing or even acquiescence. One might hazard the guess that a majority of EU citizens are not even *aware* of the existence of the social dialogue arrangements and of the identity of the European social partners. To that extent, it is difficult to sustain the idea that the general mandate resulting from the acceptance of the existence of the arrangements provides significant democratic support for the institution.[59] A greater degree of public involvement of a more routine nature is

---

[57] See the discussion below on this.

[58] See above n. 53, at 448–9.

[59] It should be noted that the support of the European Parliament for the social dialogue process is of no help here.

therefore necessary, even if this limits to some extent the autonomy of the social partners. The question is not one of incessant meddling by the Commission into agreements reached by the partners, but one of keeping sufficient powers to ensure *supervision* of the process. The Commission, however, has foreclosed this possibility. It considers that agreements reached between the social partners are cast in stone and can only be either accepted or rejected *en bloc* by the Council. It has threatened to withdraw proposals should the Council contemplate amending an Article 139 agreement. For its own part, the Commission seems to see its role in deciding whether or not to put a proposal to the Council as merely that of guardian of the Treaties: it will check, in addition to the "representativity" of the partners, whether the agreement complies with EU law but would seem to have excluded any exercise of its own *political* discretion as to whether or not the agreement should be adopted and transformed into Community law.[60] Such an approach was not mandated by the wording of Article 139. In particular, the fact that a proposal from the Commission is required could be interpreted as suggesting that there is an element of discretion that the Commission could choose to exercise. It is true that the Article 139 procedure might lose much of its "attraction" with UNICE if the deal struck in the negotiations could start to unravel in subsequent discussions with the Commission. While the hands-off attitude of the Commission thus makes sound political sense, it makes the Article 139 procedure a rather unattractive proposal from a democratic legitimation point of view.

CONCLUSION

Bercusson [61] is surely right in his view that the social dialogue has its own conceptual framework which is different from that of a parliamentary system of representation and that one should not approach the issue of legitimation of the social dialogue with the constitutional tool-kit of parliamentary representative democracy. However, approaching it with a national industrial relations toolkit would not take sufficient account of the specificity of both the EU environment and the social dialogue within it and, in doing so, would brush under the carpet some legitimate questions on the democratic legitimacy of the process. On the other hand, it seems unduly pessimistic to see, as Obradovic does,[62] the social dialogue as irremediably incapable of legitimation. To be sure, the relationship between the social dialogue and democratic theory is "messy" and the social dialogue is unlikely to fit in a blueprint for a perfectly democratic EU polity. Nevertheless, interest groups cannot simply be willed away. Structuring

---

[60] The Council also seems to have accepted the idea of the sanctity of the autonomy of the social partners and its role as mainly one of checking the "legality" of the agreement: see G Brinkmann, above n. 25, at 254.

[61] See above n. 21, and related text.

[62] See above n. 20.

group-based interest representation can therefore contribute to enhancing the democratic legitimacy of EU decision-making processes. However, greater checks than are necessary at the national level might be required in the EU polity whose democratic processes are structurally weaker than is possible within a national polity, and this may require being less fundamentalist about the sacrosanct autonomy of the social partners than we can afford to be at national level.

15

Converse Pyramids and the EU Social Constitution

BARRY FITZPATRICK[1]

INTRODUCTION

The hypothesis underlying this exploratory chapter is that, in the integrative interplay between national and Community competence which dominates the legislative, and particularly the constitution-building processes, of the European Union,[2] the Member States will strive to retain competence over areas of policy which are central to their own national hierarchies (or pyramids) of values. This is not to deny theories of multi-level governance within the EU.[3] Rather, it holds that the spectrum across which the preponderance of multi-level governance may reside at the national or supranational institutional levels is, within the context of the EU, vertical rather than horizontal, that is to say that it is a *hierarchy* of policy areas.

This EU hierarchy, or pyramid, is dependent upon the centrality of the policy area to, on the one hand, the perceived imperatives of EU integration and, on the other, embedded interests within the Member States, and, where *de jure* or *de facto* unanimity prevails, the interests of particular states. It might therefore be anticipated that what emerges, particularly with a focus upon EU social

[1] Earlier versions of this chapter were presented at a conference, "The UK and the Social Dimension of the European Union", at the University of Leeds in November 1998, a Jean Monnet Lecture at the University of Bremen in June 1999 and a postgraduate seminar at the European University Institute in January 2000. I am grateful to participants in each event for their comments and am also most grateful to my colleagues, Martin Lodge, who read an earlier draft of this chapter, and Patricia McKee, who constructed the pyramidal diagrams. All errors, presumptions and misconceptions are my own.
[2] See generally, J H H Weiler, "The Reformation of European Constitutionalism" (1996) 35 *JCMS* 97–131. Joseph Weiler (at 99) adopts Alec Sweet Stone's definition of constitutionalism (A Stone, "Constitutional Dialogues in the European Community", EUI Working Paper RSC No. 95/38 at 1) as being "the process by which the EC Treaties evolved from a set of legal arrangements binding upon sovereign states, into a vertically integrated legal regime conferring judicially enforceable rights and obligations on all legal persons and entities, public and private, within [the sphere of application of EC law]".
[3] See generally K Armstrong and S Bulmer, *The Governance of the Single European Market* (Manchester, Manchester University Press, 1998) and P Craig, "The Nature of the Community: Integration, Democracy, and Legitimacy" in P Craig and G de Búrca (eds), *The Evolution of EU Law* (Oxford, Oxford University Press, 1999) 1–54, at 16–23.

constitutionalism, will be a pyramid of policies which is, within perceived imperatives of economic integration, the converse of national pyramids. In consequence the prospects for a comprehensive and coherent regime within an area of Community policy, prerequisites for the achievement of a genuine constitution, are in turn dependent upon the position which a particular policy area takes up upon the EU pyramid. A uni-centric view of the EU economic constitution or social constitution is bound to end in frustration. Of necessity, a coherent picture about how constitutional values are enunciated and protected is bound to involve an assessment of the interaction between Community and national norms, almost the marrying of the converse pyramids. On the basis of this hypothesis, it will be argued that social policy is trapped in a middle layer of the EU pyramid, in counterpoise to a middle layer of national pyramids. In consequence, constitutional and institutional restraints have thwarted the limitation of national competence in favour of comprehensive and coherent EU competence over social policy.

This converse pyramids hypothesis will be examined, both in terms of legislative provision and judicial interpretation, first, within the "grand bargains"[4] of the EC Treaty as an economic constitution and then as the source of the EU's social constitutionalism. At this level, most attention is centred upon the secondary role of social policy within the EU constitution and less upon the role of the European Court of Justice in pursuit of the social objectives within the constitutional framework. Secondly, a core value of Community social policy, the fundamental principle of equality irrespective of sex, is considered to establish the extent to which the EU legislator and the European Court have respected perceived converse pyramidal values, particularly in the period since the enactment of the Maastricht Treaty during which time the Member States can be seen to have exercised a more persistent "voice"[5] over social policy issues.

THE EC TREATY AS AN ECONOMIC/MARKET INTEGRATION PYRAMID

Given the failure of the grand designs of the European Defence Community and the European Political Community, there was inevitability about the limited neo-functionalist objectives of the European Economic Community.[6] From the EU's inception, a balance was struck between integrationist pressures towards a common market and the retention of sovereignty over issues of national sensitivity, a line of least resistance begotten out of bitter experience of more ambitious aspirations, a limitation of sovereignty, in the famous words of the European Court, "albeit in limited fields".[7] It can be seen that, as these "limited

---

[4] Armstrong and Bulmer, above n. 3, at 30.

[5] J H H Weiler, "The Transformation of Europe" (1991) 100 *Yale LJ* 2403, at 2411, drawing on A E Hirschmann, *Exit, Voice and Loyalty—Responses to Decline in Firms, Organizations and States* (Cambridge, MA, Harvard UP, 1970).

[6] See Craig, above n. 3, at 5–7.

[7] Case 6/64 *Costa v. ENEL* [1964] ECR 585. See Weiler, above n. 2, at 124.

fields" have expanded, partly through inventive use of Article 308 (ex 235) EC,[8] but primarily through Treaty amendment, there has developed:

> "a continuum between pure intergovernmental politics at one end of the spectrum and supranational politics at the other . . . It is therefore perfectly possible for different areas of Community policy to be located at different points along the spectrum".[9]

It is the central hypothesis of this chapter that this spectrum is essentially hierarchical.

An historical perspective on the development of this spectrum raises the hypothesis that a form of hierarchy of Community principles has been established, which can be epitomised as a pyramidal structure (see Figure 15.1).[10]

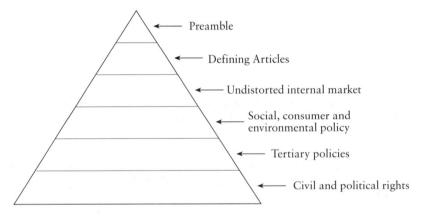

Fig. 15.1. *EC Treaty*

At its apex is the Preamble, setting out laudable aspirations such as "an ever closer union among the peoples of Europe"[11] and, most notably for social lawyers, "the essential objective of their efforts the constant improvement of the living and working conditions of their peoples".[12] The Preamble might have had nothing more than some stratospheric significance, hovering over the Community pyramid without making any contribution to the hierarchy of norms within it. But, on numerous occasions, most notably for social lawyers, the European Court has treated the Preamble as an overarching set of defining Community aspirations.[13] Nevertheless, the recitals of the Treaty's Preamble

---

[8] Weiler, above n. 5.

[9] Craig, above n. 3, at 21.

[10] Some of this analysis is rehearsed in B Fitzpatrick, "The Community's Social Policy: Recent Developments and Remaining Problems" in S Konstadinidis (ed.), *A People's Europe: Tuning a Concept into Content* (Aldershot, Dartmouth, 1999) 29–66.

[11] First recital of the Preamble of the EC Treaty.

[12] Third recital of the Preamble.

[13] Case 43/75 *Defrenne* v. *Sabena* [1976] ECR 455. In para. 10 of its judgment, the Court invoked the third recital of the Preamble to justify the social objective of Art. 119 EC.

resonate with the sound of *economic* aspirations of "steady expansion, balanced trade and fair competition",[14] "unity of their economies" and "their harmonious development",[15] hardly surprising in what was, and still is, despite a change in nomenclature, an overwhelmingly economic Treaty and hence a hierarchy of norms within which economic objectives take priority.

The opening Articles, at this defining level of the Community pyramid, concretise how these aspirations are to be achieved.[16] In the original EC Treaty, they were devoid of any quasi-political or even social aspirations. The Maastricht Treaty added respect for the environment and "a high level of employment and of social protection" in Article 2 EC and the Amsterdam Treaty has refined these tasks further, adding "equality between men and women, . . . [and] a high degree of competitiveness and convergence of economic performance". The still predominantly economic nature of these early Articles is now disturbed by the inclusion, in what are now Articles 17–22 EC, of provisions for European citizenship, augmented by Article 13 EC, providing a treaty base for EU legislation upon non-discrimination on grounds of sex, racial or ethnic origin, religion or belief, disability, age or sexual orientation. No doubt, these developments reflect at least a cosmetic shift of emphasis away from a purely economic pyramid but without altering the economic focus of these "apex" Articles.

In the European economic constitution,[17] the top substantive layer concerns the creation of an undistorted internal market. The *fundamental* freedoms are, of necessity, economic, that is, free movement of goods,[18] persons, services and capital,[19] supported by a regime of undistorted competition.[20] This layer includes essential ancillary policies such as agricultural[21] and transport policy[22] and now the area vital to the ultimate achievement of an undistorted internal market, that of EMU.[23] It is only when these core principles of an undistorted internal market are set out that attention is diverted to secondary, "middle

[14] Fourth recital of the Preamble.

[15] Fifth recital of the Preamble.

[16] They also provide the basis upon which later, "lower" parts of the Treaty pyramid may be interpreted, see for example, Case C–202/88 *European Commission* v. *France* [1991] ECR I–1223 and Opinion 1/91 [1991] ECR I–6079, both on Art. 2 EC.

[17] See generally M P Maduro, *We, the Court, The European Court of Justice and the European Economic Constitution* (Oxford, Hart Publishing, 1998).

[18] Title I of the consolidated Treaty.

[19] Title III of the Treaty.

[20] Title VI of the Treaty.

[21] Title II of the Treaty.

[22] Title IV of the Treaty.

[23] Title VII of the Treaty. It is also significant that these regimes of free movement and undistorted competition are overwhelmingly concerned with commercial rights and obligations, within which it is only in the fields of free movement of workers (and secondary aspects of the right of establishment and the freedom to provide services) that genuine "personal", socio-economic rights can be identified. More generally, social rights in EU law are overwhelmingly socio-economic, dependent upon a labour market, rather than a social welfare, nexus. (See I Ward, *A Critical Introduction to European Law* (London, Butterworths, 1996) 147.)

layer" issues such as social policy.[24] The ambivalence of the EU towards social policy is highlighted by the absence, until the Amsterdam Treaty, of an effective Treaty base upon which a broad agenda of Community social legislation could be enacted by qualified majority voting (QMV).[25] It was the negative integrationist effects of the quest for the achievement of the internal market,[26] particularly in the field of free movement of goods, which precipitated a series of further middle layers to the EU pyramid into the realms of environmental policy[27] and consumer policy.[28] In both cases, in pursuit of positive integrationist standards, relatively unfettered competence has been given to the Community legislator to act, within the Council by QMV. Although social policy sits in this middle layer by reason of its original inclusion in the EC Treaty and the more extensive Treaty bases now available, Community social legislation seems to have been rarely motivated by internal market spill-over,[29] although the exclusion of "the rights and interests of employed persons" from QMV under Article 95 EC (ex 100a) EC contributed to this lack of "spill-over". Nonetheless, internal market issues retain the potential to create such "spill-over" controversies in the future.[30]

The three amending Treaties have brought a range of "bottom layer" competences into the EC Treaty. Policy areas such as economic and social cohesion

[24] For a definitive analysis of the "secondary" significance of social policy in early development of the Community, see P Davies, "The Emergence of European Labour Law" in W McCarthy (ed.), *Legal Interventions in Industrial Relations Gains and Losses* (Oxford, Basil Blackwell, 1992) 313–59.

[25] In this sense, "Treaty base" is used to signify a Treaty Article upon the basis of which legislation can be enacted, in the case of social policy, only Articles 100 and 235 in the original Treaty. Article 118a EC (introduced by the Single European Act (SEA) and now incorporated into Article 137 EC) provided a limited Treaty base for legislation concerning the safety and health of workers and the Social Policy Agreement (SPA), annexed to the EC Treaty by the Maastricht Treaty, gave legislative competence, of dubious constitutionality, to the Member States other than the United Kingdom to legislate upon the range of matters now incorporated within Article 137 EC.

[26] Described by some commentators as "spill-over" (e.g., A Weale, "Environmental Rules and Rule-making in the European Union", (1996) 3 *Journal of European Public Policy* 594–611), an appropriate analogy in the context of a pyramidal analysis.

[27] Title XIX of the consolidated Treaty.

[28] Title XIV of the Treaty. Both areas of competence can be seen to be a reaction to the negative integration engendered by free movement of goods, in the case of consumer policy, cases such as Case 120/78 *Rewe-Zentrale AG* v. *Bundesmonopolverwaltung für Branntwein* [1979] ECR 649 ("Cassis de Dijon") and, in the case of environmental policy, cases such as Case 302/86 *Commission* v. *Denmark (Danish Bottles)* [1988] ECR 4607. It is arguable that one of the few developments of competence brought about by the Amsterdam Treaty has been to add Title XIII (Public Health) to this middle layer of relatively unfettered competences, a natural development of pre-existing Qualified Majority Voting (QMV) over safety and health of workers.

[29] Examples are the "market upheaval" directives, the Collective Redundancies Directive 1975 (Directive 75/129/EEC), consolidated in the 1998 Directive (Directive 98/59/EC), the Transfers of Undertakings Directive 1977 (Directive 77/187/EEC), as amended by the 1998 Directive (Directive 98/50/EC) and the Insolvency Directive 1980 (Directive 80/987/EEC), and, more recently, the Posting of Workers Directive 1996 (Directive 96/71/EC).

[30] For example, in the recent clash between competition policy and the right to free collective bargaining (see Case C–67/96 *Albany International BV* v. *Stichting Bedrijfspensioenfonds Textielindustrie* judgment of 21 September 1999, not yet reported, noted by S Vousden, "*Albany*, Market Law and Social Exclusion", (2000) 29 *ILJ* 170–80).

and research and technological development[31] can be relegated to this layer because the outcomes of the policy-making process have little impact on the legal systems of the Member States.[32] On the other hand, the tertiary nature of areas such as education, vocational training and youth[33] is exemplified through the absence of the competence to legislate so as to harmonise national law. None of these additions has challenged the economic core of the pyramid itself, if anything re-emphasised by the push towards the achievement of the internal market following the SEA, and of EMU after the Maastricht Treaty.

Despite the efforts of the Court to give extensive substance to the more social aspects of the Treaty, i.e. free movement of persons and equal pay, the Treaty is deliberately silent on many core issues of social rights, for example as enunciated in the International Covenant on Economic, Social and Cultural Rights,[34] the European Social Charter[35] or the International Labour Organisation Declaration on Fundamental Principles and Rights at Work.[36] Equally predictably, the Treaty still lacks a substantive code of fundamental human rights,[37] even though some recognition is now given to such rights, both in the Maastricht Treaty[38] and on the basis of a code of binding general principles that the Court has developed.[39] It is only in the "top level" of the EU pyramid, within

[31] Respectively in Titles XVII and XVIII.

[32] K Armstrong and S Bulmer, above n. 3, at 25–6, describe competence over environmental policy and research and technological development as relating to "second level legislation", a description broadly in line with the analysis in this chapter, but subject to a distinction made here between "second level" competence in which significant inroads are made into national competence and "third level" in which they are not.

[33] Respectively Chapter 3 of Title XI and Title XII.

[34] See generally, M Craven, *The International Covenant on Economic, Social and Cultural Rights* (Oxford, Clarendon Press, 1995).

[35] For example, the European Committee of Social Rights categorises the "hard core" Articles of the Social Charter to be Article 1 (the right to work), Article 5 (the right to organise), Article 6 (the right to bargain collectively), Article 12 (the right to social security), Article 13 (the right to social and medical assistance), Article 19 (the right of migrant families and their families to protection and assistance) and, in the Revised Charter, Article 20 (the right to equal opportunities and equal treatment in matters of employment and occupation without discrimination on grounds of sex), of which only Articles 19 and 20 are covered, in a labour market context, within the EU constitution.

[36] *ILO Declaration on Fundamental Principles and Rights at Work and its Follow-up* (Geneva, ILO, 1998), focusing on freedom of association, effective recognition of the right to collective bargaining, elimination of all forms of forced and compulsory labour, effective abolition of child labour and elimination of discrimination in respect of employment and occupation.

[37] See now, Simitis Report, *Affirming Fundamental Rights in the European Union Time to Act* (Brussels, European Commission, 1999), including the right to equality of opportunity and treatment, freedom of choice of occupation, the right to determine use of personal data, the right to family reunion, the right to bargain collectively, and to resort to collective action in the event of a conflict of interests; and the right to information, consultation and participation, in respect of decisions affecting the interests of workers.

[38] Article 6(2) of the Maastricht Treaty, as amended by the Amsterdam Treaty, referring to the European Convention of Human Rights (ECHR). See also the explicit reference to the European Social Charter and the Community Charter of Fundamental Social Rights 1989 in Article 136 EC.

[39] See the debate between Jason Coppel and Aidan O'Neill (J Coppell and A O'Neill, "Taking Rights Seriously" (1992) 29 *CMLRev* 669), and Joseph Weiler and Nicolas Lockhart (J H H Weiler and N Lockhart, "'Taking Rights Seriously' 'Seriously'" (1995) 32 *CMLRev* 51–94 (Part I) and 579–627 (Part II)).

the scope of an undistorted internal market, that the EU legal system achieves a level of comprehensiveness and coherence which justifies the designation of "constitution". Since the earliest days of the European Court, it is this economic pyramid, a European economic constitution, which takes precedence over a subsequent, inconsistent national law.[40]

A POLITICO-SOCIO-ECONOMIC/CITIZENSHIP PYRAMID

Stepping away from this well-understood structure, one is struck by the fact that, if one was to be asked to prepare, on a blank sheet of paper, a pyramid of fundamental political, social and economic principles upon which citizenship within a society (or constitution) was to be built, one might well emerge with a pyramidal structure which is the converse of the EU structure.

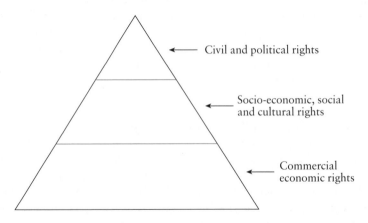

Fig. 15.2. *A citizenship pyramid*

It is most likely that the presentation of such rights would begin with civil rights such as right to life,[41] freedom from unlawful arrest[42] and right to a fair trial[43] and political rights, such as freedom of association[44] and the right to

---

[40] Norbert Reich has also constructed a valuable model to identify levels of Community competence, using the analogy of a "Russian doll", placing in order, from the innermost, consumer rights, social policy, environmental policy and civil and political rights (N Reich, "A European Constitution for Citizens: Reflections on the Rethinking of Union and Community Law" (1997) 3 *ELJ* 131–64, at 133). For a less pejorative categorisation of Community rights, see G de Búrca, "The Language of Rights and European Integration" in J Shaw and G More (eds), *New Dynamics of European Union* (Oxford, Clarendon Press, 1995) 29–54.

[41] Article 2 ECHR.

[42] Article 5 ECHR.

[43] Article 6 ECHR.

[44] Article 11 ECHR.

vote.[45] Once these civil and political rights had been asserted, for example as in the Universal Declaration of Human Rights or the European Convention of Human Rights, one might wish to move on to fundamental social rights, such as a right to minimum subsistence, to housing, health and education, to work, to join trade unions, to equality of treatment, to employment protection etc.[46] It might only be when these social and socio-economic rights had been codified that our attention might shift to fundamental economic rights, largely of a personal, socio-economic nature, such as rights to property,[47] to manage a business, even to move freely to undertake economic activities. It is difficult to imagine essentially commercial rights, such as free movement of goods and rights to undistorted competition, figuring at all in a national constitutional structure. This is also the case within the instruments of international law, given the perceived higher status of the International Covenant of Civil and Political Rights over the International Covenant of Economic, Social and Cultural Rights and the perceived higher status of the European Convention of Human Rights over the European Social Charter, even if the subservience of social rights to civil and political rights in international law is increasingly contested.[48] Both within a grand sweep through the EC Treaty, and but also within the minutiae of it, the EU's economic pyramid is almost precisely the *converse* of what we might reasonably expect to find in a "traditional" constitutional structure, reflecting the national pyramids of fundamental values within the Member States.

Such a hypothesis is hardly surprising. A pragmatic, functionalist and later neo-functionalist approach was adopted by the founders of the European Economic Community and those who followed them. Given the persistent requirement of unanimity in Intergovernmental Conferences, the history of the development of the Community pyramid has been one of following a line of least resistance towards what the Member States have perceived to be issues of high national priority, at least in comparison with the acknowledged dictates of European economic integration.[49] Indeed, as we shall consider below, in social

[45] Article 3 of the First Protocol to the ECHR.

[46] It is instructive, although not necessarily consistent with a hierarchical analysis, that nearly every Constitution set out by the Council of Europe in its publication, *The Rebirth of Democracy: Twelve Constitutions of Central and Eastern Europe* (Strasbourg, Council of Europe Press, 1995), places civil and political rights before economic, social and cultural rights.

[47] See Carol Harlow's discussion of the "late arrival" of property rights in the First Protocol of the European Convention of Human Rights (C Harlow, "*Francovich* and the Problem of the Disobedient State" (1996) 2 *ELJ* 199–225, at 211–12).

[48] See P Alston and J H H Weiler, "An EU Human Rights Policy" in P Alston (ed.), *The EU and Human Rights* (Oxford, Oxford University Press, 1999) 1–66, at 31–4 and the Simitis Report, above n. 37, section 8, on "indivisibility". The reason why this hierarchy operates in international law, but not EU law, is that, as Alan Milward points out (A Milward, *The European Rescue of the Nation-State* (London, Routledge, 1994) 439), in the latter, states are placing themselves under a legally enforceable regime while, in the former, they are not.

[49] What Harlow calls questions of "low policy" as opposed to "high policy", Harlow, above n. 47, at 224. See also E Meehan, *Citizenship and the European Community* (London, Sage, 1993) 140. It follows from this analysis that a European level emphasis in multi-level governance will be stronger in areas of national "low policy" which broadly coincide with European "high policy".

policy legislative processes, and hence within the Community's social policy pyramid, a similar reconciliation of Community and national imperatives can be identified. This conclusion is consistent with the seminal analysis by Professor Sir Otto Kahn-Freund of the "transplantation" of law between societies.[50] What Kahn-Freund's "tough law" categories, for example such as collective labour law,[51] come down to are merely examples of the proposition that the higher up a national pyramid a set of laws reside, the more cherished they are within that system and the greater will be the resistance to their transplantation into equally elevated positions within other legal systems.[52] In the context of European integration, it therefore requires powerful integrative forces to bring about Community competence over the harmonisation of (or even minimum guarantees within) particular areas of law. The "tougher" the area of law and policy, the less likely it is that these integrative forces will be sufficiently powerful.[53]

It was not particularly controversial for the European Court to assert the supremacy of the EU economic pyramid over national economic concerns in commercial cases concerning reclassification of customs duties[54] and obscure arguments over nationalisation of an electricity supply industry.[55] Such matters, although of practical significance, do not impinge upon fundamental values within national pyramids. Even a fundamental freedom to move in search of work,[56] to receive medical services,[57] or to market a liquor of one strength as opposed to another,[58] may raise *theoretical* constitutional problems, but not national angst over an assault upon fundamental values. Such economic questions are near the bottom of national constitutional pyramids and hence assertions of Community law supremacy of the economic pyramid, from the top of

---

[50] O Kahn-Freund, "On the Uses and Misuses of Comparative Law", (1974) 37 *MLR* 1–27, both in relation to the distribution of political and judicial power and the role of "organised interests" (at 12).

[51] *Ibid.*, 13–27.

[52] These tensions are obviously exacerbated by the fact that there are relatively coherent "legal families" in the broad areas of labour law (B Fitzpatrick, "Community Social Policy after Maastricht", (1992) 21 *ILJ* 199–213) and welfare law (see T Hervey, "Sex Equality in Social Protection: New Institutionalist Perspectives on Allocation of Competence", (1998) 4 *ELJ* 196–219, at 200–1) thereby raising obstacles to the development of an EU social model even where QMV applies in the Council of Ministers, let alone where unanimity survives. Such tensions will also emerge within the "Social Dialogue" under Articles 138–139 EC.

[53] In Kahn-Freund's terms, it can be argued that consumer and environmental law are relatively new areas of law, which are not embedded into national legal systems. Once subjected to intense negative integrationist pressures, they have been elevated into the middle layer of the EU pyramid. Social policy has, by way of contrast, maintained its "tough law" status and hence has failed to mature into a coherent and comprehensive system of law because integrationist pressures have been weaker and embedded interests have been stronger. Once again, a European focus within a system of multi-level governance will be weaker where "tough law" issues apply (see the EU social pyramid in Figure 15.3).

[54] Case 26/62 *Van Gend en Loos* v. *Nederlands Administratie der Belastingen* [1963] ECR 1.

[55] *Costa*, above n. 7.

[56] Case C–292/89 *R* v. *Immigration Appeal Tribunal, ex parte Antonissen* [1991] ECR I–745.

[57] Cases 286/82 and 26/83 *Luisi and Carbone* v. *Ministero del Tesoro* [1984] ECR 377.

[58] *Rewe-Zentrale AG*, see above n. 28.

one but in contradiction to the bottom of the other, have not precipitated significant national resistance.[59] Stein famously described this period as one of "benign neglect",[60] explained as being to some extent due to the "technicality" of the subject matter of the case law of the European Court.[61] As the scope of Community law has expanded, partly as a natural consequence of accelerating economic integration but also in response to a notion of European citizenship, these tensions between the Community pyramid and the national pyramids have intensified. It is only when these fundamental economic freedoms run counter to genuinely respected national values,[62] be it a general constitutional principle of proportionality,[63] protection of the unborn child[64] or even social regulation of shopping hours,[65] that the illusion of the supremacy of this predominantly economic pyramid is revealed.[66]

The Court finds various safety value mechanisms to allow respect for superior national pyramidal values under the guise of the assertion of the continuing supremacy of EU law. This is achieved most obviously through interpretation of derogations, for example, on grounds of public policy in relation to free move-

---

[59] Weiler explains this in terms of "exit", "the organizational abandonment in the face of unsatisfactory performance" and "voice", as the "intraorganizational correction and recuperation" (J H H Weiler, "The Transformation of Europe" (1991) 100 *Yale LJ* 2403, at 2411, based upon the seminal analysis of A O Hirschman, *Exit, Voice and Loyalty, Responses to Decline in Firms, Organizations and States* (Cambridge, Mass, Harvard University Press, 1970)). On the one hand, Community law supremacy prevents "selective exit" from the central norms of the Community pyramid. On the other hand, it is subject to extensive "voice" on the part of the Member States, particularly through unanimity requirements upon the exercise of Article 308 (ex 235) EC expansion of competence and an increasing willingness to argue national positions before the European Court. It might be argued that the Member States were prepared to forego "selective exit" from the rigours of the economic pyramid secure in the knowledge that they retained extensive control over what were, in reality, more immediately significant national pyramidal values.

[60] E Stein, "Lawyers, Judges and the Making of a Transnational Constitution", (1981) 75 *American Journal of International Law* 1.

[61] Harlow, above n. 47, at 224.

[62] This chapter would not wish to give exclusive significance to objective notions of hierarchical, constitutional values. In reality, the "voice" of the Member States has been directed towards a range of state interests. In this sense, there are at least "twin peaks", if not a "range of peaks", of national sovereignty in terms of both fundamental constitutional values and also particularly sensitive political values in all or some Member States. Indeed, many aspects of the legislative and judicial systems in the Member States encourage assertions of state, as opposed to constitutional, interests (see generally Milward, above n. 48). Nevertheless, there is hopefully some coincidence in democratic societies between a perceived hierarchy of constitutional values and what the state is prepared to defend within the EU's institutional processes.

[63] Case 11/70 *Internationale Handelsgessellschaft mbH* v. *Einfuhr- und Vorratsstelle für Getreide und Futtermittel* [1970] ECR 1125.

[64] Case C–159/90 *Society for the Protection of Unborn Children (Ireland) Limited (SPUC)* v. *Grogan* [1991] ECR I–4685. See D. Phelan, "Right to Life of the Unborn v Promotion of Trade in Services: The European Court of Justice and the Normative Shaping of the European Union", (1992) 55 *MLR* 670 at 689.

[65] Case C–169/91 *Stoke-on-Trent and Norwich City Councils* v. *B & Q plc.* [1992] ECR I–6635.

[66] As Harlow states (Harlow, above n. 47, at 211): "With the possible exception of free movement, EC rights have emerged as primarily economic in character; indeed, I have already argued that property/economic values nourish an ideology of EC law. A grave danger necessarily arises of serious clashes of value."

ment of persons[67] or the discovery of mandatory requirements of national policy in the context of free movement of goods.[68] So also the "defensive use" of fundamental rights[69] and even the wholesale reinterpretation of Article 28 (ex 30) EC[70] can be seen as safety valve mechanisms, acknowledging that market-driven, negative integration had spilled too far over the EU pyramid, particularly into areas where no competence (or no practical possibilities of legislation) existed to provide minimum, positive integrationist Community standards. Although this horizontal interaction is a battle of "two constitutionalisms",[71] it remains the case that each constitutionalism is based on a hierarchy of values and that these sets of values broadly complement each other.

In a sense, social rights are the sandwich both in the middle of the Community pyramid and also in the interaction between these converse pyramids. Despite occasional willingness to use safety valves to protect significant national pyramidal values, "middle layer" areas of competence are intrinsically vulnerable to apparently superior EU economic values. Therefore social law values have to fight their way on to an internal market agenda, for example, in the recent conflict between competition policy and the right to free collective bargaining.[72] So also, it is here that the middle layer of the Community pyramid of secondary significance meets the middle layer of the national pyramids, still of sufficient national pyramidal value to justify intense national "voice" in its defence. In its most progressive phase, from the mid-1980s until the early 1990s, the European Court took an expansive approach in its assertion of Community values.[73] Indeed, in its enthusiastic development of social and even constitutional principles,[74] the Court itself may have been, at least subliminally, seeking to convert the Community pyramid,[75] imposing restrictions upon "selective exit" in areas where Community legitimacy and competence were weaker than at the top of

---

[67] Case 30/77 *R* v. *Bouchereau* [1977] ECR 1999, so long as the national pyramidal value is "affecting one of the fundamental interests of the society". It is instructive that the Irish High Court, in *Attorney General* v. *X* [1992] ILRM 401, utilised the public policy derogation as a basis for giving primacy to the protection of the unborn child in the Irish Constitution over the supposedly fundamental freedom to move in receipt of services.

[68] For example in the Sunday trading cases, such as *Stoke-on-Trent and Norwich City Councils*, above n. 65, which were ostensibly about trading on Sundays but in reality were also concerned about employment on Sundays and cultural values towards a day of rest.

[69] Coppel and O'Neill, above n. 39, at 670.

[70] Case C–267 and 268/91 *Criminal Proceedings Against Keck and Mithouard* [1993] ECR I–6097. So also the Court's ruling in *Grogan*, above n. 64, can be seen as an example of a narrow interpretation of the socio-economic right to receive services in order to insulate, on the facts of the case, a deeply-held national principle from Community challenge.

[71] N MacCormick, "The Maastricht Urteil: Sovereignty Now", (1995) 1 *ELJ* 259, discussed by Weiler, above n. 2, at 111.

[72] *Albany International BV*, above n. 30. For a wider analysis of clashes between market integration and labour law values, see also P Davies, "Market Integration and Social Policy in the Court of Justice", (1995) 24 *ILJ* 49–77.

[73] F Mancini, "The Making of a Constitution for Europe", (1989) 26 *CMLRev* 595.

[74] Most pronounced in Opinion 1/91 *Re Draft Agreement on a European Economic Area* [1991] ECR I–6079.

[75] Described by Federico Mancini, above n. 73, at 596, as an attempt to "constitutionalise the Treaty".

the Community pyramid but where national legitimacy was still intensely strong.

That era was brought to a close by a wave of post-*Barber* trauma.[76] Most overtly, the inclusion of a principle of subsidiarity[77] in the EC Treaty following the Maastricht Treaty reflected a redetermination on the part of the Member States to protect their core national pyramidal values from Community intrusion. More covertly, although *Barber* was "only" about arguably inflated costs to UK, Dutch and German pension funds, the *Barber* Protocol in the Maastricht Treaty reflected the end of what might be described as a thirty-three-year honeymoon for a Court in the "fairyland Duchy of Luxembourg"[78] and the decisive assertion of national "voice" at the expense of European constitutionalism.[79] As will be examined below, in relation to the Court's consideration of Community sex equality norms, the period since the Maastricht Treaty has been one of broad deference to national pyramidal values on the part of the Court, particularly where Community values appear to lack sufficient pyramidal legitimacy to withstand entrenched national interests.

CONVERSE PYRAMIDS WITHIN THE EU SOCIAL CONSTITUTION

In each area of Community policy, it is possible to construct a pyramid of Community values and contrast it with pyramids of national values. This is particularly the case in relation to EU social constitutionalism. In the legislative sphere, it is possible to see converse pyramids at work.

What was previously the Social Policy Agreement[80] reflects the converse priorities of the Member States over issues upon which they are prepared to release sovereignty and those upon which they are not. In a genuine social constitution, freedom of association might well come at the top of a social pyramid. It is protected by the ECHR[81] and perceived as a core value within ILO Conventions[82] and the European Social Charter.[83] So also, some protection for other aspects of collective labour law, for example the right to strike, would, at least traditionally, be high up the agenda, in the spirit of the European Social Charter.[84] Both

[76] Case C–262/88 *Barber* v. *Guardian Royal Exchange Insurance* [1990] ECR I–1889.

[77] Article 5 (ex 3b) EC. See N Bernard, "The Future of European Economic Law in the Light of the Principle of Subsidiarity" (1996) 33 *CMLRev*. 633–66.

[78] E Stein, above n. 60, at 1.

[79] What Ian Ward describes as "a triumph of economic and political expediency" (Ward, above n. 23, at 172).

[80] Now Articles 136–145 EC.

[81] Article 11.

[82] Conventions 87 and 98. See also *ILO Declaration on Fundamental Principles and Rights at Work and its Follow-up*, above n. 36.

[83] Article 5. See L Samuel, *Fundamental Social Rights Case Law of the European Social Charter* (Strasbourg, Council of Europe Publishing, 1997) 105–42.

[84] Article 6(4) of the Charter. See Samuel, *ibid.*, 161–84. See also M P Maduro, "Striking the Elusive Balance Between Economic Freedom and Social Rights in the EU" in Alston above, n. 48, 449–72 and S Sciarra, "From Strasbourg to Amsterdam: Prospects for the Convergence of European Social Policy Rights Policy" in Alston, above n. 48, 473–501.

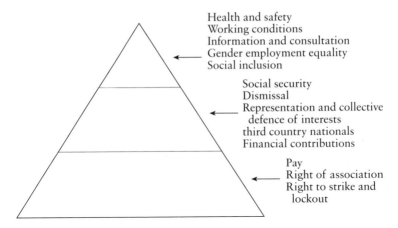

Fig. 15.3. *The EU social pyramid*

issues were totally excluded from the SPA[85] and are also excluded from the so-called Social Chapter in the consolidated Treaty[86]. Equally pertinently, issues high up the national pyramids, such as social security and dismissal law,[87] are conveniently placed within the scope of unanimity rules, as is the non-discrimination clause[88] in the consolidated Treaty. So also distinctions are made between the more significant (and more contentious) "representation and collective defence of the interests of workers and employers, including co-determination, [but still] subject to [the total exclusion of the right to strike]",[89] governed by unanimity and the less controversial "information and consultation of workers"[90] governed by QMV.

Given that the social constitution can itself only be amended by unanimity in an Intergovernmental Conference, it follows that the legislative structures which emerge will reflect a line of least resistance towards the creation of Community competence. Indeed, collective labour law is the quintessential "tough law" area of policy as enunciated by Kahn-Freund.[91] The Community Charter of Fundamental Social Rights for Workers can be seen as a more meaningful attempt to convert the Community pyramid but its own flaws merely reinforce the pyramidal analysis. First, it is non-binding and indeed was not even subscribed to by the United Kingdom. Secondly, it is subject to subsidiarity[92] and, in

---

[85] Article 2(6) SPA.

[86] Article 137(6) EC.

[87] Article 137(3) EC.

[88] New Article 13 EC.

[89] Article 137(3) EC.

[90] Article 137(1) EC.

[91] Kahn-Freund, above n. 50, 13–27.

[92] Fifteenth recital of the Preamble to the Charter. See L Betten and N Grief, *EU Law and Human Rights* (London, Longman, 1998) 71. Nevertheless, the Community Charter has been invoked in all EU social policy measures since its enactment (Betten and Grief, at 73).

consequence, the accompanying Action Programme[93] left the most contentious areas of social policy firmly in the hands of the Member States.[94] The prospects of the Charter being utilised as a source of general principles of fundamental social rights, thereby enriching social citizenship within the EU, are limited by its uncertain status.[95] It may yet form the basis, along with the European Social Charter, for a social dimension to the proposed EU Charter of Rights, a more determined bid to bring about a conversion of the EU converse pyramid.

There are some other indications within the legislative framework of an attempt to infuse some elements of a Community social citizenship model into the Community pyramid. Arguably, those directives, such as the equal treatment directives, based upon Article 308 (ex 235) EC, reflect an approach not solely based upon the economic criteria of market integration. More interestingly, Article 137(1) (ex 118a) EC also eschewed a market integration approach in favour of one based upon the intrinsic social value of health and safety protection.[96] Equally, despite the critique above of the substance of the SPA, as now enacted in Articles 136–145 EC, it must at least be said that it was modelled upon Article 118a EC rather than a mere repeal of Article 100a(2) EC, which would have driven most social law developments back into the realms of market integration.[97] Nonetheless, these elements of social citizenship within the Community social pyramid hardly compensate for the intrinsically converse nature of the pyramid. In consequence, neither a recognisable hierarchy of fundamental social rights nor a consistent and coherent system of social law has emerged from this process. Clearly some attempts have been made by the Court to convert the pyramid, particularly in sex equality law. And yet, sex equality norms themselves are subject to a pyramidal analysis.

THE CONVERSE PYRAMIDS OF COMMUNITY SEX EQUALITY NORMS

The notion of a converse pyramid applies also to Community sex equality law, at the heart of Community social policy. If one was once again to prepare, on a blank sheet of paper, a pyramid of social rights within which one would wish to see equality irrespective of sex, one would probably wish to start with subsistence-based (social protection) welfare benefits, followed perhaps by work-based (social insurance) welfare benefits (followed perhaps by occupational social security (OSS) entitlements). Only then might one move on to labour mar-

---

[93] Commission Communication, *Concerning its Action Programme Relating to the Implementation of the Community Charter of Basic Social Rights for Workers* (COM(89) 568).

[94] See, e.g., Section 6 on "Freedom of Association and Collective Bargaining". See Ward, above n. 23, at 160.

[95] Opinion of Advocate General Jacobs in *Albany International BV*, above n. 30.

[96] Armstrong and Bulmer, above n. 3, refer to safety and health measures as being "socially solidaristic" (at 29).

[97] M Weiss, "The Significance of Maastricht for European Community Social Policy", (1992) 8 *IJCLLIR* 3–14.

ket entitlements, objectively preferring to deal next with equal treatment in working conditions and, subsumed within it, the question of equal pay (and possibly OSS within that heading).[98] It is surprising, from this citizenship perspective, but totally comprehensible within the labour market-driven economic pyramid of Community law, that once again our Community pyramid is the almost precise converse that of national pyramids.

National/citizenship model   *Community/market integration model*

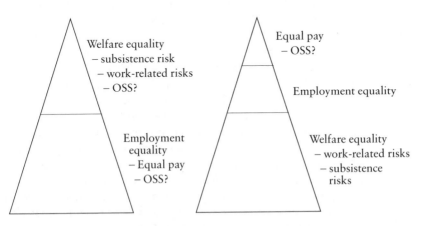

Fig. 15.4. *Converse sex equality pyramids*

The interaction between these two opposing pyramids can best be seen in relation to both the legislative and judicial treatment of the areas as a whole and the judicial treatment of the principle of indirect discrimination. Initially the principle of equal pay irrespective of sex was unceremoniously shifted from a draft part of the EC Treaty on "distortions of competition" and included, in Article 119 EC, within the otherwise weakly drafted Social Policy provisions.[99] It was later elevated by the European Court into a fundamental social right.[100] Possibly, the Court was able to give such significance to equal pay, arguably more appropriate as a political objective than as a justiciable legal concept, because of its perceived relative unimportance in national pyramidal thinking. As part of a transient attempt to add substance to the middle layer of the Community economic pyramid in the wake of the first Social Action Programme in 1973, the Council grasped this opportunity to enact two directives on equality. It was content to rely upon Article 94 (ex 100) EC and a market

---

[98] See B Fitzpatrick, "Summary of the Conference" in *Beyond Equal Treatment: Social Security in a Changing Europe*, Report of Conference of the Irish Presidency of the European Union, Dublin, 10–12 October 1996 (Department of Social Welfare, Dublin, 1996) 12–19, at 13–14.

[99] C Hoskyns, *Integrating Gender* (London, Verso, 1996) 57.

[100] *Defrenne*, above n. 13.

integration rationale for the Equal Pay Directive 1975 (75/117/EEC) but struggled to find a rationale even for the use of Article 308 (ex 235) EC in relation to the Equal Treatment in Working Conditions Directive 1976 (76/207 EEC), falling back upon the Preamble's "essential objective" as "one of the objectives" on the basis of which Article 235 EC could be invoked. In pyramidal terms, the equal pay principle was uncluttered by limitations; the principle of equal treatment in working conditions was also undistorted by significant exceptions.

However, as the Community and national pyramids collided, the quality of the legislation deteriorated, albeit enacted in more difficult times both economically and politically. The Equal Treatment in Social Security Directive 1979 (79/7/EEC) seeks to achieve "the progressive implementation"[101] of the principle of equal treatment in matters of social security. Subsistence-based benefits, by way of social assistance, are only governed by the 1979 Directive to the extent that they are "intended to supplement or replace"[102] the "work-related" statutory schemes governed by Article 3(1)(a) of the Directive. This focus is confirmed by the application of the Directive to the "working population".[103] So also, the 1979 Directive and the Equal Treatment in Occupational Social Security Directive 1986 (86/378/EEC) contain significant exceptions to the principle of *direct* discrimination, for example, on issues of retiring ages,[104] survivors' benefits[105] and actuarial reductions.[106] The European Court, in its immediate pre-post-*Barber* trauma period, sought to bypass these derogations through imaginative, and, within its own "fairyland logic", totally predictable, exploitation of its earlier case law on pure equal pay questions,[107] once again a conversion of low policy into high policy. It was only then that the *de facto* superiority of the national pyramids became apparent. The Court, in elevating OSS within the scope of an already elevated principle of equal pay, broke the rules of converse pyramids and sought to restrict "selective exit" from superior Community competence over significant national values, albeit initially financial, but with knock-on effects into the nationally significant arena of welfare equality. Although the Court has been much slower, and more reticent, in

---

[101] Article 1(2) of the 1976 Directive and Article 1 of the 1979 Directive.

[102] Article 3(1)(b) of the 1979 Directive.

[103] Article 2 of the Directive. Indeed, any ambiguity in the Directive as to its scope beyond work-related risks in the field of social security to include subsistence risks in the field of social assistance has been resolved by the European Court in favour of a narrow work-related approach (see Hervey, above n. 52, 202–3 and, more generally, J Sohrab, *Sexing the Benefit* (Aldershot, Dartmouth, 1996).

[104] Article 7(1)(a) of the 1979 Directive; Article 9(a) of the 1986 Directive (see now Directive 96/97 EC).

[105] Article 7(1)(c) of the 1979 Directive; Article 9(b) of the 1986 Directive.

[106] Article 9(c) of the 1986 Directive. It is also notable that the Burden of Proof Directive 1997, incorporating a modest reversal of the burden of proof in sex equality cases and a statutory definition of the principle of indirect discrimination, does not apply to the 1979 and 1986 Directives.

[107] Arguably from Case 12/81 *Garland* v. *British Rail Engineering* [1982] ECR 359. See B Fitzpatrick, "Equality in Occupational Pensions—The New Frontiers after *Barber*", (1991) 54 MLR 271–80. See generally, E A Whiteford, *Adapting to Change: Occupational Schemes, Women and Migrant Workers* (The Hague, Kluwer, 1996).

acknowledging the fundamental nature of the principle of equal treatment in working conditions,[108] let alone the principle of equal treatment in social security,[109] one can read the post-*Barber* cases from beginning to end and barely find a reference to the fundamental nature of the *equal pay* principle, which was being reconstituted into the image compatible with national pyramids, as ordained in the *Barber* Protocol.[110]

Nevertheless, Article 141 (ex 119) EC is of no consequence outside the field of employment equality, even subsuming OSS within it. In the field of welfare equality, we find entrenched not only derogations from the principle of direct discrimination, as set out above, but also the virtual neutralisation of the principle of indirect discrimination.[111] Once again, this neutralisation is an instructive exercise in pyramidal interaction. As in earlier discussion, it has been in the interpretation of a safety valve between purportedly superior Community concepts and national issues of high pyramidal value, in this case, the principle of objective justification, that the middle layer status of Community social policy is highlighted. At one end of the Community gender equality pyramid, the European Court established an extensive definition of the indirect discrimination principle[112] within the relatively safe area of equal pay, albeit a case involving OSS.[113] The Court allowed the equal pay principle to trickle down the Community pyramidal structure rather more dramatically in *Rinner-Kühn*,[114] not merely by converting an essentially welfare equality issue concerning a *statutory* sick pay scheme into an equal pay controversy in litigation against the *employer* which was faithfully applying it but also by requiring the *Member*

---

[108] Case 152/84 *Marshall* v. *Southampton and South West Hampshire Area Health Authority* [1986] ECR 723.

[109] Case C–343/92 *De Weerd, née Roks* v. *Bestuur van de Bedrijfsvereniging voor de Gezondheid, Geestelijke en Maatschappelijke Belangen* [1994] ECR I–571.

[110] See B Fitzpatrick, "Equality in Occupational Pensions Schemes: Still Waiting for *Coloroll*", (1994) 23 *ILJ* 155–163, 204. This is particularly the case in the Court's rulings in Case C–109/91 *Ten Oever* v. *Stichting Bedrijfspensioenesfonds voor het Glazenwassers-en Schoonmaakbedriif* [1993] ECR I–4879 in which the Court "reinterpreted" its *Barber* ruling on prospective effect (see E Whiteford, "Occupational Pensions and European Law: Clarity at Last?" in T Hervey and D O'Keefe (eds), *Sex Equality Law in the European Union* (Chichester, Wiley, 1996) 21–34) and in Case C–408/92 *Smith* v. *Avdel Systems Ltd* [1994] ECR I–4435 in which it permitted "adverse equalisation" of OSS retiring ages.

[111] Fitzpatrick, above n. 98; S Spiliotopoulos "Can Sex Equality Justify Levelling-Down Survivors' Benefits?", in Department of Social Welfare, above n. 98, 171–9. See also Hervey, above n. 52, at 210–14.

[112] There is an oblique reference to the principle in Article 2(1) of the 1976 Directive, with particular reference to marital or family status.

[113] Case 170/84 *Bilka-Kaufhaus GmbH* v. *Karin Weber von Hartz* [1986] ECR 1607, in which the Court defined the principle of indirect discrimination, in relation to the facts of the case, in the following terms (at para. 36): "If the national court finds that the measures chosen by Bilka correspond to a real need on the part of the undertaking, are appropriate with a view to achieving the objectives pursued and are necessary to that end, the fact that the measures affect a far greater number of women than men is not sufficient to show that they constitute an infringement of Article 119".

[114] Case 171/88 *Rinner-Kühn* v. *FWW Spezial Gebäudereinigung GmbH* [1989] ECR 2743.

State to provide the objective justification for it.[115] And yet, at the other end of the Community pyramid, in relation to subsistence-based welfare benefits, the Court was giving an extensive freedom to the Member States through a significantly different formulation of the objective justification test.[116]

So also, in *Commission v. Belgium*,[117] the Court refused to distinguish the Belgian scheme from the Dutch scheme in *Teuling*. By now, the *Rinner-Kühn* test had been diluted to one of "a *legitimate* objective of social policy"[118] as opposed to a *necessary* one. The Court went on to assert that, in the present state of Community law, the Member States continued to enjoy a "reasonable measure of discretion" over social policy matters.[119] This assertion, in the context of challenges to fundamental aspects of national policies of social protection, effectively neutralised the assault upon structural discrimination in relation to the *social protection* aspects of social security schemes.[120]

As part of a retreat from judgments such as *Rinner Kühn*,[121] the Court effectively neutralised the indirect discrimination principle in relation to *employment-related* social security schemes in *Megner*.[122] The Court was considering the provisions of German social security law whereby those involved in "minor employment"[123] were excluded from a series of German social insurance benefits. Here we find the enunciation of an even weaker definition of objective

---

[115] "However, if the Member State can show that the means chosen meet a necessary aim of its social policy and that they are suitable and requisite for attaining that aim, the mere fact that the provision affects a much greater number of female workers than male workers cannot be regarded as constituting an infringement of Article 119" (at para. 14). This was giving the Member States "voice" but not perhaps in a fashion which they anticipated.

[116] In *Teuling* (Case 30/85 *Teuling v. Bedrijfsvereniging voor de Chemische Industrie* [1987] ECR 2497), the Court was concerned with the disproportionate effect on women of Dutch social security rules which provided minimum subsistence against the threat of poverty on the basis of dependency principles. In this category, of *subsistence-based* welfare benefits, the Court was content (at para. 16) to accept that protection against the risks of poverty was "an integral part of the social policy of the Member States".

[117] Case C–228/89 *Commission v. Belgium* [1991] ECR I–2205.

[118] Emphasis added.

[119] At para. 22.

[120] Karen Banks (K Banks, "Social Security—Objective Justification in the Context of Indirect Discrimination", (1991) 20 *ILJ* 220–3) prophetically commented, that this reminder of national competence was "ominous in relation to future enforcement of the principle of equal treatment in relation to social security matters", at 23.

[121] See, for example, H Fenwick and T Hervey, "Sex Equality in the Single Market: New Directions for the European Court of Justice", (1995) 32 *CMLRev* 443–70.

[122] Case C–444/93 *Megner and Scheffel* v. *Innungskrankenkasse Rheinhessen-Pfalz* [1995] ECR I–4741. See also Case C–31/93 *Nolte* [1995] ECR I–4625.

[123] "Minor employment" was defined as employment "where it is normally engaged in for less than 15 hours a week and the monthly remuneration does not exceed one-seventh of the average monthly salary of persons insured under the statutory old-age insurance scheme during the reference calendar year" (in 1993, DM 530 in the Original *Länder*) (Opinion of the Advocate General in paras 4 and 5). Those in "minor employment" were excluded from compulsory invalidity and old-age insurance and sickness insurance and unemployment insurance. Those in "short-term employment", defined as employment "normally restricted, by virtue of its nature or under a contract of employment, to 18 hours a week" (Opinion of the Advocate General at para. 8) were excluded from unemployment insurance.

justification for indirect discrimination, amounting to little more than "reasonable subjective justification".[124]

In the employment sphere, involving cases higher up the Community pyramid but lower down the national pyramids, we find evidence of the *Megner* approach in employment regimes which have a *statutory* basis, as in *Rinner-Kühn*[125] but not in those based purely on collective agreements and employer prerogative.[126] Has the converse pyramids hypothesis survived this analysis? In *Krüger*, the Court sought to distinguish *Megner* on the basis that the case did not involve "a question of either a measure adopted by the national legislature in the context of its discretionary power or a basic principle of the German social security system".[127] What can be said is that the contrast between the top and bottom layers of the respective pyramids vindicates a converse pyramids analysis and that the contrast between welfare and employment equality generally is still strong, as shown by the reason given by the Court in *Kruger*. In this sense, in the allocation of competence between the EU and the Member States, welfare equality is still a "tough law" area of policy in comparison with employment equality.[128] The rationale behind the converse pyramids hypothesis is that the Member States will seek to establish maximum "voice" where they feel that their "selective exit" is being imperilled and, as the *Barber* saga shows, the Court can be receptive to powerfully expressed national concerns, in this case using the safety valve of objective justification to protect national interests. There is an apparent perversity in applying stricter standards of objective justification to private parties than the Member States themselves, cloaked in the legitimacy of statutory enactment.[129] Nevertheless, the Court has allowed its restrictive approach to objective justification in the intrinsically statutory field of welfare equality to be forced up the Community pyramid into the arena of statutory

---

[124] "It should be noted that the social and employment policy aim relied on by the German government is objectively unrelated to any discrimination on grounds of sex and that, in exercising its competence, the national legislature was reasonably entitled to consider that the legislation in question was necessary in order to achieve that aim" (para. 35).

[125] For example, in Case C–457/93 *Kuratorium für Dialyse und Nierentransplantation eV* v. *Lewark* [1996] ECR I–243, the Court adopted the "legitimate aim" approach from *Megner* but the "appropriate and necessary means" approach from *Bilka*. In the widely anticipated judgment in Case C–167/97 *R* v. *Secretary of State for Employment, ex p Seymour-Smith* [1999] ECR I–623, the Court appears to revert to a *Megner*-style test of objective justification.

[126] In Case C–281/97 *Krüger* v. *Kreiskrankenhaus Ebersberg* [1999] IRLR 808, the circumstances in *Megner* were transposed into a pure employment situation, albeit in the public sector. A collective agreement excluded those in "minor employment" from the grant of a special annual bonus. The defendant sought to rely on *Megner* to argue that the same margin of discretion should be granted to the negotiators of the agreement, a proposition which the Court was unable to accept.

[127] At para. 29 of the judgment.

[128] See Hervey, above n. 52, at 213–14.

[129] Indeed, the intrusion of a *Megner* approach into the field of employment equality undermines its constitutional coherence in a policy area where some degree of coherence has been established, albeit that the Burden of Proof Directive (Directive 97/80/EC) may reestablish a more coherent approach.

employment schemes.[130] It can be argued that the perceived peripheral nature of sex equality in the 1970s and 1980s allowed the development of Community sex equality law both legislatively and judicially. Once its intrusiveness, particularly in relation to structural discrimination, became apparent, the retreat back "up" the Community pyramid and more significantly "down" the national pyramids began. Hence, the Court is less autonomous than might otherwise be anticipated, even in relation to a fundamental social right such as equality irrespective of sex. It can be strongly responsive to national pyramidal interests,[131] particularly since the post-*Barber* trauma of the early 1990s.

W(H)ITHER THE EU SOCIAL CONSTITUTION?[132]

The central thesis of this chapter is first that it is helpful, in considering the interaction between Community and national norms, both in the legislative and the judicial spheres, to attempt to assemble a hierarchy or pyramid of priorities both at Community and national levels. The Community pyramid is likely to be reasonably discernible but each Member State may have a range of pyramids depending upon the perspective adopted, be it constitutional, governmental, judicial etc. It is suggested here that there is a broad, sometimes crude, converse relationship between Community and national pyramids. Integrative momentum, and a European focus in multi-level governance, have greater force the closer one comes to the apex of the Community pyramid, at the heart of internal market-making. A second proposition in this chapter is that social policy is stranded as a middle layer policy area, sufficiently significant to have generated considerable energy at the Community level but of too vital an importance to the Member States to be allowed to mature into an EU social constitution. This analysis is sustainable within social policy itself and even within the hierarchy of values underpinning the fundamental principle of equality irrespective of sex. In middle layer pyramidal politics, the "tough law" constraints upon the development of Community norms are too strong. At this level, the institutional structures of the EU give a primacy to national "voice" which, despite a significant body of EU law, thwarts attempts at coherence and consistency. Arguably, the EC Treaty and indeed the European Court had an easy law ride through the formative years of the EU and its legal system. A market integration model worked well so long as issues of marginal national pyramidal value were being subjected to superior Community economic norms. As the Community pyramid has risen like a subterranean mountain through Treaty amendment and extensive judicial interpretation, the top layer of economic rights has been developed. The existing social middle layer of the Community pyramid has been exploited,

---

[130] This analysis supports a "twin peaks" approach whereby it is possible to construct a range of hierarchies (or pyramids) of national priorities.

[131] Hervey, above n. 52, at 203, n. 38.

[132] See E Whitford, "W(h)ither Social Policy?" in Shaw and More, above n. 40, at 111–28.

at least from the first Social Action Programme onwards, in recognition of the converse nature of the pyramid and areas of middle layer competence have been added. Both the force of market integration and a growing perception of European citizenship brought the Community pyramid in the late 1980s into conflict with the top level and middle level values of national pyramids. The route of "selective exit" was progressively closed off by imaginative interpretation of Community law by the European Court. This friction has led to a galvanised reassertion of Member State "voice" over social policy issues, not merely in the Council of Ministers but also before the Court, which has proved to be responsive to such reassertions of national priorities.

In a regime of Treaty amendment governed by unanimity rules, it is difficult to see the conversion of the Community social policy pyramid. As such, the EU's social constitution, as an amalgam of EU and predominantly national norms, may be ill-equipped to confront the challenges of intensified market integration, particularly in the era of EMU.[133] In particular it is difficult to see how collective labour law rights, which are not even on the Community pyramid at present, can be elevated to its apex. Nor can we expect the European Court to be in a position to convert the Community pyramid in contradiction to the political will of the Member States.[134] A first telling test of the willingness of the Member States to contemplate some conversion of the pyramid comes with their reaction to the Commission's proposals on a general framework non-discrimination directive and a race and ethnic origin directive,[135] both inspired by notions of citizenship and fundamental rights but subject to a Treaty base requiring unanimity. A second telling test will be the fate of economic, social and cultural rights within the proposed EU Charter of Rights.[136] Both initiatives may prove to be either the salvation or nemesis of the EU social constitution. Certainly, the approach of the EU towards the human rights aspects of enlargement would indicate that indivisibility of civil, political, economic, social and cultural rights is not prominent on the EU agenda.[137] So also, social rights have been given "a very low priority" in the EU's external human rights policy.[138] It is possible to envisage a situation in which civil and political rights, plucked from Community

---

[133] Mundell's seminal analysis of EMU indicates that labour market policy may prove to be a vital instrument of national policy in circumstances in which recourse to interest rate controls are neutralised: R Mundell, "A Theory of Optimal Currency Areas", (1961) *American Economic Review* 51, discussed by P de Grauwe, *The Economics of Monetary Integration* (3rd edn., Oxford, Oxford University Press, 1997) 1–11.

[134] An under-developed aspect of this chapter concerns the ability of Social Dialogue to provide the momentum towards an EU social constitution, a prospect not sustained by its output since its inception (see B Bercusson, "The European Community's Charter of Fundamental Social Rights of Workers", (1990) 53 *MLR* 624 at 641).

[135] COM(99) 565; COM(99) 566.

[136] See L Betten and D Mac Devitt, *The Protection of Fundamental Social Rights in the European Union* (The Hague, Kluwer, 1996) in which the failure to constitutionalise social rights in the EU is well-documented. See also Betten and Grief, above n. 92.

[137] Alston and Weiler, above n. 48, at 32. Editorial (M Marijke), "The Social Dimension of the Enlargement of the European Union", (1998) 5 *MJ* 107–9.

[138] Alston and Weiler, above n. 48, at 32.

obscurity by the European Court through its fundamental rights jurisprudence, are elevated to the apex of the EU pyramid but second generation, largely programmatic[139] economic, social and cultural rights are left once again stranded in the middle layer of the EU pyramid. This converse pyramid hypothesis need not be deterministic. Non-discrimination law may be revolutionised by Article 13 directives.[140] The Charter of Rights may be inspired by indivisibility, fundamentally altering the focus of multi-level governance on social policy issues.[141] But in two environments governed by unanimity, it is largely a matter of political will[142] whether meaningful progress can be achieved in relation to issues upon which national pyramidal values continue to hold a consistent stranglehold over EU social constitutionalism.

---

[139] K Lenaerts, "Fundamental Rights to be Included in a Community Catalogue", (1991) 16 *ELRev* 367–90.

[140] The Race and Ethnic Origin Directive (Directive 2000/43, OJ 2000 L180/22) was agreed in June 2000. There is less optimism in relation to the prospects for the enactment of the horizontal framework proposal by the end of 2000.

[141] The draft Charter, now being negotiated (*The Times*, 1 June 2000), contains within its 50 Articles significant social rights, including a wide-ranging non-discrimination provision, even wider than the categories of inequality in Article 13 EC (Article 22) and more specific social rights on freedom to choose an occupation (Article 32), workers' right to information and consultation (Article 33), the right to bargain collectively including the right to take collective action (Article 34), rights to rest periods and annual leave (Article 35), rights to safe and healthy working conditions (Article 36), protection of young people (Article 37), the right to protection against unjustified or abusive termination of employment (Article 38), the right to reconcile family and domestic life (Article 39), rights of migrant workers to equal treatment (Article 40), rights to social security and social assistance (Article 41), rights to health provision (Article 42) and rights for the disabled (Article 43). The eventual status and the substance of the Charter remain matters of speculation.

[142] D Harris, "The European Social Charter and Social Rights in the European Union", in Betten and Mac Devitt, above n. 136, at 107–11.

16

Europe's Social Self: "The Sickness Unto Death"

MIGUEL POIARES MADURO

The Sickness Unto Death is the title of the famous book written by Søren Kierkegaard in the middle of the last century.[1] The sickness to which Kierkgaard refers is that of a human being who is unable to believe in his own destiny beyond physical death. A human being who, in his view, refuses to accept the meaning of his or her life. That meaning is, in Kierkegaard's writings, closely associated with the Christian faith but the metaphor of the sickness unto death can be used in a broader context. In this chapter I use it in two ways: first, to highlight the fact that many of the European Union's current social policy problems stem from its own refusal to accept the conclusions which follow from its internally developed political identity; and second to stress that current social debates risk begging the question if they continue to ignore, and do not discuss, the question of Europe's social self and advance proposals that are instead based on quite different assumptions. The risk, as Kierkgaard would say, is that of constantly discussing the "rest" while losing oneself. This argument, applied in my own terms, goes so far as to say that this is a foundational moment for Europe, in which it can either "accept" its selfhood or deny it with a risk that a split may occur between its self (which guarantees social legitimacy) and its emerging political form.

It has often been argued that the impact of EU law on social policies has been a functional one with regard to economic integration and the general promotion of economic freedom and social deregulation. At the same time, it is historically known that economic integration has, on other occasions, provided a rationale for the promotion of social rights in Europe in order to guarantee a level playing field and to avoid distortions of competition. Furthermore, European integration has also been conceived of as a safeguard of the welfare state. In the latter perspective, the European Union is the new forum in which social rights, no longer viable at the national level, are reintroduced. These different perspectives of Europe's social policy are also associated with a broader debate on the

---

[1] S Kierkegaard (ed.), *The Sickness Unto Death: a Christian Psychological Exposition for Edification and Awakening/ by Anti-Climacus* (A Hannay (trans.), Harmondsworth, Penguin Books, 1989).

nature of European integration: some conceive of European integration exclusively as economic integration; others argue that economic integration needs to be complemented by some form of political integration which must include a system of social entitlements. But this political integration can still be conceived of either as a functional necessity deriving from economic integration, or as arising from an independent political claim which stresses the need for solidarity in Europe.

This chapter approaches the debates on the nature and position of social policy in the EU from a different perspective. It puts them in the context of a discussion on Europe's constitutional identity and its social self. In this way, the chapter relates the current debates on the European Union's social policy to other recent or anticipated constitutional developments. The chapter also identifies a series of dilemmas and problems in Europe's social policy the solution of which, it is argued, requires us to focus on the contested social identity of Europe. Are the different aspects of the social impact of European integration and the social policies of the EU based on some agreement regarding a core set of shared European social values? What rationale has commanded the different social developments involved in European integration? Does European integration need some criterion of distributive justice?

The main normative argument of this chapter will be that it is no longer possible to evade the debate on Europe's social identity at the risk of putting at stake the overall integration project itself. *The Sickness Unto Death* to which this chapter refers is Europe's refusal to face and discuss its integration identity in the social sphere. Kierkegaard identifies the crisis of one's search for one's identity in three types of despair: "being unconscious in despair of having a self (inauthentic despair), not wanting in despair to be oneself, and wanting in despair to be oneself".[2] I will argue below that Europe's dilemma in defining its social identity lies in the two forms of authentic despair highlighted by Kierkegaard.

In the first section of the chapter I will concentrate on contrasting Europe's social self with Europe's social policy and the concept of European citizenship. Raising awareness of one's identity is the first step in making a true choice of one's self. This section will additionally review the emergence of a European social policy from the perspective of the debate between negative and positive integration. I will review the evolution of the different dilemmas at the core of this policy and highlight the current strains within the EU's traditional approach to social issues in light of the fact that European social policy has been developed in a functional relation to market integration. The second section will review the emergence of the concept of European citizenship in relation to social rights. It will highlight the under-developed nature of European social citizenship and the confused and ambiguous character of the current set of European social rights. Again, the underlying paradoxes and dilemmas will be related to

---

[2] Kierkegaard, above n. 1, at 43.

other aspects of the political and constitutional development of the EU and I will argue that those paradoxes and dilemmas can only be properly addressed in the context of a debate on Europe's social self. The last section of the chapter will relate the normative and political paradoxes of European social policy to the debate on Europe's constitutional model. It will be argued that present developments of the EU's constitutional model (to be reinforced in the planned institutional reform) are producing a change in the dominant conceptions of the *demos* and *telos* of the European Union, and can only be fully legitimised if this is reflected in the degree of European solidarity and if the question of Europe's social self is finally addressed.

FROM NEGATIVE TO POSITIVE INTEGRATION:
THE EMERGENCE OF EUROPE'S SOCIAL POLICY

It has now become common to hear about Europe's social deficit. Either as result of legal constraints or the constraints of economic competition, European economic integration (in parallel with global economic integration) has generated pressures towards deregulation and has challenged social standards and welfare. This has not been (totally) compensated for by social policies arising at the level of the European Union. It is easier to promote integration by reducing state legislation interfering with economic activities (negative integration) than by creating common standards and regulatory frameworks for economic agents (positive integration). The latter requires an agreement on social policies and rights normally expressed in the form of legislation, and is difficult to achieve in the EU context of different national interests and ideological standpoints.

The impact of Community law on national social rights, through negative market integration, has generally been seen as "negative" by social lawyers because it has restricted the capacity of states to enact social provisions. However, the opposite has normally occurred when Community law is addressed by social lawyers from the perspective of positive market integration in the form of social legislation enacted at the EU level.[3] This is so, even though the competence of the EU on social issues has generally been limited and moves at a slow pace. Community law has been seen, mainly among labour lawyers, as a source for the defence and promotion of social policies against the predominantly deregulatory ideologies at the national level. The ideology of deregulation is not uniform among the Member States and labour lawyers hope to mobilise the more "social" states to push, at the European level, for social rights and policies that they are not able to establish at the national level. At the same time, the arguments in favour of deregulation often stress the need to be competitive in the European market, which requires states with more protective

---

[3] See P Davies, "Market Integration and Social Policy in the Court of Justice", (1995) 24 *Industrial Law Journal* 49.

social rights to reduce their degree of protection. Thus, labour lawyers try to reinstall the primacy of social rights over the market through common regulations at the European level.

Nevertheless, the core of the European economic constitution lies in market integration. It was under the legitimacy granted by market integration and through the rules provided in the Treaties for its achievement that the European Court has developed the notion of a European constitution.[4] Although the original EC Treaty also contained social provisions (for example former Articles 117 to 119 EC), the core of market integration has been the free movement provisions promoting market access to the different national markets. However, the borderline between securing access to the market to further market integration and securing access to the market to enhance economic freedom is thin and often non-existent. When reviewing national measures which have an effect on free movement, the European Court is deciding both on the acceptable degree of restriction on trade and on the level of market regulation. The fundamental rights character granted to the free movement provisions and the widening of its scope of action in order to extend European supervision over national regulation and support the constitutionalisation of Community law has led to a spill-over of market integration rules into virtually all areas of national law. As a consequence, many national social rights and policies have been challenged under the free movement provisions. The extension of the scope of action of the free movement of goods and services has raised a challenge to almost any regulation of the market and has limited the social and economic policies of Member States. Several non-discriminatory national regulations protecting or promoting social rights have been challenged as giving rise to restrictions on free movement. This has been the case with legislation regarding the working hours of workers,[5] the organisation of work and the monopoly of workers associations,[6] public systems of labour procurement services[7] or price regulations,[8] all of which can be said to be related to social rights. In general, the application of some of the free movement rules has been seen as promoting deregulation and as preventing Member States from pursuing national social policies, even those which are non-protectionist. The same has occurred with the application of Community competition rules which has led to challenges to different national labour law provisions.[9] In some cases, it has been common for social provisions

---

[4] See M P Maduro, *We The Court, The European Court of Justice and the European Economic Constitution* (Oxford, Hart Publishing, 1998).

[5] See the Sunday Trading cases, notably Case C–145/88 *Torfaen Borough Council* v. *B&Q plc.* [1989] ECR 3851.

[6] Case C–179/90 *Merci Convenzionali Porto di Genova SpA* v. *Siderurgica Gabrielli SpA* [1991] ECR I–5889.

[7] Case C–41/90 *Höfner and Elser* v. *Macroton GmbH* [1991] ECR I–197 and Case C–134/95 *USSL* v. *INAIL* [1997] ECR I–195.

[8] See, e.g., Case 65/75 *Tasca (Ricardo)* [1976] ECR 291; Cases 88–90/75 *Sadam* [1976] ECR 323; Case 13/77 *GB-INNO-BM* v. *ATAB* [1977] ECR 2115; Case 82/77 *Openbaar Ministerie* v. *Van Tiggele* [1978] ECR 25.

[9] See the various examples given by Davies, above n. 3, mainly at 58.

to be challenged through a coordinated application of free movement and competition rules.

Such deregulatory consequences *at the national level* are not, however, a product of a neo-liberal vision of the economic constitution by the Court, but are instead the functional result of the need to promote integration—requiring negative integration in the form of judicial review of divergent state regulations restricting trade—coupled with the absence of a distributive justice criterion which could guide the Court in authorising some of those restrictions on the basis of socio-economic grounds. Market integration generates competition between the national economic and legal systems subject to the goal of efficiency. This is a process which is reinforced if such market integration is achieved mainly through negative integration (accepting products complying with different social and labour standards) and not through positive integration (introducing common social standards). The consequences of this process are deregulation at the national level and a reduction in the political control over the economic sphere.

The arguments in favour of a European social policy attempt to reintroduce such political control over the economic sphere at the EU level and, in such an instance, the EU would become the relevant level for the establishment and protection of social policies. Negative integration would be followed by positive integration. On the other hand, those arguing against the development of a European social policy and European social rights prefer to subject those policies and rights to market competition itself.

Much of the current status of social values in the European Union is a consequence of the balance between negative and positive integration. There is nothing new about this debate. When the EC Treaty was drafted there were two divergent opinions on whether the prior harmonisation of social policy was necessary. One side (coinciding with the French who had the most protective social legislation) argued in favour of European legislative harmonisation of social policies. The other side (Germany) opposed such harmonisation, preferring to "rely on normal competitive forces to achieve it in the long run".[10] What became Article 119 EC, requiring equal pay for men and women (now Article 141 EC), was a result of the compromise reached in the Treaty.

In reality, both systems of managing economic and regulatory competition in integrated markets generate harmonisation of social rights and policies. The difference lies in the institutional framework through which such harmonisation arises and its impact on the final outcome of harmonisation. As stated by Trubek:

"Once economic interdependence reaches a certain point, and borders no longer serve as major barriers to economic movement, there is a pressure towards uniformity in economic policies. These pressures may come about to ensure fair competition and the

---

[10] E B Haas, *The Uniting of Europe* (Stanford, Stanford University Press, 1968) (first published 1958) 516.

smooth functioning of economic enterprises that span national borders ('level playing field'), or they may be the result of 'regulatory competition' among sovereignties in a unified space".[11]

One of the questions to be addressed in the context of the European Union is whether we should accept competition among the different states even with respect to social rights and policies or whether should we establish common rights and policies to which such competition should conform. For a long time, this balance between positive and negative integration and its impact on social policies has been decided on the basis of the institutional problems linked to positive integration coupled with a vision of negative integration as the only available alternative to integrate the market. However, this state of the affairs has slowly changed and today there are enhanced legislative competences for the EU to intervene in the social sphere.[12] At the same time, incentives have been created for social partners to shift their social dialogue into the European arena.[13]

These developments have, however, remained prisoners of the logic of market integration whereby they secure equal conditions of competition while imposing common social standards which are to be secured and guaranteed by the different Member States. This emerging social policy is not one in which the EU takes into hand the job of guaranteeing a minimum safety net and social protection for all European citizens. Instead, it is a social policy in which the EU requires its Member States to comply with certain social standards in order to benefit fully from their membership of the internal market. This is why Europe's social policy is built upon the joint efforts of two different forces: European states which have an interest in promoting higher social standards to secure their competitive position; and national social actors who use European social policy as an alternative political process to promote social rights. But the alliance between these two forces is only possible with regard to social rights which can be constructed as preventing unfair competition in the internal market. Rights which could promote redistribution in European terms and would require a commitment of the EU to distributive justice are excluded from European social policy. Moreover, even the social rights which are enacted as part of that social policy are, as a consequence of the limits under which such social policy is conceived, understood so as to restrict their potential for redistribution within the EU. Moebius and Szyszczak have recently reviewed the concept of "worker" in Community legislation and the rights it affords to European citizens.[14] In their article, they argue against the limited interpretation of the concept of work which is usually assumed to underpin Community rights and policies. They favour a concept of work and worker to include people under-

---

[11] D Trubeck, *Social Justice "After" Globalization—The Case of Social Europe* (mimeo, November 1996) 5.
[12] See, notably, Article 137 EC.
[13] See Articles 138 and 139 EC.
[14] I Moebius and E Szyszczak, "Of Raising Pigs and Children", (1998) 18 *YEL* 125.

taking unpaid care work. The difference between the traditional concept of Community worker and that proposed by Moebius and Szyszczak lies in the different identities of European social policy which those concepts reflect. The policy developments proposed by Moebius and Szyszczak require a European social policy which pursues independent political goals of the EU and which the EU is ready to assume, if necessary by "paying the bill" and setting up a criterion of distributive justice to allocate it. Instead, the continuing dominating paradigm of European social policy is not based upon a criterion of European distributive justice but only upon assuring the incorporation of some common social standards at the national level to the extent that they do not imply an additional burden for the EU and may help to secure a "level playing field" within the EU. According to this paradigm, the costs of social policies are distributed by the market and supported by the different states independently of their welfare position. A different paradigm, such as that underlying the proposal of Moebius and Szyszczak, would require the EU to assume independent social goals and figure out a method of distributive justice to allocate its costs.

The debate between negative and positive integration and its effect on social policy has usually underscored the consequences of the definition of distributive justice in Europe. Independently of the preferred method of integration chosen, it is obvious that the dominant political arena for the determination of social values shifts to the European level. The notion that negative integration will protect the various states' political autonomy (by recognising their different rules) is artificial since the balance between efficiency-enhancing and redistributive policies is no longer a choice dependent on those policies but a functional result of the degree of negative market integration and its system of competition among rules. Negative integration already implies a shift in the relevant political arena of social policies. It therefore becomes crucial to discuss what legitimises that political arena and the social values to be taken into account therein. But positive integration also requires more than the setting of common social standards to be secured by the different Member States. Once European economic integration develops its own social policies and erodes the capacity of nation states for redistribution, the relevant question becomes, what should guide the framing of those policies, and how should mechanisms of redistribution at the European level be reintroduced? Those who focus on the EU exclusively as an area of free trade and a common market envision the EU as an instrument of efficiency and wealth maximisation. But can and should the EU only be about increasing societal net gain through market integration without concerns about how such wealth is distributed within the EU? And, if, as it will be shown, European rights and policies have redistributive consequences, should these not be based on a European criterion of distributive justice instead of being decided by the market and the power of the different states?

FROM FREE MOVEMENT TO SOCIAL RIGHTS:
THE DIFFERENT FACES OF EUROPEAN CITIZENSHIP

The foundations for the construction of the European citizen and the status of citizenship are to be found in the free movement rules. This provides the best starting point for an enquiry into the social identity of Europe and the ranking and character of social rights in its legal order. A comparative analysis of the treatment given to the different free movement rules and its redistributional impact already highlights the subsidiary and under-developed nature of Europe's social citizenship when compared with its original market citizenship[15] and the emerging political citizenship. The European Court has referred to the free movement provisions as "fundamental freedoms"[16] granting them a status similar to that of fundamental rights in national constitutions. This conception of the free movement provisions as fundamental rights has played a key role both as an instrument of market integration (in cooperation with individual litigants and national courts) and, at the same time, as a form of legitimation of Community law and market integration. However, the character of such fundamental freedoms has, to a certain extent, remained unclear and the Court has for some while favoured the promotion of the free movement of goods and, to a lesser extent, the free movement of services over the free movement of persons.

Until the case of *Keck and Mithouard*,[17] the Court adopted an interpretation of the rule of the free movement of goods that subjected almost any national regulation to a test of proportionality similar to cost/benefit analysis.[18] This brought virtually any public regulation of the market under close scrutiny and promoted deregulation of the market *at the national level*. As we have seen in the previous section, the expansion of free movement rules has had an impact on other areas of the law related to social concerns and not just trade protectionism and has promoted economic freedom.[19]

Market integration can also be used to promote the development of European social rights but the functional use of market integration rules to further social rights has been limited. The Court has mainly required the abolition of discrimination based on nationality among workers in one Member State, albeit expanding the prohibition of discrimination beyond the issues mentioned in Article 39 EC: "employment, remuneration, and other conditions of work and employment". For some time the Court has been giving a more restrictive interpretation of the rules regarding the free movement of persons than its interpre-

---

[15] The expression belongs to M Everson, "The Legacy of the Market Citizen" in J Shaw and G More (eds), *New Legal Dynamics of European Union* (Oxford, Oxford University Press, 1995) 73.

[16] See, e.g., Case C–55/94 *Gebhard* [1995] ECR I–4165, at para. 34.

[17] Joined Cases C–267 and C–268/91 *Keck and Mithouard* [1993] ECR I–6097.

[18] See Maduro, above n. 4, at 61–8.

[19] See Davies, above n. 3.

tation of the free movement of goods and the freedom to provide services. As we have seen, in the field of the free movement of goods (and to a more limited extent, services), the Court has considered as restrictions to trade national regulations that do not discriminate against imports but may, nevertheless, affect trade by affecting market access in general. In this way, many national regulations limiting economic freedom (including regulations protecting social rights) have been challenged under Community rules since the limits to economic freedom are also conceived of as limits to free trade and market access. The same broad scope has not been given to the free movement of workers which could be used to challenge national regulations restricting certain social rights. In fact, in the same way that it is possible to argue that regulation of the market creates barriers to trade, it would be possible to argue that workers will need a minimum degree of protection to exercise effectively free movement. For example, the argument could be made that a prohibition, in a Member State, to strike or to be become a union member could deter workers from other Member States, where those rights existed, from moving to that Member State.[20] This argument may seem remote from the original wording and intent of the Treaty rules on the free movement of workers but it is in no way different from the arguments, in favour of deregulation, which have been accepted in the context of the free movement of goods.[21]

The broader scope granted to the free movement of goods and services in comparison to the free movement of workers has, however, had redistributional effects; the wealth generated by economic integration has mainly gone to those who benefit from the free movement of goods and services. The more restricted development of the free movement of workers when compared to other free movement rules has, in fact, reinforced the exclusionary character of the free movement rules with regard to some categories of people, such as the unemployed who were not included in the original free movement provisions. The more cautious interpretation of the European Court in the area of the free movement of persons may have simply reflected the political sensibility of some states with regard to this issue; this can be seen in parts of the Treaty such as the unanimity requirement for the adoption of Community legislation in much of this area.[22] This attitude on the part of some Member States departs from their

---

[20] Note that the two examples of social rights given do not require any type of legislative action (as normally happens with social rights of a programmatic character) and could be established simply by judicial recognition.

[21] It is sufficient to think of the arguments, regarding Article 28 (ex 30) EC, used to challenge national regulations which prohibited shops from opening on Sundays, prevented certain marketing and advertising methods, or imposed the use of recyclable bottles.

[22] See Articles 42, 47 and 95 EC.

[23] *Keck and Mithouard*, above n. 17. In this decision, the Court restricted the scope of application of what was then Article 30 EC with regard to national measures regulating "selling arrangements" and which do not discriminate against imports (no longer considered as capable of restricting trade in the context of the free movement of goods). The traditional interpretation of Article 30 is, however, maintained with regard to national measures on product characteristics. On *Keck* see S Weatherill, "After *Keck*: Some Thoughts on How to Clarify the Clarification", (1996) 33 *CMLRev* 885; Gormley, "Two Years After Keck", (1996) 19 *Fordham International Law Journal*

concern about the redistributional effects which a general principle of the free movement of persons could have within the EU but, at the same time, it appears to *ignore* the redistributional effects which the current status quo already promotes and which tends to create a category of European people excluded from the full benefits of European Union. The extent to which this state of the affairs can be maintained is dubious in view of the political growth of the EU and the current dilemmas facing both its political and judicial processes.

The recent case law of the European Court signals a shift in its judicial activism towards favouring a limitation of the scope of the application of the free movement of goods and a broader application of the free movement of persons. The limits set in *Keck* to challenges, under Article 28 (ex 30) EC, to national rules the effect of which is to limit the commercial freedom of traders,[23] will reduce the impact of the free movement of goods on national legislation protecting social rights. Instead, a broader use of the free movement of workers is now available to promote social rights in the European common market. The *Bosman* decision is a good example, supporting a right to work and the freedom of workers to choose their work and employment.[24] This decision prohibited rules that, albeit not discriminating against workers of other Member States, reduced their free movement by imposing limits on their freedom to leave their employer and to choose among different employment contracts. The consequence of the recent expansion of the free movement of persons provisions beyond the simple prohibition of discrimination on the basis of nationality may be the recognition of a set of European social rights required for an effective protection of the free movement of persons. Developments in this sense will depend largely on the sophistication and capacity of social actors to raise litigation combining Community law arguments with fundamental social rights.[25] But they will also depend on the notion of the underlying European political community which the Court and the political process will construct to support and mould the rights of market integration.

What is clear is that the most important developments in the area of social rights have also come from the core of market integration. It is the relationship established between free movement of persons and the principle of non-discrimination on the basis of nationality that has mainly been the driving force

---

866; M Mattera, "De l'arrêt 'Dassonville' à l'arrêt Keck: l'obscure clarité d'une jurisprudence riche en principes novateurs et en contradictions", (1994) *Revue du Marché Unique Européen* 117; D Chalmers, "Repackaging the Internal Market—The Ramifications of the *Keck* Judgment", (1994) 19 *ELRev* 385; M Lopez Escudero, "La jurisprudencia *Keck* y *Mithouard*: Una Revision del Concepto de Medida de Efecto Equivalente", (1994) *Revista de Instituciones Europeas* 379; N Bernard, "Discrimination and Free Movement in EC Law", (1996) 45 *International and Comparative Quarterly* 82; Higgins, "The Free Movement of Goods Since *Keck*", (1997) 6 *IJEL*; and M P Maduro, "*Keck*: The End? The Beginning of the End? Or Just the End of the Beginning?", (1994) 1 *IJEL* 30.

[24] Case C–415/93 *Bosman* [1995] ECR I–4921.

[25] That has not been the case up to now. In this sense, see E Szyszczak, "Future Directions in European Union Social Policy Law", (1995) 19 *ILJ* 31.

behind some of the most important developments on the protection of social rights in the European Union and the construction of a European citizenship. The prohibition of discrimination on the basis of nationality (Article 12 EC) has been used by the Court to extend the protection conferred by social rights in a given Member State to nationals of any Member State in that state.[26] This has been furthered by the direct effect granted to the principle of non-discrimination on the basis of nationality established in Article 12 EC. Such a principle is only effective within the scope of the application of the Treaty but, once a certain social right can be conceived, for example, as being instrumental to the protection of the free movement of an individual included in one of the categories of persons covered by the Treaty, such a right must be applied in a non-discriminatory manner. This process culminated in the *Martínez Sala* decision where the Court appeared to confer almost absolute protection against discrimination by a Member State to a national of another Member State lawfully resident in that state. So long as that is the case, a national of any Member State in another Member State is granted the same social rights and protection accorded by that state to its own nationals. Discussing what are now Articles 17(2) and 12 EC, the Court stated:

"Article 8(2) of the Treaty attaches to the status of citizen of the Union rights and duties laid down by the Treaty, including the right, laid down in Article 6 of the Treaty, not to suffer discrimination on grounds of nationality within the scope of application *ratione materiae* of the Treaty.

It follows that a citizen of the European Union . . . lawfully resident in the territory of the host Member State, can rely on Article 6 of the Treaty in all situations which fall within the scope *ratione materiae* of Community law, including the situation where that Member State delays or refuses to grant to that claimant a benefit that is provided to all persons lawfully resident in the territory of that State on the ground that the claimant is not in possession of a document which nationals of that same State are not required to have and the issue of which may be delayed or refused by the authorities of that State.

Since the unequal treatment in question thus comes within the scope of application of the Treaty, it cannot be considered to be justified: it is discrimination directly based on the appellant's nationality and, in any event, nothing to justify such unequal treatment has been put before the Court".[27]

The limit posed by the condition that the "unequal treatment in question comes within the scope of application of the Treaty"[28] is much less significant

---

[26] In the words of Carlos Ball, "The Court of Justice has interpreted Community Law provisions that provide individuals with justiciable economic rights in a way that prohibits Member States from treating their own citizens better than the citizens from other Member States working within their borders. This has contributed significantly to the formation of a European social citizenship", in "The Making of a Transnational Capitalist Society: The Court of Justice, Social Policy, and Individual Rights Under the European Community's Legal Order", (1996) 37 *Harvard International Law Journal* 307 at 314.

[27] Case C–85/96 *Martínez Sala* [1998] ECR I–2708, paras 62–4.

[28] The Court established two conditions: that the facts of the case must fall within the scope *ratione materiae* and *ratione personae* of the Treaty. The latter is linked to the interpretation to be

than one could initially think, as the case in question confirms. In fact, it is difficult to conceive of any area which is still *ratione materiae* outside the scope of Community law,[29] much less when any unequal treatment among nationals of different Member States in a Member State can be said to restrict the free movement of persons. In this area, the scope of application *ratione materiae* of Community law will basically depend on its scope of application *ratione personae*. In other words, it will depend on the extent to which all European citizens are given a general right of free movement. If they are granted a general right of free movement, the logical consequence will be that they should not be discriminated against independently of the state in which they choose to live.

However, even this basic right to free movement of European citizens (the right to freely take up residence where he or she wishes) is doubtful. Although the Maastricht Treaty proclaimed the general principle of the free movement of persons, it is not clear whether this principle has direct effect and the conditions upon which its exercise are made dependent are equally uncertain.[30] This uncertainty comes directly from the ambiguous nature of Europe's social identity and the incapacity to face the questions immediately raised by general principles such as the free movement of persons: can European citizens choose whatever national model of social protection they prefer? Would some type of harmonisation of national social policies be required? And will that not require, in turn, an exercise at the European level of a redistributive function to be supported by some European criterion of distributive justice? My argument, to be developed below, is that it is no longer possible for the European Union to avoid these questions and the definition of its social self.

At the moment, the traditional "unbearable" status quo still dominates; although the Court has extended the protection granted by Community law to students or job-searchers, there is no general right of free movement of persons granted with direct effect even, arguably, after the *Martínez Sala* decision in which the Court did not consider it necessary to clarify the status of what was then Article 18 (ex 8a) EC.[31] So long as the free movement of persons continues to be developed as a function of market integration and economic efficiency, the intention is an optimal allocation of labour under the mechanisms generated by market integration. There is no free movement of persons conceived of as a right to choose among different models of life and regulatory regimes (including social protection). Neither is such a principle accepted to entail a form of redistribution by allowing people to locate themselves optimally in view not only of labour demand but also of social protection. At the same time, however, it is becoming more and more difficult to explain the "status of apartheid" of the free

given by the Court to the general right of free movement of persons established in Article 18 (ex 8a) EC which the Court considered unnecessary to consider in this case (see below).

[29] It is not required for specific Community rules to address an issue for it to come under its scope of application. Otherwise, the Court would not need independently to apply Article 6.

[30] See J Shaw and S Fries, "Citizenship of the Union: First Steps in the European Court of Justice", (1994) 4 *European Public Law* 533.

[31] See paras 58–9.

movement of persons in the context of an EU with growing spheres of competence and an increasingly majoritarian institutional framework (which however still does not largely apply to free movement of persons). The answers to these questions require us to face different redistributional consequences and to discuss the nature of the European social contract, something which the EU continues to avoid.

As things stand, and to use the raw Marxist language of Gustav Peebles, "people primarily gain rights within the European Union by demonstrating that they embody exchange value and are therefore personified commodities; people are not accorded rights merely for being human".[32] The extension of rights performed by the European Court has gone hand in hand with an extension of the economic and market rationale into other areas of human interaction.[33] It was the latter that made the former possible, but it also made the European constitution and its "citizens" prisoners of the functional logic of the Treaties. Therefore, the development of social rights in the EU does not come about as a consequence of a political conception of the social and economic protection deserved by any European citizen. An overview of the status and position of classical social rights in the EU confirms this.

The classic example of a social right enshrined in the Treaty is Article 141 EC which establishes "the principle that men and women should receive equal pay for equal work". However it is well known that the origin of this norm is to be found in the aim of protecting equal conditions of competition. Even if the Court's case law and Community legislation have, in effect, partly raised it into the status of a true fundamental social right, this principle has always appeared a "lone ranger" in the otherwise empty and foggy landscape of European social rights. Moreover, its unique status and the absence of an underlying rational and coherent construction of the legitimacy of Europe's social rights has limited the development of this principle of equal treatment between men and women with regard to work into a prohibition of other forms of work discrimination, such as discrimination on the basis of sexual orientation.[34] Only a perception of strong limits on the legitimacy of European social rights may justify the reluctance of the Court to extend the prohibition of discrimination into other categories of people. A broader understanding of the legitimacy of social Europe would have allowed the Court to fill in the gaps in the protection afforded by current European legislation to cases of work discrimination on the basis of the general principles of the European legal order.

The picture is even more complex and confused if we look at the broader status and catalogue of European social rights. It is well known that the European

---

[32] G Peebles, "A Very Eden of Innate Rights of Man? A Marxist Look at the European Union Treaties and Case Law" (1997) 22 *Law & Soc. Inquiry* 581.

[33] *Ibid.*, 586–7.

[34] See Case C–249/96 *Grant* v. *South West Trains* [1998] ECR I–62. The Court has, however, accepted a partial extension of the prohibition to discriminate on the basis of sex to cover transsexuals in Case C–13/94 *P* v. *S and Cornwall County Council* [1996] ECR I–2143.

Court has developed a catalogue of fundamental rights as legal principles of the Community legal order with which Community acts, and, in some cases, national acts have to conform. This judicially constructed protection of fundamental rights has been transplanted into the Treaties. However, social rights have always appeared to assume a secondary position in the context of that catalogue. It has even been argued that the Court's jurisprudence has generated some confusion between its fundamental human rights doctrine and its fundamental economic rights doctrine and, in effect, has made the former dependent on the economic objectives of the EU.[35] There is, however, a core of social rights which have been tentatively developed by the Court in different circumstances and under different doctrines. We have already highlighted the right not to be discriminated against on the basis of nationality, equality between men and women, free movement of persons (with some limits to be clarified),[36] the right to work and the right to choose freely a job and employment. Other rights (such as those regarding workers' participation) have been affirmed by the Court but only following Community legislation and without the recognition of a constitutional and fundamental rights status. Both the European Court of Justice and the Court of First Instance have also referred to general sources of social rights protection such as the European and Community Social Charters.[37] Such references have, however, been limited and rarely has the European Court affirmed, as general principles of Community law, fundamental social rights. This contrasts sharply with its approach to property rights or to economic activity which have been frequently applied in the review of Community acts and legislation.

It is this uncertainty regarding the status and catalogue of fundamental social rights in the EU legal order that has led to calls for the introduction of a list of fundamental social rights in the Treaties.[38] This is reflected in the proposals of the Comité des Sages responsible for the report on a Europe of Civic and Social Rights prepared before the Amsterdam Intergovernmental Conference. The Committee argued that it was necessary to provide the Court with a stronger legal basis in the Treaties empowering it to review Community legislation (and national legislation within the scope of Community law)[39] under the criteria of fundamental social rights. The Amsterdam Treaty did not, however, include a list of social rights and fewer steps were taken than the Committee had proposed. Nevertheless a relevant novelty was the insertion into the EC Treaty of a

---

[35] See Ball, above n. 26, at 315.

[36] See the discussion below.

[37] See, e.g., Case C–246/96 *Magorrian and Cunningham* v. *Eastern Health and Social Service Board and the Department of Health and Social Services* [1997] ECR I–7153; Case C–191/94 *AGF Belgium* [1996] ECR I–1859; Case T–135/96 *UEAPME* [1998] ECR II–2335. See also Szyszczak, above n. 25, at 31 and references therein.

[38] See B Hepple, "Social Values and European Law", (1995) 39 *Current Legal Problems*, 39; R Blanpain, B Hepple, S Sciarra and M Weiss, *Fundamental Social Rights: Proposals for the European Union* (Leuven, Walter Lëen Fonds, 1996). See also the *Molitor Group Report*, "Labour Law, Proposal 1" (Agence Europe/Documents, No 1947, 4 August 1993).

[39] Thus, the degree of incorporation of EU fundamental rights in national legal orders would not be changed.

general principle prohibiting discrimination on the basis of sex, race, ethnic origin, religion, beliefs, disabilities, age or sexual orientation.[40] But such a principle does not appear to have direct effect and is more a clause of empowerment for future Community action in this area. The Social Chapter was also inserted into the Treaties and Article 136 (in the Title on social policy) now includes a reference to "fundamental social rights such as those set out in the European Social Charter signed at Turin on 18 October 1961 and in the 1989 Community Charter of the Fundamental Social Rights of Workers". Contrary to the proposals of the Committee, no catalogue of fundamental social rights was inserted, nor were they given the same status as other fundamental rights whose respect by the EU is imposed in Article 6 of the Maastricht Treaty. Moreover, the reference in Article 136 must be read in light of the fact that the European Court has considered that such a provision "is essentially in the nature of a programme".[41] As to rights which could promote a European function of distributive justice, the Treaty is completely silent. The idea of a European safety net is far from even being considered a topic of debate and redistribution is still to be constructed in cross-national terms and is limited to regional and cohesion funds.

The overall picture remains ambiguous and confused. The status of Europe's social rights and its relation with other fundamental rights is still unclear. The legitimacy constraints which limit the potential of Europe's social policy will continue to restrain the development of Europe's social rights and will provide misguided results between the ambitions of the independent goals commanding some of those social rights and the limits on their interpretation and application derived from the ambiguous and limited nature of the legitimacy underlying such rights at a European level. At the same time, the growth of the number of such rights without an appropriate framework of legitimacy identifying their status and overall placing in the European political project will raise potential conflicts of rights without appropriate criteria to regulate them. The new Charter of Fundamental Rights may bring some certainty and coherence into this confused panorama with the introduction of a catalogue of fundamental rights but it will not solve any of the underlying dilemmas if it does not use the opportunity to start a deliberative moment in which the legitimacy of social Europe is discussed, including the lack of a criterion of distributive justice. This is also required to complete the construction of European citizenship and the social legitimacy of its supportive demos.

Citizenship is normally defined in reference to a certain demos and developed in a political and social status derived from the social contract of that political community. But one of the originalities of European integration was an evolving notion of citizenship referring not to a *demos* but, to use the expression of

---

[40] Article 13 EC as introduced by the Amsterdam Treaty.
[41] See Case 149/77 *Defrenne* v. *Sabena* [1978] ECR 1365; Case 170/84 *Bilka-Kaufhaus* v. *Weber von Hartz* [1986] ECR I–1607; Case 126/86 *Gimenez Zaera* v. *INSS* [1986] ECR I–2261, para. 13.

Peebles, to a "community of economic circulation".[42] This corresponds to what Everson has termed as the "market citizen". This is a citizenship whose status corresponds to the set of rights granted to individuals as participants and beneficiaries of the process of economic integration. The political spill-over of European integration has stressed the inadequacy of this limited version of citizenship and reinforced the claims for political and social rights in the European Union. The "Maastricht citizen" was an attempt to answer those claims by formally establishing a European citizenship and a limited status of political rights which can be related to other institutional changes (such as the reinforcement of the European Parliament's powers). But it is still unclear to which dominant demos these political rights relate.[43] Furthermore, apart from the still contested and ambiguous principle of the free movement of persons there is no real social content given to European citizenship. Again, the reason probably lies in the difficulty of elaborating a principle of distributive justice within the emerging European political community. The crucial question becomes whether there can be a European citizenship deprived of a social content. This is not to say that there are no European social rights. In fact, as we have seen, there are several of such rights. The problem is that they arise and are defined not in reference to independent political goals associated to a social status attributed to any European citizen *vis-à-vis* the emerging European political community, but in reference to ad hoc political bargains that are aimed at binding the states but not the EU and which are legitimised via market integration. As a consequence, their redistributive effects are not really thought out in accordance with a criterion of distributive justice for the EU.

DEMOS, TELOS AND EUROPE'S SOCIAL SELF

If one looks at Marshall's well known description of the three waves of fundamental rights associated with citizenship one is bound to notice that, whilst political rights are emerging in the European Union, social rights continue to be the main gap in the process of constructing European citizenship.[44] Even the arguments in favour of European social rights refer mainly to the need to create a set of rights in relation to which the EU can ensure *states*' compliance. The idea of European social rights as European social entitlements arising from a

---

[42] The expression is drawn from Peebles, above n. 32.

[43] Everson, above n. 15, at 76, talks about a conceptual obscurity which raises two contrasting possibilities: "First, Union citizenship may relate to a common but limited European society, which does not supersede but exists alongside its national counterparts. Secondly, Union citizenship may yet be associated with national societies".

[44] An application of Marshall's theory to the EU has recently been attempted by Duarte Bué Alves in an LLM thesis dissertation at the Universidade Católica Portuguesa. A short version of the thesis will be published as a Working Paper of the Faculdade de Direito da Universidade Nova di Lisboa (http://www.fd.unl.pt/pt/wps/wps.htm).

criterion of distributive justice agreed among all citizens of the EU is rarely, if ever, discussed.

The recognition of a set of social rights accorded to all European citizens both with regard to the different national *demos'* and the emerging European *demos* must follow from a notion of citizenship that is not simply inclusive of those wealthy enough to enjoy the elitist free movement and (currently) limited citizenship provisions. If citizenship *is* narrowly inclusive, many Europeans will feel estranged from European citizenship. Naturally, this will be a hotly debated issue: debates on efficiency *versus* distributive justice never have been peaceful and are not likely to be in the context of a "contested" European political community whose degree of cohesion and solidarity can only be said to be weak. The main problem is that decisions on these issues are *already* being taken at the European level. In the absence of an agreed European social contract those decisions simply flow from the functional ideology of market integration. Moreover, European integration has reached a point where its emerging European *demos* and its redistributive and majoritarian elements can no longer be socially accepted and legitimised without an underlying social contract and a criterion of distributive justice.

The rhetoric of the Treaties has seen a progressive reinforcement of the social goals of European integration included in the Preambles and initial Articles. This social rhetoric goes beyond the simple safeguard of social values in light of the regulatory challenges brought by economic integration. The current rhetoric is even partially linked with a notion of European solidarity whereby the goal of economic and social cohesion is entrusted to the EU.

Article 2 of the EC Treaty states that the Community shall "promote throughout the Community a harmonious, balanced, and sustainable development of economic activities, a high level of employment and of social protection . . . and economic and social cohesion and solidarity among Member States". This provision is reflected in Title XVII but also in the conception of the Community's social policy as aiming at "the promotion of employment, improved living and working conditions, so as to make possible their harmonisation while the improvement is being maintained, proper social protection, dialogue between management and labour, the development of human resources with a view to a lasting employment and the combating of exclusion" (Article 136(1) EC). A goal which the Member States recognise will not only ensue from the functioning of the common market but will require direct Community action (Article 136(3) EC).

However, this rhetoric has much of the symbolic about it, lacking any real correspondence with the other provisions of the Treaties or the policies of the EU,[45] and it is clear that Jacques Delors' goal of a European social area has not moved much beyond words. Still, one must not ignore the powerful consequences which may be derived from this rhetoric as a legitimating factor for

---

[45] In this sense, see J Shaw, "Twin-track Social Europe—the Inside Track" in D O'Keeffe and P Twomey (eds), *Legal Issues of the Maastricht Treaty* (London, Chancery, 1994) 295.

the European Union. In combination with human rights and citizenship, the reinforcement of the goal of economic and social cohesion is one of the key instruments written in at the Maastricht and Amsterdam Intergovernmental Conferences to promote the social legitimacy of the integration process in light of its economic and institutional developments. Maastricht saw the reinforcement of the structural funds and an increased stress on the social and economic cohesion of the EU as a necessary complement to EMU, vital to safeguard its feasibility and social acceptance.[46] But the redistributive function of the EU (although not its redistributive effects) is still fundamentally restricted to the structural funds which form the basis of a policy of economic and social cohesion much more modest than the name leads us to assume.[47] In fact, the redistributive function performed by the structural funds appears as part of package-deals agreed in the context of broader reforms within the EU and to guarantee support for other substantive and institutional developments. In spite of the rhetoric of social and economic cohesion included in Articles 2, 3, and 158 *et seq* EC, that goal is not reflected in the different policies of the EU and its pursuit appears to be committed only to the structural funds. In this way, that redistributive policy is not part of a criterion of distributive justice which could coordinate all the policies of the EU but is, instead, a compensation which is given to some states which could lose more or gain less from other specific policies or institutional choices of the EU. Redistribution in the EU occurs as a result of ad hoc intergovernmental bargaining and not as a constitutive element of an emerging polity founded upon a social contract which includes a criterion of distributive justice. This form of redistributive policies could fit well with the original foundations of the European Communities, but it is doubtful whether it is adequate for the political form and redistributive effects of the contemporary European integration project.

If it is usual to see critiques of the current status quo refer to a European social deficit, the same is true that few of those critiques address the question of distributive justice at a European level. Bob Hepple, for example, argues that "until such time as European social policy is explicitly based on general principles which reflect common social values, there will be no rational basis for Community legislation and judicial interpretation in the social field".[48] However even Hepple appears to concentrate on the protection of a common set of social values (which he derives from the different Member States) from the intrusion of market integration and efficiency enhancing policies and not on the establishment of European policies which would promote a European dimension of that common set of social values.[49] The social constitution of Europe to which this author refers will serve as a yardstick for the protection of social

---

[46] See C Mestre and Y Petit, "La cohésion économique et sociale après le Traité sur l'Union européenne" (1995) 31 *RTD eur.* 207.

[47] See Shaw, above n. 46, at 305.

[48] Hepple, above n. 38, at 40.

[49] *Ibid.*, mainly at 40–4, 52 and 60.

rights at the national level and Community norms but would not, itself, promote forms of redistribution and social allocation at the European level. It would therefore preserve the idea of Europe's social policy as establishing a common set of social values to be achieved and safeguarded by the different Member States, and not as promoting a European ideal of distributive justice expressed in independent political and social goals. In other words, that social constitution of Europe will guarantee a level playing field within Europe and impose on all states a core set of social values to be respected by all but would not entrust to the EU a function of redistribution to be achieved in accordance with a European criterion of distributive justice. The social perspective underlying this limited conception of Europe's social self is that which merges the interests of those who want to guarantee a level playing field in the internal market with regard to social standards, with the interests of those who want to use Europe to promote more social rights at the national level. This limited version of the European social self does not really recognise Europe's right and legitimacy to establish and exercise an independent redistributive function.

The reality, however, is that European policies already have broad redistributive effects and what appears to be lacking is an overall criterion of distributive justice to assess and coordinate those redistributive effects. Is the lack of a real agreement on a criterion of distributive justice for Europe acceptable in light of the political and economic developments of the EU? Is the current and expected future model of the EU compatible with the lack of identification of its social self expressed in a criterion of distributive justice? Or will that social self come about as a creation of the functional method without a true European social contract? Does European despair (following Kierkegaard) come from not wanting to be itself as it has now become or does European despair come from wanting to be itself? The latter, as Kierkegaard noted, entails a higher level of consciousness of the self. In our case, it departs from recognising the political form that Europe has already attained and the redistributive impact it has in the different states and among European citizens. But can this political form continue to emerge and have redistributive effects without a form of social legitimation? To use the words of Kierkegaard, this despair arises in the context of "severing the self from any relation to the power which has established it, or severing itself from the conception that there is such a power". How, therefore, can this relation be established and Europe become itself? The answer given by Kierkegaard, in relation to human beings, is faith. This is what, in his view, allow us to leave despair and relates us to the power that created us, thus gaining perfect conscience and acceptance of our self. This is not an easy concept to transfer into a political project. Here, the power lies in the people (the *demos*) and, at least in my view, the relation between the *demos* and the polity must be rational. The form of the polity must come about through a form of deliberation among the members of the *demos*. But the individual reasons for giving our allegiance to that polity and acceptance of being part of that *demos* may vary. What are the conditions for European citizens to have "faith" in the current

European Union? To answer this we must ask both what the European self already is (to improve consciousness of that self) and what it needs to find out about itself if it wants to secure the relation with the power that created it (the European *demos*, however it may be understood).[50] This raises several broad and difficult questions which there is not space to address here; I instead wish simply to raise awareness of the European social self and to highlight its relation with other political and constitutional developments of the EU in a way that may contribute to reshaping the current constitutional debates of the EU and the understanding and role of social policies. The focus is on assuming that distributive justice has to become part of the European social self.

The assumption of economic integration was, as stated before, increased growth without interference in the distributional function. But a viable and sustainable integration is only workable if the effects of economic growth are fairly distributed. The issue of redistribution is therefore present from the outset of any project of economic integration. It is well known in economic theory that, although all may gain from economic integration and trade liberalisation, it is to be expected that richer and more competitive countries may gain more than less developed countries.[51] Still, as I have mentioned before, the focus of the project of European economic integration has been on efficiency enhancing and wealth maximisation. The economic growth to be expected from market integration was to be beneficiary to all, albeit not in equal terms. Moreover, the degree of economic and social cohesion of the starting members of the project would create reassurance that the redistributive effects would not impose an undue burden on any of the members. In most economic integration agreements, states make their cost/benefit analyses at the time of signing and, if necessary, obtain specific compensations for agreeing to certain areas of economic integration. The fact that redistributive effects have taken place as a consequence of developments in other policies of the EU could also be legitimised in light of the adoption of unanimous voting procedures for decision-making in the EU. In this case, states could either prevent policies which could have adverse redistributive effects on their own welfare or could subject their agreement to the receipt of some form of compensation in other areas of European policies (something referred to as issue-linkage).[52] It is this that has determined the pattern of both goal determination and the institutional development of the European Communities. Taking as our basis the traditional standards of efficiency, we can make reference to Pareto superiority, Pareto optimality, Kaldor-Hicks efficiency and Pigou optimality in determining the different goals and

---

[50] As the sum of national *demos*, the constituency of European citizens is a community identified by history or other factors.

[51] See Mestre and Petit, above n. 47, at 241.

[52] According to S Weber and H Wiesmeth, "an international regime . . . provides a political environment that naturally promotes issue linkage: by affecting 'transaction costs', the costs associated with acts of non-co-operative behaviour, it makes it easier to link particular issues and to negotiate side-payments that allow some actors to extract positive gains on one issue in return for the favours expected on another", in "Issue Linkage in the European Community", (1991) 25 *JCMS* 258.

decision-making procedures which can be adopted in the project of European integration. They can be seen as rules orientating decision-making procedures or decision-making outcomes.[53] In the latter, Pareto superiority is assured if no one is worse off and at least one person is better off. Pareto optimality exists once there is no conceivable state (*n*) in which anyone will be worse off. A decision is Kaldor-Hicks efficient if those that are better off win sufficiently to compensate the losers so that they are not worse off. Finally there is a Pigou optimal as long as there is a net benefit, that is those better off win more than those worse off lose. The original model of European integration and its patterns of decision-making emphasised a kind of Pareto or Kaldor-Hicks efficiency. In the absence of a common belief in some kind of European ideal or political concept of European integration, integration could only proceed if it pragmatically satisfied as many people or groups as possible.[54] This could be achieved either by guaranteeing that all would have to agree to a specific decision (an institutional rule promoting Pareto efficiency) or by agreeing on mechanisms of compensation to those who would be worse off by virtue of a certain decision (subordinating institutional and substantive developments to a form of Kaldor-Hicks efficiency). The leading idea justifying free trade is a kind of Pareto or Kaldor-Hicks effciency. Free trade and economic integration will maximise total net benefits but not necessarily in a even way. With the development of European economic integration and its institutional and political spill-overs, redistributive concerns arose and the solution was the introduction of redistributive policies which have been developed as compensating some states and which still correspond to an overall Kaldor-Hicks form of efficiency.

However, the development of European integration has strained this form of relation between the model and degree of integration and its ideals. The degree of integration, the expansion of the scope of action of the European Union and its institutional changes are producing redistributive effects which are no longer predictable as part of ad hoc political bargaining that may then be legitimised through appropriate forms of compensation. Instead, the degree of majoritarian decision-making and the scope of European policies require an overall criterion of distributive justice which may legitimise those different policies and their redistributive effects. The institutional shift to majoritarian decision-making (both through the extension of majority voting and parliamentary intervention) and the growth of Community competences tend to subordinate the EU to a societal goal such as Pigou optimality and to have a redistributive impact larger than that which could be functionally legitimised.

In this respect, by increasing majoritarian decision-making and parliamentary intervention, the Amsterdam Treaty may have a constitutional importance

---

[53] Coleman speaks of the distinction between teleological (or consequentialist) modes of justification and consensual modes of justification. See J L Coleman, "The Foundations of Constitutional Economics" in R B Mckenzie (ed.), *Constitutional Economics—Containing the Economic Powers of Government* (Lexington, Mass, Toronto, Lexington Books, 1984) at 141. See also the description of Pareto superiotity, Pareto optimality and Kaldor-Hicks efficiency, *ibid.* at 143–4.

[54] See Haas, above n. 10, at xxiv.

well beyond that which is usually attributed to it.[55] Renaud Dehousse has identified two models in the European institutional architecture: the parliamentary
system and the regulatory structure. As this author remarks, "the regulatory
approach is primarily a functional one: the European Union should concentrate
on activities in which it can hope to achieve greater efficiency than can the
Member States".[56] The parliamentary system entails a move towards forms of
traditional democratic legitimacy such as those involving majoritarian decision-
making and direct representation. According to Dehousse once more, the
Amsterdam Treaty has, in many ways, confirmed and reinforced the role of the
parliamentary system which was already indicated at Maastricht.[57] The current
2000 Intergovernmental Conference's focus on institutional issues appears destined to further that parliamentary and majoritarian model. But, in my view, the
change towards a parliamentary and majoritarian system cannot be separated
from a debate on the *telos* of the EU and its social self. Those institutional
changes also involve a move towards Pigou-optimal decisions which tend to
have stronger redistributive effects since they do not require the agreement of all
parties involved. However, these redistributive effects will not be guided by a
criterion of distributive justice. In the absence of this, the redistributive effects
of the majoritarian system will simply favour the interests of the majority without taking into account the intensity to which different interests are affected by
the decisions of the majority or the departing status quo of those called to participate in the decisions. A majoritarian system needs an underlying social contract based on a criterion of distributive justice to guarantee the social
legitimacy of the majority decisions. Such a social contract guarantees the allegiance of all to the polity by stipulating forms of long term compensation and
by protecting the interests of those minorities which may at times be unduly bur-
dened by the redistributive effects of the majoritarian decisions. One of the key
elements of such a social contract is the setting up of overall mechanisms and
criteria of distributive justice.

Up to now it has been possible for European integration to comply with the
requirements of both formal and social legitimacy through its recourse to the
regulatory model, functional legitimacy and national input. The redistributive
impact of European policies was legitimised both by recourse to functional
goals and national direct or indirect agreement. Issue-linkage provided the relation between the two: the unintended redistributive effects of some European
policies were compensated for with other policies and, in this way, such redistributive impact could, one way or the other, be legitimised by an agreement of
the states. In this way, functional legitimacy both limited the redistributive
impact of European integration and subjected it to trade-offs and agreements

---

[55] In this sense, Jean-Claude Piris, " Does the European Union have a Constitution? Does it Need
One?", (1999) 24 *ELRev* 557 at 564.

[56] R Dehousse, "European Institutional Architecture After Amsterdam: Parliamentary System or
Regulatory Structure?", (1998) 35 *CMLRev* 595 at 599.

[57] *Ibid.*, 624.

between the states. The increased majoritarian and parliamentary character of the European Union make this traditional form of legitimacy more difficult. At the same time, the extension of the scope of Community competences and its growing role as a new political arena mean that it will be increasingly used by different political and social groups to promote independent political goals, and not only those which are functionally attached to the construction of a common market. This emerging political and majoritarian character of the European Union can only be fully legitimised if it is based on a social contract. As Hirschman would put it: less voice would either lead to exit or be replaced by loyalty.[58] And loyalty can only come to the European Union through the means of a social contract. In my view the institutional and social challenges currently faced by the EU require it to also address its underlying *telos* and social identity. This constitutive moment of the EU arises out of the exhaustion of the functional model and its incapacity to legitimise the current institutional and political developments of the EU.

The result of this constitutive moment is unclear, but what must be included is a debate on the social identity of Europe and its reflection on a criterion of distributive justice.[59] Without such debate there can be no true social contract capable of legitimising the emerging European polity[60] and the consequences would be either a return to a less advanced form of integration (including a reduction of majoritarian decision-making and stricter limits on European competences) or, if the current model continues to be stretched, a crisis of social legitimacy which may manifest itself in increased national challenges to European policies (whose redistributive effects are not understood and accepted).

There are, however, good reasons to suppose that it will be possible to develop such a social contract (which does not necessarily require a constitutional project or referendum) and to agree on a criterion of distributive justice for the EU. Recent work by Habermas has developed this argument, departing from the current global challenges to the national welfare state. According to Habermas,[61] it will not continue to be possible for the nation state to guarantee the mechanisms and instruments of social solidarity on which the welfare state has been founded. But this affects the legitimacy of the nation state which requires social justice to secure its own survival. The alternative, for Habermas,

---

[58] A Hirschman, *Exit, Voice and Loyalty—Responses to Decline in Firms, Organizations and States* (Cambridge, Mass, Harvard University Press, 1970).

[59] In a different sense from that argued here but also claiming that "the Union's social policy now stands at a crossroads (and) requires courageous decisions" at the risk of creating "a policy vacuum and leading to the disenchantment among those very citizens who have had their expectations awakened", see C Barnard, "EC 'Social' Policy", in P Craig and G de Búrca (eds), *The Evolution of EU Law* (Oxford, OUP, 1999) 47, at 511.

[60] For Habermas, "the only kind of democratic process that will count as legitimate, and that will be able to provide its citizens with solidarity, will be one that succeeds in an appropriate allocation and a fair distribution of rights", in *The Postnational Constellation* (Polity Press, 2000, forthcoming).

[61] See above n. 61.

lies in the project of European integration, but for this the reinforcement of its capacity for political action must go hand in hand with the development of a form of civil solidarity among European citizens which will secure and express itself in different redistributive policies.

I argue that the project foreseen by Habermas is not only a possible answer to the global challenges faced by the nation state but a choice which the Member States can no longer ignore in view of their own construction of the European Union. Once a certain degree of economic and political integration is achieved, the competition among states generated by that economic integration and the redistributive effects of the policies of the new political entity, will make it difficult for the different Member States to carry on with successful independent redistributive policies.[62] It is this that explains the fears of some who foresee the likelihood of a general principle of free movement of persons hinted at in the *Martínez Sala* decision of the European Court.[63] But this is so only if we refuse to accept that the EU entails in itself a degree of solidarity between its citizens that must, at least, extend to full European citizenship for all, if necessary, by imposing a redistributive burden that is to be legitimised by a criterion of distributive justice among all European citizens. The masters of the EU (citizens and Member States) may deny that such civil solidarity is possible within the EU but they may not evade the question any longer. Whatever the perspective adopted, it is now clear that we must link European social expectations to principles of social justice[64] and that this requires a debate on Europe's social contract.

The promotion of economic integration through free trade is understood to increase efficiency and wealth maximisation. However, many fear that such gains may occur at the cost of weaker social groups and may not be fairly distributed among all the members of society. At the same time, the institutional developments of the EU have promoted forms of decision-making with redistributive effects. Without an agreement on a criterion of distributive justice, these decisions will be seen as a simple reflection of the balance of power in the EU and as lacking general social legitimacy. This is not to say that the EU needs some kind of supportive communitarian ideal or cultural or historical identity. The European *demos* and its social contract may result from the free allegiance of all European citizens with regard to a set of political and social values. But whatever the structure of the European *demos* it needs an underpinning social contract which, in its turn, must entail some criterion of distributive justice. In my view, this requires the replacement of the current redistribution policies based on trade-offs and issue-linkages by redistribution policies which are no

---

[62] On the problems and virtues of competition among states and competition among rules see Maduro, above n. 4, at 126.

[63] See Shaw and Fries, above n. 30, at 533.

[64] See S. Sciarra, "European Social Policy and Labour Law—Challenges and Perspectives", *Collected Courses of the Academy of European Law*, vol. IV, Book 1 (Academy of European Law, The Hague, Kluwer Law International, 1996) 301 at 310.

longer conceived of as state to state but as citizen to citizen and are embodied by a criterion of distributive justice which can be used in creating, interpreting and applying all European policies. In this sense, such a social contract does not necessarily require, for example, an immediate system of taxation and social security. It requires above all, a reconstruction of all current policies (directly redistributive or not) in light of that overall criterion of distributive justice among European citizens and not states. Only this transformation will give the EU the legitimacy basis for the political powers which it is currently acquiring.

Simply stated, Europe must, as Kierkegaard would say, discuss its identity. It can no longer remain with the intellect of a child and the body of an adult. As it now stands, and in Kierkegaard's terms, it faces despair: the despair of wanting to be oneself and the despair of not wanting to be oneself. I do not know the resolution but I believe that future developments of the EU depend on a discussion of this identity or, perhaps better, on a discussion of its underlying social contract. The content of that social contract will both define and be defined by the model and ideal of European integration adopted and, in general, our preferences with regard to efficiency and distributive justice. There are two basic dilemmas that intersect each other in this issue: the first concerns the choice between wealth maximisation and distributive justice; the second is to do with whether we favour a model of economic integration or a model of political integration for Europe. What is clear is that the present status quo is no longer viable as it no longer fits with the impact of European integration. The erosion of national powers and Europe's impact on the exercise of national redistribution policies will bring increased pressures in favour of the assumption of a redistributive function at the European level. This claim will be reinforced by the need to complement the wealth maximisation brought about by economic integration with some form of distributive fairness. Furthermore, the coming institutional developments of the EU are bound to reinforce its majoritarian and supranational characteristics, thereby increasing the redistributive impact of European policies. This institutional development can only be fully legitimised and accepted if its redistributive effects are guided by a socially agreed criterion of distributive justice.

To ignore this "social identity question" in the forthcoming constitutional debates of the European Union may well correspond to the dangerous path of which Kierkegaard warned: "The biggest danger, that of losing oneself, can pass off in the world as quietly as if it were nothing; every other loss, an arm, a leg, five dollars, a wife, etc., is bound to be noticed".

Index